THE TREND OF
ECONOMIC THINKING

F. A. HAYEK

THE COLLECTED WORKS OF

F. A. Hayek

THE TREND OF
ECONOMIC THINKING

Essays on Political Economists and
Economic History

F. A. HAYEK

Edited by W. W. Bartley III and Stephen Kresge

Liberty Fund

INDIANAPOLIS

This book is published by Liberty Fund, Inc., a foundation established to encourage study of the ideal of a society of free and responsible individuals.

The cuneiform inscription that serves as our logo and as the design motif for our endpapers is the earliest-known written appearance of the word "freedom" (*amagi*), or "liberty." It is taken from a clay document written about 2300 B.C. in the Sumerian city-state of Lagash.

The Trend of Economic Thinking is volume 3 of The Collected Works of F. A. Hayek, published by The University of Chicago Press.

This Liberty Fund paperback edition of *The Trend of Economic Thinking* is published by arrangement with The University of Chicago Press and Taylor & Francis Books, Ltd., a member of the Taylor & Francis Group.

Frontispiece: Friedrich Hayek © Bettmann/CORBIS
Cover photo: Friedrich August von Hayek © Hulton-Deutsch Collection/CORBIS

P   1   2   3   4   5   6   7   8   9   10

Library of Congress Cataloging-in-Publication Data

Hayek, Freidrich A. von (Friedrich August), 1899–1992.
The trend of economic thinking: essays on political economists and economic history/F. A. Hayek; edited by W. W. Bartley III and Stephen Kresge.
    p.   cm.—(The collected works of F. A. Hayek)
Originally published: London: Routledge, 1991.
Includes bibliographical references and index.
ISBN 978-0-86597-742-6 (pbk.: alk. paper)
1. Economics—History.   2. Economists—History.   3. Economic history.   I. Bartley, William Warren, 1934–   II. Kresge, Stephen.   III. Title.
HB75.H36   2009
330.15—dc22   2008028280

Liberty Fund, Inc.
8335 Allison Pointe Trail, Suite 300
Indianapolis, Indiana 46250-1684

This book is printed on paper that is acid-free and meets the requirements of the American National Standard for Permanence of Paper for Printed Library Materials, Z39.48-1992. ⊚

Cover design by Erin Kirk New, Watkinsville, Georgia
Printed and bound by Thomson-Shore, Inc., Dexter, Michigan

THE COLLECTED WORKS OF F. A. HAYEK

General Editor: W. W. Bartley, III
The Hoover Institution on War, Revolution and Peace,
Stanford University

Editors of the German edition: Alfred Bosch and Reinhold Veit
The Walter Eucken Institute, Freiburg im Breisgau

Editor of the Japanese Edition: Chiaki Nishiyama
The Hoover Institution on War, Revolution and Peace,
Stanford University

Associate Editor: Stephen Kresge

Assistant Editor: Gene Opton

Published with the support of

The Hoover Institution on War, Revolution and Peace,
Stanford University
Anglo American and De Beers Chairman's Fund, Johannesburg
Cato Institute, Washington, D.C.
The Centre for Independent Studies, Sydney
Chung-Hua Institution for Economic Research, Taipei
Earhart Foundation, Ann Arbor
Engenharia Comércio e Indústria S/A, Rio de Janeiro
Escuela Superior de Economia y Administración de Empresas
(ESEADE), Buenos Aires
The Heritage Foundation, Washington, D.C.
The Institute for Humane Studies, George Mason University
Institute of Economic Affairs, London
Instituto Liberal, Rio de Janeiro
Charles G. Koch Charitable Foundation, Wichita
The Vera and Walter Morris Foundation, Little Rock
Swedish Free Enterprise Foundation, Stockholm
Verband der Österreichischen Banken und Bankiers, Vienna
The Wincott Foundation, London

CONTENTS

CONTENTS

EDITORIAL FOREWORD

I

The Trend of Economic Thinking, a new collection of essays by Hayek concerning political economists and economic history, is the third volume of The Collected Works of F. A. Hayek, a new standard edition of his writings, and the second volume in order of appearance. The first volume, *The Fatal Conceit*, was published in Britain in 1988 and in the United States in 1988.

Of the work's fifteen chapters, five have never previously been published, and another two have never before been published in English. Most of the remaining chapters are difficult to obtain, only three of them being readily available in other Hayek collections. These three essays are placed here as part of the more systematic presentation aimed for in the Collected Works.

II

The Collected Works of F. A. Hayek attempts to make virtually the entire Hayek corpus available to the reader for the first time. The chief organisation is thematic, but within this structure a chronological order is followed where possible.

The series opens with two closely-related books on the limits of reason and planning in the social sciences—*The Fatal Conceit*, a new work, and *The Uses and Abuses of Reasons: The Counter-Revolution of Science and Other Essays*, a work never previously published in Britain. The series continues with two collections of historical and biographical essays (*The Trend of Economic Thinking: Essays on Political Economists and Economic History* and *The Fortunes of Liberalism and the Austrian School*).

The bulk of Hayek's contributions to economics are contained in the four volumes *Nations and Gold*; *Money and Nations*; *Investigations in Economics*; and *Monetary Theory and Industrial Fluctuations*.

These volumes are followed by two volumes of documentation, historical record, and debate: *Contra Keynes and Cambridge* and *Socialism and War*. The texts will be published in corrected, revised and annotated form, with introductions by distinguished scholars intended to place them in their historical and theoretical context.

It is the intention of the editors that the series of volumes be complete in so far as that is reasonable and responsible. Thus essays which exist in slightly variant forms, or in several different languages, will be published always in English or in English translation, and only in their most complete and finished form unless some variation, or the timing thereof, is of theoretical or historical significance. Some items of ephemeral value, such as short newspaper articles and book notices of a few lines written when Hayek was editing *Economica*, will be omitted. And of course the correspondence to be published will be mainly that which bears significantly on Hayek's literary and theoretical work in economics, psychology, biography and history, political theory, and philosophy.

III

The preparation of a standard edition of this type is a large and also expensive undertaking. First and foremost amongst those to be thanked for their very great assistance are W. Glenn Campbell, Director Emeritus of the Hoover Institution on War, Revolution and Peace, Stanford University, and John Raisian, Acting Director of the Hoover Institution, for the generous decision to provide the principal underlying support for this project. The presiding genius behind the larger project, without whose advice and support it never could have been organised or launched, is Walter S. Morris, of the Vera and Walter Morris Foundation. Another institution whose directors watched carefully over the inception of the project, and whose advice has been invaluable, is the Institute for Humane Studies, George Mason University. The editor is particularly indebted to Leonard P. Liggio, Walter Grinder, and John Blundell, of the Institute for Humane Studies. Equally important has been the unflagging support and advice of Norman Franklin, former Head of Routledge & Kegan Paul, who had been Hayek's publisher for many years. I should also like to express my deep thanks to Mrs. Penelope Kaiserlian, Associate Director of the University of Chicago Press, and to Mr. Peter Sowden, of Routledge. Finally, the project could not have been carried through successfully without the generous financial assistance of the supporting organisations, whose names are listed prominently at the beginning of the volume, and to which all associated with the volume are deeply grateful. The support of these sponsors—institutions and foundations from six continents—

not only acknowledges the international appreciation of Hayek's work, but also provides very tangible evidence of the 'extended order of human cooperation' of which Hayek writes.

W. W. Bartley, III

F.A. HAYEK

THE TREND OF ECONOMIC THINKING

Essays on Political Economists and Economic History

INTRODUCTION

Friedrich August von Hayek was born in 1899 in what was then Vienna. The name is still in use, unlike, say, Saigon; and, unlike, say, Angkor Wat, there is still an inhabited city in the same location; but the Vienna into which Hayek was born, the city which that name conjures up in our memory and imagination, survives no more than the fabled Trebizond. Hayek has lived most of his life, as have many civilised people of the twentieth century, in a kind of exile. England is his adopted country, but he made his last home in Freiburg.

"What a small group!" Hayek has recalled, of his family and friends in that long-lost Vienna. "[Konrad] Lorenz I first encountered when he was a boy of four or five; [Otto] Frisch, the youngest brother of friends of my father; [Ludwig] Wittgenstein, a second cousin of my mother whom I first remember in 1918 when we were both ensigns in the artillery of the Austro-Hungarian army; Böhm-Bawerk, my maternal grandfather's colleague and mountaineering companion; [Erwin] Schrödinger, the son of my father's botanical colleague who occasionally accompanied his father to the botanists' teas at our house. . . ."

What made Vienna the distinctive city that it was, as much as any other the fount of Western culture, is a question to be kept in mind, but it is not the subject here under discussion. What we might observe is that a milieu such as that in which Hayek spent his childhood and youth, a society in which family and associates, position and accomplishment, knowledge and history were so tightly intertwined, meant that the members of such a society were quickly and always apprised of what *mattered*. This is no small feat, as any teacher of the present generation of youth knows too well. It is the *significance* of knowledge and information that leads to the evolution of understanding. Indifference cannot produce the sort of inquiry, the criticism and dissent that is necessary for the growth of knowledge.

What has given Hayek's writing its enduring value is this sense of what matters. Economists cannot point to a sterling record of prescience. Classical theory foundered on the rocks of a world depression; Keynesian economics on the phenomenon inelegantly referred to as 'stagflation'; and as for Marxism, the year of 1989 has finally brought the collapse of a system that extracted inhuman costs to enforce a fanatical blunder. For Hayek, it is no consolation to have been right all along. It is in his criticisms of socialism, of the attempt to control by fiat the relations among human beings, that Hayek has demonstrated his keen sense of significance, of the compelling need to define the *problem* faced. Only if a problem has been clearly defined can we know if we have found an answer. This is by no means the simple practice the statement suggests. In wanting the world to conform to our expectations, we too often craft a problem to accept the solution we want, rather than face an unacceptable truth. In his preface to *Conjectures and Refutations*,[1] the work which Sir Karl Popper dedicated to Hayek, Popper observes that his book is largely a variation on one very simple theme—the thesis that we can learn from our mistakes. But then, how do we know when we are mistaken, and when can we afford to admit a mistake? The growth of knowledge is forced through a painful need generated by error, and the lessons of economics can be swift and unsparing. Even so, why should we bother with history, particularly with the history of theories, which is what many of the essays collected in this volume are about? There are several aspects to an answer to this question.

In the chapter "History and Politics", Hayek observes that historical myths have perhaps played nearly as great a role in shaping opinion as historical facts; and that even new ideas reach wider circles usually not in their abstract form but as the interpretations of particular events. Is it then not as important to know the lineage of an idea as the idea itself; to be able to assess its staying power and to observe whether the problem addressed has become a problem solved?

Herewith, then, to compare, a passage from David Hume and one from Richard Cantillon:

> Accordingly we find that, in every kingdom into which money begins to flow in greater abundance than formerly, everything takes a new face: labour and industry gain life; the merchant becomes more enterprising, the manufacturer more diligent and skilful, and even the farmer follows his plough with greater alacrity and attention. . . . From the whole of this reasoning we may conclude,

[1] K. R. Popper, *Conjectures and Refutations* (New York and London: Basic Books, 1962).

that it is of no manner of consequence, with regard to the domestic happiness of a state, whether money be in a greater or less quantity. The good policy of the magistrate consists only in keeping it, if possible, still encreasing; because, by that means, he keeps alive a spirit of industry in the nation, and encreases the stock of labour, in which consists all real power and riches.[2]

But Cantillon, foreseeing a less happy outcome, provides an antidote; and completes the economist's 'dismal task':

> When a State has arrived at the highest point of wealth (I assume always that the comparative wealth of States consists principally in the respective quantities of money which they possess) it will inevitably fall into poverty by the ordinary course of things. The too great abundance of money, which so long as it lasts forms the power of States, throws them back imperceptibly but naturally into poverty. Thus it would seem that when a State expands by trade and the abundance of money raises the price of Land and Labour, the Prince or the Legislator ought to withdraw money from circulation, keep it for emergencies, and try to retard its circulation by every means except compulsion and bad faith, so as to forestall the too great dearness of its articles and prevent the drawbacks of luxury.[3]

There is hardly a country in the world today where these two positions are not—still!—under interminable debate. The terms in which the debates are conducted do change, as politics and economic theory continue their three-legged race to define terms of success and escape the rude revelation of a problem for which no solution ever seems forthcoming. The problem is the determination of monetary standards; the rise and fall of prices must be conveyed by some instrument, something with more staying power than, say, a tuning fork. There is a difference between money and a monetary standard; and the dawn of the history of the problem is to be found in Hayek's chapter on the genesis of the gold standard. But it is also in the essay on Dr. Bernard Mandeville where Hayek finds "the definite breakthrough in modern thought of the twin ideas of evolution and of the spontaneous formation of an order", an order which is the result of human action, but not of human design.

---

[2] David Hume, *Essays Moral, Political, and Literary*, ed. Eugene F. Miller (Indianapolis, Ind.: Liberty*Classics*, 1985), pp. 286-288.

[3] Richard Cantillon, *Essai sur la Nature du Commerce en Général*, ed. Henry Higgs (London: Frank Cass, 1959), p. 185.

England did not establish the gold standard by any conscious and deliberate act. In fact, it came about as the unintended consequence of the attempt to secure a silver standard through the recoinage of 1695, which was a deliberate, and rather costly, act, the result of an argument by John Locke that a monetary standard was a matter of principle, and that a standard once established in which contracts are made should be upheld. The establishment of Locke's principle did not secure its objective—a silver standard for the shilling, which Sir Isaac Newton, too, tried to secure in his role as Master of the Mint—but it did have the fortuitous outcome of securing for London the leading role in the world's financial markets, since it led much of the world to believe that if they lent their money to London they could be reasonably assured of getting it back. The principle was invoked in 1844 when England returned to the gold standard after the Napoleonic wars, and again in 1926 with not so favourable an outcome. Alas, the principle, like all such, contained premises the implications of which were not, perhaps still are not, known. Since the shilling—or any denomination of any currency—must be a fixed number, to fix that number relative to any other convertible value is a mysterious achievement for which there is no reliable recipe. Yet a principle, once accepted, takes on the same objective reality as any other event, thus muddying the ancient distinction between 'natural' and 'artificial' laws, the dichotomy which Hayek has found so poisonous in the Aristotelian menu.

The lessons of history are not, or not only, to avoid repeating the mistakes of the past. Whatever history has left to teach—and that value cannot be over-estimated—derives largely from what was not, perhaps could not have been, understood in the first place. Since we cannot predict all of the consequences of any act, or all of the implications of any theory, and do not, therefore, *know* what we are doing, we do not know what we have done.[4]

Consider the difficulties faced by economic forecasters extrapolating economic trends from estimates of present activity which are derived from statistics which in turn undergo endless revisions. In the words of one, "In theory, you're trying to find out what the future is going to be like. That's difficult when the past keeps changing."[5] The assumption that *economists* can find predictable solu-

---

[4] For a full discussion of this thesis and its implications for economic theory, see W. W. Bartley, III, *Unfathomed Knowledge, Unmeasured Wealth* (La Salle, Ill., and London: Open Court, 1990).

[5] Martin Zimmerman, chief economist at Ford Motor Co., quoted in *The Wall Street Journal*, August 31, 1989, p. A2.

tions to economic problems is undoubtedly the most inhibiting force in the present curriculum for students of economics. It has led to the increasing isolation of theoretical economists from the day-to-day practitioners of the subject—the actual participants in an economy, the consumers and the producers. It is the growth of *their* knowledge which is all important both for the success of an economy and the validity of any economic theory. And the fact that this knowledge is so widely dispersed and ever-changing lies at the core of much of Hayek's most important work, for example his famous essays, "The Use of Knowledge in Society"[6] and "The Meaning of Competition".[7] Yet it is the unpredictable character of the growth of knowledge which requires that from time to time we return our thoughts to the past, to rediscover in the terms set by our original problems whether we are still on course.

We can find no better introduction to the rewards of reading Hayek's historical studies—many of which are collected in this volume, and some of which appear here for the first time in English—than to repeat the gracious acknowledgement given to Hayek by Sir John Clapham in the preface to his definitive history of the Bank of England. "His masterly knowledge of our economic literature has been at my command; and to him I owe a number of pamphlet and press references. His edition of Henry Thornton's *Paper Credit* was always on my table for the period 1780-1820."[8] The essays in this volume—including Hayek's essay on Henry Thornton—are not printed in chronological order (though for the convenience of students of Hayek's work a table of the contents in chronological sequence is provided), since Hayek was not primarily concerned with establishing a sequential view of economic cause and effect. His concern here, and throughout most of his work, is with the development of concepts and their role in determining the evolution of economic and political order. With an historical context in view we may attempt to escape from the limits of our own parochial assumptions about human behaviour; investigating, as it were, the fossil remains for clues about evolution, to try to evade our own extinction.

Hayek's Vienna was not so lucky. The Great War and the Second World War severed Vienna's links with its former domain. But wars

---

[6] In F. A. Hayek, *Individualism and the Economic Order*, Gateway edition (Chicago: Henry Regnery, 1972), pp. 77-91.

[7] Op. cit., pp. 92-106.

[8] Sir John Clapham, *The Bank of England* (Cambridge: Cambridge University Press, 1944), p. viii.

are effects as well as causes, and Vienna's links with the former provinces of the Austro-Hungarian empire had already begun to loosen. There is perhaps yet another economic history lesson to be found in causes of the eventual collapse of all the great nineteenth-century empires, one that heretofore has not received sufficient attention, one that might reawaken an interest in economic history and the history of economic theory. Hayek, as we have said, had a keen sense of what mattered. In fact, the primary function of the capital city of an empire, such as Vienna or London, has been to bring together all the information necessary to maintain the political and economic order upon which the survival of the empire depends. Understanding the significance of information was the job of everyone in a capital; their own careers depended on it. But an invention of the nineteenth century changed the world forever in ways that we only now—with the development of the computer—begin to comprehend. Economists of the time did not. Ricardo had changed the focus of economic theory to an investigation of how economic gain is shared among the factors of production. Marx compounded the felony with his focus on industrial production. In fact, the investment of capital in manufacturing is but one of a set of interdependent relations which we might call the *dispersal of consumption*—and, although not identified as such in classical theory, is the necessary condition for the division of labour to be profitable. In short, it was the development of railroads that fundamentally changed the means of production of goods, and necessarily the consumption of those goods. (A thorough discussion of this economic process is beyond the intent of this introduction. However, examples are necessary to understand the importance of our subject, the unlearned lessons of history.)

More important than the railroad, ultimately, was the telegraph. For the first time, information could be conveyed over long distances without something or someone having to be physically transported. Once this possibility existed, the financial, political and military justification for empire vanished. Think of the Roman road and the British navy; think of the early banking families, the Rothschilds, for example; think of the incredible intelligence network of Lloyd's of London.

Now consider the instantaneous transmission of financial information by computer and satellite. And consider why this is valuable enough to have repaid the enormous investment it has required to bring it into being. For an explanation, we can retrace the development of economic theory, to writers before Ricardo, to Adam Smith, of course, but also to Richard Cantillon, about whom Hayek's essay is one of the treasures of this collection.

> Suppose now that the circulation of money in the provinces and in the Capital is equal both in quantity of money and speed of circulation. The balance will be first sent to the Capital in cash and this will diminish the quantity of money in the Provinces and increase it in the Capital, and consequently the raw material and commodities will be dearer in the Capital than in the Provinces, on account of the greater abundance of money in the Capital. The difference of prices in the Capital and in the Provinces must pay for the costs and risks of transport, otherwise cash will be sent to the Capital to pay the balance and this will go on till the prices in the Capital and the Provinces come to the level of these costs and risks. Then the Merchants or Undertakers of the Market Towns will buy at a low price the products of the Villages and will have them carried to the Capital to be sold there at a higher price: and this difference of price will necessarily pay for the upkeep of the Horses and Menservants and the profit of the Undertaker, or else he would cease his enterprise.
>
> It will follow from this that the price of raw Produce of equal quality will always be higher in the Country places which are nearest the Capital than in those more distant in proportion to the costs and risks of transport; and that the Countries adjacent to Seas and Rivers flowing into the Capital will get a better price for their Produce in proportion than those which are distant (Other things being equal) because water transport is less expensive than land transport. On the other hand the Products and small wares which cannot be consumed in the Capital, because they are not suitable or cannot be sent thither on account of their bulk, or because they would be spoiled on the way, will be infinitely cheaper in the Country and distant Provinces than in the Capital, owing to the amount of money circulating for them which is much smaller in the distant Provinces.
>
> So it is that new laid eggs, game, fresh butter, wood fuel, etc. will generally be much cheaper in the district of Poitou than in Paris, whilst Corn, Cattle and Horses will be dearer at Paris only by the difference of the cost and risk of carriage and the dues for entering the City.[9]

(It should also be observed that in this passage Cantillon points to the source of the seasonal flow of money that so plagued early banking.)

And he observes as well:

---

[9] Cantillon, op. cit., pp. 152-153.

> England today consumes not only the greatest part of its own small produce but also much foreign produce, such as Silks, Wines, Fruit, Linen in great quantity, etc. while she sends abroad only the produce of her Mines, her work and Manufactures for the most part, and dear though Labour be owing to the abundance of money, she does not fail to sell her articles in distant countries, owing to the advantage of her shipping, at prices as reasonable as in France where these same articles are much cheaper.[10]

Hayek has written at some length about the role of prices as signals for altering economic responses. The primary signal is the existence of two different prices for the same good. If the cost of transport is less than the difference between the two prices, a profit can be made. That profit is the fundamental gain of capitalism. It is why capitalism can improve the welfare of all without shifting the burden of cost within an economy.

Agreed, the above discussion is simplified. A price difference cannot always be discovered in an instant. There is the complication of the monetary standard; and prices alone do not tell one all that one needs to know in order to make efficient choices. Most troubling of all, there are unforeseen and unintended consequences which follow from any change in—or from a failure to change—economic behaviour; or from some at once improbable, yet unprepossessing, invention.

The troubling history of England in the twentieth century provides an example. For an empire which thrived on its ability to develop knowledge and to comprehend the significance of information, there was a disastrous lapse at the end of the Second World War. Recall the signal flags that Nelson used to win the battle at Trafalgar; the critical role that radar played in the Battle of Britain; and the decisive role that codebreaking played, first against the Japanese in the Pacific by the United States; secondly against the German U-boats by the British in the Atlantic, using a primitive computer developed by Alan Turing. The British failed to understand what they had been given. It was left for an Hungarian refugee, John von Neumann—not in Vienna but in America—to continue the revolution begun by the invention of the telegraph.

Of course, the sun did not begin to set on the British Empire because it failed to develop the computer. The empire dissolved when the costs of maintaining the economic and political order

---

[10] Op. cit., p. 171.

embodied in the structure became greater than the benefits: the telegraph, wireless, and then, of course, television so accelerated economic processes that even the Concorde supersonic transport was obsolete by the time Britain and France had developed it at a cost of billions. Widely dispersed information can now be brought together instantly, and new intelligence can be broadcast so efficiently that it is beyond the ability of any central power to control. This has raised 'opportunity cost' above any cost of production as the critical factor in the success of any new enterprise, commercial or military. Surprising anyone—except economists—has become more difficult and more costly. Stealth aircraft were the inevitable response to radar, and when fax machines replace posters, dictators learn that the handwriting is on the wall.

Has not something been lost in this instantaneous transmission of information? There is now such a welter of facts, images, disasters, space launches, children fallen in wells, dictators shot or not shot, oil prices up and oil prices down, how is anyone to make sense of it all? Will not even the lessons of the present, to say nothing of history, disappear in the banality of 'sound bytes', homilies made urgent through a wilful distortion of a sensory order. When we come to the realisation that so many of the enduring economic problems have *not* been solved, contrary to the assumptions of the economics textbooks, what will the undignified scramble for the exits leave trampled underfoot?

What is becoming a scarce resource is any sense of the significance of this welter of information. We are losing the sense of what matters, of the habits of mind that can identify problems and learn from mistakes. Some of this can be traced to a loss of context; abstract ideas are not easily conveyed absent a recognisable embodiment, and the subtext, that which is not said, may be missing. Hayek's quarrels with Aristotle are of the same character as his conversations with Sir Karl Popper and Milton Friedman: the welcome criticism of peers, those who can recognise the same premises needed to define a given problem, however they may come to differ over their conclusions. Only now do we begin to realise that something valuable may have been driven from the world when the continuity and tradition of Western civilisation was shattered in the same blows that destroyed unwanted empires. Now in Eastern Europe there is nostalgic talk of the good old days under the Hapsburg empire.

The evolution of knowledge is inseparable from the evolution of language, and something invaluable is lost when 'sound bytes' replace the human voice, heard in face-to-face discussion of mutual concerns. Inflection counts for much, and what is *not* said can only be recognised when allusion and irony are possible. So Vienna waltzes.

"Carl Menger", Hayek has recalled, "I saw only once, shortly after I had read his *Grundsätze*, when he marched in procession at the unveiling at the university of a monument of his brother Anton. He was so dignified and impressive with his long beard that later in my biographical essay I described him . . . as tall—the only wrong statement and the only one based on personal knowledge in that essay. I was however later brought in to advise on the sale of his library—so I saw the studies of all three founders of the Austrian school, but two of them only after their deaths. . . .

"The lady, Mrs. Menger, allowed me, as a reward for my efforts, to pick one attractive seventeenth-century duodecimo volume from his shelf of duplicates. It happened to be the to me still unknown essay by Richard Cantillon, which at once greatly fascinated me. . . ."

Stephen Kresge

PART I

THE ECONOMIST AND HIS DISMAL TASK

ONE

THE TREND OF ECONOMIC THINKING[1]

I

The position of the economist in the intellectual life of our time is unlike that of the practitioners of any other branch of knowledge. Questions for whose solution his special knowledge is relevant are probably more frequently encountered than questions related to any other science. Yet, in large measure, this knowledge is disregarded and in many respects public opinion even seems to move in a contrary direction. Thus the economist appears to be hopelessly out of tune with his time, giving unpractical advice to which his public is not disposed to listen and having no influence upon contemporary events. Why is this?

The situation is not without precedent in the history of economic thought; but it cannot be considered as normal, and there is strong reason to believe that it must be the result of a particular historical situation. For the views at present held by the public can clearly be traced to the economists of a generation or so ago. So that the fact is, not that the teaching of the economist has no influence at all; on the contrary, it may be very powerful. But it takes a long time to make its influence felt, so that, if there is change, the new ideas tend to be swamped by the domination of ideas which, in fact, have

[1] [Inaugural lecture delivered at the London School of Economics and Political Science on March 1, 1933. The Chair was taken by Dr. James Bonar. This essay was published in *Economica*, vol. 13, May 1933, pp. 121-137. The title of the lecture may possibly allude to an anthology edited by R. G. Tugwell, *The Trend of Economics* (New York: Alfred A. Knopf, 1924), published when Hayek was a student at New York University and attending seminars at Columbia University, where Tugwell was Assistant Professor of Economics. For a study of the significance of this lecture in the development of Hayek's thought, see Bruce J. Caldwell, "Hayek's 'The Trend of Economic Thinking'", *Review of Austrian Economics*, vol. 2, 1988, pp. 175-178. -Ed.]

become obsolete. Hence the recurring intellectual isolation of the economist. The problem of the relation between the economist and public opinion today resolves itself, therefore, into a question of the causes of the intellectual changes which have conspired to bring about this cleavage. It is this subject which I have chosen as the main theme of this lecture.

II

The subject is a vast one, but the aspect which I wish chiefly to emphasise is that which the economist must, naturally, be most anxious to make clear to the public: i.e., the role played by purely scientific progress—the growth of our insight into the interdependence of economic phenomena—in bringing about these changes in his attitude to practical problems.

At first sight there seem to be only two reasons why economists should change their attitude towards questions of economic policy: either they may find that their knowledge has been inadequate, or their views on the fundamental ethical postulates (upon which, of course, every practical conclusion is based) may undergo a change. In either case the role played by science would be clear. But, in fact, the cause of the great historical changes which I am discussing seems to me to be of a more subtle kind. It consists neither of a change in the underlying ethical valuations nor of a refutation of the validity of certain analytical propositions, but rather in a change of view regarding the relevance of that knowledge for practical problems. It was not a change of ideals nor a change of reasoning but a change of view with regard to the applicability of such reasoning which was responsible for the characteristic features of the popular economics of today. How did this come about?

It is a common belief that, about the middle of last century, perhaps under the influence of socialistic ideas, the social conscience was aroused by the existence of human misery which had previously escaped recognition, and it was decided no longer to tolerate it. Hence the decline of 'the old political economy' which had been blind to these considerations. But, in fact, nothing could be farther from the truth. No serious attempt has ever been made to show that the great liberal economists were any less concerned with the welfare of the poorer classes of society than were their successors. And I do not think that any such attempt could possibly be successful. The causes of the change must be sought elsewhere.

III

It is probably true that economic analysis has never been the product of detached intellectual curiosity about the *why* of social phenomena, but of an intense urge to reconstruct a world which gives rise to profound dissatisfaction. This is as true of the phylogenesis of economics as of the ontogenesis of probably every economist. As Professor Pigou[2] has aptly remarked: "It is not wonder, but the social enthusiasm which revolts from the sordidness of mean streets and the joylessness of withered lives, that is the beginning of economic science."[3] The mere existence of an extremely complicated mechanism which led to some kind of coordination of the independent action of individuals was not sufficient to arouse the scientific curiosity of men. While the movement of the heavenly bodies or the changes in our material surroundings excited our wonder because they were evidently directed by forces which we did not know, mankind remained—and the majority of men still remain—under the erroneous impression that, since all social phenomena are the product of our own actions, all that depends upon them is their deliberate object.

It was only when, because the economic system did not accomplish all we wanted, we prevented it from doing what it had been accomplishing, in an attempt to make it obey us in an arbitrary way, that we realised that there was anything to be understood. It was only incidentally, as a by-product of the study of such isolated phenomena, that it was gradually realised that many things which had been taken for granted were, in fact, the product of a highly complicated organism which we could only hope to understand by the intense mental effort of systematic inquiry. Indeed, it is probably no exaggeration to say that economics developed mainly as the outcome of the investigation and refutation of successive Utopian proposals—if by 'Utopian' we mean proposals for the improvement of undesirable effects of the existing system, based upon a complete disregard of those forces which actually enabled it to work.

---

[2] [Arthur C. Pigou (1877-1959), Professor of Political Economy, Cambridge University, 1908-1944. -Ed.]

[3] [Arthur C. Pigou, *The Economics of Welfare*, fourth edition (London: Macmillan, 1932), p. 5. -Ed.]

IV

Now, since economic analysis originated in this way, it was only natural that economists should immediately proceed from the investigation of causal interrelationships to the drawing of practical conclusions. In criticising proposals for improvement, they accepted the ethical postulates on which such proposals were based and tried to demonstrate that these were not conducive to the desired end and that, very often, policies of a radically different nature would bring about the desired result.

Such a procedure does not in any way violate the rule, which Professor Robbins[4] has so effectively impressed upon us, that science by itself can never prove what ought to be done.[5] But if there is agreement on ultimate aims, it is clearly scientific knowledge which decides the best policy for bringing them about. No doubt the economist should always be conscious of this distinction; but it would certainly have been nothing but intolerable pedantry if, in discussing practical problems, the economist had always insisted that science by itself proves nothing, when in fact it was only the newly gained knowledge which was decisive in bringing about the change in their attitude towards practical affairs.

The attitude of the classical economists to questions of economic policy was the outcome of their scientific conclusions. The presumption against government interference sprang from a wide range of demonstrations that isolated acts of interference definitely frustrated the attainment of those ends which all accepted as desirable.

[4] [Lionel Robbins (1898-1984), later Lord Robbins of Clare Market, Professor of Economics at the London School of Economics and Political Science, University of London, 1929-61; later chairman of the *Financial Times* and President of the Royal Economic Society; for many years one of Hayek's closest friends and associates. Among his works are *An Essay on the Nature and Significance of Economic Science* (London: Macmillan, 1932), *The Great Depression* (London: Macmillan, 1934), and *Autobiography of an Economist* (London: Macmillan, 1971). -Ed.]

[5] [Lionel Robbins, *An Essay on the Nature and Significance of Economic Science* (London: Macmillan, 1932). -Ed.]

V

But the position of the young science which led to conclusions so much in conflict with the result of more primitive reflections was bound to become difficult as soon as—following its first triumphant success—it became more conscious of its remaining defects. And those who disliked its conclusions were not slow in making the most of all the defects they could find. It was not the practical preoccupations of the economist which were responsible for this result. It is by no means certain that economics would have been less disliked if economists had been more careful to distinguish the pure theory from the more applied parts of their conclusions. It is true that economics was contemptuously dubbed a mere utilitarian science because it did not pursue knowledge for its own sake. But nothing would have aroused more resentment than if economists had tried to do so. Even today it is regarded almost as a sign of moral depravity if the economist finds anything to marvel at in his science; i.e., if he finds an unsuspected order in things which arouses his wonder. And he is bitterly reproached if he does not emphasise, at every stage of his analysis, how much he regrets that his insight into the order of things makes it less easy to change them whenever we please.

The attack on economics sprang rather from a dislike of the application of scientific methods to the investigation of social problems. The existence of a body of reasoning which prevented people from following their first impulsive reactions, and which compelled them to balance indirect effects, which could be seen only by exercising the intellect, against intense feeling caused by the direct observation of concrete suffering, then as now, occasioned intense resentment. It was against the validity of such reasoning in general that the emotional revolt was directed. Thus, temporarily, social enthusiasm succeeded in destroying an instrument created to serve it because it had been made impatient by the frequent disappointments which it had occasioned.

It is not to be denied that, at this early stage, economists had not yet become quite conscious of the precise nature of their generalisations. Nor can it be questioned that on some points, such as the theory of value, they proceeded on very unsatisfactory general assumptions. To what extent the actual foundations of the classical system were influenced by the fashionable philosophy of the day has been made clear by the distinguished author of *Philosophy and Politi-*

cal Economy.[6] But the abandonment *en bloc* of analytical economics was mainly due, not to the detection of faults in the foundation of concepts, but to the fact that, just at the time of this revolt, what professed to be a substitute method of analytical reasoning offered itself to the more practical-minded economist—a method which, from their point of view, had none of the objectionable features of the existing body of economics. I refer to the methods of the famous Historical School in Economics.[7] Although in the proper sense of a school aiming at the *replacement* of theoretical analysis by description, this is now a thing of the past, yet it is of tremendous historical importance because of its influence on popular thought at the present time.

It is clear that anything which justified the treatment of practical problems as something unique, determined only by their own historical development, was bound to be greeted as a welcome relief from the necessity of controlling emotions by difficult reasoning. It was just this advantage which the historical method afforded. Refusing to believe in general laws, the Historical School had the special attraction that its method was constitutionally unable to refute even the wildest of Utopias, and was, therefore, not likely to bring the disappointment associated with theoretical analysis. Its emphasis on the unsatisfactory aspects of economic life, rather than upon what was owed to the working of the existing system, and what would be the consequences if we tried directly to control some of the recognised evils, strongly recommended it to all those who had become impatient.

VI

For a considerable time, mainly during the last third of the nineteenth century, the two schools which now existed not only employed different methods, but also turned their attention to different problems. The more theoretically minded had to concentrate rather on the revision of the fundamental principles which had been damaged by decades of attack, and had to leave the more applied parts to others who were coming more and more under the influ-

---

[6] [James Bonar, *Philosophy and Political Economy in Some of their Historical Relations* (London: S. Sonnenschein; New York: Macmillan, 1893). -Ed.]

[7] [The German economists Wilhelm Roscher (1817-1894), Bruno Hildebrand (1812-1878), Karl Knies (1821-1898), Gustav Schmoller (1838-1917), and their followers. -Ed.]

ence of the historical method. So long, however, as this part of the task was left to men who had previously become acquainted with the general principles of analysis—and who were, therefore, immune from the more popular fallacies—the full effect of this change did not become apparent. The distinguished economist to whose memory this chair[8] is dedicated, and with whose long and fruitful career Professor Gregory has made us familiar,[9] offers a conspicuous example of the nature of this change. Thomas Tooke could never have become one of the leaders of the free-trade movement in his early years, and remained its lifelong advocate, if he had applied to the problems of international trade the same purely inductive methods which, in his later years, he considered as exclusively decisive in the discussion of monetary problems.

As so frequently happens, it was only in the second generation of the new school that the lack of the tools necessary for the interpretation of the intricate phenomena they were busy describing made itself felt. And so it came about that, just at the time when the theorists were most successful in constructing a sounder analytical basis for their science, the superstructure of more concrete applications which had been left in the hands of the more practical-minded men fell gradually, more discredited than disproved, into oblivion. And, in consequence, many of the palliatives and quack remedies which, in the past, had been rejected because, even judged by the analysis of the classical system, their indirect effects were seen to be obviously more objectionable than their immediate benefits, were introduced by the new generation of historical economists, until the reaction was carried to a point at which the futile attempts to redress special grievances by short-sighted State action could hardly have been more numerous if an analytical science of economics had never existed. It is no accident that the return of protectionism which followed the free-trade era of the nineteenth century was the work of men under the influence of this school.

---

[8] [Thomas Tooke (1774-1858), after whom Hayek's chair in Economic Science and Statistics was named. -Ed.]

[9] [Theodor Emmanuel Gugenheim Gregory, *An Introduction to Tooke and Newmarch's A History of Prices and of the State of the Circulation from 1792 to 1856* (London: P. S. King, 1928). -Ed.]

VII

It takes a long time to rebuild the structure of a science if one starts by revising the fundamental concepts. And the modern revision of theoretical economics has occupied sufficient time to allow what was at first the heretical view of a number of radical economists—who had to fight what was then the conservatism of the practical men who were still under the influence of economic liberalism—to pervade the thought of the public and to establish itself as the dominating doctrine, not only among advanced social reformers, but even among the most conservative businessmen. The public mind in all the leading countries of the world is now completely under the domination of the views which spring from the revolt against the classical economics of seventy years ago.

But, in the meantime, theorists have carried their work to a more realistic stage and have discovered with surprise how often the older writers, with their cruder instruments, had come to the right conclusions with regard to the concrete problems of the day. And this advance of theoretical reasoning has been borne out by the practical experience of our time. Times of great upheaval sometimes afford clearer demonstration of the broad principles of economic analysis than times when the movement of things is much less perceptible. In what, following a phrase used by Alfred Marshall in a similar connexion regarding the Napoleonic period,[10] we may call the temporary return of Europe to a reign of violence, the old doctrines have been once more tested; and while the descriptive-interventionist school had nothing to contribute, many of the classical maxims have emerged with renewed credit.

But while the task of the historical economist was comparatively simple because what he had to say on all problems of policy was not, and could not be, in any way different from what the man in the street would want if he had never heard of economics; that is, while the task of the historical school could be accomplished by simply waiting until the public had forgotten what it had previously learned, the task of the theoretical economist is a much more difficult one. It consists essentially in the demonstration of inconsistencies in a kind of ordinary reasoning which everybody employs

---

[10] [Alfred Marshall, *Industry and Trade: A Study of Industrial Technique and Business Organization; and of their Influences on the Conditions of Various Classes and Nations* (London: Macmillan, 1920), p. 674. -Ed.]

and the validity of which no one would ever doubt were it applied to simple cases where it can easily be understood. The difficulty really arises from the fact that the same kind of reasoning from familiar and undoubted facts, which even those who are most scornful of theoretical reasoning cannot avoid applying to simple cases, becomes suspect and calls for empirical confirmation as soon as it is applied to somewhat more complicated phenomena where it cannot be followed without some effort, or even special training.

And yet it is nothing but this that the economist does. By combining elementary conclusions and following up their implications he gradually constructs, from the familiar elements, a mental model which aims at reproducing the working of the economic system as a whole. Whether we use as a basis facts which are known from everyday experience or facts which have been laboriously collected by statistical or historical research, the importance and the difficulty of this further task remains the same, and the only test of its usefulness as a tool of interpretation is whether, by impeccable logic, it yields a model which reproduces movements of the type which we observe in the modern world. Only when we have carried to its logical conclusion this task of fitting the known parts together, so that we realise all the implications of their coexistence, are we able to say whether the known facts from which we have started are sufficient for the explanation of the more complicated phenomena.

The process of reasoning might, of course, have been carried out by some superhuman master-mind in a second, just as the whole structure of mathematics might be deduced from a few fundamental axioms.[11] But, in fact, its development has been the slow and gradual work of generations. But the very fact that economic theory consists merely of ordinary reasoning from commonly known facts—but carried beyond the point at which it is immediately obvious, and even beyond the point which an ordinary thinker would reach unaided by the work of earlier generations of economists—makes it very difficult for the non-economist to believe that economics can teach him anything. It explains why he is always likely to feel injured if the economist implies that there are interrelations between things which he does not see; and why the economist—unlike the

[11] [But see now Kurt Gödel, "Die Vollständigkeit der Axiome des logischen Funktionenkalküls", *Monatshefte für Mathematik und Physik*, vol. 37, 1930, pp. 349-360; and "Über formal unentscheidbare Sätze der Principia Mathematica und verwandter Systeme", *Ibid.*, vol. 38, 1931, pp. 173-198. Hayek took note of Gödel's proofs in his later work. See for example *Studies in Philosophy, Politics, and Economics* (Chicago: University of Chicago Press; London: Routledge & Kegan Paul, 1967), p. 62. -Ed.]

practitioners of the other sciences—is almost expected to apologise if he disagrees with the more hastily reached conclusions of lay thought. What is even more resented is the mental shorthand and the conventional formulae which the economist uses as an indispensable part of his technique, in place of the explicit development on every occasion of all his arguments—a process which, of course, would be inimical to the formulation of any conclusions whatever.

VIII

Now, pursued in the way I have explained, economic analysis provides particular answers to particular questions. But it does more than this. By bringing out the interdependence of the particular phenomena, one upon the other, it provides insight of a much wider character: an insight into the nature of the economic system as a whole, which affords a refutation of the more naive beliefs regarding economic phenomena to which minds trained in purely descriptive disciplines seem subject. It is exceedingly difficult to explain this in a form which is unexceptionable. But it is necessary to understand it if we are to comprehend the general effects which preoccupation with theoretical analysis tends to have upon the attitude of the economist to practical questions. Let me try to make it clear.

From the time of Hume and Adam Smith, the effect of every attempt to understand economic phenomena—that is to say, of every theoretical analysis—has been to show that, in large part, the coordination of individual efforts in society is not the product of deliberate planning, but has been brought about, and in many cases could only have been brought about, by means which nobody wanted or understood, and which in isolation might be regarded as some of the most objectionable features of the system. It showed that changes implied, and made necessary, by changes in our wishes, or in the available means, were brought about without anybody realising their necessity. In short, it showed that an immensely complicated mechanism existed, worked and solved problems, frequently by means which proved to be the only possible means by which the result could be accomplished, but which could not possibly be the result of deliberate regulation because nobody understood them. Even now, when we begin to understand their working, we discover again and again that necessary functions are discharged by spontaneous institutions. If we tried to run the system by deliberate regulation, we should have to invent such institutions, and yet at first we did not even understand them when we saw them.

Unfortunately, this oldest and most general result of the theory of social phenomena has never been given a title which would secure it an adequate and permanent place in our thinking. The limitations of language make it almost impossible to state it without using misleading metaphorical words. The only intelligible form of explanation for what I am trying to state would be to say—as we say in German—that there is *sense* [*Sinn*] in the phenomena; that they perform a necessary *function*. But as soon as we take such phrases in a literal sense, they become untrue. It is an animistic, anthropomorphic interpretation of phenomena, the main characteristic of which is that they are not willed by any mind. And as soon as we recognise this, we tend to fall into an opposite error, which is, however, very similar in kind: we deny the existence of what these terms are intended to describe.

It is, of course, supremely easy to ridicule Adam Smith's famous "invisible hand"—which leads man "to promote an end which was no part of his intention".[12] But it is an error not very different from this anthropomorphism to assume that the existing economic system serves a definite function only in so far as its institutions have been deliberately willed by individuals. This is probably the *last* remnant of that primitive attitude which made us invest with a human mind everything that moved and changed in a way adapted to perpetuate itself or its kind. In the natural sciences, we have gradually ceased to do so and have learned that the interaction of different tendencies may produce what we call an order, without any mind of our own kind regulating it. But we still refuse to recognise that the spontaneous interplay of the actions of individuals may produce something which is not the deliberate object of their actions but an organism in which every part performs a necessary function for the continuance of the whole, without any human mind having devised it. In the words of an eminent Austrian economist, we refuse to recognise that society is an organism and not an organisation[13] and that, in a sense, we are part of a 'higher' organised system which, without our knowledge, and long before we tried to understand it,

---

[12] [Adam Smith, *An Inquiry Into the Nature and Causes of the Wealth of Nations* [1776], book IV, chapter ii, in *The Glasgow Edition of the Works and Correspondence of Adam Smith*, vol. 2:1 (Oxford: Clarendon Press, 1976), p. 456. -Ed.]

[13] [Ludwig von Mises, *Gemeinwirtschaft* (Jena: Gustav Fischer, 1923), p. 280 et seq. (second edition, 1932, p. 265). See English translation: *Socialism* (Indianapolis, Ind.: Liberty*Classics*, 1981), pp. 261-263. -Ed.]

solved problems the existence of which we did not even recognise, but which we should have had to solve in much the same way if we had tried to run it deliberately.

IX

The recognition of the existence of this organism is the recognition that there is a subject-matter for economics. It is one of the causes of the unique position of economics that the existence of a definite object of its investigation can be realised only after a prolonged study, and it is, therefore, not surprising that people who have never really studied economic theory will necessarily be doubtful of the legitimacy of its existence, as well as of the appropriateness of its method. A real proof for all I have said and for all the economist contends can, therefore, be given only by means of a complete exposition of his science. Hence I must content myself here with illustrating the meaning of what I have said by means of a few general references and one more concrete example.

In the whole body of economics, there is probably no part which shows better how our inability to understand the working of the existing system leads to dissatisfaction with it and also to action which can only make the situation worse, than that most difficult part, the theory of capital and interest. It is in this field that, during the past fifty years, decisive advances have been made which have put on a sound basis much that was divined rather than demonstrated by the earlier economists. I do not think that this belief—as might, perhaps, be suspected—is due to a personal predilection for those problems. It is, of course, true that I should not be standing here today if I had not had the good fortune to receive my training in economics in an atmosphere which was still full of the influence of the man to whom these advances are mainly due.[14] And if I needed anything to remind me of this, the presence in the chair of the distinguished economist to whom the introduction of

[14] [Eugen von Böhm-Bawerk (1851-1914), Austrian minister of finance and later Professor of Economics at the University of Vienna along with Hayek's teacher Friedrich von Wieser. His works include the multi-volume *Kapital und Kapitalzins* [1884-1912], translated as *Capital and Interest*, 3 vols (South Holland, Ill.: Libertarian Press, 1959), and "Zum Abschluß des Marxschen Systems", in *Staatswissenschaftliche Arbeiten, Festgaben für Karl Knies*, ed. O. von Boenigk (Berlin: Haering, 1896), translated as *Karl Marx and the Close of His System* (London: Fisher Unwin, 1898) and reprinted in *Karl Marx and the Close of His System and Böhm-Bawerk's Criticism of Marx*, ed. Paul Sweezy (New York: Augustus M. Kelley, 1949). -Ed.]

these doctrines into the English-speaking world is chiefly owing could not fail to make me vividly conscious of the situation.[15]

But I think that there is ample objective evidence of the extraordinary part which this theory has played in the progress of our insight into the economic process. There is probably no better instance of how the study of economic theory compels socialist thinkers to realise that, in their attempts to construct a positive plan of their ideal society, they can solve some of the main problems in no better way than by copying as closely as possible even what seemed to them before some of the most objectionable features of the existing system—including interest. And, on the other hand, there can be little doubt at the present day that the prevalent tendency to discredit the accumulation of wealth, to belittle the need for capital, and to discourage saving—not only in times of depression[16]—which is clearly an effect of the lack of understanding of the functions of capital, is one of the main destructive forces leading the world to misery.

Let me try to state in more detail an example which is typical of the errors in reasoning which lead, in most cases, to the demand for planning. It has the rare advantage of being capable of explanation in few words. For a most impressive array of further examples of a similar nature, I need only remind you of the last inaugural address of an economist at this School—that of Professor Plant—delivered at the beginning of last session.[17] My example relates to the theory of technical progress and depreciation. In the popular discussion of competitive capitalism, it is often complained that entrepreneurs go on using obsolete machinery when better machines are available. Side by side with such complaints are others to the effect that capital is 'wasted' by replacing existing machinery when it is still fit for many years' use. Each of these obviously incompatible criticisms is made a plea for centralised planning. Each implies that competition leads to uneconomic production which a wise planner would avoid. Closer analysis, however, reveals the fact that either of the alternatives which the intelligent planner is supposed to adopt

[15] [James Bonar was in the chair when Hayek delivered this Inaugural Address. See footnotes 1 and 6 above. -Ed.]

[16] [See "Spending and Savings: Public Works from Rates", Letter, with T. E. Gregory, Arnold Plant, and Lionel Robbins, to *The Times* of London, October 19, 1932, replying to "Private Spending: Money for Productive Investment", letter in *The Times*, October 17, 1932, by D. H. MacGregor, A. C. Pigou, J. M. Keynes, Walter Layton, Arthur Salter, and J. C. Stamp. -Ed.]

[17] [See Arnold Plant, "Trends in Business Administration", *Economica*, vol. 35, no. 12, February 1932, pp. 45-62. -Ed.]

would lead to a waste of resources, and that the wisest thing he could do would be to bring about, by delicate regulation, what is accomplished spontaneously by competition. It reveals, too, that he would lack the most important guide to such action which the competitive system affords.

In either case, of course, what we want to do is to make the best possible use of the available resources. And whatever criterion we adopt as to the relative importance of different needs, this means that a given result ought, in every case, to be obtained with the least possible sacrifice of other ends.

In the case under consideration, competition will obviously mean that the new invention will be introduced in *all* cases where it reduces current costs of production; i.e., where the cost of the capital required for the new invention is smaller than the saving on other costs made possible by the new machinery; and it will be introduced *only* in such cases. But the cost of capital, as well as other costs (such as the wages of labour) which are saved, is evidently determined by the competing demand from other industries. This in fact means, in the first place, that our problem is to determine whether, and to what extent, in the industry in question, labour (or other factors which can be used elsewhere) is to be replaced by new capital; and secondly, that the question depends upon the relative addition to the total product which either of these two will contribute elsewhere. If the cost of capital—interest and amortisation—invested in it is less than the cost of the other factors it replaces, the new machinery will be introduced *not* in order to do the work of machinery which is already in existence, but because it does that work *plus* the work of a quantity of other factors which will produce elsewhere more than the new capital could have done. It is obvious that a wise planner would have to act on the same principles, and that he could only do so on the basis of a given rate of interest, expressing the productivity of capital. But it is difficult to see how this could be obtained save by a competitive capital market. The best the dictator could do in such a case would be to imitate as closely as possible what would happen under free competition. Yet having regard to the extent to which legislative action is demanded, at the present time, to protect invested capital against obsolescence caused by the introduction of more modern technical methods, it is not possible to be very optimistic about the outcome.

X

This example of analysis will, perhaps, be sufficient to explain why the economist will come to very different conclusions from those reached by those to whom economic phenomena represent a number of independent events, explained by their individual historical causes, and in no way implied by the inherent logic of the system. This does not by any means imply that the economist will arrive at a purely negative attitude towards any kind of deliberate interference with the working of the system. But it may, and very likely will, mean an almost consistently negative attitude towards those proposals for interference which are not based upon an understanding of the working of the system; namely, the proposals which spring most readily and regularly to the lay mind. Further, in view of the incomplete nature of our knowledge, it will mean that, in all doubtful cases, there will exist a presumption against interference. However, this by no means does away with the positive part of the economist's task, the delimitation of the field within which collective action is not only unobjectionable but actually a useful means of obtaining the desired ends. Unfortunately, at the present time, as at the time when theoretical economics was first in the ascendancy, the effects of an extensive State activity which is based upon a quite inadequate understanding of the coherence of economic phenomena are so preponderantly more harmful than the absence of any new form of State activity which he might like to suggest, that the economist is, in practice, almost inevitably driven into a mainly negative position. But it is certainly to be hoped that this practical necessity will not again prevent economists from devoting more attention to the positive task of delimiting the field of useful State activity.

There can be no doubt that after Bentham's early distinction between the *agenda* and the *non-agenda* of government, the classical writers very much neglected the positive part of the task and thereby allowed the impression to gain ground that *laissez-faire* was their ultimate and only conclusion—a conclusion which, of course, would have been invalidated by the demonstration that, in any single case, State action was useful. To remedy this deficiency must be one of the main tasks of the future.

XI

But while I certainly do not wish to minimise this part of the economist's task, I still think that our present knowledge justifies us in saying that the field for rational State activity in the service of the ethical ideals held by the majority of men is not only different from, but is also very much narrower than is often thought. It is, of course, on this point that an increasing number of economists so completely disagree with the current popular opinion which considers a progressive extension of State control as inevitable.

Characteristically enough, this belief in the inevitability of more State control is, in most cases, based not so much upon a clear notion of the supposed advantages of planning as upon a kind of fatalism: upon the idea that 'history never moves back'—another legacy of the belief in historical laws which dominated the thinking of the last two generations. But in an age where we are rapidly returning to the conditions of mercantilism, this argument against the possibility of a return to conditions similar to those existing sixty years ago is probably bound to lose its force. More important is the fact that the other source of the belief in the inevitability of the ultimate victory of planning, the conviction that, since where there is no directing Will there must be chaos, deliberate planning will necessarily mean an improvement on existing conditions, is more and more recognised to be the result of our insufficient understanding of the existing system.

I have discussed planning here rather than its older brother socialism, not because I think that there is any difference between the two (except for the greater consistency of the latter), but because most of the planners do not yet realise that they are socialists and that, therefore, what the economist has to say with regard to socialism applies also to them. In this sense, there are, of course, very few people left today who are not socialists.

Indeed, it seems to me to be almost inevitable that, on the basis of such economic ideas as are imbibed as part of the general education of the day, every warm-hearted person, as soon as he becomes conscious of the existing misery, should become a socialist. This has certainly been the experience of a great many economists of the younger generation to whom, when they took up their study, economics meant little else but more information about these deplorable facts which cried aloud for a remedy. But the conclusion to which the study of economics leads some of them seems so violently in contrast with the reasons which led them to embark upon their study of economics that most people conclude that their ethical standards must have undergone a complete change. It is, indeed, one of the interesting facts of the present time that a growing number of economists of the younger generation who have not the slightest sentimental attachment to conservatism—and many of whom began as socialists—feel more and more compelled by their reasoning to take a conservative attitude towards many problems—or rather an attitude which, a generation ago, would have been called conservative. And this happens with men who not only have all possible sympathy with the ethical motives from which economic radicalism springs, but who would be only too glad if they could believe that socialism or planning can do what they promise to do, because they probably realise better than any non-economist that, for a considerable time at least, development will tend in this direction and will be revised, if ever, only at the cost of bitter experience and grave disillusionment.

That such an intellectual reaction is on the way and that it is not merely the experience of one or two individuals is perhaps somewhat difficult to see if one looks at a single country; but it becomes fairly clear if one compares countries in different phases of development of economic thought.[18] If one compares, for example, Germany, where the influences which led to the decline of analytical insight originated, with, say, the United States, where they have been felt only in comparatively recent times, or even with England—which, in this respect, occupies a kind of intermediate position—one cannot help noticing how far the cycle has already swung round in Germany and how completely the relative position of the intellectual radicals and popular opinion has changed. In Germany—and to a certain extent in England also—the people who call for a further extension of governmental control of economic life have certainly ceased to be in any way intellectual path-breakers. They are most definitely the expression of the spirit of the age, the ultimate product of the revolutionary thinking of an earlier generation. To recognise their position in this respect, of course, does nothing to decide the question whether the future belongs to them—as it well may. But it throws an interesting light on the role played by the progress of knowledge in this development. For, whatever we may think about particular problems, there can be no doubt that recent additions to knowledge in this respect have made the probability of a solution of our difficulties by planning appear less, rather than more, likely. What seemed minor difficulties to the

[18] [This essay was written in 1933. -Ed.]

33

economist of a generation ago have since been recognised—by socialists as well as by non-socialists—as crucial problems which some may, perhaps, hope to solve in the future, but the complete neglect of which certainly invalidates much of the popular confidence of the present.[19]

And so I come back to the point from which I started—the isolation of the contemporary economist and the refusal of modern progressivism to avail itself of the knowledge he can provide—a knowledge which is the product of the only persistent attempt systematically to explore the possibilities of change. The peculiar historical development which I have sketched has brought it about that the economist frequently finds himself in disagreement in regard to means with those with whom he is in agreement with regard to ends; and in agreement in regard to means with those whose views regarding ends are entirely antipathetic to him—men who have never felt the urge to reconstruct the world and who frequently support the forces of stability only for reasons of selfishness. In such a situation, it is perhaps inevitable that he should become the object of dislike and suspicion. But if he recognises the circumstances from which they spring, he will be able to bear them with patience and understanding, confident that he possesses in his scientific knowledge a solvent for differences which are really intellectual, and that although, at present, his activities have little effect, yet in course of time they will come to be recognised as serving more consistently than the activities of those he opposes, the ends which they share in common.

[19] [See F. A. Hayek, ed., *Collectivist Economic Planning* (London: Routledge & Kegan Paul, 1935). -Ed.]

TWO

ON BEING AN ECONOMIST[1]

It is reported of the greatest economist whom I have personally known[2] that he used to say that if he had seven sons they should all study economics. If this was meant to suggest the magnitude of the task economists have to solve, this heroic resolution cannot be highly enough commended. If it was meant to suggest that the study of economics is a sure path to personal happiness, I am afraid I have no such cheerful message for you. And it may be that Carl Menger himself later changed his views: when at last, at the age of sixty-two, he produced one son, this son did not become an economist, though the father lived to see him become a promising mathematician.

There is at least one kind of happiness which the pursuit of most sciences promises but which is almost wholly denied to the economist. The progress of the natural sciences often leads to unbounded confidence in the future prospects of the human race, and provides the natural scientist with the certainty that any important contribution to knowledge which he makes will be used to improve the lot of men. The economist's lot, however, is to study a field in which, almost more than any other, human folly displays itself. The scientist has no doubt that the world is moving on to better and finer things, that the progress he makes today will tomorrow be recognised and used. There is a glamour about the natural sciences which expresses itself in the spirit and the atmosphere in which it is pursued and received, in the prizes that wait for the successful as in the satisfaction it can offer to most. What I want to say to you tonight is a warning that, if you want any of this, if to sustain you

---

[1] [An address delivered to the Students' Union of the London School of Economics, February 23, 1944. The address was presumably delivered at Peterhouse, Cambridge University, where the LSE was lodged during the war. This essay has not previously been published. -Ed.]

[2] [Carl Menger, founder of the Austrian School, is being referred to, but what Hayek says is an exaggeration. Hayek saw Menger on a formal occasion, but did not meet him. He did know the family, was asked to help in estimating the value of Carl Menger's library, and knew Menger's son, Karl Menger, Jr., quite well. -Ed.]

in the toil which the prolonged pursuit of any subject requires, you want these clear signs of success, you had better leave economics now and turn to one of the more fortunate other sciences. Not only are there no glittering prizes, no Nobel prizes[3] and—I should have said till recently—no fortunes and no peerages,[4] for the economist. But even to look for them, to aim at praise or public recognition, is almost certain to spoil your intellectual honesty in this field. The dangers to the economist from any too strong desire to win public approval, and the reasons why I think it indeed fortunate that there are only few marks of distinction to corrupt him, I shall discuss later. But before that I want to consider the more serious cause for sorrow to the economist, the fact that he cannot trust that the progress of his knowledge will necessarily be followed by a more intelligent handling of social affairs, or even that we shall advance in this field at all and there will not be retrograde movements. The economist knows that a single error in his field may do more harm than almost all the sciences taken together can do good—even more, that a mistake in the choice of a social order, quite apart from the immediate effect, may profoundly affect the prospects for generations. Even if he believes that he is himself in possession of the full truth—which he believes less the older he grows—he cannot be sure that it will be used. And he cannot even be sure that his own activities will not produce, because they are mishandled by others, the opposite of what he was aiming at.

I shall not argue that the economist has no influence. On the contrary, I agree with Lord Keynes that "the ideas of economists and political philosophers, both when they are right and when they are wrong, are more powerful than is commonly understood. Indeed the world is ruled by little else."[5] The only qualification I want to add, and with which Lord Keynes would probably agree, is that economists have this great influence only in the long run and only indirectly, and that when their ideas begin to have effect, they

---

[3] [This was written in 1944, long before the establishment of the Nobel Memorial Prize in Economic Science which Hayek himself was awarded in 1974. Hayek accepted the prize with some reservations, expressing in his acceptance speech in Stockholm some of the reluctance stated in this lecture. See "The Pretence of Knowledge", chapter 2 of his *New Studies in Philosophy, Politics, Economics and the History of Ideas* (Chicago: University of Chicago Press; London: Routledge & Kegan Paul, 1978). -Ed.]

[4] [The reference is obviously to Keynes, who was created a Baron in 1942. -Ed.]

[5] *The General Theory of Employment Interest and Money* (London: Macmillan, 1936), p. 383 [reprinted as vol. 7 of *The Collected Writings of John Maynard Keynes* (London: Macmillan, 1973). -Ed.].

have usually changed their form to such an extent that their fathers can scarcely recognise them.

This is closely connected with the fact, inevitable I believe in a democracy, that those who have to apply economic theory are laymen, not really trained as economists. In this economics differs from other disciplines. We do not, as the other sciences do, train practitioners who are called in when an economic problem arises—or they can at most be called in as advisers- while the actual decisions must be left to the statesman and the general public. However attractive the ideal of a government by experts may have appeared in the past—it even induced a radical liberal like John Stuart Mill to state that "of all governments, ancient and modern, the one by which this excellence [i.e., that political questions are decided 'by the deliberately formed opinion of a comparatively few, specially educated for the task'] is possessed in the most eminent degree is the government of Prussia—a most powerfully and skilfully organised aristocracy of all the most highly educated men in the kingdom".[6] We know now where this leads. And we prefer, I think rightly, an imperfect government by democratic methods to a real government by experts.

But this has consequences of which economists more than others ought to be aware. We can never be sure what our suggestions will produce and whether our best meant efforts may not result in something very different from what we wish. It is, in fact, quite conceivable that advance in social knowledge may produce a retrogression in social policy, and this has indeed happened more than once. I will give you only one example. About seventy years ago economists began seriously to urge certain exceptions to the free-trade argument then almost universally accepted. I am not concerned here whether they were right or wrong. The point I want to make is merely that when after the usual interval of a generation or so their ideas began to take effect they produced a state of affairs which, I believe, even the most extreme protectionists would agree to be greatly inferior to the conditions of near free trade they had attacked. It may be true that some little protection, or some little flexibility in exchange rates, judiciously administered, may be better than free trade or the gold standard. I don't believe it, but it may

---

[6] [John Stuart Mill, "Rationale of Representation" [1835], in *Essays on Politics and Society* (Toronto: University of Toronto Press; London: Routledge & Kegan Paul, 1977), p. 23, which is vol. 18 of *The Collected Works of John Stuart Mill*. The quotation as given weaves together a full sentence by Mill with the quotation in brackets which precedes it by a few lines. The meaning is not altered. -Ed.]

be true. But this does not exclude that the advocacy of these modifications may have most regrettable effects. The attack against the principle, or perhaps half-truth, of the free-trade doctrine has certainly had the effect that the public forgot even a great deal of the elementary economics it had learnt, and became once more ready to assent to absurdities which seventy years ago it would have laughed out of court.

I have just referred to the interval of a generation or so which usually elapses before a new opinion becomes a political force. This phenomenon will be familiar to the readers of Dicey's *Law and Opinion*,[7] and I could add many further instances to those given there. But it is perhaps specially necessary to remind you of it, because the unique rapidity with which, in our own time, the teaching of Lord Keynes has penetrated into public consciousness may a little mislead you about what is the more regular course of things. I shall presently have to suggest an explanation of this exceptional case.

Another point to which I have indirectly referred already, but on which I must dwell a little, is the fact that in our field no knowledge can be regarded as established once and for all, and that, in fact, knowledge once gained and spread is often, not disproved, but simply lost and forgotten. The elements of the free-trade argument, at one time nearly understood by every educated man, are a case in point. The reason why in our field knowledge can be so lost is, of course, that it is never established by experiment, but can be acquired only by following a rather difficult process of reasoning. And while people will believe a thing if you just tell them 'it has been shown by experiment'—although they may understand nothing about it—they will not accept in the same manner an argument, even though that argument may have convinced everybody who has understood it. The result is that in economics you can never establish a truth once and for all but have always to convince every generation anew—and that you may find much more difficult when things appear to yourself no longer so simple as they once did.

I cannot attempt here more than to touch upon the inexhaustible subject of *Economists and the Public*, a subject on which Professor W. H. Hutt of Capetown has written a thoughtful book, which contains many wise things and some not so wise—and which I

---

[7] [A. V. Dicey, *Lectures on the Relation Between Law & Public Opinion in England During the Nineteenth Century* (London: Macmillan, 1914). -Ed.]

strongly recommend to your attention.[8] There are very interesting points in this connexion, which have considerable bearing on our professional position as economists, such as the special difficulty, in our field, to distinguish between the expert and the quack—and the equally important fact of the traditional unpopularity of the economists. You probably all know the remark of Walter Bagehot[9] that the public has never yet been sorry to hear of the death of an economist. In fact, the dislike for most of the teaching of the economists in the past has built up a picture of the economist as a sort of monster devouring children. There is little to justify it in the facts. One of the great liberal politicians of the early nineteenth century (Sir James Mackintosh[10]) has said that "he had known Smith slightly, Ricardo well and Malthus intimately and found them about the best men he had known". I can to some extent confirm this. As you perhaps know I have amused myself at times to dig into the history of economics, and during the past twenty-five years I have had the opportunity to know not only a good many economists of this and the past generation but also to compare them with scholars in other fields. And I must say I have found them on the whole a surprisingly nice, sensitive and sane lot of people, less crotchety and mad than other scientists. Yet they still enjoy a reputation worse than almost any other profession and are imagined to be particularly hard, prejudiced, and devoid of feeling. And it was, and still is, the most eminent of economists in an academic sense, towards whom these reproaches were most frequently directed, while nothing is easier than for a crank to acquire the reputation of being a friend of the people. Things are in this respect still very much the same as they were in Adam Smith's time, and what he said about the relation of an M.P. to monopolies applies very much to the relation of the economist to the practical 'interests'—and not only the capitalist interests: "The member of parliament", you will find it

---

[8] [W. H. Hutt, *Economists and the Public: A Study of Competition and Opinion* (London: Jonathan Cape, 1936). Hutt was one of Hayek's earliest associates at the London School of Economics and a life-long friend and collaborator. -Ed.]

[9] [Walter Bagehot (1826-1877), English economist, banker and essayist, editor of *The Economist* and author of *Lombard Street* (London: P. S. King, 1873), reprinted in *The Collected Works of Walter Bagehot* (London: The Economist, 1978), vol. 9, pp. 45-233. This is perhaps the best-known book on English central banking. -Ed.]

[10] [Sir James Mackintosh (1765-1832), English jurist and abolitionist, author of *Vindiciae Gallicae: Defence of the French Revolution and its English Admirers against the Accusations of the Right Hon. Edmund Burke* (London: G. G. J. and J. Robinson, 1791), and *History of the Revolution in England in 1688* (London: Longmans, Rees, Orme, Brown, Green, & Longman, 1834). -Ed.]

said in the *Wealth of Nations*,[11] "who supports every proposal for strengthening this monopoly (of house manufacturers), is sure to acquire not only the reputation of understanding trade, but great popularity and influence with an order of men whose number and wealth render them of great importance. If he opposes them, on the contrary, and still more if he has authority enough to thwart them, neither the most acknowledged probity, nor the highest rank, nor the greatest public services, can protect him from the most infamous abuse and detraction, from personal insults, nor sometimes real danger, arising from the insolent outrage of furious and disappointed monopolists."

Before I pursue this subject of the effect of public opinion and political bias on the work of the economist I must for a moment pause to consider the various reasons and purposes which make us study economics. It is probably still true of most of us—and in this, too, economics differs from most other subjects—that we did not turn to economics for the fascination of the subject as such. Whatever may guide us later, few do—or at least did in my time—turn to economics for that reason—simply because we usually don't quite know what economics is. Indeed I remember that when I first borrowed during the last war from a fellow officer a textbook on economics[12] I was strongly repelled by the dreariness of what I found, and my social enthusiasm was hardly sufficient to make me plod through the tome in which I hoped to find—and needless to say, did not find—the answer to the burning problem of how to build a juster society for which I really cared. But while the motives which have led most of us—and I hope most of you—to the study of economics are highly commendable, they are not very conducive to real advance of insight. The fact which we must face is that nearly all of us come to the study of economics with very strong views on subjects which we do not understand. And even if we make a show of being detached and ready to learn, I am afraid it is almost always with a mental reservation, with an inward determination to prove that our instincts were right and that nothing we learn can change our basic convictions. Though I am verging dangerously on preaching, let me nevertheless implore you to make

[11] [Adam Smith, *An Inquiry into the Nature and Causes of the Wealth of Nations* [1776], book IV, chapter ii, in *The Glasgow Edition of the Works and Correspondence of Adam Smith*, vol. 2:1 (Oxford: Clarendon Press, 1976), p. 471. -Ed.]

[12] [This happened during a quiet period on the Italian front, on the Piave. The two books were by Grunzl and Jentsch. Hayek later told us, "I still marvel that these particular books did not give me a permanent distaste for the subject". -Ed.]

a determined effort to achieve that intellectual humility which alone helps one to learn. Nothing is more pernicious to intellectual honesty than pride in not having changed one's opinions—particularly if, as is usually the case in our field, these are opinions which in the circles in which we move are regarded as 'progressive' or 'advanced' or just modern. You will soon enough discover that what you regard as specially advanced opinions are just the opinions dominant in your particular generation and that it requires much greater strength and independence of mind to take a critical view of what you have been taught to be progressive than merely to accept them.

But back to my main topic. The great majority of you necessarily study the social sciences not with the intention of going on to study them for the rest of your lives, but with a view to a job in which in the near future you can use your knowledge. You will then be entirely concerned with what is practical and will have to take the dominant ideals and ideas of your time for granted. Though in the long run it may be the economist who creates these ruling ideas, what he can do in practice is determined by the ideas created by his fathers or grandfathers. Does that mean that in academic study, too, we ought to be concerned with the immediately practical, take the current of ideas for granted, and prepare ourselves for the particular job we shall probably be called upon to perform? Now I do not believe that the universities can do this or that they would perform their proper function if they attempted to do it. I do not think that in the social sciences the universities could give an effective 'professional training' or that persons so trained would be of much use except for subordinate jobs. The practical aspects of a particular job are much better learnt on the job—and that is even true of many of the more general concrete aspects of the society in which we live. What you need, if through that inevitable apprenticeship you hope ultimately to rise to more responsible positions, is a capacity to interpret the detail with which you will be concerned and to see through the catchwords and phrases which govern everyday life. Does the study of the social sciences as it is now pursued provide this education—or how can it be made to do so?

This raises immediately the vexed problem of specialisation versus a general and all-round education, much more acute and difficult in the social sciences than anywhere else. Let me at once meet a common misunderstanding: it is often argued that in social life everything hangs so closely together that society can only be studied 'as a whole'.[13] If that were really the case it would mean that it could not be studied at all. Nobody is capable of really understanding all aspects of society, and so far as advancement of knowledge is concerned specialisation is in the social sciences as necessary as anywhere, and becomes daily more necessary. But in another sense the contention that exclusive knowledge of a single sector of the social sciences is of little use is perfectly true. While you may be a very useful member of society if you are a competent chemist or biologist but know nothing else, you will not be a useful member of society if you know only economics or political science and nothing else. You cannot successfully use your technical knowledge unless you are a fairly educated person, and, in particular, have some knowledge of the whole field of the social sciences as well as some knowledge of history and philosophy. Of course real competence in some particular field comes first. Unless you really know your economics or whatever your special field is, you will be simply a fraud. But if you know only economics and nothing else, you will be a bane to mankind, good, perhaps, for writing articles for other economists to read, but for nothing else. If you have only three years[14] this double task of acquiring technical competence in a narrow field *plus* a general education is a formidable task. But you will find it will for long be the only opportunity you have to collect a great deal of varied knowledge whose meaning and significance you will recognise only later. And if you mean to make the academic study of one of the subjects your life-work, it is even more important that during your undergraduate years you let your interests range rather widely. Any successful original work on one of the social sciences requires now many years of exacting and exclusive attention to a narrow field, and it will be only after ten or fifteen years in which by such work you have become entitled to

---

[13] [This is an allusion to K. R. Popper's discussion of 'holism' in his three articles on "The Poverty of Historicism". Hayek, then editor of *Economica*, published the first two of these in that journal in 1944, and the third in 1945. Popper's essays were later republished in book form as *The Poverty of Historicism* (London: Routledge & Kegan Paul, 1957). In 1943 and 1944 Hayek assisted Popper in three fundamental ways which Popper later described as "having saved my life". The first was to publish "The Poverty of Historicism", which G. E. Moore had refused for publication in *Mind*; the second was to persuade Sir Herbert Read, at Routledge, to agree to publish *The Open Society and Its Enemies* (London: Routledge & Kegan Paul, 1945), which had been been turned down by twenty publishers; the third was to secure for Popper, then in New Zealand, a Readership at the London School of Economics. - Ed.]

[14] [The length of the usual undergraduate degree programme in Britain. -Ed.]

regard yourself as a creative economist that you once again emerge as a man who can look at things in a wider perspective and can broaden out beyond your narrow specialism. It is in the years before you have become specialists, before you have tied yourself to a particular field or a particular purpose, that you must acquire what general education you will have to guide you in the most active and productive part of your life.

What I want to plead for here is that in this you should let yourself be guided not by any fixed purpose but mainly by intellectual curiosity and a spirit of exploration. Apart from what you need for examination purposes there is no definite field of knowledge which you can hope to have 'covered' by the time you complete your course. And you will derive infinitely more profit if you allow yourself to follow up problems which at the moment interest you, or interest yourself in questions which you feel are definitely interesting, than if you make it a set purpose to master a definite subject. That you do enough of that the impending examinations see to. But no man or woman deserves to be at a university whose intellectual energy is completely absorbed by that except in the last months before the exams, in work for the exam. Unless you use the opportunities you now have in this respect you will never make the gain which I still regard as the greatest of all that the university can give: the discovery that to learn, to come to understand things, can be the greatest of human pleasures, and the only one that will never be exhausted.

But I see I let myself again and again be drawn away from what I wanted to talk more about than anything, and as time is now getting short I must concentrate entirely on that one point. It is a point connected with the one I have just discussed—the way in which, not as beginners, but in our original work as economists, we should guide and direct our interests. Should we aim at immediate usefulness, should we concern ourselves mainly with what is immediately practicable? Or should we pursue whatever intellectual difficulty we feel we might be able to solve, follow up problems where we see accepted views are defective or muddled and where, therefore, we can hope to effect some theoretical improvement, irrespective of whether we can now see what its practical significance will be or not? The question is, of course, closely connected with whether the economist should strive for immediate influence or whether he should be content to work in effect for a distant future in which he has little personal interest. This is, of course, a choice which only the academic economist, the 'don', has to make; but it is nevertheless of some importance.

When I stress the unpopular and unfashionable answer to these questions I do not, of course, mean to imply that these are really exclusive alternatives and that a sensible person will not aim at some judicious balance between the two. What I want to suggest is merely that the 'academic' attitude which I shall favour is being unduly disparaged at the moment and the dangers to full intellectual integrity and independence which the more 'practical' attitude involves are perhaps not fully enough recognised.

The reason why I think that too deliberate striving for immediate usefulness is so likely to corrupt the intellectual integrity of the economist is that immediate usefulness depends almost entirely on influence, and influence is gained most easily by concessions to popular prejudice and adherence to existing political groups. I seriously believe that any such striving for popularity—at least till you have very definitely settled your own convictions, is fatal to the economist and that above anything he must have the courage to be unpopular. Whatever his theoretical beliefs may be, when he has to deal with the proposals of laymen the chance is that in nine out of ten cases his answer will have to be that their various ends are incompatible and that they will have to choose between them and to sacrifice some ambitions which they cherish. This is an inevitable consequence of the type of problems with which he has to deal: problems which are well described by the lines of Schiller that

> With ease by one another dwell the thoughts
> But hard in space together clash the things.

The economist's task is precisely to detect such incompatibilities of thoughts before the clash of the things occurs, and the result is that he will always have the ungrateful task of pointing out the costs. That's what he is there for and it is a task from which he must never shirk, however unpopular and disliked it may make him. Whatever else you may think of the classical economists you must admit that they never feared being unpopular.

It is fashionable now to sneer at their 'non-conformist conscience' or 'self-castigating spirit' which found pleasure in recommending all sorts of self-denial. And perhaps at a time when to adhere to their doctrines was essential to respectability there really was not as much merit in their stern attitude as some of them might claim. But the pendulum has now so much swung in the opposite direction, the fashion is now so much to give the public what it wants rather than to warn it that it cannot have all, that it is worth remembering how much easier this is than to take the unpopular course. I think as economists we should at least always suspect ourselves if we find that we are on the popular side. It is so much easier to believe pleasant conclusions, or to trace doctrines which others like to believe, to concur in the views which are held by most people of good will, and not to disillusion enthusiasts, that the temptation to accept views which would not stand cold examination is sometimes almost irresistible.

It is the desire to gain influence in order to be able to do good which is one of the main sources of intellectual concessions by the economist. I do not mean, and do not wish to argue, that the economist should entirely refrain from making value judgements or from speaking frankly on political questions. I do not believe that the former is possible or the latter desirable. But I think he ought to avoid committing himself to a party—or even devoting himself predominantly to some one good cause. That not only warps his judgement—but the influence it gives him is almost certainly bought at the price of intellectual independence. Too much anxiety to get a particular thing done, or to keep one's influence over a particular group, is almost certain to be an obstacle to his saying many unpopular things he ought to say—and leads to his compromising with 'dominant views' which have to be accepted, and even accepting views which would not stand serious examination.

I trust you will forgive me if I seriously suggest that the danger of such intellectual corruption, of concession made to the desire of gaining influence, is today greater from what are known as the left or progressive parties than from those of the right. The forces of the right are usually neither intelligent enough to value the support of intellectual activities, nor have they the sort of prizes to offer which are likely to influence honest people. But the fact that, whatever may be true of the country as a whole, the 'intelligentsia' is predominantly left means that you are certain to have much greater influence, and therefore apparently chances to be useful, if you accept the sort of views which are generally regarded as 'progressive'. There are now, and probably always will be, any number of attractive jobs, such as various sorts of research or adult education, in which you will be welcomed if you hold the right kind of 'progressive' views, and will have a better chance of getting on various committees or commissions if you represent any known political programme than if you are known to go your own way. Never forget that the reputation of being 'progressive' adheres almost always to people or movements which have already half succeeded in converting people.[15]

There can be no question that in resisting the inclination to join in with some popular movement one deliberately excludes oneself from much that is pleasant, profitable and flattering. Yet I believe that in our field more than in any other this is really essential: if anyone, the economist must keep free not to believe things which it would be useful and pleasant to believe, must not allow himself to encourage wish-dreams in himself or others. I don't think the work of the politician and the true student of society are compatible. Indeed it seems to me that in order to be successful as a politician, to become a political leader, it is almost essential that you have no original ideas on social matters but just express what the majority feel. But I have perhaps said already more than enough about the external temptations and I want to say only a few more words about the internal ones, the seductive attraction exercised by the pleasantness of certain views. Here, too, there has recently been a great change of attitude. While the classical economists were perhaps a little too apt to feel 'that is too good to be true', I believe this attitude is still a safer one than the feeling that the conclusions of an argument are so desirable that they must be true.

I can illustrate this position only from my own experience and that will probably be different from yours. From all considerations other than the purely scientific one I have every reason to wish that I were able to believe that a planned socialist society can achieve what its advocates promise. If I could convince myself that they are right this would suddenly remove all the clouds which to me blacken all the prospects of the future. I should be free to share in the happy confidence of so many of my fellow men and to join with them in the work for a common end. As an economist such a situation would indeed have a double attraction. As I am again and

---

[15] "Students of social science must fear popular approval; evil is with them when all men speak well of them. If there is any set of opinions by the advocacy of which a newspaper can increase its sale, then the student . . . is bound to dwell on the limitations and defects and errors, if any, in that set of opinions: and never to advocate them unconditionally even in an *ad hoc* discussion. It is almost impossible for a student to be a true patriot and to have the reputation of being one at the same time." —Alfred Marshall. [Quoted in A. C. Pigou, "In Memoriam: Alfred Marshall", in A. C. Pigou, *Memorials of Alfred Marshall* (New York: Kelley & Millman, 1956), p. 89. For more on Marshall's views of the duties of the economist see John K. Whitaker, "Some Neglected Aspects of Alfred Marshall's Economic and Social Thought", *History of Political Economy*, vol. 9, no. 2, Summer 1977, pp. 161-197, esp. pp. 185-190. -Ed.]

again reminded by some socialist colleagues, our special knowledge would secure us a much more important position and I might rise to be a trusted leader instead of a hated obstructionist. You will probably say that of course it is only pride which, once I have staked my professional reputation on a certain view, now prevents me from seeing the truth. But it was not always so. And I have indeed been mainly thinking of the extremely painful process of disillusionment which led me to my present views.

You will probably not have the experience in the same connexion, but I am sure that, if you do not regard your economics just as a given instrument to achieve given ends, but as a continuous adventure in the search for truth, you will sooner or later have a similar experience in one connexion or another. It will be for you as well a choice between cherished and pleasant illusions on the one side and the ruthless pursuit of an argument which will lead you almost certainly into isolation and unpopularity and which you do not know where else it will lead. I believe this duty to face and think through unpleasant facts is the hardest task of the economist and the reason why, if he fulfils it, he must not look for public approval or sympathy for his efforts. If he does he will soon cease to be an economist and become a politician—a very honourable and useful calling, but a different one, and not one which gives the kind of satisfaction we expect when we embark on an intellectual pursuit. It is this choice about which I wanted to talk and of the necessity of which I mainly wanted to warn you. There are, as you will realise more and more, many self-denying ordinances which the economist must pass on himself if he wants to remain true to his vocation. But the most important of them seems to me that he must never directly aim at immediate success and public influence. I do not go as far as Professor Hutt in the book mentioned who wants the economists to submit to an almost monastic discipline in order to protect them from corruption. But I believe there is more truth in what he says than is commonly admitted. And I don't know that any economist will be happy in his profession till he has made the choice and, if he chooses the pursuit of light rather than of fruits, reconciles himself with these limitations.

If he is able to do so I believe he has a better chance in the long run to contribute to the improvement of our social problems than if he more directly strove for it. I am also convinced that if he has made the renunciation there is a great deal of real pleasure in his work, just as there would be if he had equally wholeheartedly devoted himself to any more tangible and definite goal. So far as I myself am concerned, at any rate, and in spite of what I have said,

I have never really regretted that I became an economist, or really wished to change with anybody else.

But I have been long enough. It was not my intention when I started to preach a sermon, and if I have sometimes more than verged on it, you must forgive me. It was the first and I trust will be the last sermon I shall ever preach. And it has taken this form, not because I am anxious to convert you to my point of view, but rather because I had to talk about questions which have deeply concerned me and where it has cost me considerable efforts to clear my own mind, and on which in consequence I feel strongly.

THREE

TWO TYPES OF MIND[1]

Accident had early drawn my attention to the contrast between two types of scientific thinking which I have since again and again been watching with growing fascination. I have long wished to describe the difference but have been deterred by the egotistic character such an account is bound to assume. My interest in it is largely due to the fact that I myself represent a rather extreme instance of the more unconventional type, and that to describe it inevitably means largely talking about myself and must appear like an apology for not conforming to a recognised standard. I have now come to the conclusion, however, that the recognition of the contribution students of this type can make may have important consequences for policy in higher education, and that for this reason such an account may serve a useful purpose.

There exists a stereotype of the great scientist which, though overdrawn, is not entirely wrong. He is seen, above all, as the perfect master of his subject, the man who has at his ready command the whole theory and all the important facts of his discipline and is prepared to answer at a moment's notice all important questions relating to his field. Even if such paragons do not really exist, I have certainly encountered scientists who closely approach this ideal. And many more, I believe, feel that this is the standard at which they ought to aim, and often suffer from a feeling of

---

[1] Reprinted with additions from *Encounter*, vol. 45, September 1975, pp. 33-35. Since the first publication my attention has been drawn to the fact that there is some similarity between the distinction drawn in this article and that drawn by Sir Isaiah Berlin in his well-known essay, "The hedgehog and the fox". This had not occurred to me but is probably true. But if I had been aware of it I would certainly not have wished to claim on my behalf that in contrast to the "foxes" who know many things, I was a *hedgehog who knows one big thing*. [The revised version of this essay appeared in *New Studies in Philosophy, Politics, Economics and the History of Ideas* (Chicago: University of Chicago Press; London: Routledge & Kegan Paul, 1978). Readers may find some corroboration of Hayek's experience in the anecdotes and quotations provided by Ben-Ami Scharfstein in his *The Philosophers: Their Lives and the Nature of Their Thought* (Oxford: Oxford University Press, 1980), especially chapter 1, section "Creative Resistance to Persuasion". -Ed.]

inadequacy because they fail to attain it. It is also the type we learn to admire because we can watch him in operation. Most of the brilliant expositors, the most successful teachers, writers and speakers on science, the sparkling conversationalists belong to this class. Their lucid accounts spring from a complete conspectus of the whole of their subject which comprehends not only their own conceptions but equally the theories of others, past and present. No doubt these recognised masters of the existing state of knowledge include also some of the most creative minds, but what I am not certain is whether this particular capacity really helps creativity.

Some of my closest colleagues and best friends have belonged to this type and owe their well-deserved reputations to accomplishments I could never try to emulate. In almost any question about the state of our science I regard them as more competent to provide information than a person of my own sort. They certainly can give a more intelligible account of the subject to an outsider or young student than I could, and are of much greater help to the future practitioner. What I am going to plead is that there is a place in the various institutions for a few specimens of minds of a different type.[2]

In my private language I used to describe the recognised standard type of scientists as the memory type. But this is somewhat unfair because their ability is due to a particular kind of memory, and there are also other kinds. I shall therefore here call this type simply the 'master of his subject'. It is the kind of mind who can retain the particular things he has read or heard, often the particu-

---

[2] The first instances of this contrast to strike me were E. von Böhm-Bawerk and F. von Wieser. The former, whom I saw only when I was a boy, was evidently an eminent "master of his subject", while the latter, my teacher, was in many respects rather a puzzler. J. A. Schumpeter, another representative 'master of his subject', once described him as follows: "The fellow economist who enters Wieser's intellectual world at once finds himself in a new atmosphere. It is as if one entered a house which nowhere resembles the houses of our time and the plan and furniture of which is strange and not at once intelligible. There is hardly another author who owes as little to other authors as Wieser, fundamentally to none except Menger and to him only a suggestion—with the result that for a long time many fellow economists did not know what to do with Wieser's work. Of his edifice everything is his intellectual property, even where what he says has already been said before him." (From an article in a Viennese newspaper on the occasion of Wieser's seventieth birthday, quoted at somewhat greater length in my obituary of Wieser reprinted as an introduction to his *Gesammelte Abhandlungen* (Tübingen: J. C. B. Mohr, 1929).) A similar contrast appears to have existed between the two influential Chicago teachers of economics, Jacob Viner, very much a 'master of his subject', and Frank H. Knight, a puzzler if there ever was one.

lar words in which an idea has been expressed, and retain them for a long time. This capacity one may lack, though one may possess a very good short-term memory even for isolated facts, as I know from my own experience, at least when I was a very young man. I owe it largely to the capacity to swot up in a few weeks before the end-of-the-year examinations the whole substance of a year's teaching in several subjects in which I had done no work whatever that I managed to complete a school education which gave me access to a university. But I forgot such knowledge as rapidly as I had acquired it; and I always lacked the capacity to retain, for any length of time, the successive steps of a complex argument, or to store in my mind useful information which I could not place into a framework of ideas with which I was familiar.

What preserved me from developing an acute sense of inferiority in the company of those more efficient scholars was that I knew that I owed whatever worthwhile new ideas I ever had to *not* being able to remember what every competent specialist is supposed to have at his fingertips. Whenever I saw a new light on something it was as the result of a painful effort to reconstruct an argument which most competent economists would effortlessly and instantly reproduce.

What, then, does my knowledge consist of on which I base my claim to be a trained economist? Certainly not in the distinct recollection of particular statements or arguments. I generally will not be able to reproduce the contents of a book I have read or a lecture I have heard on my subject.[3] But I have certainly often greatly profited from such books or lectures, of the contents of which I could not possibly give an account even immediately after I had read or heard them. In fact the attempt to remember what the writer or speaker said would have deprived me of most of the benefit of the exposition, at least so far as it was on a topic on which I had already some knowledge. Even as a student I soon gave up all attempts to take notes of lectures—as soon as I tried I ceased to understand. My gain from hearing or reading what other

---

[3] This may sound a curious confession from a university teacher who for some forty years regularly lectured on the history of economic thought and enjoyed so doing. I was indeed always greatly interested in the works of earlier students, and learnt a great deal from them. And somehow I enjoyed reconstructing their lives and personalities, although I had no illusions that this in any way explained their scientific beliefs. I believe I also gave in my lectures a fairly adequate picture of their influence on the development of economics by discussing their effect on others. But what I told my students was essentially what I had learnt from those writers and not what they chiefly thought, which may have been something quite different.

people thought was that it changed, as it were, the colours of my own concepts. What I heard or read did not enable me to reproduce their thought but altered my thought. I would not retain their ideas or concepts but modify the relations among my own.

The result of this manner of absorbing ideas is best described by comparing it to the somewhat blurred outlines of a composite photograph: that is, the results of superimposing prints of different faces which at one time were popular as a means of bringing out the common features of a type or a race. There is nothing very precise about such a picture of the world. But it provides a map or a framework in which one has to discover one's path rather than being able to follow a rigidly defined established one. What my sources give me are not definite pieces of knowledge which I can put together, but some modification of an already existing structure inside of which I have to find a way by observing all sorts of warning posts.

Alfred North Whitehead is quoted as saying that "muddleheadedness" is a condition precedent to independent thought. That is certainly my experience. It was because I did not remember the answers that to others may have been obvious that I was often forced to think out a solution to a problem which did not exist for those who had more orderly minds. That the existence of this sort of knowledge is not wholly unfamiliar is shown by the only half-joking description of an educated person as one who has forgotten a great deal.[4] Such submerged memories may be quite important guides of judgement.

I am inclined to call minds of this type the 'puzzlers'. But I shall not mind if they are called the muddlers, since they certainly will often give this impression if they talk about a subject before they have painfully worked through to some degree of clarity.

Their constant difficulties, which in rare instances may be rewarded by a new insight, are due to the fact that they cannot avail themselves of the established verbal formulae or arguments which lead others smoothly and quickly to the result. But being forced to find their own way of expressing an accepted idea, they sometimes discover that the conventional formula conceals gaps or unjustified tacit presuppositions. They will be forced explicitly to answer questions which had been long effectively evaded by a plausible but ambiguous turn of phrase of an implicit but illegitimate assumption.

---

[4] [Hayek is probably referring to the aphorism that an educated person is one who has forgotten more than he knows. -Ed.]

People whose minds work that way seem clearly to rely in some measure on a process of wordless thought, something the existence of which is occasionally denied but which at least bilingual persons seem to me often to possess. To 'see' certain connexions distinctly does not yet mean for them that they know how to describe them in words. Even after long endeavour to find the right form of words they may still be acutely aware that the expression adopted does not fully convey what they really mean. They also show another somewhat curious feature which I believe is not rare but which I have never seen described: that many of their particular ideas in different fields may spring from some single more general conception of which they are themselves not aware but which, like the similarity of their approach to the separate issues, they may much later discover with surprise.

Since I wrote the preceding sections I have been struck by a further observation that certainly those of my close friends in my subject whom I regard as eminently 'masters of their subject', and by watching whom I have largely formed these ideas, seem also to be particularly susceptible to the opinions dominant in their environment and the intellectual fashions of their time generally. This is perhaps inevitable in persons who strive to command all the relevant knowledge of their time and who usually are inclined to believe that if an opinion is widely held there must be something in it, while the 'muddleheads' are much more apt stubbornly and undisturbed to go on in their own way. I do not know what significance this may have, except, perhaps, merely that the second type rarely takes the trouble carefully to study views which do not fit into their scheme of thought.

If there really are two such different types of mind which both have their contributions to make to the growth of knowledge, it may well mean that our present system of selecting those to be admitted to the universities may exclude some who might make great contributions. There are of course also other reasons which make one feel doubtful about the principle that all those, and only those, who can pass certain examinations should have a claim to a university education. The number of great scientists who were bad pupils at school and might not have passed such a test is large—and the proportion of the children who were at school very good at all subjects and later became intellectually eminent comparatively small. It seems to me also clear that the application of the now accepted principle is, in fact, lowering the proportion of the students who study because of a passionate interest in their subject.

At any rate, while I have serious doubts whether we ought to increase further the number of those who acquire a claim to a university education by passing certain examinations, I feel strongly that there ought to be a second way where the intensity of the desire for the acquisition of scientific knowledge counts decisively. This means that it should be possible to acquire this right by some sacrifice of one's own. I readily admit that there is little relation between the strength of this wish and the capacity to pay for its satisfaction. Nor is the possibility of financing the study by current earnings from other work an adequate solution—certainly not in the demanding experimental subjects. In professional schools like law or medicine, loans to be repaid from later earnings may solve the financial problem. Yet this hardly helps in the selection of those to be enabled to devote themselves to theoretical work.

There are sacrifices, however, which are in everybody's power and which might be deemed to give a claim to the opportunity to devote oneself for a time wholly to the study of a chosen subject. If this privilege could be earned by pledging oneself for a number of years to an austere life of semi-monastic character, denying oneself many of the pleasures and amusements which at our present level of wealth youth often takes for granted, it would truly be by an effort of one's own and not by somebody else's judgement of his capacity that the passionate interest in a subject would come to count; a chance would thus be given to those whose talent will show itself only after they can immerse themselves in their special subject.

What I envisage is an arrangement by which those who chose this course would have such essentials as housing, simple food, and an ample credit for books and the like provided for them, but would have to pledge themselves to live beyond this on a very restricted budget. It seems to me that the readiness to give up for a few years some of the usual pleasures of the young is a better indication of the probability of an individual profiting from a higher education than the success in examinations in a variety of school subjects. I should also not be surprised if those who earned their right to study by such a personal sacrifice would be more respected by their fellows than those who had acquired it by passing examinations. It is probably still true and recognised that most great achievements as well as high esteem are due to a self-discipline which puts a single-minded pursuit of a self-chosen goal above most other pleasures—a sacrifice of many other human values which many of the great scientists had to bring at the most productive stage of their careers.

To be sure, even with such a system admission would require some proof of competence in the chosen field and recurrent evidence of progress in the course of the study. I would also hold up to those who, for some four years or so, stand the course with faithful observance of the special discipline, and who then show great ability, the prospect of an ample graduate scholarship with complete freedom. Even if a large proportion of those who started on this scheme fell by the wayside and either did not complete the course or showed no more than average performance, I believe such an institution would enable us to find and develop talents which without it may be lost. Indeed, it seems to me that the type that would be attracted thereby should constitute an important ingredient of any scholarly community—and a safeguard against the good examinees being able to establish a reign of sacred formulae under which all minds move in the accustomed grooves.

FOUR

HISTORY AND POLITICS[1]

Political opinion and views about historical events ever have been and always must be closely connected. Past experience is the foundation on which our beliefs about the desirability of different policies and institutions are mainly based, and our present political views inevitably affect and colour our interpretation of the past. Yet, if it is too pessimistic a view that man learns nothing from history, it may well be questioned whether he always learns the truth. While the events of the past are the source of the experience of the human race, their opinions are determined not by the objective facts but by the records and interpretations to which they have access. Few men will deny that our views about the goodness or badness of different institutions are largely determined by what we believe to have been their effects in the past. There is scarcely a political ideal or concept which does not involve opinions about a whole series of past events, and there are few historical memories which do not serve as a symbol of some political aim. Yet the historical beliefs which guide us in the present are not always in accord with the facts; sometimes they are even the effects rather than the cause of political beliefs. Historical myths have perhaps played nearly as great a role in shaping opinion as historical facts. Yet we can hardly hope to profit from past experience unless the facts from which we draw our conclusions are correct.

The influence which the writers of history thus exercise on public opinion is probably more immediate and extensive than that of the political theorists who launch new ideas. It seems as though even such new ideas reach wider circles usually not in their abstract form but as the interpretations of particular events. The historian is in this respect at least one step nearer to direct power over public opinion than is the theorist. And long before the professional

---

[1] [First published as the introduction to *Capitalism and the Historians*. Essays by T. S. Ashton, L. M. Hacker, W. H. Hutt, and B. de Jouvenel (London and Chicago: University of Chicago Press, 1954). -Ed.]

historian takes up his pen, current controversy about recent events will have created a definite picture, or perhaps several different pictures, of these events which will affect contemporary discussion as much as any division on the merits of new issues.

This profound influence which current views about history have on political opinion is today perhaps less understood than it was in the past. One reason for this probably is the pretension of many modern historians to be purely scientific and completely free from all political prejudice. There can be no question, of course, that this is an imperative duty of the scholar in so far as historical research, that is, the ascertainment of the facts, is concerned. There is indeed no legitimate reason why, in answering questions of fact, historians of different political opinions should not be able to agree. But at the very beginning, in deciding which questions are worth asking, individual value judgements are bound to come in. And it is more than doubtful whether a connected history of a period or of a set of events could be written without interpreting these in the light, not only of theories about the interconnexion of social processes, but also of definite values—or at least whether such a history would be worth reading. Historiography, as distinguished from historical research, is not only at least as much an art as a science; the writer who attempts it without being aware that his task is one of interpretation in the light of definite values also will succeed merely in deceiving and will become the victim of his unconscious prejudices.

There is perhaps no better illustration of the manner in which for more than a century the whole political ethos of a nation, and for a shorter time of most of the Western world, was shaped by the writings of a group of historians than the influence exercised by the English 'Whig interpretation of history'. It is probably no exaggeration to say that, for every person who had firsthand acquaintance with the writings of the political philosophers who founded the liberal tradition, there were fifty or a hundred who had absorbed it from the writings of men like Hallam[2] and Macaulay[3], or Grote[4] and

---

[2] [Henry Hallam (1777-1859), English historian. -Ed.]

[3] [Thomas Babington Macaulay, 1st Baron Macaulay (1800-1859), English essayist, historian, and politician, author of the *History of England from the Accession of James II* (London: Longman, Brown, Green & Longmans, 1849-1861). -Ed.]

[4] [George Grote (1794-1871), English classicist, historian, and politician, author of *A History of Greece*, 12 vols (London: John Murray, 1846-56) and *Plato and the Other Companions of Socrates*, in 3 vols (London: John Murray, 1865). See also H. Grote, *The Personal Life of George Grote* (London: John Murray, 1873). -Ed.]

Lord Acton[5]. It is significant that the modern English historian who more than any other has endeavoured to discredit this Whig tradition later came to write that "those who, perhaps in the misguided austerity of youth, wish to drive out that Whig interpretation . . . are sweeping a room which humanly speaking cannot long remain empty. They are opening the doors for seven devils which, precisely because they are newcomers, are bound to be worse than this first."[6] And, although he still suggests that "Whig history" was "wrong" history, he emphasises that it "was one of our assets" and that "it had a wonderful effect on English politics".[7]

Whether in any relevant sense "Whig history" really was wrong history is a matter on which the last word has probably not yet been said but which we cannot discuss here. Its beneficial effect in creating the essentially liberal atmosphere of the nineteenth century is beyond doubt and was certainly not due to any misrepresentation of facts. It was mainly political history, and the chief facts on which it was based were known beyond question. It may not stand up in all respects to modern standards of historical research, but it certainly gave the generations brought up on it a true sense of the value of the political liberty which their ancestors had achieved for them, and it served them as a guide in preserving that achievement.

The Whig interpretation of history has gone out of fashion with the decline of liberalism.[8] But it is more than doubtful whether, because history now claims to be more scientific, it has become a more reliable or trustworthy guide in those fields where it has exercised most influence on political views. Political history indeed has lost much of the power and fascination it had in the nineteenth century; and it is doubtful whether any historical work of our time has had a circulation or direct influence comparable with, say, T. B. Macaulay's *History of England*.[9] Yet the extent to which our present

---

[5] [See Hayek's "The Actonian Revival: On Lord Acton", in vol. 4 of *The Collected Works of F. A. Hayek*. -Ed.]

[6] Herbert Butterfield, *The Englishman and His History* (Cambridge: Cambridge University Press, 1944), p. 3.

[7] *Ibid.*, p. 7.

[8] [Hayek refers here to liberalism in its nineteenth-century sense. "In 1860 a liberal, of whatever nationality, was one who favoured free trade, a market economy with little or no government intervention, a limited constitutional state, and a social policy based on self-help. . . . Those who espoused the views defined as liberal in 1860 were, by the mid-twentieth century, now commonly labelled as conservatives." Stephen Davies, in "Bibliographic Essay: The Decline of Classical Liberalism: 1860-1940", *Humane Studies Review*, vol. 5, no. 2, Winter 1987-8, pp. 1-19. -Ed.]

[9] Macaulay, op. cit.

political views are coloured by historical beliefs has certainly not diminished. As interest has shifted from the constitutional to the social and economic field, so the historical beliefs which act as driving forces are not mainly beliefs about economic history. It is probably justifiable to speak of a socialist interpretation of history which has governed political thinking for the last two or three generations and which consists mainly of a particular view of economic history. The remarkable thing about this view is that most of the assertions to which it has given the status of 'facts which everybody knows' have long been proved not to have been facts at all; yet they still continue, outside the circle of professional economic historians, to be almost universally accepted as the basis for the estimate of the existing economic order.

Most people, when being told that their political convictions have been affected by particular views on economic history, will answer that they never have been interested in it and never have read a book on the subject. This, however, does not mean that they do not, with the rest, regard as established facts many of the legends which at one time or another have been given currency by writers on economic history. Although in the indirect and circuitous process by which new political ideas reach the general public the historian holds a key position, even he operates chiefly through many further relays. It is only at several removes that the picture which he provides becomes general property; it is via the novel and the newspaper, the cinema and political speeches, and ultimately the school and common talk, that the ordinary person acquires his conceptions of history. But in the end even those who never read a book and probably have never heard the names of the historians whose views have influenced them come to see the past through their spectacles. Certain beliefs, for instance, about the evolution and effects of trade unions, the alleged progressive growth of monopoly, the deliberate destruction of commodity stock as the result of competition (an event which, in fact, whenever it happened, was always the result of monopoly and usually of government-organised monopoly), about the suppression of beneficial inventions, the causes and effects of 'imperialism', and the role of the armament industries or of 'capitalists' in general in causing war, have become part of the folklore of our time. Most people would be greatly surprised to learn that most of what they believe about these subjects are not safely established facts but myths, launched from political motives and then spread by people of goodwill into whose general beliefs they fitted. It would require several books like the present one to show how most of what is commonly believed on these questions, not merely by radicals but also by many conservatives, is not history but political legend. All we can do here with regard to these topics is refer the reader to a few works from which he can inform himself about the present state of knowledge on the more important of them.[10]

There is, however, one supreme myth which more than any other has served to discredit the economic systems to which we owe our present-day civilisation and to the examination of which the present volume[11] is devoted. It is the legend of the deterioration of the position of the working classes in consequence of the rise of 'capitalism' (or of the 'manufacturing' or 'industrial' system). Who has not heard of the 'horrors of early capitalism' and gained the impression that the advent of this system brought untold new suffering to large classes who before were tolerably content and comfortable? We might justly hold in disrepute a system to which the blame attached that even for a time it worsened the position of the poorest and most numerous class of the population. The widespread emotional aversion to 'capitalism' is closely connected with this belief that the undeniable growth of wealth which the competitive order has produced was purchased at the price of depressing the standard of life of the weakest elements of the society.

That this was the case was at one time indeed widely taught by economic historians. A more careful examination of the facts, however, has led to a thorough refutation of this belief. Yet, a generation after the controversy has been decided, popular opinion still continues as though the older belief had been true. How this belief should ever have arisen and why it should continue to determine the general view long after it has been disproved are both problems which deserve serious examination.

---

[10] Cf. M. Dorothy George, "The Combination Laws Reconsidered", *Economic History* (supplement to the *Economic Journal*), vol. 1, May 1927, 214-228; W. H. Hutt, *The Theory of Collective Bargaining* (London: P. S. King, 1930) and *Economists and the Public* (London: Jonathan Cape, 1936); L. C. Robbins, *The Economic Basis of Class Conflict* (London: Macmillan, 1939) and *The Economic Causes of War* (London: Jonathan Cape, 1939); Walter Sulzbach, *"Capitalistic Warmongers": A Modern Superstition* (Public Policy Pamphlets, No. 35 (Chicago: University of Chicago Press, 1942)); G. J. Stigler, "Competition in the United States", in *Five Lectures on Economic Problems* (London and New York: Longmans, Green, 1949); G. Warren Nutter, *The Extent of Enterprise Monopoly in the United States, 1899-1939* (Chicago: University of Chicago Press, 1951); and, on most of these problems, the writings of Ludwig von Mises, especially his *Socialism* (London: Jonathan Cape, 1936; reprinted Indianapolis, Ind.: LibertyClassics, 1981). -Ed.]

[11] [That is, to *Capitalism and the Historians*, the volume of essays to which this essay first served as an introduction. -Ed.]

This kind of opinion can be frequently found not only in the political literature hostile to capitalism but even in works which on the whole are sympathetic to the political tradition of the nineteenth century. It is well represented by the following passage from Ruggerio's esteemed *History of European Liberalism*:

> Thus it was precisely at the period of intensest industrial growth that the condition of the labourer changed for the worse. Hours of labour multiplied out of all measure; the employment of women and children in factories lowered wages: the keen competition between the workers themselves, no longer tied to their parishes but free to travel and congregate where they were most in demand, further cheapened the labour they placed on the market: numerous and frequent industrial crises, inevitable at a period of growth, when population and consumption are not yet stabilised, swelled from time to time the ranks of the unemployed, the reserves in the army of starvation.[12]

There was little excuse for such a statement even when it appeared a quarter-century ago. A year after it was first published, the most eminent student of modern economic history, Sir John Clapham, rightly complained:

> The legend that everything was getting worse for the working man, down to some unspecified date between the drafting of the People's Charter and the Great Exhibition, dies hard. The fact that, after the price fall of 1820-21, the purchasing power of wages in general—not, of course, of everyone's wages—was definitely greater than it had been just before the revolutionary and Napoleonic wars, fits so ill with the tradition that it is very seldom mentioned, the works of statisticians of wages and prices being constantly disregarded by social historians.[13]

In so far as general public opinion is concerned, the position is scarcely better today, although the facts have had to be conceded even by most of those who had been mainly responsible for spreading the contrary opinion. Few authors have done more to create the

---

[12] Guido de Ruggiero, *Storia del liberalism europeo* (Bari, 1925), trans. R. G. Collingwood under the title *The History of European Liberalism* (London: Oxford University Press, 1927), p. 47, esp. p. 85. It is interesting that Ruggiero seems to derive his facts mainly from another supposedly liberal historian, Elie Halévy, although Halévy never expressed them so crudely.

[13] J. H. Clapham, *An Economic History of Modern Britain* (Cambridge: Cambridge University Press, 1926), vol. 1, chapter 7.

belief that the early nineteenth century had been a time in which the position of the working class had become particularly bad than Mr. and Mrs. J. L. Hammond; their books are frequently quoted to illustrate this. But towards the end of their lives they admitted candidly that

> statisticians tell us that when they have put in order such data as they can find, they are satisfied that earnings increased and that most men and women were less poor when this discontent was loud and active than they were when the eighteenth century was beginning to grow old in a silence like that of autumn. The evidence, of course, is scanty, and its interpretation not too simple, but this general view is probably more or less correct.[14]

This did little to change the general effect their writing had on public opinion. In one of the latest competent studies of the history of the Western political tradition, for instance, we can still read that, "like all the great social experiments, however, the invention of the labour market was expensive. It involved, in the first instance, a swift and drastic decline in the material standard of living of the working classes."[15]

I was going to continue here that this is still the view which is almost exclusively represented in the popular literature when the latest book by Bertrand Russell came to my hands in which, as if to confirm this, he blandly asserts:

> The industrial revolution caused unspeakable misery both in England and in America. I do not think any student of economic history can doubt that the average happiness in England in the early nineteenth century was lower than it had been a hundred years earlier; and this was due almost entirely to scientific technique.[16]

The intelligent layman can hardly be blamed if he believes that such a categorical statement from a writer of this rank must be true. If a Bertrand Russell believes this, we must not be surprised that the versions of economic history which today are spread in hundreds of

---

[14] J. L. Hammond and Barbara Hammond, *The Bleak Age* (1934) (revised edition, London: Pelican Books, 1947), p. 15.

[15] Frederick Watkins, *The Political Tradition of the West* (Cambridge, Mass.: Harvard University Press, 1948), p. 213.

[16] Bertrand Russell, *The Impact of Science on Society* (New York: Columbia University Press, 1951), pp. 19-20.

thousands of volumes of pocket editions are mostly of the kind which spread this old myth. It is also still a rare exception when we meet a work of historical fiction which dispenses with the dramatic touch which the story of the sudden worsening of the position of large groups of workers provides.

The true fact of the slow and irregular progress of the working class which we now know to have taken place is of course rather unsensational and uninteresting to the layman. It is no more than he has learned to expect as the normal state of affairs; and it hardly occurs to him that this is by no means an inevitable progress, that it was preceded by centuries of virtual stagnation of the position of the poorest, and that we have come to expect continuous improvement only as a result of the experience of several generations with the system which he still thinks to be the cause of the misery of the poor.

Discussions of the effects of the rise of modern industry on the working classes refer almost always to the conditions in England in the first half of the nineteenth century; yet the great change to which they refer had commenced much earlier and by then had quite a long history and had spread far beyond England. The freedom of economic activity which in England had proved so favourable to the rapid growth of wealth was probably in the first instance an almost accidental by-product of the limitations which the revolution of the seventeenth century had placed on the powers of government; and only after its beneficial effects had come to be widely noticed did the economists later undertake to explain the connexion and to argue for the removal of the remaining barriers to commercial freedom. In many ways it is misleading to speak of 'capitalism' as though this had been a new and altogether different system which suddenly came into being towards the end of the eighteenth century; we use this term here because it is the most familiar name, but only with great reluctance, since with its modern connotations it is itself largely a creation of that socialist interpretation of economic history with which we are concerned. The term is especially misleading when, as is often the case, it is connected with the idea of the rise of the propertyless proletariat which by some devious process have been deprived of their rightful ownership of the tools for their work.

The actual history of the connexion between capitalism and the rise of the proletariat is almost the opposite of that which these theories of the expropriation of the masses suggest. The truth is that, for the greater part of history, for most men the possession of the tools for their work was an essential condition for survival or at least for being able to rear a family. The number of those who could maintain themselves by working for others, although they did not themselves possess the necessary equipment, was limited to a small proportion of the population. The amount of arable land and of tools handed down from one generation to the next limited the total number who could survive. To be left without them meant in most instances death by starvation or at least the impossibility of procreation. There was little incentive and little possibility for one generation to accumulate the additional tools which would have made possible the survival of a larger number to the next, so long as the advantage of employing additional hands was limited mainly to the instances where the division of the tasks increased the efficiency of the work of the owner of the tools. It was only when the larger gains from the employment of machinery provided both the means and the opportunity for their investment that what in the past had been a recurring surplus of population doomed to early death was in an increasing measure given the possibility of survival. Numbers which had been practically stationary for many centuries began to increase rapidly. The proletariat which capitalism can be said to have 'created' was thus not a proportion of the population which would have existed without it and which it had degraded to a lower level; it was an additional population which was enabled to grow up by the new opportunities for employment which capitalism provided. In so far as it is true that the growth of capital made the appearance of the proletariat possible, it was in the sense that it raised the productivity of labour so that much larger numbers of those who had not been equipped by their parents with the necessary tools were enabled to maintain themselves by their labour alone; but the capital had to be supplied first before those were enabled to survive who afterwards claimed as a right a share in its ownership. Although it was certainly not from charitable motives, it still was the first time in history that one group of people found it in their interest to use their earnings on a large scale to provide new instruments of production to be operated by those who without them could not have produced their own sustenance.

Of the effect of the rise of modern industry on the growth of population, statistics tell a vivid tale. That this in itself largely contradicts the common belief about the harmful effect of the rise of the factory system on the large masses is not the point with which we are at present concerned. Nor need we more than mention the fact that, so long as this increase of the numbers of those whose output reached a certain level brought forward a fully corresponding increase in population, the level of the poorest fringe could not be substantially improved, however much the average might rise. The point of immediate relevance is that this increase of population and particularly of the manufacturing population had proceeded in England at least for two or three generations before the period of which it is alleged that the position of the workers seriously deteriorated.

The period to which this refers is also the period when the problem of the position of the working class became for the first time one of general concern. And the opinions of some of the contemporaries are indeed the main sources of the present beliefs. Our first question must therefore be how it came about that such an impression contrary to the facts should have become widely held among the people then living.

One of the chief reasons was evidently an increasing awareness of facts which before had passed unnoticed. The very increase of wealth and well-being which had been achieved raised standards and aspirations. What for ages had seemed a natural and inevitable situation, or even an improvement upon the past, came to be regarded as incongruous with the opportunities which the new age appeared to offer. Economic suffering both became more conspicuous and seemed less justified, because general wealth was increasing faster than ever before. But this, of course, does not prove that the people whose fate was beginning to cause indignation and alarm were worse off than their parents or grandparents had been. While there is every evidence that great misery existed, there is none that it was greater than or even as great as it had been before. The aggregations of large numbers of cheap houses of industrial workers were probably more ugly than the picturesque cottages in which some of the agricultural labourers or domestic workers had lived; and they were certainly more alarming to the landowner or to the city patrician than the poor dispersed over the country had been. But for those who had moved from country to town it meant an improvement; and even though the rapid growth of the industrial centres created sanitary problems with which people had yet slowly and painfully to learn to cope, statistics leave little doubt that even general health was on the whole benefited rather than harmed.[17]

More important, however, for the explanation of the change from an optimistic to a pessimistic view of the effects of industrialisation than this awakening of social conscience was probably the fact that

[17] Cf. M. C. Buer, *Health, Wealth and Population in the Early Days of the Industrial Revolution* (London: Routledge, 1926).

this change of opinion appears to have commenced, not in the manufacturing districts which had firsthand knowledge of what was happening, but in the political discussion of the English metropolis which was somewhat remote from, and had little part in, the new development. It is evident that the belief about the 'horrible' conditions prevailing among the manufacturing populations of the Midlands and the north of England was in the 1830s and the 1840s widely held among the upper classes of London and the south. It was one of the main arguments with which the landowning class hit back at the manufacturers to counter the agitation of the latter against the Corn Laws and for free trade. And it was from these arguments of the conservative press that the radical intelligentsia of the time, with little firsthand knowledge of the industrial districts, derived their views which were to become the standard weapons of political propaganda.

This position, to which so much even of the present-day beliefs about the effects of the rise of industrialism on the working classes can be traced, is well illustrated by a letter written about 1843 by a London lady, Mrs. Cooke Taylor, after she had for the first time visited some industrial districts of Lancashire. Her account of the conditions she found is prefaced by some remarks about the general state of opinion in London:

> I need not remind you of the statements put forward in the newspapers, relative to the miserable conditions of the operatives, and the tyranny of their masters, for they made such an impression on me that it was with reluctance that I consented to go to Lancashire; indeed these misrepresentations are quite general, and people believe them without knowing why or wherefore. As an instance: just before starting I was at a large dinner party, at the west end of the town, and seated next a gentleman who is considered a very clever and intelligent man. In the course of the conversation I mentioned that I was going to Lancashire. He stared and asked, "What on earth could take me there? That he would as soon think of going to St. Giles's; that it was a horrid place—factories all over; that the people, from starvation, oppression, and over-work, had almost lost the form of humanity; and that the mill-owners were a bloated, pampered race, feeding on the very vitals of the people." I answered that this was a dreadful state of things; and asked "In what part he had seen such misery?" He replied that "he had never *seen* it, but had been *told* that it existed; and that for his part he never had been in the manufacturing districts, and that he never would." This gentleman was one of the very numerous body

of people who spread reports without ever taking the trouble of inquiring if they be true or false.[18]

Mrs. Cooke Taylor's detailed description of the satisfactory state of affairs which to her surprise she found ends with the remark:

> Now that I have seen the factory people at their work, in their cottages and in their schools, I am totally at a loss to account for the outcry that has been made against them. They are better clothed, better fed, and better conducted than many other classes of working people.[19]

But even if at the time itself the opinion which was later taken over by the historians was loudly voiced by one party, it remains to explain why the view of one party among the contemporaries, and that not of the radicals or liberals but of the Tories, should have become the almost uncontradicted view of the economic historians of the second half of the century. The reason for this seems to have been that the new interest in economic history was itself closely associated with the interest in socialism and that at first a large proportion of those who devoted themselves to the study of economic history were inclined towards socialism. It was not merely the great stimulus which Karl Marx's 'materialist interpretation of history' undoubtedly gave to the study of economic history; practically all the socialist schools held a philosophy of history intended to show the relative character of the different economic institutions and the necessity of different economic systems succeeding each other in time. They all tried to prove that the system which they attacked, the system of private property in the means of production, was a perversion of an earlier and more natural system of communal property; and, because the theoretical preconceptions which guided them postulated that the rise of capitalism must have been detrimental to the working classes, it is not surprising that they found what they were looking for.

But not only those by whom the study of economic history was consciously made a tool of political agitation—as is true in many

---

[18] This letter is quoted in "Reuben", *A Brief History of the Rise and Progress of the Anti-Corn-Law League* (London [1845]). Mrs. Cooke Taylor, who appears to have been the wife of the radical Dr. Cooke Taylor, had visited the factory of Henry Ashworth at Turton, near Bolton, then still a rural district and therefore probably more attractive than some of the urban industrial districts.

[19] *Ibid.*

instances from Marx and Engels to Werner Sombart[20] and Sidney and Beatrice Webb[21]—but also many of the scholars who sincerely believed that they were approaching the facts without prejudice produced results which were scarcely less biased. This was in part due to the fact that the 'historical approach' which they adopted had itself been proclaimed as a counterblast to the theoretical analysis of classical economics, because the latter's verdict on the popular remedies for current complaints had so frequently been unfavourable.[22] It is no accident that the largest and most influential group of students of economic history in the sixty years preceding the First World War, the German Historical School, prided themselves also on the name of the 'socialists of the chair' (*Kathedersozialisten*); or that their spiritual successors, the American 'institutionalists', were mostly socialists in their inclination. The whole atmosphere of these schools was such that it would have required an exceptional independence of mind for a young scholar not to succumb to the pressure of academic opinion. No reproach was more feared or more fatal to academic prospects than that of being an 'apologist' of the capitalist system; and, even if a scholar dared to contradict dominant opinion on a particular point, he would be careful to safeguard himself against such accusation by joining the general condemnation of the capitalist system.[23] To treat the existing economic order as merely a 'historical phase' and to be able to predict from the 'laws of historical development' the emergence of a better future system became the hallmark of what was then regarded as the truly scientific spirit.

Much of the misrepresentation of the facts by the earlier economic historians was, in reality, directly traceable to a genuine endeavour to look at these facts without any theoretical preconceptions. The idea that one can trace the causal connexions of any events

[20] [Werner Sombart (1863-1941), German economist and sociologist. -Ed.]

[21] [Sidney (1859-1947) and Beatrice (1858-1943) Webb, early and major members of the Fabian socialist movement in Britain, and co-founders of the London School of Economics. -Ed.]

[22] Merely as an illustration of the general attitude of that school a characteristic statement of one of its best-known representatives, Adolf Held, may be quoted. According to him, it was David Ricardo "in whose hand orthodox economics became the docile servant of the exclusive interests of mobile capital", and his theory of rent "was simply dictated by the hatred of the moneyed capitalist against the landowners" (*Zwei Bücher zur sozialen Geschichte Englands* (Leipzig: Duncker & Humblot, 1881), p. 178).

[23] A good account of the general political atmosphere prevailing among the German Historical School of economists will be found in Ludwig Pohle, *Die gegenwärtige Krise in der deutschen Volkswirtschaftslehre* (Leipzig: A. Deichert, 1911).

without employing a theory, or that such a theory will emerge automatically from the accumulation of a sufficient amount of facts, is of course sheer illusion.[24] The complexity of social events in particular is' such that, without the tools of analysis which a systematic theory provides, one is almost bound to misinterpret them; and those who eschew the conscious use of an explicit and tested logical argument usually merely become the victims of the popular beliefs of their time. Common sense is a treacherous guide in this field, and what seem 'obvious' explanations frequently are no more than commonly accepted superstitions. It may seem obvious that the introduction of machinery will produce a general reduction of the demand for labour. But persistent effort to think the problem through shows that this belief is the result of a logical fallacy, of stressing one effect of the assumed change and leaving out others. Nor do the facts give any support to the belief. Yet anyone who thinks it to be true is very likely to find what seems to him confirming evidence. It is easy enough to find in the early nineteenth century instances of extreme poverty and to draw the conclusion that this must have been the effect of the introduction of machinery, without asking whether conditions had been any better or perhaps even worse before. Or one may believe that an increase of production must lead to the impossibility of selling all the product and, when one then finds a stagnation of sales, regard this as a confirmation of the expectations, although there are several more plausible explanations than general "overproduction" or "underconsumption".

There can be no doubt that many of these misrepresentations were put forward in good faith; and there is no reason why we should not respect the motives of some of those who, to arouse public conscience, painted the misery of the poor in the blackest colours. We owe to agitation of this kind, which forced unwilling eyes to face unpleasant facts, some of the finest and most generous acts of public policy—from the abolition of slavery to the removal of taxes on imported food and the destruction of many entrenched privileges and abuses. And there is every reason to remember how miserable the majority of the people still were as recently as 100 or 150 years ago. But we must not, long after the event, allow a distortion of the facts, even if committed out of humanitarian zeal, to affect our view of what we owe to a system which for the first

[24] See K. R. Popper, *The Logic of Scientific Discovery* [1934] (London: Hutchinson, 1959).

time in history made people feel that this misery might be avoidable. The very claims and ambitions of the working classes were and are the result of the enormous improvement of their position which capitalism brought about. There were, no doubt, many people whose privileged position, whose power to secure comfortable income by preventing others from doing better what they were being paid for, was destroyed by the advance of freedom of enterprise. There may be various other grounds on which the development of modern industrialism might be deplored by some; certain aesthetic and moral values to which the privileged classes attached great importance were no doubt endangered by it. Some people might even question whether the rapid increase of population, or, in other words, the decrease in infant mortality, was a blessing. But if, and in so far as, one takes as one's test the effect on the standard of life of the large number of the toiling classes, there can be little doubt that this effect was to produce a general upward trend.

The recognition of this fact by the students had to wait for the rise of a generation of economic historians who no longer regarded themselves as the opponents of economics, intent upon proving that the economists had been wrong, but who were themselves trained economists who devoted themselves to the study of economic evolution. Yet the results which this modern economic history had largely established a generation ago have still gained little recognition outside professional circles. The process by which the results of research ultimately become general property has in this instance proved to be even slower than usual.[25] The new results in this case have not been of the kind which is avidly picked up by the intellectuals because it readily fits into their general prejudices but, on the contrary, are of a kind which is in conflict with their general beliefs. Yet, if we have been right in our estimate of the importance which erroneous views have had in shaping political opinion, it is high time that the truth should at last displace the legend which has so long governed public belief.

The recognition that the working class as a whole benefited from the rise of modern industry is of course entirely compatible with the fact that some individuals or groups in this as well as other classes may for a time have suffered from its results. The new order meant an increased rapidity of change, and the quick increase of wealth

[25] On this, cf. my essay, "The Intellectuals and Socialism", *University of Chicago Law Review*, vol. 16, 1949. [Reprinted in *Studies in Philosophy, Politics, and Economics* (Chicago: University of Chicago Press; London: Routledge & Kegan Paul, 1967). -Ed.]

was largely the result of the increased speed of adaptation to change which made it possible. In those spheres where the mobility of a highly competitive market became effective, the increased range of opportunities more than compensated for the greater instability of particular jobs. But the spreading of the new order was gradual and uneven. There remained—and there remain to the present day—pockets which, while fully exposed to the vicissitudes of the markets for their products, are too isolated to benefit much from the opportunities which the market opened elsewhere. The various instances of the decline of old crafts which were displaced by a mechanical process have been widely publicised (the fate of the hand-loom weavers is the classical example always quoted). But even there it is more than doubtful whether the amount of suffering caused is comparable to that which a series of bad harvests in any region would have caused before capitalism had greatly increased the mobility of goods and of capital. The incidence on a small group among a prospering community is probably felt as more of an injustice and a challenge than was the general suffering of earlier times which was considered as unalterable fate.

The understanding of the true sources of the grievances, and still more the manner in which they might be remedied so far as possible, presupposes a better comprehension of the working of the market system than most of the earlier historians possessed. Much that has been blamed on the capitalist system is in fact due to remnants or revivals of pre-capitalistic features: to monopolistic elements which were either the direct result of ill-conceived state action or the consequence of a failure to understand that a smooth-working competitive order required an appropriate legal framework. We have already referred to some of the features and tendencies for which capitalism is usually blamed and which are in fact due to its basic mechanism not being allowed to work; and the question, in particular, why and to what extent monopoly has interfered with its beneficial operation is too big a problem for us to attempt to say more about it here.

This introduction is not intended to do more than to indicate the general setting in which the more specific discussion of the following papers[26] must be seen. For its inevitable tendency to run in generalities I trust these special studies will make up by the very concrete treatment of their particular problems. They cover merely part of

[26] [I.e., the essays by T. S. Ashton, L. M. Hacker, W. H. Hutt, and B. de Jouvenel in *Capitalism and the Historians*. See footnote 1. -Ed.]

the wider issue, since they were intended to provide the factual basis for the discussion which they opened. Of the three related questions—What were the facts? How did the historians present them? and Why?—they deal primarily with the first and chiefly by implication with the second. Only the paper by M. de Jouvenel,[27] which therefore possesses a somewhat different character, addresses itself mainly to the third question; and, in so doing, it raises problems which reach even beyond the complex of questions which have been sketched here.

[27] [Bertrand de Jouvenel, "The Treatment of Capitalism by Continental Intellectuals", *ibid.* -Ed.]

PART II

THE ORIGINS OF
POLITICAL ECONOMY IN BRITAIN

FIVE

FRANCIS BACON: PROGENITOR OF SCIENTISM (1561-1626)[1]

Practising scientists sometimes imagine that they are following the 'Baconian empirical method'. It is doubtful whether any successful scientist ever did so. Certainly Francis Bacon himself was not a scientist but a lawyer, at one time Lord Chancellor of England—and a man with little sympathy for the work of the true great scientists of his age, of a Galileo, a Harvey, or a Gilbert. But he was a man who wrote a great deal about what science ought to do and he was a great phrasemaker, a man who believed himself called upon to direct other men's scientific work and thereby to recognise scientific effort so as to make it more beneficial to mankind.

The interesting point, which is not often perceived, is the connexion of this conception of science with Bacon's political views. We come to understand its significance when we read in A. V. Dicey's account of seventeenth-century English constitutional history that "the real subject in dispute between statesmen such as Bacon and Wentworth[2] on the one hand, and Coke[3] and Eliot[4] on the other,

---

[1] [Published as "Progenitor of Scientism", *National Review*, July 16, 1960, pp. 23-24, as a review of J. G. Crowther, *Francis Bacon, The First Statesman of Science* (London: Cresset Press, 1960). Among J. G. Crowther's other books are *An Outline of the Universe* (London: Paul, French, & Trubner, 1931); *Scientists of the Industrial Revolution* (London: Cresset, 1962); *Six Great Scientists: Copernicus, Galileo, Newton, Darwin, Curie, Einstein* (London: Hamish Hamilton, 1961); *British Scientists of the 20th Century* (London: Routledge & Kegan Paul, 1952); *A Short History of Science* (London: Methuen, 1969); *Founders of British Science* (London: Cresset, 1960). -Ed.]

[2] [Peter Wentworth (1530-1596), Puritan parliamentary leader from 1571 to 1593. Wentworth was sent to the Tower repeatedly for insisting on parliamentary exemption from royal prerogative, and for demanding that Elizabeth name a successor in 1593. -Ed.]

[3] [Sir Edward Coke (1552-1634), English judge, appointed Attorney-General in 1594 (an appointment for which Bacon was also vying). He became Chief Justice of the King's bench in 1613, but friction with the King forced his resignation and imprisonment. After later joining parliament he became a leader in the popular movement against the arbitrary powers of the court. He is author of the *Reports* (1600-15) and of *Institutes of the Law of England* (1628). See Stephen D. White, *Sir Edward Coke and 'The Grievances of the Commonwealth' 1621-28* (Chapel Hill, N.C.:

was whether a strong administration of the Continental type should, or should not, be permanently established in England".

We owe it to the victory of Coke and Eliot that the English-speaking world did not develop the tyranny of a 'scientific' administration. Indeed, except for his one-time secretary, Thomas Hobbes, neither the political nor the scientific views of Bacon carried much weight in England. Fortunately, it was the successors of his great opponent Edward Coke—Matthew Hale[5] and David Hume, Adam Smith and Edmund Burke—who fashioned the political tradition of the English-speaking world.

The latest book devoted to Bacon by one of his contemporary admirers,[6] J. G. Crowther, says revealingly: "Bacon's influence may have been more widely and deeply realised through the French Encyclopaedia than through the Royal Society. But the complete realisation of his aims, so far, is to be found in the new socialist states, where social life has been reorganised on scientific lines, and science is pursued according to a comprehensive plan, for the endowment of human life 'with new discoveries and powers'." Later in the book the Chinese of 1958 are cited for a modern expression of Bacon's ideas; and one suspects that the author generally regards Bacon more as the predecessor of what he discreetly calls "non-egalitarian socialism" than of the democratic socialism of the West.

What is so interesting about this book is not the description of the character of Bacon, which is probably just, but that he should be praised for it. This becomes significant if one learns more about the author. Mr. J. G. Crowther has for many years been prominent as 'a scientific journalist of the new type' who, in his own words, "tries by continuous unpersonal accounts to create the scientific attitude required to solve present social problems". He has long been one of the most active members of a small but influential group

University of North Carolina Press, 1974). See also William Holdsworth, *History of English Law* (London: Methuen, 1909-72), and Louis Knafla, *Law and Politics in Jacobean England* (Cambridge: Cambridge University Press, 1977). -Ed.]

[4] [Sir John Eliot (1592-1632), leader of the Constitutional Party in the second parliament of Charles I (1626). He strongly attacked royal misgovernment and wrote the bulk of the Remonstrance and Petition of Right. Imprisoned when parliament was dissolved, he wrote in prison a treatise on constitutional monarchy, *Monarchy of Men* (1632). -Ed.]

[5] [Sir Matthew Hale (1609-1676), judge of the common bench under Cromwell, Lord Chief Justice under Charles II. Author of *History of the Common Law* (1739) and *Please of the Crown* (1736). See Edmund Heward, *Matthew Hale* (London: Robert Hale, 1972). -Ed.]

[6] [J. G. Crowther, *Francis Bacon, The First Statesman of Science*, op. cit. -Ed.]

which spread the Marxist message so successfully introduced by the Russians at the Congress of the History of Science in London thirty years ago. Ten years later with his *The Social Relations of Science*[7] he produced one of the standard works of that school and he is now able to list no less than twenty-four other books he has published on various aspects of the 'statesmanship of science'. (This does not quite measure up to Bacon's ambitions, who at one stage proposed to write books on the various departments of science at the rate of one a month!)

Mr. Crowther rightly sees in Bacon primarily "one of the forerunners of the modern art of propaganda", especially important to a generation for whom "propaganda for science in the development and government of human affairs is as important as technical skill". He admires him as a man anxious to command other men's wits and to organise a "mass-production of discoveries by machines, along industrial lines", even though he has to admit that Bacon "almost certainly [*sic*] did not succeed in discovering . . . an automatic method of discovery, in which imagination plays no part". He nevertheless is represented as "the first to outline the chief aims of modern man, which are taking shape so swiftly in the twentieth century . . . closer to the ideas of today than of the last three centuries", or even as "the greatest prophet of the modern age" and the "forerunner of Hegel, and of Marx and Engels".

One should not for this reason dismiss this book too lightly as just Marxist propaganda. It is in fact extraordinarily instructive on one of the most significant phenomena of our time, the great fascination which the idea of a centrally directed society has exercised over some of the best scientific men of our time—although the worst excesses come rarely from working scientists but usually from the kind of lay enthusiasts for science of whom Francis Bacon is the great prototype. It is surely no accident that he was probably the first to argue that it was not to be "left (as heretofore) to the pleasure of the undertakers and adventurers, where and how to build and plant; but that they do it according to a prescript and formulary".

It is surely also no accident that Bacon's great opponent, Sir Edward Coke, "though a conservative in law, emerged as the champion of liberty and progress", and had the insight to write on the title page of the copy of the *Novum Organon* which Bacon had presented to him:

---

[7] (New York: Macmillan, 1941; revised edition, London: Cresset, 1967).

It deserveth not to be read in Schooles
But to be freighted in the ship of Fooles.

Mr. Crowther's portrait of Bacon is not of the quality of the great biography of Coke which Catherine Drinker Bowen gave us a few years ago.[8] Yet the two make fascinating reading side by side. Neither, however, has quite brought out the nature of a contrast of intellectual types which has played a great role ever since, and of which Bacon and Coke are perhaps historically both the first and the most interesting examples.[9] It is fundamentally a difference of attitude to knowledge, which both men in their different ways revered.

To the pseudo-scientist it is a tool which he can manipulate and through which he can manipulate society. Bacon was thinking in terms of the master-mind who commands and consciously applies all knowledge. To Coke, most of the knowledge of mankind is embodied rather in the cultural tradition of which the lawyer in particular is the tool and instrument. To him the process in which knowledge grows is something greater than individual man and beyond the capacity of the control of any one mind.

For the past 350 years it has been on the whole the ideals of Coke which have governed the West. I believe they are also closer to those of the really great scientists, who usually are informed with humility. But are not perhaps the great number of the scientists who are not so great, but who are likely to rule us in the future, generally closer to Bacon than to Coke?

---

[8] *The Lion and the Throne* (Boston: Little, Brown, 1957; London: Hamish Hamilton, 1957).

[9] [See this volume, chapter 3, "Two Types of Mind". -Ed.]

SIX

DR. BERNARD MANDEVILLE[1]
(1670-1733)

I

It is to be feared that not only would most of Bernard Mandeville's contemporaries turn in their graves if they could know that he is today presented as a master-mind to this august body, but that even now there may have been some raising of eyebrows about the appropriateness of such a choice. The author who achieved such a *succès de scandale* almost 250 years ago is still not quite reputable. Though there can be no doubt that his works[2] had an enormous

---

[1] [This essay was first printed in *Proceedings of the British Academy* (London: Oxford University Press), vol. 52, 1966, pp. 125-141, being the Lecture on a Master Mind delivered to the Academy on March 23, 1966. Reprinted as chapter 15 of *New Studies in Philosophy, Politics, Economics and the History of Ideas* (Chicago: University of Chicago Press; London: Routledge & Kegan Paul, 1978); German translation in F. A. Hayek, *Freiburger Studien* (Tübingen: J. C. B. Mohr [Paul Siebeck] Verlag, 1969). Spanish translation, *Estudios Públicos*, Santiago, Chile, 1986. -Ed.]

[2] Any serious work done today on Mandeville must be deeply indebted to the splendid edition of *The Fable of the Bees* which the late Professor F. B. Kaye published in 1924 through the Oxford University Press. All information about Mandeville and his work used in this lecture is taken from this edition and references to its two volumes will be simply 'i' and 'ii'. Though my opinion of Mandeville's importance is based on earlier acquaintance with most of his works, when I came to write this lecture I had access only to this edition of the *Fable* and two modern reprints of *A Letter to Dion*; all quotations from other works are taken from Kaye's Introduction and Notes to his edition. At least Mandeville's *Origin of Honour* (1732) and his *Free Thoughts on Religion etc.* (1720), and probably also some of his other works, would, however, deserve to be made more accessible; it would be a great boon if the Oxford University Press could be persuaded to expand its magnificent production of the *Fable* into an edition of Mandeville's collected works. [Hayek also included in his bibliography in the original article *An Enquiry into the Causes of the Frequent Executions at Tyburn* (London, 1725) and *A Letter to Dion* (London, 1732), new edition by B. Dobrée (Liverpool, 1954). Among recent reprints of Mandeville's works are *The Virgin Unmask'd* [1709] (Delmar, N.Y.: Scholars' Facsimiles and Reprints, 1975); *The Mischiefs that Ought Justly to be Apprehended From a Whig-Government* [1714] (Los Angeles: published for the William Andrews Clark Memorial Library, University of California, by Augustan Reprint Society, 1975); *Free Thoughts on Religion, the Church, and National Happiness* [1720] (Delmar, N.Y.: Scholars' Facsimiles and Reprints, 1981); *A Modest*

circulation and that they set many people thinking on important problems, it is less easy to explain what precisely he has contributed to our understanding.

Let me say at once, to dispel a natural apprehension, that I am not going to represent him as a great economist. Although we owe to him both the term 'division of labour' and a clearer view of the nature of this phenomenon, and although no less an authority than Lord Keynes[3] has given him high praise for other parts of his economic work, it will not be on this ground that I shall claim eminence for him. With the exception I have mentioned—which is a big one—what Mandeville has to say on technical economics seems to me to be rather mediocre, or at least unoriginal—ideas widely current in his time which he uses merely to illustrate conceptions of a much wider bearing.

Even less do I intend to stress Mandeville's contributions to the theory of ethics, in the history of which he has his well-established place. But though a contribution to our understanding of the genesis of moral rules is part of his achievement, it appears to me that the fact that he is regarded as primarily a moralist has been the chief obstacle to an appreciation of his main achievement.

I should be much more inclined to praise him as a really great psychologist,[4] if this is not too weak a term for a great student of human nature; but even this is not my main aim, though it brings me nearer to my contention. The Dutch doctor, who about 1696, in his late twenties, started to practise in London as a specialist in the diseases of the nerves and the stomach, that is, as a psychiatrist,[5]

Defence of Publick Stews [1724] (Los Angeles: published for the William Andrews Clark Memorial Library, University of California, by Augustan Reprint Society, 1973); and An Enquiry into the Origin of Honour and the Usefulness of Christianity in War [1732] (London: Cass, 1971). Kaye's edition of The Fable of the Bees, recently reprinted (2 vols; Indianapolis, Ind.: LibertyClassics, 1988), is still considered the definitive edition of Mandeville's work. -Ed.]

[3] [John Maynard Keynes (1883-1946). -Ed.]

[4] Professor Kaye has duly drawn attention to the more remarkable of Mandeville's psychological insights, especially to his modern conception of an ex post rationalization of actions directed by emotions (see i, p. lxxvii, and cf. pp. lxiii-lxiv), to which I would like to add references to his observations of the manner in which a man born blind would, after gaining sight, learn to judge distances (i, p. 227), and to his interesting conception of the structure and function of the brain (ii, p. 165).

[5] Mandeville's work on psychiatry seems to have had a considerable reputation. A Treatise of Hypochondriac and Hysteric Passions which he published in 1711 had to be reprinted in the same year and was republished in an enlarged version in 1730 with the word 'Diseases' substituted for 'Passions' in the title. [See reprints: A Treatise of the Hypochondriack and Hysterick Diseases (Delmar, N.Y.: Scholars' Facsimiles and Reprints,

and continued to do so for the following thirty-seven years, clearly acquired in the course of time an insight into the working of the human mind which is very remarkable and sometimes strikingly modern. He clearly prided himself on this understanding of human nature more than on anything else. That we do not know why we do what we do, and that the consequences of our decisions are often very different from what we imagine them to be, are the two foundations of that satire on the conceits of a rationalist age which was his initial aim.

What I do mean to claim for Mandeville is that the speculations to which that *jeu d'esprit* led him mark the definite breakthrough in modern thought of the twin ideas of evolution and of the spontaneous formation of an order, conceptions which had long been in coming, which had often been closely approached, but which just then needed emphatic statement because seventeenth-century rationalism had largely submerged earlier progress in this direction. Though Mandeville may have contributed little to the answers of particular questions of social and economic theory, he did, by asking the right questions, show that there was an object for a theory in this field. Perhaps in no case did he precisely show *how* an order formed itself without design, but he made it abundantly clear that it *did*, and thereby raised the questions to which theoretical analysis, first in the social sciences and later in biology, could address itself.[6]

II

Mandeville is perhaps himself a good illustration of one of his main contentions in that he probably never fully understood what was his main discovery. He had begun by laughing about the foibles and pretences of his contemporaries, and that poem in Hudibrastic verse which he published in 1705 as *The Grumbling Hive, or Knaves Turned Honest* was probably little more than an exercise in the new language he had come to love and of which in so short a time he had acquired a remarkable mastery. Yet though this poem is all that

1976); *A Treatise of Hypochondriack and Hysterick Passions* (New York: Arno Press, 1976). -Ed.]

[6] Cf. Leslie Stephen, *History of English Thought in the 18th Century*, second edition (London: Smith, Elder, 1881), vol. 1, p. 40: "Mandeville anticipates, in many respects, the views of modern philosophers. He gives a kind of conjectural history describing the struggle for existence by which man gradually elevated himself above the wild beasts, and formed societies for mutual protection."

most people today know about him, it gives yet little indication of his important ideas. It also seems at first to have attracted no attention among serious people. The idea that

> The worst of all the multitude
> Did something for the common good

was but the seed from which his later thought sprang. It was not until nine years later, when he republished the original poem with an elaborate and wholly serious prose commentary, that the trend of his thought became more clearly visible; and only a further nine years later, with a second edition of *The Fable of the Bees, or Private Vices Public Benefits*, a book about twenty times as long as the original poem, that his ideas suddenly attracted wide attention and caused a public scandal. Finally, it was really only after yet another six years, when in 1728, at the age of fifty-eight, he added a second volume to it, that the bearing of his thought became quite clear. By that time, however, he had become a bogey man, a name with which to frighten the godly and respectable, an author whom one might read in secret to enjoy a paradox, but whom everybody knew to be a moral monster by whose ideas one must not be infected.

Yet almost everybody read him[7] and few escaped infection. Though the very title of the book, as the modern editor observes,[8] was apt "to throw many good people into a kind of philosophical hysterics which left them no wit to grasp what he was driving at", the more the outraged thundered, the more the young read the book. If Dr. Hutcheson[9] could give no lecture without attacking *The Fable of the Bees*, we may be sure that his student Adam Smith very soon turned to it. Even half a century later Dr. Samuel Johnson[10] is said to have described it as a book that every young man had on his shelves in the mistaken belief that it was a wicked book.[11] Yet by

---

[7] There is perhaps no other comparable work of which one can be equally confident that all contemporary writers in the field knew it, whether they explicitly refer to it or not. Alfred Espinas ("La Troisième phase de la dissolution du mercantilisme", *Revue internationale de sociologie*, 1902, p. 162) calls it "un livre dont nous nous sommes assurés que la plupart des hommes du XVIII⁰ siècle ont pris connaissance".

[8] F. B. Kaye in i, p. xxxix.

[9] [Francis Hutcheson (1694-1746), Professor of Moral Philosophy at Glasgow University. -Ed.]

[10] [(1709-1784). -Ed.]

[11] I borrow this quotation, which I have not been able to trace, from Joan Robinson, *Economic Philosophy* (London: C. A. Watts, 1962), p. 15.

then it had done its work and its chief contributions had become the basis of the approach to social philosophy of David Hume[12] and his successors.

III

But does even the modern reader quite see what Mandeville was driving at? And how far did Mandeville himself? His main general thesis emerges only gradually and indirectly, as it were as a by-product of defending his initial paradox that what are private vices are often public benefits. By treating as vicious everything done for selfish purposes, and admitting as virtuous only what was done in order to obey moral commands, he had little difficulty in showing that we owed most benefits of society to what on such a rigoristic standard must be called vicious. This was no new discovery but as old almost as any reflection on these problems. Had not even Thomas Aquinas had to admit that *multae utilitates impedirentur si omnia peccata districte prohiberentur*—that much that is useful would be prevented if all sins were strictly prohibited?[13] The whole idea was so familiar to the literature of the preceding century, particularly through the work of La Rochefoucauld[14] and Bayle[15], that it was not difficult for a witty and somewhat cynical mind, steeped from early youth in the ideas of Erasmus[16] and Montaigne[17], to develop it into a grotesque of society. Yet by making his starting-point the particular moral contrast between the selfishness of the motives and the benefits which the resulting actions conferred on others, Mandeville saddled himself with an incubus of which neither he nor his successors to the present day could ever quite free themselves.

It was in the elaboration of this wider thesis that Mandeville for the first time developed all the classical paradigmata of the spontaneous growth of orderly social structures: of law and morals, of language, the market, of money, and also of the growth of technological knowledge. To understand the significance of this it is

---

[12] [See this volume, chapter 7. -Ed.]

[13] *Summa Theologia*, II. ii, q. 78 i.

[14] [François de Marsillac, duc de La Rochefoucauld (1613-1680), French courtier, soldier, and moralist, author of *Réflexions ou sentences et maximes morales* (1678, numerous editions). -Ed.]

[15] [Pierre Bayle (1647-1706), French Protestant scholar and philosopher, author of the *Dictionnaire historique et critique* (Rotterdam: R. Leers, 1697). -Ed.]

[16] [Desiderius Erasmus (1466?-1536). -Ed.]

[17] [Michel Eyquem de Montaigne (1533-1592). -Ed.]

necessary to be aware of the conceptual scheme into which these phenomena had somewhat uneasily been fitted during the preceding 2,000 years.

IV

The ancient Greeks, of course, had not been unaware of the problem which the existence of such phenomena raised; but they had tried to cope with it with a dichotomy which by its ambiguity produced endless confusion, yet became so firm a tradition that it acted like a prison from which Mandeville at last showed the way of escape.

The Greek dichotomy which had governed thinking so long, and which still has not lost all its power, is that between what is natural (*physei*) and that which is artificial or conventional (*thesmoi* or *nomoi*).[18] It was obvious that the order of nature, the *kosmos*, was given independently of the will and actions of men, but that there existed also other kinds of order (for which they had a distinct word, *taxis*, for which we may envy them) which were the result of the deliberate arrangements of men. But if everything that was clearly independent of men's will and their actions was in this sense obviously 'natural', and everything that was the intended result of men's action 'artificial', this left no distinct place for any order which was the result of human actions but not of human design. That there existed among the phenomena of society such spontaneous orders was often perceived. But as men were not aware of the ambiguity of the established natural/artificial terminology, they endeavoured to express what they perceived in terms of it, and inevitably produced confusion: one would describe a social institution as 'natural' because it had never been deliberately designed, while another would describe the same institution as 'artificial' because it resulted from human actions.

It is remarkable how close, nevertheless, some of the ancient thinkers came to an understanding of the evolutionary processes that produced social institutions. There appears to have existed in all free countries a belief that a special providence watched over

[18] Cf. F. Heinimann, *Nomos und Physis* (Basel: F. Reinhardt, 1945), and my essay "The Result of Human Action But Not of Human Design" in my *Studies in Philosophy, Politics, and Economics* (London and Chicago: University of Chicago Press; London: Routledge & Kegan Paul, 1967).

their affairs which turned their unsystematic efforts to their benefit. Aristophanes refers to this when he mentions that[19]

> There is a legend of the olden time
> That all our foolish plans and vain conceits
> Are overruled to work the public good.

—a sentiment not wholly unfamiliar in [Britain]. And at least the Roman lawyers of classical times were very much aware that the Roman legal order was superior to others because, as Cato is reported to have said, it[20]

> was based upon the genius, not of one man, but of many: it was founded, not in one generation, but in a long period of several centuries and many ages of men. For, said he, there never has lived a man possessed of so great a genius that nothing could escape him, nor could the combined powers of all men living at one time possibly make all the provisions for the future without the aid of actual experience and the test of time.

This tradition was handed on, chiefly through the theories of the law of nature; and it is startling how far the older theorists of the law of nature, before they were displaced by the altogether different rationalist natural law school of the seventeenth century, penetrated into the secrets of the spontaneous development of social orders in spite of the handicap of the term 'natural'. Gradually even this unfortunate word became almost a technical term for referring to human institutions which had never been invented or designed by men, but had been shaped by the force of circumstances. Especially in the works of the last of the Schoolmen, the Spanish Jesuits of the sixteenth century, it led to a systematic questioning of how things would have ordered themselves if they had not otherwise been arranged by the deliberate efforts of government; they thus produced what I should call the first modern theories of society if their

---

[19] *Ecclesiazusae*, 473; the translation is that by B. B. Rogers in the Loeb edition (Cambridge, Mass.: Harvard University Press; London: William Heinemann, 1924), vol. 3, p. 289.

[20] M. Tullius Cicero, *De re publica* ii, I, 2, Loeb edition by C. W. Keyes (London: W. Heinemann; New York: G. Putnam's Sons, 1928), p. 113. Cf. also the Attic orator Antiphon, *On the Choreutes*, par. 2 (in *Minor Attic Orators*, Loeb edition by K. J. Maidment (Cambridge, Mass.: Harvard University Press; London: William Heinemann, 1941), p. 247), where he speaks of laws having "the distinction of being the oldest in this country, . . . and that is the surest token of good laws, as time and experience show mankind what is imperfect".

teaching had not been submerged by the rationalist tide of the following century.[21]

V

Because, however great an advance the work of a Descartes, a Hobbes, and a Leibniz may have meant in other fields, for the understanding of social growth processes it was simply disastrous. That to Descartes Sparta seemed eminent among Greek nations because its laws were the product of design and "originated by a single individual, they all tended to a single end"[22] is characteristic of that constructivistic rationalism which came to rule.[23] It came to be thought that not only all cultural institutions were the product of deliberate construction, but that all that was so designed was necessarily superior to all mere growth. Under this influence the traditional conception of the law of nature was transformed from the idea of something which had formed itself by gradual adaptation to the 'nature of things', into the idea of something which a natural reason with which man had been originally endowed would enable him to design.

I do not know how much of the older tradition was preserved through this intellectual turmoil, and particularly how much of it may still have reached Mandeville. This would require an intimate knowledge of the seventeenth-century Dutch discussion of legal and social problems which is still largely inaccessible to one who does not read Dutch. There are many other reasons why a thorough study of this period of Dutch thought, which probably had great influence on English intellectual development at the end of that and the beginning of the next century, has long seemed to me one of the great desiderata of intellectual history. But until that gap is filled I can, so far as my particular problem is concerned, only surmise that a closer study would probably show that there are some threads connecting Mandeville with that group of late School-

---

[21] On Luis Molina, from this angle the most important of these sixteenth-century Spanish Jesuits, and some of his predecessors see my essay "The Result of Human Action But Not of Human Design", in *Studies in Philosophy, Politics, and Economics*, op. cit.

[22] René Descartes, *A Discourse on Method*, part II, Everyman edition (London: J. M. Dent; New York: E. P. Dutton, 1912), p. 11.

[23] [See Hayek's account of constructivism in this volume, chapter 8. -Ed.]

men and particularly its Flemish member, Leonard Lessius of Louvain.[24]

Apart from this likely connexion with the older continental theorists of the law of nature, another probable source of inspiration for Mandeville was the English theorists of the common law, particularly Sir Matthew Hale.[25] Their work had in some respects preserved, and in other respects made unnecessary in England, a conception of what the natural law theorists had been aiming at; and in the work of Hale Mandeville could have found much that would have helped him in the speculations about the growth of cultural institutions which increasingly became his central problem.[26]

Yet all these were merely survivals of an older tradition which had been swamped by the constructivistic rationalism of the time, the most powerful expositor of which in the social field was the chief target of Hale's argument, Thomas Hobbes.[27] How ready men still were, under the influence of a powerful philosophy flattering to the human mind, to return to the naive design theories of human institutions, much more in accord with the ingrained propensity of our thinking to interpret everything anthropomorphically, we will understand better when we remember that distinguished renaissance scholars could still as a matter of course search for personal inventors of all the institutions of culture.[28] The renewed efforts to trace the political order to some deliberate act, an original agreement or contract, was much more congenial to this view than the more sophisticated accounts of their evolution which had been attempted earlier.

[24] Leonard Lessius, *De justitia et jure*, 1606.

[25] [Sir Matthew Hale (1609-1676). -Ed.]

[26] On Sir Matthew Hale see now particularly J. G. A. Pocock, *The Ancient Constitution and the Feudal Law* (Cambridge: Cambridge University Press, 1957), esp. pp. 171 *et seq.* I would like to make amends here for inadvertently not referring to this excellent book in *The Constitution of Liberty* (Chicago: University of Chicago Press, 1960), for the final revision of which I had much profited from Mr. Pocock's work.

[27] [Thomas Hobbes (1588-1679). -Ed.]

[28] Cf. Pocock, op. cit., p. 19: "This was the period in which Polydore Vergil wrote his *De inventoribus rerum* on the assumption that every invention could be traced to an individual discoverer; and in the field of legal history Macchiavelli would write with what seems singular naivete of the man "chi ordinó" so complex a creation of history as the monarchy of France"—with footnote references to Denys Hay, *Polydore Vergil* (Oxford: Clarendon Press, 1952), chapter 3, Niccoló Macchiavelli, *Discorsi* I, xvi, and Pierre Mesnard, *L'Essor de la philosophie politique au XVI° siècle* (Paris: J. Vrin, 1951), p. 83.

VI

To his contemporaries "Mandeville's reduction of all action to open or disguised selfishness"[29] may indeed have seemed little more than another version of Hobbes, and to have disguised the fact that it led to wholly different conclusions. His initial stress on selfishness still carried a suggestion that man's actions were guided by wholly rational considerations, while the tenor of his argument becomes increasingly that it is not insight but restraints imposed upon men by the institutions and traditions of society which make their actions appear rational. While he still seems most concerned to show that it is merely pride (or "self-liking")[30] which determines men's actions, he becomes in fact much more interested in the origin of the rules of conduct which pride makes men obey but whose origin and rationale they do not understand. After he has convinced himself that the reasons for which men observe rules are very different from the reasons which made these rules prevail, he gets increasingly intrigued about the origin of these rules whose significance for the orderly process of society is quite unconnected with the motives which make individual men obey them.

This begins to show itself already in the prose commentary on the poem and the other pieces which make up part I of the *Fable*, but blossoms forth in full only in part II. In part I Mandeville draws his illustrations largely from economic affairs because, as he thinks, "the sociableness of man arises from those two things, *viz.*, the multiplicity of his desires, and the continuous opposition he meets with in his endeavours to satisfy them".[31] But this leads him merely to those mercantilist considerations about the beneficial effects of luxury which caused the enthusiasm of Lord Keynes. We find here also that magnificent description of all the activities spread over the whole earth that go to the making of a piece of crimson cloth[32] which so clearly inspired Adam Smith and provided the basis for the explicit introduction of the division of labour in part II.[33]

---

[29] F. B. Kaye, i, p. lxiii.

[30] See Chiaki Nishiyama, *The Theory of Self-Love: an Essay in the Methodology of the Social Sciences, and especially of Economics, with special Reference to Bernard Mandeville*, University of Chicago, Ph.D. thesis (mimeographed), 1960.

[31] i, p. 344.

[32] i, p. 356. Already Dugald Stewart in his *Lectures on Political Economy* (*Collected Works*, vii, p. 323) suggests that this passage in Mandeville "clearly suggested to Adam Smith one of the finest passages of *The Wealth of Nations*".

[33] ii, p. 284.

Already underlying this discussion there is clearly an awareness of the spontaneous order which the market produces.

VII

I would not wish to dwell on this at any length, however, if it were not for the fact that Mandeville's long recognised position as an anticipator of Adam Smith's argument for economic liberty has recently been challenged by Professor Jacob Viner,[34] than whom there is no greater authority on such matters. With all due respect, however, it seems to me that Professor Viner has been misled by a phrase which Mandeville repeatedly uses, namely his allusions to the "dextrous management by which the skilful politician might turn private vices into public benefits".[35] Professor Viner interprets this to mean that Mandeville favours what we now call government interference or intervention, that is, a specific direction of men's economic activities by government.

---

[34] Introduction to Bernard Mandeville, *A Letter to Dion* (1732), edited for the Augustan Reprint Society, Los Angeles, University of California, 1953, and reprinted in Professor Viner's *The Long View and the Short* (Glencoe, Ill.: The Free Press, 1958), pp. 332-342. For the predominant and, I believe, truer opinion, cf. Albert Schatz, *L'Individualisme économique et social* (Paris: A. Colin, 1907), p. 62, who describes the *Fable* as "l'ouvrage capital où se trouvent tous les germes essentiels de la philosophie économique et sociale de l'individualisme". [I am grateful to Mr. Douglas Irwin, of the Federal Reserve System in Washington, for pointing out to me that the late Professor Viner, an associate and correspondent of Hayek's since 1931, replied to this passage, and Hayek's argument as a whole, in a letter (January 23, 1967) that is preserved, with the Viner papers, in the Archives of Princeton University Library, as well as with the Hayek papers at the Hoover Institution, Stanford University. Unfortunately, Hayek's reply is not to be found in either location. "As things stand now", Viner wrote, "I see nothing to withdraw, to amend, or to justify, in what I have written about Mandeville...". Viner requests clarification of (1) what Hayek means by "interventionism", "management", or "laissez faire"; (2) whether Hayek has a definition of intervention that excludes activity by government of ancient origin, or which if new is "improvement", or is not "deliberate"—in the sense, say, of being impulsive, or is local rather than central, or has been introduced by mediocrities, or is according to the rule of law; (3) why mercantilist intervention is not relevant or important in interpreting Mandeville's position. "All the evidence", Viner insists, "points to Mandeville having been a staunch Whig of his time. I know of no interventionist law on the books in his time which he criticized, except as it involved discrimination against dissenters or exclusion of Protestant immigrants. He was, of course, an immigrant himself, and he says somewhere that he was 'a part of the dissenters,' but unlike many dissenters, I am sure he had too little religious faith to practice religious intolerance of any kind, even against Puritans, had he the power." -Ed.]

[35] i, pp. 51, 369; ii, p. 319; also *A Letter to Dion*, op. cit., p. 36.

This, however, is certainly not what Mandeville meant. His aim comes out fairly unmistakably already in the little-noticed subtitle to the second 1714 printing of the *Fable*, which describes it as containing "Several Discourses, to demonstrate, that Human Frailties, . . . may be turned to the Advantage of the Civil Society, and made to supply the Place of *Moral Virtues*".[36] What I believe he wants to say by this is precisely what Josiah Tucker expressed more clearly forty years later when he wrote that "that *universal* mover in human nature, SELF-LOVE, may receive such a direction in this case (as in all others) as to promote the public interest by those efforts it shall make towards pursuing its own".[37] The means through which in the opinion of Mandeville and Tucker individual efforts are given such a direction, however, are by no means any particular commands of government but institutions and particularly general rules of just conduct. It seems to me that Mr. Nathan Rosenberg is wholly right when, in his reply to Professor Viner, he argues that in Mandeville's view, just as in Adam Smith's, the proper function of government is "to establish the rules of the game by the creation of a framework of wise laws", and that Mandeville is searching for a system where "arbitrary exertions of government power would be minimised".[38] Clearly an author who could argue, as Mandeville had already in part I of the *Fable*, that "this proportion as to numbers in every trade finds itself, and is never better kept than when nobody meddles or interferes with it",[39] and who in conclusion of part II speaks

[36] Cf. the title page reproduced in ii, p. 393. It is not described as a second edition, which term was reserved to the edition of 1723.

[37] Josiah Tucker, *The Elements of Commerce and Theory of Taxes* (1755), in R. L. Schuyler, *Josiah Tucker, a Selection from his Economic and Political Writings* (New York: Columbia University Press, 1931), p. 92.

[38] Nathan Rosenberg, "Mandeville and laissez faire", *Journal of the History of Ideas*, vol. 24, 1963, pp. 190, 193. Cf. ii, p. 335, where Mandeville argues that, though it would be preferable to have all power in the hands of the good, "the best of all then not being to be had, let us look out for the next best, and we shall find, that of all possible means to secure and perpetuate to nations their establishment, and whatever they value, there is no better method than with wise laws to guard and entrench their constitution and to contrive such forms of administration, that the common-weal can receive no great detriment from the want of knowledge or probity of ministers, if any of them should prove less able and honest than we would wish them." [In the letter mentioned above, Jacob Viner also disputes Hayek's interpretation of Tucker. Viner writes: "If you read on a few pages after the citation you made I think you will find that this is one of the many occasions in which freedom meant for him avoidance of outright prohibitions or commands or physical constraint where taxes and subsidies could do the job, but did not mean non-regulation." -Ed.]

[39] i, pp. 299-300.

about "how the shortsighted wisdom, of perhaps well-meaning people, may rob us of a felicity, that would flow spontaneously from the nature of every large society, if none were to divert or interrupt this stream",[40] was quite as much (or as little)[41] an advocate of *laissez faire* as Adam Smith.

I do not attach much importance to this question and would have relegated it to a footnote if in connexion with it the baneful effect of the old dichotomy of the 'natural' and the 'artificial' had not once again made an appearance. It was Elie Halévy who had first suggested that Mandeville and Adam Smith had based their argument on a "natural identity of interests", while Helvetius (who undoubtedly was greatly indebted to Mandeville and Hume), and, following Helvetius, Jeremy Bentham, were thinking of an "artificial identification of interests";[42] and Professor Viner suggests that Helvetius had derived this conception of an artificial identification of interests from Mandeville.[43] I am afraid this seems to me the kind of muddle to which the natural/artificial dichotomy inevitably leads. What Mandeville was concerned with was that institutions which man had not deliberately made—though it is the task of the legislator to improve them—bring it about that the divergent interests of the individuals are reconciled. The identity of interests was thus neither 'natural' in the sense that it was independent of the institutions which had been formed by men's actions, nor 'artificial' in the sense that it was brought about by deliberate arrangement, but the result of spontaneously grown institutions which had developed because they made those societies prosper which tumbled upon them.

VIII

It is not surprising that from this angle Mandeville's interest became increasingly directed to the question of how those institutions grew up which bring it about that men's divergent interests are reconciled. Indeed this theory of the growth of law, not through the design of some wise legislator but through a long process of trial

[40] ii, p. 353.

[41] Cf. J. Viner, "Adam Smith and laissez faire", *Journal of Political Economy*, vol. 35, 1927, and reprinted in *The Long View and the Short*, op. cit.

[42] Elie Halévy, *The Growth of Philosophic Radicalism* (London: Faber & Gwyer, 1928), pp. 15-17.

[43] *The Long View and the Short*, op. cit., p. 342.

and error, is probably the most remarkable of those sketches of the evolution of institutions which make his investigation into the origin of society which constitutes part II of the *Fable* so remarkable a work. His central thesis becomes[44]

> That we often ascribe to the excellency of man's genius, and the depth of his penetration, what is in reality owing to the length of time, and the experience of many generations, all of them very little differing from one another in natural parts and sagacity.

He develops it with reference to laws by saying that[45]

> there are very few, that are the work of one man, or of one generation; the greatest part of them are the product, the joint labour of several ages. . . . The wisdom I speak of, is not the offspring of a fine understanding, or intense thinking, but of sound and deliberate judgement, acquired from a long experience in business, and a multiplicity of observations. By this sort of wisdom, and length of time, it may be brought about, that there may be no greater difficulty in governing a large city, than (pardon the lowness of the simile) there is in weaving of stockings.

When by this process the laws "are brought to as much perfection, as art and human wisdom can carry them, the whole machinery can be made to play of itself, with as little skill, as is required to wind up a clock".[46]

Of course Mandeville is not fully aware of how long would be the time required for the development of the various institutions—or of the length of time actually at his disposal for accounting for it. He is often tempted to telescope this process of adaptation to circumstances,[47] and does not pull himself up to say explicitly, as Hume later did in a similar context, that "I here only suppose those reflections to be formed at once, which in fact arise insensibly and by degrees".[48] He still vacillates between the then predominant

---

[44] ii, p. 142.

[45] ii, p. 322.

[46] ii, p. 323.

[47] N. Rosenberg, loc. cit., p. 194.

[48] David Hume, *A Treatise on Human Nature*, ed. T. H. Green and T. H. Grose (London: Longmans, Green, 1882), vol. 2, p. 274.

pragmatic-rationalist and his new genetic or evolutionary view.[49] But what makes the latter so much more significant in his work than it was in the application to particular topics by Matthew Hale or John Law,[50] who probably did it better in their particular fields, is that he applies it to society at large and extends it to new topics. He still struggles to free himself from the constructivistic preconceptions. The burden of his argument is throughout that most of the institutions of society are not the result of design, but how "a most beautiful superstructure may be raised upon a rotten and despicable foundation",[51] namely men's pursuit of their selfish interests, and how, as "the order, economy, and the very existence of civil society . . . is entirely built upon the variety of our wants . . . so the whole superstructure is made up of the reciprocal services which men do to each other".[52]

IX

It is never wise to overload a lecture with quotations which, taken out of their context, rarely convey to the listener what they suggest to the reader of the consecutive exposition. So I will merely briefly mention the further chief applications to which Mandeville puts these ideas. Starting from the observation of how the skills of sport involve movements the purpose of which the acting person does not know,[53] and how similarly the skills of the arts and trades have been raised to "prodigious height . . . by the uninterrupted labour and joint experience of many generations, though none but men of ordinary capacity should ever be employed in them",[54] he maintains that manners in speaking, writing, and ordering actions are general-

---

[49] Cf. Paul Sakmann, *Bernard de Mandeville und die Bienenfabel-Controverse* (Freiburg i.B., Leipzig, and Tübingen: J. C. B. Mohr, 1897), p. 141. Although partly superseded by Kaye's edition, this is still the most comprehensive study of Mandeville.

[50] In his *Money and Trade Considered: With a Proposal for Supplying the Nation with Money* (Edinburgh: Printed by the Heirs and Successors of Andrew Anderson, 1705), which thus appeared in the same year as Mandeville's original poem, John Law gave what Carl Menger rightly described as the first adequate account of the development of money. There is no ground for believing that Mandeville knew it, but the date is interesting as showing that the evolutionary idea was somehow 'in the air'.

[51] ii, p. 64.

[52] ii, p. 349.

[53] ii, pp. 140-141.

[54] ii, p. 141.

ly followed by what we regard as "rational creatures . . . without thinking and knowing what they are about".[55] The most remarkable application of this, in which Mandeville appears to have been wholly a pioneer, is to the evolution of language which, he maintains, has also come into the world "by slow degrees, as all other arts and sciences".[56] When we remember that not long before even John Locke had regarded words as arbitrarily "invented",[57] it would seem that Mandeville is the chief source of that rich speculation on the growth of language which we find in the second half of the eighteenth century.[58]

All this is part of an increasing preoccupation with the process which we would now call cultural transmission, especially through education. He explicitly distinguishes what is "adventitious acquired by culture"[59] from what is innate, and makes his spokesman in the dialogue of part II stress that "what you call natural, is evidently artificial and acquired by education".[60] All this leads him in the end to argue that "it was with our thought as it is with speech"[61] and that[62]

> human wisdom is the child of time. It was not the contrivance of one man, nor could it have been the business of a few years, to establish the notion, by which a rational creature is kept in awe for fear of itself, and an idol is set up, that shall be its own worshipper.

Here the anti-rationalism, to use for once the misleading term which has been widely used for Mandeville and Hume, and which we had now better drop in favour of Sir Karl Popper's "critical rationalism",[63] comes out most clearly. With it Mandeville seems to me to have provided the foundations on which David Hume was

---

[55] ii, p. 287.

[56] ii, p. 287.

[57] John Locke, *Essay Concerning Human Understanding*, III, ii, I.

[58] [Compare, however, G. A. Wells, *The Origins of Language* (La Salle, Ill.: Open Court, 1987). -Ed.]

[59] ii, p. 89.

[60] ii, p. 270.

[61] ii, p. 269.

[62] *The Origin of Honour* (1732), quoted, i, p. 47n.

[63] [See K. R. Popper, *The Open Society and Its Enemies*, fourth and subsequent editions (London: Routledge & Kegan Paul, 1962). See also Hayek's "Kinds of Rationalism", in *Studies in Philosophy, Politics, and Economics* (Chicago: University of Chicago Press; London: Routledge & Kegan Paul, 1967), pp. 82-95. - Ed.]

able to build. Already in part II of the *Fable* we meet more and more frequently terms which are familiar to us through Hume, as when Mandeville speaks of "the narrow bounds of human knowledge"[64] and says that

> we are convinced, that human understanding is limited; and by the help of very little reflection, we may be as certain, that the narrowness of its bounds, its being so limited, is the very thing, the sole cause, which palpably hinders us from driving into our origins by dint of penetration.[65]

And in *The Origin of Honour*, which came out when Hume was twenty-one and according to his own testimony was "planning" the *Treatise on Human Nature*, but had not yet started "composing" it,[66] we find the wholly Humean passage that[67]

> all human creatures are swayed and wholly governed by their passions, whatever fine notions we may flatter ourselves with; even those who act suitably to their knowledge, and strictly follow the dictates of their reason, are not less compelled to do so by some passion or other, that sets them to work, than others, who bid defiance and act contrary to both, and whom we call slaves to their passions.

X

I do not intend to pitch my claim on behalf of Mandeville higher than to say that he made Hume possible.[68] It is indeed my estimate of Hume as perhaps the greatest of all modern students of mind

---

[64] ii, p. 104. Cf. David Hume, "Enquiry", in *Essays, Moral, Political, and Literary*, ed. T. H. Green and T. H. Grose (London: Longmans, Green, 1875), vol. 2, p. 6: "Man is a reasonable being; and as such, receives from science his proper food and nourishment: But so narrow are the bounds of human understanding, that little satisfaction can be hoped for in this particular, either from the extent or security of his acquisitions."

[65] ii, p. 315.

[66] Cf. E. C. Mossner, *The Life of David Hume* (London: Nelson, 1954), p. 74.

[67] *The Origin of Honour*, p. 31, quoted, i, p. lxxix.

[68] Cf. Simon N. Patten, *The Development of English Thought* (New York: Macmillan, 1910), pp. 212-213: "Mandeville's immediate successor was Hume. . . .If my interpretation is correct, the starting-point of Hume's development lay in the writings of Mandeville." Also O. Bobertag's observation in his German translation *Mandeville's Bienenfabel* (Munich: Georg Muller, 1914), p. xxv: "Im 18. Jahrhundert gibt es nur einen Mann, der etwas gleich Grosses—und Grösseres—geleistet hat, David Hume."

and society which makes Mandeville appear to me so important. It is only in Hume's work that the significance of Mandeville's efforts becomes wholly clear, and it was through Hume that he exercised his most lasting influence. Yet to have given Hume[69] some of his leading conceptions seems to me sufficient title for Mandeville to qualify as a master-mind.

How much Mandeville's contribution meant we recognise when we look at the further development of those conceptions which Hume was the first and greatest to take up and elaborate. This development includes, of course, the great Scottish moral philosophers of the second half of the century, above all Adam Smith and Adam Ferguson, the latter of whom, with his phrase about the "results of human action but not of human design",[70] has provided not only the best brief statement of Mandeville's central problem but also the best definition of the task of all social theory. I will not claim in favour of Mandeville that his work also led via Helvetius to Bentham's particularistic utilitarianism which, though the claim is true enough, meant a relapse into that constructivistic rationalism which it was Mandeville's main achievement to have overcome. But the tradition which Mandeville started includes also Edmund Burke, and, largely through Burke, all those 'historical schools' which, chiefly on the Continent, and through men like Herder[71] and Savigny[72], made the idea of evolution a commonplace in the social

[69] The same may also be true concerning Montesquieu. See on this Joseph Dedieu, *Montesquieu et la tradition politique anglaise* (Paris: J. Gabalda, 1909), pp. 260-261, and 307n.

[70] Adam Ferguson, *An Essay on the History of Civil Society* (Edinburgh: Edinburgh University Press, 1767), p. 187: "Every step and every movement of the multitude, even in what are termed enlightened ages, are made with equal blindness to the future; and nations stumble upon establishments, which are indeed the result of human action, but not the execution of any human design. If Cromwell said, That a man never mounts higher than when he knows not wither he is going; it may with more reason be affirmed of communities, that they admit of the greatest revolutions where no change is intended, and that the most refined politicians do not always know wither they are leading the state by their projects."

[71] It may deserve notice that J. G. Herder seems to have been the earliest instance where the influence of Mandeville joined with that of the somewhat similar ideas of G. Vico.

[72] It would seem as if it had been largely by way of Savigny that those ideas of Mandeville and Hume eventually reached Carl Menger and thus returned to economic theory. It was in the sociological parts of his *Untersuchungen über die Methode* (1883), translated as *Problems of Economics and Sociology*, ed. Louis Schneider (Urbana, Ill.: University of Illinois Press, 1963), that Carl Menger not only restated the general theory of the formation of law, morals, money, and the market in a manner which, I

sciences of the nineteenth century long before Darwin. And it was in this atmosphere of evolutionary thought in the study of society, where 'Darwinians before Darwin' had long thought in terms of the prevailing of more effective habits and practices, that Charles Darwin at last applied the idea systematically to biological organisms.[73] I do not, of course, mean to suggest that Mandeville had any direct influence on Darwin (though David Hume probably had). But it seems to me that in many respects Darwin is the culmination of a development which Mandeville more than any other single man had started.

Yet Mandeville and Darwin still have one thing in common: the scandal they caused had ultimately the same source, and Darwin in this respect finished what Mandeville had begun. It is difficult to remember now, perhaps most difficult for those who hold religious views in their now prevailing form, how closely religion was not long ago still associated with the 'argument from design'. The discovery of an astounding order which no man had designed was for most men the chief evidence for the existence of a personal creator. In the moral and political sphere Mandeville and Hume did show that the sense of justice and probity on which the order in this sphere rested was not originally implanted in man's mind but had, like that mind itself, grown in a process of gradual evolution which at least in principle we might learn to understand. The revulsion against this suggestion was quite as great as that caused more than a century later when it was shown that the marvels of the organism could no longer be adduced as proof of special design. Perhaps I should have said that the process began with Kepler and Newton. But if it began and ended with a growing insight into what determined the kosmos of nature, it seems that the shock caused by the discovery that the moral and political kosmos was also the result

---

believe, had never again been attempted since Hume, but that he also expressed the fundamental insight that (p. 94 of the translation): "This genetic insight is inseparable from the idea of theoretical science." Perhaps it also deserves notice here, since this seems not to be generally known, that, through his pupil Richard Thurnwald, Menger exercised some influence on the rise of modern cultural anthropology, the discipline which more than any other has in our day concentrated on what were the central problems of the Mandeville-Hume-Smith-Ferguson tradition. Cf. also the long extracts from Mandeville now given in J. S. Slotkin, ed., *Readings in Early Anthropology* (Chicago: Aldine Publishing, 1965).

[73] On the influence on Charles Darwin of conceptions derived from social theory see E. Radl, *Geschichte der biologischen Theorien*, ii (Leipzig: W. Engelmann, 1909), esp. p. 121.

of a process of evolution and not of design contributed no less to produce what we call the modern mind.

Addendum: Bernard Mandeville[74]

Bernard Mandeville was born in 1670 in Rotterdam as the scion of a family of medical doctors named 'de Mandeville'—a title that he himself did not use—that had been active in Holland for at least three generations. He studied medicine at the University of Leiden, where in 1691 he achieved the rank of doctor, specialising in nervous and digestive illnesses. Not long afterwards he moved to London, where within a few years he attained a successful practice and distinguished position. After publishing three Latin essays on medical questions while still living in Holland, and also a few minor literary essays in English, his work in social philosophy began in 1705 with his publication of a satirical poem called "The Grumbling Hive, or Knaves turn'd Honest". Although this work already contained the basic ideas of his later work and was a popular success, it nonetheless found hardly any serious attention. Similarly, the first book edition of 1714—published under the title *The Fable of the Bees: or, Private Vices, Publick Benefits*, in which the poem was followed by a detailed commentary entitled "An Inquiry into the Origin of Moral Virtue", as well as a series of "Remarks"—enjoyed little real notice. Only the third edition of 1723 (which was designated as the second edition) aroused not only great attention but even public scandal. In this edition the "Remarks" were substantially expanded and an "Essay on Charity Schools" was added. Overlooking a few minor works, this was followed in 1729 by *The Fable of the Bees, Part II*, Mandeville's most mature work, and in 1732, the year of his death, *A Letter to Dion*, a debate with an anonymous critic about the philosophy of Bishop Berkeley.

The subtitle of *The Fable of the Bees*—"Private Vices, Publick Benefits"—expresses in paradoxical form Mandeville's main thesis, which, set out in the original poem in half-jesting form, led to ever more serious philosophical considerations about questions of ethics and social philosophy. In the realm of ethics Mandeville failed to resolve the paradox which is posed by the opposition between a rigorous ethics of duty and a study of human actions from the standpoint of utility.

The lively contrast between the self-interested motives and the beneficent consequences of human action was nonetheless exceptionally influential and

---

[74] [Hayek published this brief article on Mandeville in the *Handwörterbuch der Sozialwissenschaften* (Stuttgart-Tübingen-Göttingen), vol. 7, 1959, pp. 116-117. It is translated into English for the first time here. The translation is by the General Editor. -Ed.]

the discussion of ethical and social philosophy in the middle of the eighteenth century is dominated by its influence, even where Mandeville's book, branded as immoral and godless, went unmentioned.

The significance of Mandeville lies not so much in his particular contribution to economic theory, where he generally (as in the discussion of luxury) introduces only prevailing and often erroneous opinions to illustrate his thesis and really only achieved an important contribution in his working out of the concept of division of labour. The significant step forward which he represents consists in the general application of the idea of *development* to social arrangements, something which before him had been attempted only in the area of the law.

Not only in the areas of morality and convention, but also for language and money, he shows clearly how the preservation of more advantagous and the elimination of less profitable practices and usages leads to cumulative growth of extremely complicated structures which serve human goals and form the basis of culture without ever having been consciously designed. This methodological position, developed in deliberate opposition to the rationalism of Thomas Hobbes, René Descartes, and in part also of John Locke, has become of the greatest importance for the theory of the social sciences. From Mandeville there flows a direct line to David Hume and then on the one side to Adam Smith, Adam Ferguson, and Edmund Burke, and on the other side to Jeremy Bentham and the utilitarians.

Bibliographical Note:

About Mandeville:

Paul Sakmann, *Bernard de Mandeville und die Bienenfabelkontroverse* (Freiburg: J. C. B. Mohr, 1897).

Albert Schatz, "Bernard de Mandeville", *Vierteljahreschrift für Soziale- und Wirtschaftsgeschichte*, Stuttgart, 1903.

Rudolf Stammler, *Mandeville's Bienenfabel. Die letzten Gründe einer wissenschaftlich geleiteten Politik* (Berlin: O. Reichl, 1918).

Frederick Benjamin Kaye, "Mandeville and the Origin of Language", *Modern Language Notes*, vol. 39, 1924.

——, "The Mandeville Canon: A Supplement", *Notes and Queries*, London, 1924.

Arthur K. Rogers, "The Ethics of Mandeville", *International Journal of Ethics*, Chicago, 1925-6.

Sterling Power Lamprecht, "The Fable of the Bees", *Journal of Philosophy*, New York, 1926.

Vinzenz Rufner, "Die soziologische Stellung von Mandevilles Bienenfabel", *Archiv für Geschichte der Philosophie und Soziologie*, Berlin, 1929-30.

Wilhelm Deckelmann, "Untersuchungen zur Bienenfabel Mandevilles zu ihrer Entstehungsgeschichte im Hinblick auf die Bienenfabelthese". Dissertation, Hamburg, 1933.

[Hayek appended the above references to his original article. For recent studies of Mandeville, see M. M. Goldsmith, *Private Vices, Public Benefits: Bernard Mandeville's Social and Political Thought* (Cambridge and New York: Cambridge University Press, 1985); Thomas A. Horne, *The Social Thought of Bernard Mandeville: Virtue and Commerce in Early Eighteenth-Century England* (London: Macmillan, 1978); Harry Landreth, "The Economic Thought of Bernard Mandeville", *History of Political Economy*, vol. 7, no. 2, Summer 1975, pp. 193-208; Irwin Primer, ed., *Mandeville Studies* (The Hague: Martinus Nijhoff, 1975); N. Rosenberg, "Mandeville, Bernard", in *The New Palgrave: A Dictionary of Economics*, ed. Eatwell, Milgate, and Newman (London: Macmillan, 1987), vol. 3, pp. 297-298; and Louis Schneider, *Paradox and Society: The Work of Bernard Mandeville* (New Brunswick, N.J.: Transaction Books, 1986). -Ed.]

SEVEN

THE LEGAL AND POLITICAL PHILOSOPHY OF DAVID HUME (1711-1776)[1]

It is always misleading to label an age by a name which suggests that it was ruled by a common set of ideas. It particularly falsifies the picture if we do this for a period which was in such a state of ferment as was the eighteenth century. To lump together under the name of 'enlightenment' (or *Aufklärung*) the French philosophers from Voltaire to Condorcet on the one hand, and the Scottish and English thinkers from Mandeville through Hume and Adam Smith to Edmund Burke on the other, is to gloss over differences which for the influence of these men on the next century were much more important than any superficial similarity which may exist. So far as David Hume in particular is concerned, a much truer view has recently been expressed when it was said that he "turned against the enlightenment its own weapons" and undertook "to whittle down the claims of reason by the use of rational analysis".[2]

---

[1] A public lecture delivered at the University of Freiburg on July 18, 1963, and published in *Il Politico*, vol. 28, no. 4, 1963. The reference to the philosophical works of Hume will be throughout to the editions of T. H. Green and T. H. Grose, namely, *A Treatise of Human Nature*, 2 vols, London, 1890 (which will be referred to as I and II) and *Essays, Moral, Political, and Literary*, 2 vols, London, 1875 (which will be referred to as III and IV). The references to Hume's *History of England* will be to the quarto edition in six volumes, London, 1762.

Since the first publication of this essay a number of Continental studies of Hume's legal philosophy have come to my notice, of which the most important is Georges Vlachos, *Essai sur la politique de Hume* (Paris: Domat-Montchretien, 1955). Others are: G. Laviosa, *La filosofia scientifica del diritto in Inghilterra, Parte I, Da Bacone a Hume* (Turin, 1897), pp. 697-850; W. Wallenfels, *Die Rechtsphilosophie David Humes*, Doctoral Dissertation at the University of Göttingen, 1938; L. Bagolini, *Esperienza giuridica ed esperienza politica nel pensioro di David Hume* (Sienna, 1947); and Silvana Castignone, "La Dottrina della o giustizia in D. Hume", *Rivista Internazionale di Filosofia di Diritto*, vol. 38, 1960, and "Diritto naturale e diritto positivo in David Hume", *ibid.*, vol. 39, 1962. [This essay has been republished previously in F. A. Hayek, *Studies in Philosophy, Politics, and Economics* (Chicago: University of Chicago Press; London: Routledge & Kegan Paul, 1967). -Ed.]

[2] S. S. Wolin, "Hume and Conservatism", *American Political Science Review*, vol. 48, 1954, p. 1001.

The habit of speaking of the *Aufklärung* as if it represented a homogeneous body of ideas is nowhere so strong as it is in Germany, and there is a definite reason for this. But the reason which has led to this view of eighteenth-century thought has also had very grave and, in my opinion, regrettable consequences. This reason is that the English ideas of the time (which were, of course, mainly expounded by Scotsmen—but I cannot rid myself of the habit of saying 'English' when I mean 'British') became known in Germany largely through French intermediaries and in French interpretations—and often misinterpretations. It appears to me to be one of the great tragedies of intellectual and political history that thus the great ideals of political freedom became known on the Continent almost exclusively in the form in which the French, a people who had never known liberty, interpreted traditions, institutions and ideas which derived from an entirely different intellectual and political climate. They did this in a spirit of constructivist intellectualism, which I shall briefly call rationalism, a spirit which was thoroughly congenial to the atmosphere of an absolute state which endeavoured to design a new centralised structure of government, but entirely alien to the older tradition which ultimately was preserved only in Britain.

The seventeenth century, indeed, had on both sides of the Channel been an age in which this constructivist rationalism dominated. Francis Bacon and Thomas Hobbes were no less spokesmen of this rationalism than Descartes or Leibniz—and even John Locke could not entirely escape its influence. It was a new phenomenon which must not be confused with ways of thought of earlier times which are also described as rationalism. Reason was for the rationalist no longer a capacity to recognise the truth when he found it expressed, but a capacity to arrive at truth by deductive reasoning from explicit premises.[3] The older tradition, which had been represented by the earlier theorists of the law of nature, survived chiefly in England in the works of the great common lawyers, especially Sir Edward Coke and Matthew Hale, the opponents of Bacon and Hobbes, who were able to hand on an understanding of the growth

---

[3] John Locke seems to have been clearly aware of this change in the meaning of the term 'reason'. In *Essays on the Law of Nature* (ed. W. von Leyden (Oxford: Clarendon Press, 1954), p. 111) he wrote: "By reason, however, I do not think is meant here that faculty of the understanding which forms trains of thought and deduces proofs, but certain definite principles of action from which spring all virtues and whatever is necessary for the proper moulding of morals."

of institutions which was elsewhere displaced by the ruling desire deliberately to remake them.

But when the attempt to create also in England a centralised absolute monarchy with its bureaucratic apparatus had failed, and what in Continental eyes appeared as a weak government coincided with one of the greatest upsurges of national strength and prosperity which are known to history, the interest in the prevailing undesigned, 'grown' institutions led to a revival of this older way of thinking. While the Continent was dominated during the eighteenth century by constructivist rationalism, there grew up in England a tradition which by way of contrast has sometimes been described as 'anti-rationalist'.

The first great eighteenth-century figure in this tradition was Bernard Mandeville, originally a Dutchman, and many of the ideas I shall have to discuss in connection with David Hume can be found *in nuce* already in the writings of the former.[4] That Hume owes much to him seems to be beyond doubt. I shall discuss these ideas, however, in the fully developed form which only Hume gave them.

Almost all these ideas can be found already in the second part of the *Treatise on Human Nature* which he published at the age of twenty-nine in 1740 and which, though it was almost completely overlooked at first, is today universally acknowledged as his greatest achievement. His *Essays*, which began to appear in 1742, the *Enquiry concerning the Principles of Morals*, in which nine years later he attempted to restate those ideas in briefer and more popular form, and his *History of England* contain sometimes improved formulations and were much more effective in spreading his ideas; but they added little that is new to the first statement.

Hume is of course known mainly for his theory of knowledge, and in Germany largely as the author who stated the problems which Immanuel Kant endeavoured to solve. But to Hume the chief task was from the beginning a general science of human nature, for which morals and politics were as important as the sources of knowledge. And it would seem probable that in those fields he awoke Kant from his 'dogmatic slumber' as much as he had done in epistemology. Certainly Kant, but also the other two great German

---

[4] [See the preceding chapter. -Ed.] See C. Nishiyama, *The Theory of Self-Love: An Essay on the Methodology of the Social Sciences, and Especially of Economics, with Special Reference to Bernard Mandeville*, University of Chicago, Ph.D. thesis (mimeographed), 1960.

liberals, Schiller[5] and Humboldt[6], still knew Hume better than was true of later generations, which were entirely dominated by French thought, and particularly by the influence of Rousseau. But Hume as a political theorist and as a historian has never been properly appreciated on the Continent. It is characteristic of the misleading generalisations about the eighteenth century that even today it is still largely regarded as a period which lacked historical sense, a statement which is true enough of the Cartesian rationalism which ruled in France, but certainly not of Britain and least of all of Hume who could describe his as "the historical age and [his] as the historical nation".[7]

The neglect of Hume as a legal and political philosopher, however, is not confined to the Continent. Even in England, where it is now at last recognised that he is not merely the founder of the modern theory of knowledge but also one of the founders of economic theory, his political and still more his legal philosophy is curiously neglected. In works on jurisprudence we will look in vain for his name. The systematic philosophy of law begins in England with Jeremy Bentham and John Austin who were both indebted mainly to the Continental rationalist tradition—Bentham to Helvetius[8] and Beccaria[9], and Austin to German sources. But the greatest legal philosopher whom Britain produced before Bentham, and who, incidentally, was trained as a lawyer, had practically no influence on that development.[10]

---

[5] Johann Christoph Friedrich von Schiller (1759-1805).

[6] [Wilhelm von Humboldt (1767-1835). Humboldt's *Spheres and Duties of Government* (1792) is an early statement of an individualist and evolutionary case against government interference. His studies of the German and Prussian constitutions (1813 and 1819) set the tone for nineteenth-century German liberalism. Foreign minister, educational theorist, and philologist, Humboldt was also the founder of the University of Berlin. -Ed.]

[7] *The Letters of David Hume*, ed. J. Y. T. Greig (Oxford: Clarendon Press, 1932), vol. II, p. 444 (reprinted New York: Garland Publishing Company, 1983).

[8] [Claude Adrien Helvetius (1715-1771). One of Diderot's Encyclopédists, Helvetius served as Farmer-General from 1738 to 1751. The egalitarian and hedonistic doctrines of his *De l'Ésprit* (1758) strongly influenced Beccaria and the early utilitarians. -Ed.]

[9] [Cesare Bonsana, Marchesi di Beccaria (1738-1794) is known for his attacks on the inhumane conditions of eighteenth-century European prisons, *Essay on Crimes and Punishment* (1764), in which the utilitarian phrase "the greatest happiness of the greatest number" was first used. His major economic work, *Elementi di economia pubblica* (1771), was never completed. -Ed.]

[10] My attention was first directed to these parts of Hume's works many years ago by Professor Sir Arnold Plant.

This is the more remarkable as Hume gives us probably the only comprehensive statement of the legal and political philosophy which later became known as liberalism. It is today fairly generally recognised that the programme of nineteenth-century liberalism contained two distinct and in some ways even antagonistic elements, liberalism proper and the democratic tradition. Of these only the second, democracy, is essentially French in origin and was added in the course of the French revolution to the older, individualistic liberal tradition which came from England. The uneasy partnership which the two ideals kept during the nineteenth century should not lead us to overlook their different character and origin. The liberal ideal of personal liberty was first formulated in England which throughout the eighteenth century had been the envied land of liberty and whose political institutions and doctrines served as models for the theorists elsewhere. These doctrines were those of the Whig party, the doctrines of the Glorious Revolution of 1688. And it is in Hume, and not, as is commonly believed, in Locke, who had provided the justification of that revolution, that we find the fullest statement of that doctrine.

If this is not more widely recognised, it is partly a consequence of the erroneous belief that Hume himself was a Tory rather than a Whig. He acquired this reputation because in his *History*, as an eminently just man, he defended the Tory leaders against many of the unfair accusations brought against them—and, in the religious field, he chided the Whigs for the intolerance which, contrary to their own doctrine, they showed towards the catholic leanings prevalent among the Tories. He himself explained his position very fairly when he wrote, with reference to his *History*, that "my views of *things* are more conformable to Whig principles; my representations of *persons* to Tory prejudices".[11] In this respect such an arch-reactionary as Thomas Carlyle, who once described Hume as "the father of all succeeding Whigs",[12] saw his position more correctly than most of the democratic liberals of the nineteenth and twentieth centuries.

There are of course some exceptions to the common misunderstanding and neglect of Hume as the outstanding philosopher of liberal political and legal theory. One of these is Friedrich Meinecke who in his *Entstehung des Historismus* clearly describes how for Hume "der Sinn der englischen Geschichte [war], von einem

[11] E. C. Mossner, *Life of David Hume* (London: Nelson, 1954), p. 311. For a survey of Hume's relations to Whigs and Tories, see Eugene Miller, "David Hume: Whig or Tory?", *New Individualist Review*, vol. 1, no. 4 (Chicago: 1962).

[12] Thomas Carlyle, "Boswell's Life of Johnson", *Fraser's Magazine*, 1832.

government of men zu einem *government of law* zu werden. Diesen unendlich mühsamen, ja hässlichen, aber zum Guten endenden Prozess in seiner ganzen Komplikation und in allen seinen Phasen anschaulich machen, war oder wurde vielmehr sein Vorhaben . . . . Eine politische Grund- und Hauptfrage wurde so zum Generalthema seines Werkes. Nur von ihm aus ist es, was bisher immer übersehen wurde, in seiner Anlage und Stoffauswahl zu verstehen."[13]

It was not Meinecke's task to trace this interpretation of history back to Hume's philosophical work where he could have found the theoretical foundation of the ideal which guided Hume in the writing of his *History*. It may be true that through his historical work Hume did more to spread this ideal than through his philosophical treatment. Indeed, Hume's *History* did probably as much to spread Whig liberalism throughout Europe in the eighteenth century as Macaulay's *History* did in the nineteenth. But that does not alter the fact that if we want an explicit and reasoned statement of this ideal we must turn to his philosophical works, the *Treatise* and the easier and more elegant exposition in the *Essays* and *Enquiries*.

It is no accident that Hume develops his political and legal ideas in his philosophical work. They are most intimately connected with his general philosophical conceptions, especially with his sceptical views on the 'narrow bounds of human understanding'. His concern was human nature in general, and his theory of knowledge was intended mainly as a step towards an understanding of the conduct of man as a moral being and a member of society. What he produced was above all a theory of the growth of human institutions which became the basis of his case for liberty and the foundation of the work of the great Scottish moral philosophers, of Adam Ferguson, Adam Smith and Dugald Stewart, who are today recognised as the chief ancestors of modern evolutionary anthropology. His work also provided the foundation on which the authors of the American

---

13 [". . . the underlying tendency of English history was to be found in the transformation from a *government of men* to a *government of law*. It was his intention, or, to be exact, it came to be his intention, to illustrate this infinitely laborious, not to say ungainly, process in all its complications and all its phases. . . . A basic, major political question thus became the guiding theme of his work—a fact that has been overlooked hitherto, although it is crucial for understanding the organisation of his work and his choice of material." -Ed.]

Friedrich Meinecke, *Die Entstehung des Historismus* (Munich and Berlin: R. Oldenbourg, 1936), vol. I, p. 234. [Now available in a single volume, ed. Carl Hinrichs (Munich and Berlin: R. Oldenbourg, 1965). -Ed.]

constitution built[14] and in some measure for the political philosophy of Edmund Burke which is much closer to, and more directly indebted to, Hume than is generally recognised.[15]

Hume's starting point is his anti-rationalist theory of morals which shows that, so far as the creation of moral rules is concerned, "reason of itself is utterly impotent" and that "the rules of morality, therefore, are not conclusions of our reason".[16] He demonstrates that our moral beliefs are neither natural in the sense of innate, nor a deliberate invention of human reason, but an "artifact" in the special sense in which he introduces this term, that is, a product of cultural evolution, as we would call it. In this process of evolution what proved conducive to more effective human effort survived, and the less effective was superseded. As a recent writer put it somewhat pointedly, "Standards of morality and justice are what Hume calls 'artifacts'; they are neither divinely ordained, nor an integral part of original human nature, nor revealed by pure reason. They are an outcome of the practical experience of mankind, and the sole consideration in the slow test of time is the utility each moral rule can demonstrate towards promoting human welfare. Hume may be called a precursor to Darwin in the field of ethics. In effect, he proclaimed a doctrine of survival of the fittest among human conventions—fittest not in terms of good teeth but in terms of maximum social utility."[17]

It is, however, in his analysis of the circumstances which determined the evolution of the chief legal institutions, in which he shows why a complex civilisation could grow up only where certain types of legal institutions developed, that he makes some of his most important contributions to jurisprudence. In the discussion of these problems his economic and his legal and political theory are intimately connected. Hume is indeed one of the few social theorists who are clearly aware of the connection between the rules men obey and the order which is formed as a result.

The transition from explanation to ideal does not, however, involve him in any illegitimate confusion of explanation and recommendation. Nobody was more critical of, or explicit about the

---

[14] Douglass Adair, "'That politics may be reduced to a science': David Hume, James Madison and the Tenth *Federalist*", *Huntington Library Quarterly*, vol. 20, no. 4, 1957, pp. 343-360.

[15] H. B. Acton, "Prejudice", *Revue Internationale de Philosophie*, vol. 21, 1952.

[16] II, p. 235.

[17] C. Bay, *The Structure of Freedom* (Stanford, Calif.: Stanford University Press, 1958), p. 33.

impossibility of, a logical transition from the *is* to the *ought*,[18] about the fact that "an active principle can never be founded on an inactive" one.[19] What he undertakes is to show that certain characteristics of modern society which we prize are dependent on conditions which were not created in order to bring about these results, yet are nevertheless their indispensable presuppositions. They are institutions "advantageous to the public though . . . not intended for that purpose by the inventors".[20] Hume shows, in effect, that an orderly society can develop only if men learn to obey certain rules of conduct.

The section of the *Treatise* which deals "Of the Origin of Justice and Property" and which examines "the manner in which rules of justice are established by the artifice of men"[21] is his most significant contribution in this field. It sets out from the fact that it is life in society which alone gives that weak animal, man, his exceptional powers. He concisely describes the advantages of the "partition of employments"[22] (what Adam Smith was to make popular under the Mandevillian term "division of labour") and shows how the obstacles to union in society are gradually overcome. The chief ones among these are firstly every individual's predominant concern with his own needs or those of his immediate associates, and secondly the scarcity (Hume's term!) of means, i.e., the fact that "there is not a sufficient quantity of them to supply every one's desires and necessities".[23] It is thus "the concurrence of certain *qualities* of the human mind with the *situation* of external objects"[24] which forms the obstacles to smooth collaboration: "The qualities of mind are selfishness and *limited generosity*: And the situation of external objects is their *easy change*, joined to their *scarcity* in comparison of the wants and desires of men."[25] Were it not for those facts, no laws would ever have been necessary or have been thought of: "if men were supplied with everything in the same abundance, or if *every one* had the same affection and tender regard for *every one* as for himself, justice and injustice would be equally unknown among mankind."[26] "For

---

[18] II, p. 245.
[19] II, p. 235.
[20] II, p. 296.
[21] II, pp. 258-273. Note Hume's acknowledgement of his indebtedness to H. Grotius, IV, p. 275.
[22] II, p. 259.
[23] II, p. 261.
[24] II, p. 266.
[25] II, pp. 266-267.
[26] II, p. 267.

what purpose make a partition of goods, when everyone has already more than enough? . . . Why call this object *mine*, when, upon seizing of it by another, I need but stretch out my hand to possess myself of what is equally valuable? Justice, in that case, being totally *useless*, would be an idle ceremonial."[27] It is thus "only from the selfishness and confined generosity of men, along with the scanty provisions nature has made for his wants, that justice derives its origin."[28]

It is thus the nature of the circumstances, what Hume calls "the necessity of human society", that gives rise to the "three fundamental laws of nature":[29] those of "*the stability of possession, of its transference by consent, and of the performance of promises*"[30] of which the whole system of law is merely an elaboration. These rules were not, however, deliberately invented by men to solve a problem which they saw (though it has become a task of legislation to improve them). Hume takes great pains to show for each of these rules how self-interest will lead to their being increasingly observed and finally enforced. "The rule concerning the stability of possession", he writes, for instance, "arises gradually, and acquires force by slow progression, and our repeated experience of the inconvenience of transgressing it."[31] Similarly, "it is evident that if men were to regulate their conduct [as regards the keeping of promises] by the view of a particular *interest*, . . . they would involve themselves in endless confusion."[32] He points out that, in like manner as rules of justice arise, "are languages gradually established by human conventions without any promise. In like manner do gold and silver become the common measure of exchange."[33] Law and morals, like language and money, are, as we would say, not deliberate inventions but grown institutions or "formations". To guard against the impression that his emphasis on proven utility means that men adopted these institutions because they foresaw their utility, he stresses that in all

[27] IV, p. 180.
[28] II, pp. 267-268. The whole passage is in italics.
[29] Cf. II, p. 258: "Though the rules of justice be *artificial*, they are not *arbitrary*. Nor is the expression improper to call them *Laws of Nature*; if by natural we understand what is common to any species, or even if we confine it to mean what is inseparable from the species."
[30] II, p. 293.
[31] II, p. 263.
[32] II, p. 318.
[33] II, p. 263; cf. IV, p. 275.

his references to utility he "only suppose[s] those reflections to be formed at once which in fact arise insensibly and by degrees".[34]

Rules of this sort must be recognised before people can come to agree or bind themselves by promise or contract to any form of government. Therefore, "though it be possible for men to maintain a small uncultivated society without government, it is impossible they should maintain a society of any kind without justice, and the observance of those three fundamental laws concerning the stability of possession, its translation by consent, and the performance of promises. These are, therefore, *antecedent to government*, . . . though government, *upon its first establishment*, would naturally be supposed to derive its obligation from those laws of nature, and in particular from that concerning the performance of promises."[35]

Hume's further concern is chiefly to show that it is only the universal application of the same "general and inflexible rules of justice" which will secure the establishment of a general order, that this and not any particular aims or results must guide the application of the rules if an order is to be the result. Any concern with particular ends of either the individuals or the community, or a regard for the merits of particular individuals, would entirely spoil that aim. This contention is intimately bound up with Hume's belief in the short-sightedness of men, their propensity to prefer immediate advantage to distant gain, and their incapacity to be guided by a proper appreciation of their true long-run interest unless they bind themselves by general and inflexible rules which in the particular case are applied without regard to consequences.

These ideas, first developed in the *Treatise* from which I have so far mainly quoted, become more prominent in Hume's later writing, in which they are also more clearly connected with his political ideals. The most concise statement of them will be found in Appendix III to the *Enquiry concerning the Principles of Morals*.[36] I would

---

[34] II, p. 274.

[35] II, p. 306; first group of italics added.

[36] Cf. II, p. 301: men "prefer any trivial advantage that is present to the maintenance of order in society which so much depends on the observance of justice . . . .
You have the same propension I have, in favour of what is contiguous above what is
remote"; and II, p. 303: "Here then is the origin of civil government and society.
Men are not able radically to cure, either in themselves or others, that narrowness of
soul which makes them prefer the present to the remote. They cannot change their
natures. All they can do is to change their situation, and render the observance of
justice the immediate interest of some particular persons . . . . But this execution of
justice, though the principal, is not the only advantage of government. . . . not
contented to protect men in those conventions they make for their mutual interest, it

recommend to all who wish to become acquainted with Hume's legal philosophy to begin with those six pages (272-278 of volume II of the standard edition of the *Essays*) and to work backwards from them to the fuller statements of the *Treatise*. But I shall continue to quote mainly from the *Treatise*, where the individual statements often have greater freshness, even though the exposition as a whole is sometimes rather prolix.

The weakness of men's minds (or the "narrow bounds of human understanding" as Hume would say, or their inevitable ignorance, as I should prefer to express it) would, without fixed rules, have the result that they "would conduct themselves, on most occasions, by particular judgements, and would take into consideration the characters and circumstances of the persons, as well as the general nature of the question. But it is easy to observe that this would produce an infinite confusion in human society, and that the avidity and partiality of men would quickly bring disorder into the world, if not restrained by some general and inflexible principles."[37]

The rules of law, however, "are not derived from any utility or advantage which either the *particular* person or the public may reap from his enjoyment of any *particular* goods . . . . Justice in her decisions never regards the fitness or unfitness of objects to particular persons, but conducts herself by more extensive views."[38] In particular: "The relation of fitness or suitableness ought never to enter into consideration, in distributing the properties of mankind."[39] A single act of justice is even "frequently contrary to the *public interest*; and were it to stand by itself, without being followed by other acts, may, in itself, be very prejudicial to society. . . . Nor is every single act of justice, considered apart, more conducive to private interest than to public . . . . But, however single acts of

---

often obliges them to make such conventions, and forces them to seek their own advantage, by concurrence in some common end or purpose."

[37] II, pp. 298-299. Cf. also II, p. 318: "it is evident that if men were to regulate their conduct in this particular [the appointment of magistrates] by the view of a particular *interest*, either public or private, they would involve themselves in endless confusion, and would render all government, in a great measure, ineffectual. The private interest of everyone is different; and though the public interest in itself be always one and the same, yet it becomes the source of great dissensions, by reason of the different opinions of particular persons concerning it . . . were we to follow the same advantage, in assigning particular possessions to particular persons, we should disappoint our end, and perpetuate the confusion which that rule is intended to prevent. We must, therefore, proceed by general rules, and regulate ourselves by general interests."

[38] II, p. 273.

[39] II, p. 283.

justice may be contrary, either to public or to private interest, it is certain that the whole plan or scheme is highly conducive, or indeed absolutely requisite, both to the support of society and the well being of every individual."[40] Or, as Hume puts it in the Appendix to the *Enquiry*, "the benefit resulting from [the social virtues of justice and fidelity] is not the consequence of every individual single act; but arises from the whole scheme or system, concurred in by the whole, or the greater part of society . . . . The result of the individual act is here, in many instances, directly opposite to that of the whole system of actions; and the former may be extremely hurtful, while the latter is, to the highest degree, advantageous . . . . Its benefit arises only from the observance of the general rule; and it is sufficient, if compensation is thereby made for all the ills and inconveniences which flow from the particular characters and situations."[41]

Hume sees clearly that it would be contrary to the whole spirit of the system if individual merit rather than those general and inflexible rules of law were to govern justice and government: were mankind to execute a law which . . . "assigned the largest possession to the most extensive virtue, and gave everyone the power of doing good according to his inclinations . . . so great is the uncertainty of merit, both from its natural obscurity, and from the self-conceit of every individual, that no determinate rule of conduct would ever follow from it, and the total dissolution of society must be the immediate consequence."[42] This follows necessarily from the fact that law can deal only with "the external performance [which] has no merit. [While] we must look within to find the moral quality."[43] In other words, there can be no rules for rewarding merit, or no rules of distributive justice, because there are no circumstances which may not affect merit, while rules always single out some circumstances as the only relevant ones.

I cannot pursue here further the extent to which Hume elaborates the distinction between the general and abstract rules of justice and the particular and concrete aims of individual and public action. I hope what I have already said will suffice to show how central this distinction is for his whole legal philosophy, and how questionable therefore is the prevalent view which I have just found tersely expressed in an otherwise excellent Freiburg doctoral dissertation that

---

[40] IV, p. 273.
[41] IV, p. 273.
[42] IV, p. 187.
[43] II, p. 252.

"Die moderne Geschichte des Begriffes des allgemeinen Gesetzes beginnt mit Kant."[44] What Kant had to say about this seems to derive directly from Hume. This becomes even more evident when we turn from the more theoretical to the more practical part of his discussion, especially his conception of the government of laws and not of men[45] and his general idea of freedom under the law. It contains the fullest expression of the Whig or liberal doctrines which was made familiar to Continental thinking by Kant and the later theorists of the *Rechtsstaat*. It is sometimes suggested that Kant developed his theory of the *Rechtsstaat* by applying to public affairs his moral conception of the categorical imperative.[46] It probably was the other way round, and Kant developed his theory of the categorical imperative by applying to morals the concept of the rule of law which he found ready made.

I cannot deal here with Hume's political philosophy in the same detail in which I have considered his legal philosophy. It is extremely rich, but also somewhat better known than the latter. I will completely pass over his important and characteristic discussion of how all government is guided by opinion, of the relations between opinion and interest, and of how opinion is formed. The few points I will consider are those where his political theory rests directly on his legal theory and particularly his views on the relations between law and liberty.

In Hume's last statements on these problems, the essay "On the origin of Government" which he added in 1770 to his *Essays*, he defines "the government which, in common appellation, receives the appellation of free [as] that which admits of a partition of power among several members whose united authority is no less, or is commonly greater, than that of a monarch, but who, in the usual course of administration, must act by general and equal laws, that are previously known to all members, and to all their subjects. In this sense, it must be owned that liberty is the perfection of civil society."[47] Earlier he had in the same series of essays described how in such a government it is necessary "to maintain a watchful *jealousy* over the magistrates, to remove all discretionary powers, and to secure every one's life and fortune by general and inflexible laws. No action must be deemed a crime, but what the law has plainly

---

[44] Konrad Huber, *Massnahmegesetz und Rechtsgesetz* (Berlin: Duncker & Humblot, 1963), p. 133.

[45] III, p. 161.

[46] K. Huber, loc. cit.

[47] III, p. 116.

determined to be such . . . ",[48] and that "all general laws are attended with inconveniences, when applied to particular cases; and it requires great penetration and experience, both to perceive that these inconveniences are fewer than what results from full discretionary powers in every magistrate; and also to discern what general laws are, upon the whole, attended with the fewest inconveniences. This is a matter of so great a difficulty that men have made some advances, even in the sublime art of poetry and eloquence, where a rapidity of genius and imagination assists their progress, before they have arrived at any great refinement in their municipal laws, where frequent trials and diligent observation can alone direct their improvements."[49] And in his *History of England*, speaking of the Revolution of 1688, he tells us proudly how "No government, at that time, appeared in the world, nor is perhaps to be found in the records of any history, which subsisted without the mixture of some arbitrary authority, committed to some magistrate; and it might reasonably, beforehand, appear doubtful, whether human society could ever arrive at such a state of perfection, as to support itself with no other control, than the general and rigid maxims of law and equity. But the parliament justly thought, that the King was too eminent a magistrate to be trusted with discretionary power, which he might so easily turn to the destruction of liberty. And in the event it has been found, that, though some inconveniences arise from the maxim of adhering strictly to law, yet the advantages so much overbalance them, as should render the English for ever grateful to the memory of their ancestors, who, after repeated contests, at last established that noble principle."[50]

I must not tire your patience by more quotations, though the temptation is strong to show in detail how he endeavoured to distinguish sharply between, on the one hand, "all the laws of nature which regulate property, as well as all civil laws [which] are general, and regard alone some essential circumstance of the case,

---

[48] III, p. 96; cf. also *History*, vol. 5, p. 110: "in a monarchical constitution where an eternal jealousy must be preserved against the sovereign, and no discretionary powers must ever be entrusted to him by which the property or personal liberty of any subject can be affected."

[49] III, p. 178; cf. also p. 185: "To balance a large state . . . on laws, is a work of so great difficulty that no human genius, however comprehensive, is able, by the mere dint of reason and reflection, to effect it. The judgment of many must unite in this work: Experience must guide their labour, Time must bring it to perfection: And the feeling of inconveniences must correct the mistakes which they inevitably fall into, in their first trials and experiments."

[50] *History*, vol. 5, p. 280.

without taking into consideration the characters, situations, and connections of the persons concerned, or any particular consequences which may result from the determination of these laws, in any particular case which offers"[51] and, on the other hand, those rules which determine the organisation of authority;[52] and how even in the preserved manuscript corrections of his printed works he is careful to substitute "rules of justice" for "laws of society"[53] where this seemed advisable to make his meaning clear. I want in conclusion rather to turn to another point to which I referred earlier: the general significance of his "evolutionary" account of the rise of law and other institutions.

I spoke then of Hume's doctrine as a theory of the growth of an order which provided the basis of his argument for freedom. But this theory did more. Though his primary aim was to account for the evolution of social institutions, he seems to have been clearly aware that the same argument could also be used to explain the evolution of biological organisms. In his posthumously published *Dialogues on Natural Religion* he more than hints at such an application. He points out there that "matter may be susceptible to many and great revolutions, through the endless periods of eternal duration. The incessant changes to which every part of it is subject, seem to indicate some such general transformations."[54] The apparent design of the "parts in the animals or vegetables and their curious adjustment to each other" does not seem to him to require a designer, because he "would fain know how an animal could subsist unless its parts were so adjusted? Do we not find that it immediately perishes wherever this adjustment ceases, and that its matter corrupting tries some new form?"[55] And "no form . . . can subsist unless it possess those powers and organs necessary for its subsistence: some new order or oeconomy must be tried, and so on, without intermission; till at last some order which can support and maintain itself, is fallen upon."[56] Man, he insists, cannot "pretend to an exemption from the lot of all other animals . . . [the] perpetual war . . . kindled among all living creatures"[57] affects also his evolu-

---

[51] IV, p. 274.

[52] Cf. G. H. Sabine, *A History of Political Theory*, revised edition (New York: Holt, 1950), p. 604.

[53] Cf. the Appendix by R. Klibansky to Hume, *Theory of Politics*, ed. Frederick Watkins (London: Nelson, 1951), p. 246, note to p. 246 and also note to p. 88.

[54] II, p. 419.

[55] II, p. 428.

[56] II, p. 429.

[57] II, p. 436.

tion. It was still another hundred years before Darwin finally described this 'struggle for existence'. But the transmission of ideas from Hume to Darwin is continuous and can be traced in detail.[58]

Let me conclude this discussion of Hume's teaching by a glance on its fate during the last 200 years. Let me focus particularly on the year 1766, which happens to be the year when the elder Pitt for the last time defended the old Whig principles in support of the demand of the American colonies, and the year before Parliament with the assertion of its claim to omnipotence not only brought the most glorious period of the development of political principles to an abrupt close but also produced the cause for the eventual break with the American colonies. In this year David Hume, who by then had essentially completed his work and at the age of fifty-five had become one of the most celebrated figures of his age, out of sheer goodness, brought from France to England an equally famous man who was only a few months his junior but who had lived in misery and, as he thought, was generally persecuted: Jean-Jacques Rousseau. This encounter between the serene and even placid philosopher, known to the French as 'le bon David', and the emotionally unstable, unaccountable and half-mad idealist who in his personal life disregarded all moral rules, is one of the most dramatic episodes of intellectual history. It could not but end in a violent clash and there can be no question today, for anyone who reads the full story, which of the two was the greater intellectual and moral figure.

In a way their work had been directed against the same dominant rationalism of their age. But while Hume, to repeat a phrase I have already quoted, had attempted to "whittle down the claims of reason by rational analysis", Rousseau had to oppose to it only his uncontrolled emotion. Who then observing this encounter would have believed that it would be the ideas of Rousseau and not those of Hume which would govern the political development of the next 200 years? Yet this is what happened. It was the Rousseau-esque idea of democracy, his still thoroughly rationalist conceptions of the social contract and of popular sovereignty, which were to submerge the ideals of liberty under the law and of government limited by law. It was Rousseau and not Hume who fired the enthusiasm of the successive revolutions which created modern government on the Continent and guided the decline of the ideals of the older liberal-

---

[58] The most direct channel seems to have been Erasmus Darwin, who was clearly influenced by Hume and whose influence on his grandson is unquestioned.

sm and the approach to totalitarian democracy in the whole world. How did this development come about?

I believe the explanation lies largely in an accusation which with some justice has often been levelled against Hume, the accusation that his philosophy was essentially negative. The great sceptic, with his profound conviction of the imperfection of all human reason and knowledge, did not expect much positive good from political organisation. He knew that the greatest political goods, peace, liberty, and justice, were in their essence negative, a protection against injury rather than positive gifts. No man strove more ardently for peace, liberty, and justice. But Hume clearly saw that the further ambitions which wanted to establish some other positive justice on earth were a threat to those values. As he put it in the *Enquiry*: "Fanatics may suppose, that *domination is founded on grace*, and *that saints alone inherit the earth*; but the civil magistrate very justly puts these sublime theorists on the same footing with common robbers, and teaches them by the severest discipline, that a rule, which, in speculation, may seem the most advantageous to society, may yet be found, in practice, totally pernicious and destructive."[59] It was not from the goodness of men but from institutions which "made it the interest even of bad men, to act for the public good"[60] that he expected peace, liberty, and justice. He knew that in politics "*every man must be supposed a knave*"; though, as he adds, "it appears somewhat strange, that a maxim should be true in *politics* which is false in fact."[61]

He was far from denying that government had also positive tasks. Like Adam Smith later, he knew that it is only thanks to the discretionary powers granted to government that "bridges are built; harbours opened; ramparts raised; canals formed; fleets equipped; and armies disciplined; every where, by the care of government, which, though composed of men subject to all human infirmities, becomes, by one of the finest and most subtle inventions imaginable, a composition, which is, in some measure, exempted from all these infirmities."[62] This invention is that in these tasks in which positive aims and therefore expediency rule government was given no power of coercion and was subject to the same general and inflexible rules which aim at an overall order by creating its negative conditions: peace, liberty, and justice.

[59] IV, p. 187.
[60] III, p. 99.
[61] III, p. 118.
[62] II, p. 304.

Addendum: A Discovery about Hume by Keynes and Sraffa[63]

This Abstract of Hume's *Treatise*, published anonymously in 1740 but apparently unnoticed then and now forgotten for nearly 200 years is, as Messrs Keynes and Sraffa convincingly argue in the Introduction, a work of David Hume himself. In his disappointment about the poor reception of the *Treatise* he apparently decided to give it a 'puff' by reviewing it himself. That in doing so he could not resist the temptation to suggest improvements which he only introduced in volume III of the *Treatise*, which appeared some months after the pamphlet, gives him away beyond doubt even to the modern student. When the Abstract proved to be even less successful than the original, Hume seems to have successfully hushed up the whole affair. The only reference to the pamphlet in his correspondence has been misinterpreted and given rise to the legend that Adam Smith at the age of seventeen had prepared an abstract of the *Treatise* for his teacher Hutcheson, who had sent it on to Hume who in turn attempted to have it printed. It seems now clear that there is no reason to assume that Hume and Smith met earlier than about 1750, and the Mr. Smith mentioned in Hume's letter to Hutcheson appears to have been a Dublin bookseller, whom Hume had approached to get the *Treatise* reprinted in evasion of the English law of copyright, and at the same time to publish the Abstract.

[63] [Hayek published this short note in *Economica*, August 1938, pp. 364-365. It reviews *An Abstract of a Treatise of Human Nature, 1870*, A Pamphlet hitherto unknown by David Hume. Reprinted with an Introduction by J. M. Keynes and P. Sraffa (Cambridge: Cambridge University Press, 1938; reprinted Hamden, Conn.: Archon Books, 1965). -Ed.]

EIGHT

ADAM SMITH (1723-1790): HIS MESSAGE IN TODAY'S LANGUAGE[1]

During the forty-odd years over which I have been lecturing on the history of economics, I have always found the lectures on Adam Smith particularly difficult to give.

By the time one comes to him one has shown that most of the decisive insights into the technical issues that today constitute the backbone of economic theory, the problems of value and distribution and of money, had been gained a generation before him, and that he did not even always fully appreciate the importance of this earlier work. And yet, like most other economists, I strongly felt and wanted to convey that he was much the greatest of them all, not only in influence but also in penetration and clear recognition of the central problem of the science.

In some respects his immediate successors understood this more clearly than we do. As the editor of the *Edinburgh Review*, Francis Jeffrey, wrote in 1806 of the great Scottish moral philosophers, Lord Kames,[2] Adam Smith and John Millar[3] (and he ought to have added Adam Ferguson[4]), it was their great object

> to trace back the history of society to its most simple and universal elements—to resolve almost all that has been ascribed to positive

---

[1] [Printed in the *Daily Telegraph*, London, March 9, 1976, and reprinted in F. A. Hayek, *New Studies in Philosophy, Politics, Economics and the History of Ideas* (Chicago: University of Chicago Press; London: Routledge & Kegan Paul, 1978). In connexion with this chapter the reader may wish to consult Hayek's brief review of E. A. J. Johnson, *Predecessors of Adam Smith. The Growth of British Economic Thought* (New York: Prentice-Hall, 1937), in *Economica*, N.S., vol. 4, no. 16, November 1937, pp. 465-466. -Ed.]

[2] [Henry Home, Lord Kames (1696-1782), judge and prolific writer on law, history, and moral philosophy. -Ed.]

[3] [John Millar (1735-1801), Professor of Civil Law at Glasgow University. On Millar see Michael Ignatieff, "John Millar and Individualism", in I. Hont and M. Ignatieff, eds, *Wealth and Virtue: The Shaping of Political Economy in the Scottish Enlightenment* (Cambridge: Cambridge University Press, 1983). -Ed.]

[4] [Adam Ferguson (1723-1815), Professor of Moral Philosophy at Edinburgh University. -Ed.]

institution into the spontaneous and irresistible development of certain obvious principles—and to show with how little contrivance or political wisdom the most complicated and apparently artificial schemes of policy might have been erected.[5]

In applying this general approach to the market, Smith was able to carry the basic idea much further than any of his contemporaries. The great achievement of his famous discussion about the division of labour was the recognition that men who were governed in their efforts, not by the known concrete needs and capacities of their intimate fellows, but by the abstract signals of the prices at which things were demanded and offered on the market, were thereby enabled to serve the enormous field of the 'great society' that 'no human wisdom and knowledge could ever be sufficient' to survey.

In spite of the 'narrowness of his comprehension' individual man, when allowed to use his own knowledge for his own purposes (Smith wrote "pursue his own interests in his own way upon the liberal plan of equality, liberty and justice"), was placed in a position to serve men and their needs, and use men and their skills, who were wholly outside the range of his perception. The great society indeed became possible by the individual directing his own efforts not towards visible wants but towards what the signals of the market represented as the likely gain of receipts over outlay. The practices by which the great commercial centres had become rich were shown to enable the individual to do much more good and to serve much greater needs than if he let himself be guided by the observed needs and capacities of his neighbours.

It is an error that Adam Smith preached egotism: his central thesis said nothing about how the individual should use his increased product; and his sympathies were all with the benevolent use of the increased income. He was concerned with how to make it possible for people to make their contribution to the social product as large as possible; and this he thought required that they were paid what their services were worth to those to whom they rendered them. But his teaching nevertheless offended a deeply ingrained instinct that man had inherited from the earlier face-to-face society, the horde or the tribe, in which through hundreds of thousands of years the emotions were formed which still govern him after he has entered the open society. These inherited instincts

---

[5] [Review of Millar's *The Origin of the Distinction of Ranks* (London: Longman, 1806), in the *Edinburgh Review*, vol. 9, October 1806, Art. V, p. 84. -Ed.]

demand that man should aim at doing a visible good to his known fellows (the 'neighbour' of the Bible).

These are the feelings that still, under the name of 'social justice', govern all socialist demands and easily engage the sympathies of all good men, but which are irreconcilable with the open society to which today all the inhabitants of the West owe the general level of their wealth.

The demand for 'social justice', for an assignment of the shares in the material wealth to the different people and groups according to their needs or merits, on which the whole of socialism is based, is thus an atavism, a demand which cannot be reconciled with the open society in which the individual may use his own knowledge for his own purposes.

The recognition that a man's efforts will benefit more people, and on the whole satisfy greater needs, when he lets himself be guided by the abstract signals of prices rather than by perceived needs, and that by this method we can best overcome our constitutional ignorance of most of the particular facts, and can make the fullest use of the knowledge of concrete circumstances widely dispersed among millions of individuals, is the great achievement of Adam Smith.

Smith could not, of course, direct his arguments against what we now call socialism, since this was not known in his time. But he knew well the underlying general attitude which I like to call 'constructivism' and which will approve of no human institution unless it was deliberately designed and directed by men for the aims which their inherited feelings dictate. He called them 'men of system'; and this is what he had to say about them in his first great work:[6]

> The man of system . . . seems to imagine that he can arrange the different members of a great society with as much ease as the hand arranges the different pieces upon a chess-board. He does not consider that the pieces upon the chess-board have no other principle of motion besides that which the hand impresses upon them; but that, in the great chess-board of human society, every single piece has a principle of motion of its own, altogether different from that which the legislature might choose to impress upon it. If those two principles coincide and act in the same direction,

[6] [*Theory of Moral Sentiments* [1759], part VI, section ii, chapter 2, in *The Glasgow Edition of the Works and Correspondence of Adam Smith*, vol. 1 (Oxford: Clarendon Press, 1976), part VI, section ii, chapter 2, pp. 233-234. -Ed.]

the game of human society will go on easily and harmoniously, and is very likely to be happy and successful. If they are opposite or different, the game will go on miserably, and the society must be at all times in the highest degree of disorder.

The last sentence is not a bad description of our present society. And if we persevere in the atavism and, following the inherited instincts of the tribe, insist upon imposing upon the great society principles which presuppose the knowledge of all the particular circumstances which in that society the chief could know, back to the tribal society we shall go.

Addendum: Adam Smith as Student and Professor[7]

Professor Scott's long devotion to the cause of Adam Smith has been richly rewarded. In this splendidly produced volume of the University of Glasgow publications an immense wealth of hitherto unknown information on the first forty years of Smith's life is laid before the reader. For this period, that is, until Smith's visit to France, Professor Scott gives us in the first part of the volume a connected but by no means complete narrative, since he confines himself essentially to the new information which he has obtained. This account of part of the life of Smith fills, however, only little more than a fourth of the volume. The remainder reproduces a vast mass of documents, mainly connected with Smith's professorship in Glasgow, a considerable number of letters, including nearly fifty unpublished letters by Smith himself, a reprint of the already famous "Early Draft of the Wealth of Nations", the discovery of which was announced by Professor Scott some while ago, 31 pages of facsimile reproductions of various handwritings, and a number of appendices.

But although it was Professor Scott's deliberate choice to give us a full and critical presentation of all the new material he has found, rather than a revised account of the whole life of Adam Smith, it is probable that the majority of readers will regret this decision. As it is now before us, Professor Scott's presentation presupposes an intimate acquaintance with the life of Adam Smith as described by Rae.[8] And it can hardly be said that he gives his readers much help in assimilating the fruits of his painstaking research. Indeed, if he had deliberately wanted to make his readers experience all the

---

[7] [Hayek published this review of William Robert Scott, *Adam Smith as Student and Professor* (with unpublished documents, including parts of the "Edinburgh Lectures", a draft of the *Wealth of Nations*, extracts from the Muniments of the University of Glasgow and correspondence), Glasgow University Publications, vol. 46 (Glasgow: Jackson, 1937), in *Economica*, vol. 5, 1938, pp. 359-361. -Ed.]

[8] [John Rae, *Life of Adam Smith* (London: Macmillan, 1895; reprinted New York: Augustus M. Kelley, 1965). -Ed.]

joys of discovery of important facts after long search among less important details, he could hardly have succeeded better. One has to learn one's way about this volume before one can really appreciate its rich contents. The exciting announcement in the course of the introductory narrative of the discovery of a letter in which Smith gives an account of his studies after his return from France till he was settled as a Commissioner of Customs (p. 57) sends one hunting among the letters till one finds one (No. XLVII, p. 281) which approximately corresponds to that description, and is presumably the one referred to. And the even more interesting reference on the same page to "fifteen folio pages, most of which represent very early work" and which in part apparently reproduce some of the economic sections of the Edinburgh lectures, start one on another search till one discovers that only part of them has been reproduced, and that in a much reduced facsimile which makes exceedingly difficult reading. A few more cross-references would have been very helpful.

About the importance of the "Early Draft of the Wealth of Nations" and also of the newly discovered part of the Edinburgh lectures there can be no doubt. Professor Scott is now inclined to date the former to the summer of 1763, that is, after the session in which the recorded Glasgow lectures were given, and before Smith departed for France, while the latter belongs to 1755. Together with the notes of the Glasgow lectures they give us a surprisingly complete picture of the development of Adam Smith's thought on economics, and correct some of the traditional views, particularly as regards the supposed influence of the physiocrats.

There are only one or two points of detail where one might perhaps question Professor Scott's statements. The conversion of Mirabeau[9] to the physiocratic doctrine occurred in 1757 and not in 1758-59 as stated in the footnote on p. 125. The statement on p. 119 that the French author to whom Ferguson admitted indebtedness, and where "Adam Smith had been before him", was "no doubt Montesquieu", sounds somewhat too apodictic after Mrs. H. V. Roberts's plausible suggestion that it may have been Boisguilbert.[10] And why does Professor Scott keep from us the titles of the books, even if they are few, which the manuscript catalogue of Smith's library of the year 1781 adds to Dr. Bonar's catalogue, now he has succeeded in obtaining a photographic copy from Tokyo?[11] Such a list would surely have been more important than the facsimile reproduction of the title and one other page.

---

[9] [Victor Riquetti, Marquis de Mirabeau (1715-1789). On Mirabeau see this volume, chapter 13. -Ed.]

[10] H. V. Roberts, *Boisguilbert, Economist of the Reign of Louis XIV* (New York: Columbia University Press, 1935), p. 327.

[11] [James Bonar, ed., *A Catalogue of the Library of Adam Smith* (London: Macmillan, 1894; reprinted New York: Augustus M. Kelley, 1966). The Tokyo catalogue was published by Tadao Yanaihara as *A full and detailed Catalogue of Books which belonged to Adam Smith* (Tokyo: Iwanami Shoten, 1951). See also Hiroshi Mizuta, *Adam Smith's Library: A Supplement to Bonar's Catalogue with a Checklist of the whole Library* (Cambridge: Cambridge University Press, 1967). -Ed.]

Great as the amount of information in this volume is, it does not include all the material Professor Scott has unearthed. Occasional references to articles published by him in recent years (particularly the one on "Adam Smith at Downing Street"[12]) show that there is a good deal more, for which one has to go to various periodicals. Indeed one greatly misses a systematic bibliography, not only of Professor Scott's own writings on the subject, but also of the numerous other writings which, as he himself says, have each contributed its mite of detail to the general picture of Adam Smith. It seems that at least one of the more important of these contributions, Professor J. Jastrow's article on the occasion of the first announcement of Professor Scott's discovery of the "Early Draft of the Wealth of Nations",[13] in which Professor Jastrow makes some interesting suggestions on the significance of this find, has actually escaped Professor Scott's notice.

It is in the nature of a publication of historical documents that their significance cannot be adequately explained except by rewriting the history of the subject with which they deal. This is evidently not possible within the compass of a short review. May we hope that Professor Scott will not consider us ungrateful if we insist on regarding this volume as an interim report, and continue to wait for the revised survey of the whole life of Adam Smith which he better than anybody else could give us, and which, now that he has satisfied his exacting standards for the presentation of historical sources, his conscience may allow him to do in a lighter manner.

---

[12] In *Economic History Review*, vol. 6, no. 1, October 1935, pp. 79-89.
[13] *Zeitschrift für Nationalökonomie*, vol. 8, no. 3, June 1937, pp. 338-380.

PART III

ENGLISH MONETARY POLICY AND THE BULLION DEBATE

GENESIS OF THE GOLD STANDARD IN RESPONSE TO ENGLISH COINAGE POLICY IN THE 17th AND 18th CENTURIES[1]

I

England, which had been so greatly afflicted by wars and revolution during most of the seventeenth century, finally attained political stabilisation at the end of that century under the reign of William

---

[1] [This and the following three chapters have never previously been published. The German text was established from Hayek's original manuscript by Alfred Bosch and Reinhold Veit, of the Walter Eucken Institute in Freiburg im Breisgau. It was then translated for this volume by Dr. Grete Heinz. In conversations about his life and work Hayek has emphasised the importance of these chapters in shaping his intellectual development and career. After the opening of the Österreichische Konjunkturforschungsinstitut (Austrian Institute for Business-Cycle Research) in 1927, Hayek, who had been appointed its first director, found himself for several years unable to engage in theoretical research. He ran the institute single-handedly, with the assistance of two secretaries, and, beginning in 1927, wrote virtually all of the first four annual volumes of the huge *Monatsberichte des Österreichischen Institutes für Konjunkturforschung* published by the Institute. Only in 1929, when some American funds enabled Hayek to extend the Institute and to hire Oskar Morgenstern as a collaborator, was he able to return to theoretical work. These four chapters are the first result. Hayek was recruited to prepare a large volume on money and monetary theory for the great German *Grundriß der Sozialökonomik* which had been started by Max Weber. Of this Hayek completed "in something like final form" these four chapters on money and monetary theory from about 1650 to 1850. Before being able to complete the project, however, he was interrupted by his move from Vienna to London, and then "before I could resume the work the publisher asked me, in view of Hitler's advent to power, to cancel the contract. But the book on which I got my 'licence to teach' (*Privatdozentur*), the test lecture on 'The Paradox of Savings' which I gave in the same connexion and which led to my invitation to London, and the lectures on *Prices and Production* which I delivered at the London School of Economics in January 1931 were all offshoots of this uncompleted task." Later, Hayek gave his notes for the remainder of the projected book to his doctoral student at the LSE, Vera C. Smith (later Lutz), and encouraged her to take up the subject. She used them in her remarkable thesis, published as *The Rationale of Central Banking* (London: P. S. King, 1936; reprinted Indianapolis, Ind.: Liberty*Press*, 1990). The last three chapters of her book have been reprinted in Arthur A. Shenfield, *The British Monetary Experience 1797-1821* (Greenwich, Conn.: Committee for Monetary Research and Education, 1981). See the account of Vera Smith Lutz's book in Pedro Schwarz, "Central Bank Monopoly in the History of Economic Thought: A Century of Myopia in England", in Pascal Salin, ed., *Currency Competition and Monetary Union* (The Hague: Martinus Nijhoff, 1984), pp. 95-126. -Ed.]

of Orange. This political stability and the rebirth of cultural and economic life it generated led to such decisive advances in the realm of monetary institutions and in the understanding of monetary matters that the genesis of modern monetary institutions can truly be said to date from this period.

The mid-nineties of that century saw the founding of the Bank of England and the introduction of a far-sighted coinage reform, which was to start England on its course as the first country to adopt the modern gold standard.[2] But that was not all: these developments were accompanied by an extensive public discussion of currency questions, which disseminated understanding about monetary problems much more widely than had been the case until then anywhere in the world. This new insight gave impetus to the gradual development of monetary theory and could be said to represent its point of departure.[3]

These reforms and discussions were set in motion by the pitiful state of the English coinage system at the end of the seventeenth century. The constant deterioration of circulating money had finally led to an important coinage reform in the year 1663, which had not only realigned once more the relative weight of gold and silver coins but had substituted for the first time modern mintage methods for the primitive techniques in use until then. Until then coins had been produced by snipping them off from the cast metal bars with a short of shear, rounding them off with a hammer and pliers. A stamp was then impressed on them with a hammer or, very rarely, with a stamp press that had been introduced from France. Now a completely new procedure came into use. Coins were milled from rolled plates, stamped exclusively with a stamp press; they were then edged, that is, supplied with a lettering along the edge (by means of a procedure kept secret to avoid counterfeiting). The purpose of this was to protect the coins against clipping or filing, a common occurrence with the old coins, which had been quite irregularly shaped and hence easy to adulterate in this way. The new coins were also very uniform in fineness and weight, whereas under the old procedure substantial differences had been allowed to arise, as a result of which the coins with the largest content of

---

[2] [I.e., the 'classical gold standard', which prevailed in England from 1821 to 1914 and internationally from about 1880 to 1914. -Ed.]

[3] [Hayek did not find the opportunity to revise this essay and the following three chapters for publication. We can be confident that had he prepared them for an English readership he would have made numerous changes and revisions to take account of the ready availability of more detailed sources. -Ed.]

precious metal were melted down or exported, while the lighter ones remained in the country.

In view of the fact that gold coins, the market value of which compared with silver was disproportionately higher than its value as a currency, had disappeared from circulation, the gold content of the newly minted coins was reduced. Henceforth 44½ gold coins with a face value of 20 shillings were minted from a troy pound of gold, whereas previously only 41 coins had been stamped from that amount of gold. Since the gold originated from the African Guinea Coast, the newly minted coins were designated as guineas, a currency unit that has maintained itself in England down to the present day.[4] Such changes in the official valuation of the two precious metals—in this case setting a 14.5 to 1 ratio between gold and silver of the same weight, compared with the previous 13.3 to 1 ratio, as reflected by the reduced gold content of the new gold coin—had been a common occurrence in the past whenever the value of the two metals had previously undergone a revision on the free market. Gresham's law,[5] so called, thus came into play for coins made of the relatively overvalued metal.

Three years after this coinage reform, in 1666, there followed an additional important measure, which was intended to secure a harmonisation between the face value of coins and their content of precious metals. Until that time anyone was entitled to have coins minted from the corresponding quantity of gold or silver, but a fee was levied to cover the cost of mintage. The new measure provided that the minting of coins be done free of charge, with costs covered from state revenues specially set aside for this purpose. For many years England was the only country in which the minting of coins was gratuitous, an arrangement that remains in force even at the present time,[6] in contrast with most other European states. This gratuitous minting assured a perfect concordance between the face value of the coins and their value as precious metals, but it had the natural, though probably unanticipated, consequence that even a very slight rise in the value of the coin above the value of the coin's metal content was an incentive to mint new coins and, conversely,

---

[4] [It was abandoned in 1971, when Britain converted from pounds, shillings, and pence to a new decimal pounds and pence system. -Ed.]

[5] [Gresham's law, named for Sir Thomas Gresham (c. 1517-1579), a London merchant, is the dictum that 'bad money drives out the good'; that is, coins undervalued at the official rate of exchange will tend to withdraw from circulation and be replaced by coins officially overvalued. -Ed.]

[6] [I.e., 1929. -Ed.]

an equally slight rise in the value of either of the two metals gave impetus to the melting down or export of coins made from this metal—notwithstanding prohibitions of all kinds and barbaric punishments with which violators were threatened. This effect first manifested itself very quickly for the newly minted silver coins, which reached circulation alongside old eroded and clipped coins. These new silver coins almost instantly disappeared from circulation, and the same thing happened on an even larger scale with gold coins, which were almost entirely new and full-weight and therefore particularly well suited for export. As a tentative preventive measure, when the new guinea was minted at an anticipated equivalent of 20 shillings, the customary royal proclamation making this ratio official—and thereby making it an offense to accept it at a different ratio—was omitted. As a result, whenever the value of the gold content rose slightly and led to a higher valuation of the guinea on the open market, the government could empower its pay-offices to accept guineas at this higher rate and thus prevent an outflow of gold. Since silver coins in fact, if not by official verdict, served as the main form of currency, the practical consequence was that the exchange rate of the guinea was raised in terms of shillings, so that it matched the market level of 21 shillings. This parried effectively the threat of a gold drain, since, at this exchange rate, gold and silver corresponded very closely to the respective value of the two metals on the world market. A peculiar situation resulted, however, from this arrangement, reinforced by the poor condition of the silver coins that were currently in circulation. This situation was puzzling and presented the money theorists of that time with an insoluble mystery. Once the government had established the rate at which its pay-offices exchanged guineas, it had thereby created a minimum below which the guinea could not fall, since there was always an office where it would be accepted at this rate. At the same time, in the wake of the change in the valuation of the gold and silver coins currently in circulation, whereby the value of gold had risen in relation to silver, the heaviest of the silver coins remaining in circulation now became relatively overvalued and could therefore most advantageously be used for payments abroad. This export of silver coins could continue only so long as the last silver coin whose metal content exceeded its face value had not yet been exported or clipped. A normal new minting of silver coins at the full legal weight—which would have meant a loss—was out of the question, and therefore the remaining silver coins in England were almost without exception reduced to a metal content falling short of their value as coins. A shortage of silver coins also developed. These two factors combined to lead to two unhappy consequences: the deteriorated silver coins began to be profitably imitated by counterfeiters and, on the other hand, substitute instruments of payment were introduced, which depressed the value of the remaining silver coins of low denomination and thereby again led to the outflow of gold coins from the country. If the exchange rate of the guinea was then raised another notch, the whole vicious circle was repeated, with the final result that even when the guinea had been raised to 22 shillings by 1694, the debasement of silver coins could not be halted. Even at this rate of exchange, it was generally worth less than its face value and the shortage of silver money remained as acute as ever.

II

The only way to understand how the coinage system developed during these years is to examine the concurrent origins of England's banking institutions.[7] One of the consequences of the sad state of the coinage system, which had already prevailed for several centuries, was the need for special knowledge not only to execute monetary transactions without suffering serious losses, but even more to carry on the vital profession of money changer, let alone to make profits from the fluctuations in value of the various coins. It is easy to see why dealers in precious metals, the goldsmiths, occupied a central position in money deals and why they were advantageously situated to invest temporarily idle sums of money in a profitable way or at least to safeguard them in specially equipped places. It is equally natural that these men were deemed eminently suited for making payments and transfers abroad.

At the time of the Stuart Restoration, in 1660, goldsmiths were essentially performing the main functions of modern bankers and steadily increased in importance until the end of the century. They were at the time accepting interest-bearing deposits and extending loans to the government and to private individuals. They even allowed deposits to serve as a basis for money orders along the same lines as modern cheques and provided 'cash notes' or 'bills'

---

[7] [On the history of banking in England see also Andreas M. Andréadès, *History of the Bank of England* (London: P. S. King, 1909; reprinted London: Frank Cass, 1966); R. D. Richards, *The Early History of Banking in England* (London: P. S. King, 1929; reprinted New York: Augustus M. Kelley, 1965); and Sir John Clapham, *The Bank of England*, 2 vols (Cambridge: Cambridge University Press, 1944). -Ed.]

payable on presentation, which were issued even in relatively small amounts and circulated almost like cash. Locke reports that one such goldsmith issued no less than 1,000,000 pounds in these notes.

Inasmuch as those drafts were issued in terms of the official currency, that is, pounds, shillings, and pence, and only silver coins maintained this face value or were suitable for smaller payments, while the face value of gold coins fluctuated, such drafts were obviously exchangeable only against silver and therefore dependent on silver for their value. Conversely, however, the mounting utilisation of such substitute paper money, which reduced the need for silver money and hence its value, contributed to the outflow of the relatively least debased remaining silver coins and to the rise of the guinea's exchange rate. As long as the rise in the guinea's exchange rate and the corresponding decline of the value of silver money proceeded slowly, as was the case until 1694, it remained uncertain whether to attribute the displacement of good silver coins and the devaluation of the remaining silver coins to the production of debased silver money by counterfeiters or to the introduction of such substitute notes for silver money. The connexion becomes clear only when England was suddenly flooded by a large number of new paper notes in the wake of the founding in 1694 of the Bank of England. When bank notes in the most literal sense of the word began circulating, the guinea soon rose sharply.

Decades prior to 1694, various projects for the founding of a bank of this kind had already been under consideration; it owed its existence most directly to the Bank of Amsterdam, which served as its prototype. Since the ascension to the throne of William of Orange, political ties between England and Holland had become close. In 1694 William of Orange found himself in such financial difficulties that he accepted one of these projects, that of the Scot William Patterson. The project stipulated that a group of signers for a new 1,200,000 pound government loan found a company, to which the right would be granted to issue notes up to this amount, on the strength of the capital lent to the government. The government's appropriation bill for 1694, which included various new sources of revenue, had a provision empowering the government to let the signers of the loan incorporate as "The Governor and the Company of the Bank of England", which was to have the right for twelve years and on a yearly renewal basis thereafter to issue notes and take in deposits to the amount of their total capital. The company at first received no monopoly for the issuing of notes, nor were the notes declared to be official instruments of payment. The notes differed from modern bank notes, moreover, in that they bore interest (at the rate of 2 pence per 100 pounds per day, or 3 per cent per annum). In this respect, as well as in its making no pretence of accepting deposits merely for safekeeping and freely admitting that it intended to use them for extending loans to others, it differed from established banks in Venice, Genoa, and other Italian cities, as well as in Barcelona, and from banks founded in the middle of the seventeenth century in Amsterdam, Hamburg, Nuremberg, and Stockholm. That the bank in other respects modelled itself after these institutions, however, is clear from the fact that the bank's proponents claimed emphatically that the bank would contribute to lowering the rate of interest in England and that it would fall to 3 per cent soon after its founding, as was true in all other states that already had a bank. In the course of the next thirty years this argument for the founding of banks was reiterated again and again, and seemed to be confirmed shortly after the Bank of England was established. Only much later was the discovery made that such an artificial lowering of the interest rate, accomplished by the proliferation of money in circulation, was bound to be short lived and to lead to bad consequences as well.

III

At first, to be sure, only the favourable consequences of the bank's founding manifested themselves. Soon after its counters had opened in July 1694, its circulating bank notes reached the maximum sum of 1,200,000 pounds. In view of the fact that the entire circulation of gold and silver coins at this time was estimated at about 11 million pounds, this constituted a very considerable increase in the supply of money, which was bound to precipitate a further devaluation of money. As had been true in comparable cases, here too the devaluation affected only silver coins, whereas the exchange rate of the guinea with respect to silver and paper money soon resumed its upward trend. The relatively least debased silver coins in circulation were either exported, melted down, or clipped even more, thereby accelerating markedly the debasing of the circulating silver money. The guinea, whose value had been maintained at about 22 shillings until the end of 1694, had already climbed to 30 shillings by June of the following year. This rise in the value of the guinea and the concomitant rise in the general price level was attributed at the time and for many years thereafter to the accelerated debasement of the coins, though the latter was in fact merely a consequence of the devaluation of money that had been induced by the bank note issue of the Bank of England and the creation of similar payment instruments based on credit on the part of a number of private banks that had been founded somewhat prior to or about the same time as the Bank of England. Efforts were made to mitigate the shortage of small coins caused by the loss of silver coins through the issue of bank notes of smaller denomination (bank notes had previously been issued for amounts upwards of 20 pounds), but this only aggravated matters. In addition to the rise in the guinea's value and the increase in the price of commodities, which were the most conspicuous phenomena (and—as people believed—the consequence of the debasement of silver money), a huge fever of speculation swept the country, causing the shares of stock of the few well-established companies to rise sharply in value between July 1694 and June 1695. At the same time, many new companies, among them many banks, were founded in response to this speculation, triggering fantastic swindles in the process.

An even more urgent concern than the rise in commodity prices was the rise in foreign exchange rates. As the debasement of silver coins, which was considered as the cause of the rise in prices, was becoming worse every day, the English Parliament began at this time to look seriously into the question of making a fresh start with the metal currency in circulation, as had been proposed for a number of years previously. The condition of the metal currency was indeed alarming. The silver coins had been reduced on average to about half their officially established metal content. The price of silver bullion for its part had risen only 20 per cent above the official value of the coin. This meant that the cost of the amount of silver needed to mint a pound in silver coins would be no more than about 24 shillings, although the silver content of these 24 shillings was worth only about 12 shillings. The bulk of the silver coins in circulation was thus valued even higher than their silver content implied. The guinea, on the other hand, had attained, as mentioned earlier, an exchange rate of 30 shillings by June 1695. After several futile efforts by the government to set it at a lower rate, 30 shillings was finally set as a maximum rate. The population was bewildered by these confused circumstances. There were constant arguments in business transactions as to which coins were to be used for payments and complaints were widespread about the shortage of small change for very small transactions where bank notes were not suitable. The ubiquitousness of the alarm about the state of the coinage system can be seen, for example, in the sermons of various clerics, who gave this matter their fullest attention. The royal Chaplain, later Bishop W. Fleetwood, to whom we shall come back subsequently,[8] delivered a sermon at the end of 1694 which also appeared in print. The sermon offers such a telling description of current conditions and such remarkable theoretical insights that it could easily pass today as a lecture in economics.[9]

IV

Just as the deterioration of the coinage system reached its climax only in 1694, but was anticipated by many years of dissatisfaction, the public debate, which finally culminated in coinage reform, was also anticipated by many years of scholarly controversy set down in numerous tracts.[10] The first and probably most significant contemporary contribution to monetary theory is contained in the writings of Sir William Petty (1623-1687), best known as the founder of political arithmetic.[11] His most important contribution is his brief 1682 publication, *Quantulumcunque concerning Money* ("A little something about money").[12] In it he summarised views about the theory of money that he had already expressed in other writings over the previous ten or twenty years. He addressed the increasingly urgent coinage reform in a set of thirty-two questions and answers. There was no doubt in Petty's mind that fluctuations in the relative value of gold and silver were inevitable, since these were manifestations of changes in their cost of production. Both metals could therefore not serve simultaneously as a general standard of value. In keeping with prevailing opinions, he viewed silver as the intrinsic form of money,

---

[8] [See below, section VII. -Ed.]

[9] [William Fleetwood, *A Sermon against Clipping, Preach'd before the Right Honourable the Lord Mayor and Court of Alderman, at Guild-Hall Chappel, on Decemb. 16, 1694* (London: Printed by Tho. Hodgkin, 1694). Andréadès observes that people had become so tolerant of what was actually the crime of coin-clipping that "the clergy thought it incumbent upon them to protest and to recall the faithful to a truer view of the matter," op. cit., pp. 95-96. -Ed.]

[10] [For more on the theory of money during the seventeenth and eighteenth centuries, see Arthur E. Monroe, *Monetary Theory Before Adam Smith* (Cambridge, Mass.: Harvard University Press, 1923; reprinted Gloucester, Mass.: Peter Smith, 1965), and Douglas Vickers, *Studies in the Theory of Money 1690-1776* (Philadelphia: Chilton, 1959; reprinted New York: Augustus M. Kelley, 1968). -Ed.]

[11] [See Alessandro Roncaglia, *Petty: The Origins of Political Economy* (New York: Sharpe, 1985). -Ed.]

[12] [*Sir William Petty's Quantulumcunque concerning Money, 1682* (London: n. p., 1695), in *The Economic Writings of Sir William Petty*, ed. Charles H. Hull (Cambridge: Cambridge University Press, 1899; reprinted New York: Augustus M. Kelley, 1964), vol. 1, pp. 437-448. -Ed.]

while gold was envisaged as a commodity closely related to money. He considered it useless to combat fluctuations in the relative value of the two metals by regulations, but such a change was in his opinion the only instance in which it would be appropriate to reduce the weight of the coin that was currently undervalued, thereby preventing its leaving the country. Setting a wrong value relation between coins made of the two metals was bound to lead to an overabundance of one kind of coin and a disappearance of the other kind of coin.[13]

Although Petty mentioned only production costs of precious metals as determinants of the value of money, his analysis of individual problems reveals a deeper insight on his part. A case in point is his approach to the vexing problem of small coins, which, ever since the Middle Ages, had been difficult to mint at full value because of their relatively high mintage costs. He supported the canonists' view that a maximum amount be set for which small coins could be used. In addition, he urged that the quantity of small coins be proportional to the number of families in the population.[14] Another suggestion concerned the possibility of securing the value of money paid out by private individuals by guaranteeing its convertibility to full-valued coins. He was one of the first to point out that inferior copper money could retain a higher value as long as its deficit in weight was compensated for by the costs incurred in high-quality minting and the weight deficit was not excessive. On this score he already offers all the insights which, about a century later, at the end of the period we are examining, found their practical application in the introduction of small change. His arguments about the significance of international movements of precious metals and his related points about the money requirements of a given population are perhaps even more impressive. He realised that precious metals would be exported only if this were the cheapest way of acquiring foreign commodities, and therefore the merchant's profit would also be a gain for the nation as a whole.[15] He considered regulations forbidding the export of money and precious metals as pointless as well as futile;[16] there could be no danger that all money would be exported, and a reduction in the stock of money certainly need not be harmful.[17]

---

[13] [*Ibid.*, Questions 1-12. -Ed.]
[14] [*Ibid.*, Questions 19 and 31. -Ed.]
[15] [*Ibid.*, Question 7. -Ed.]
[16] [*Ibid.*, Question 22. -Ed.]
[17] [*Ibid.*, Question 23. -Ed.]

Just as individuals might consider it a saving to keep low cash reserves, a whole population, which was after all only a multiplicity of individuals, might wish to do likewise. A country's true need for money could be gauged by calculating the amounts of different kinds of payments such as house rentals, wages, etc. as such and such a fraction of the yearly sum that had to be paid repeatedly.[18] (This idea is particularly important because this is the first allusion to the concept of a given velocity in the circulation of money.) If a country has a surplus of precious metals in terms of this need for money, the precious metals can be used for other purposes or exported, while a shortage of money can be alleviated by setting up a bank. The banker's business, consisting in the trading of foreign currencies and interest-bearing loans, rested on public confidence, what is generally understood as credit. Fixed interest rates would be as useless as regulations prohibiting the export of money or officially established exchange rates, particularly since interest always included a premium for risk taking, which in the very nature of things would be different in each case. As to the question of coinage reform, which was already at that time the subject of heated debate, Petty argued in its favour in order to retain money as a trustworthy standard of value. His view, later expressed independently by Locke, that silver coins should be restored to their original weight, was based on the belief that prices would rise if a lower weight were set, thus maintaining the incentive to export silver but damaging English reputation and credit in the process.

While this point has no immediate bearing on the problems we have been discussing, it should be mentioned here that Petty was probably the first to refer to a seven-year cycle of alternating scarcity and abundance. He proposed that, for setting the normal rent on land, an average should be computed. Petty thus deserves to be considered a forerunner of later business cycle theories.

V

Petty's views were indeed far ahead of his time and earn him the right to be considered the first great monetary theorist. Nevertheless, there was one point on which he was outdistanced by a contemporary, the Italian publicist, Geminiano Montanari, professor of mathematics and astronomy at the University of Bologna. In his

---

[18] [*Ibid.*, Question 25. -Ed.]

book *Della Moneta* (1683)[19] he developed the quantity theory of money, which the Italian Bernardo Davanzati[20] had adumbrated a hundred years earlier. While Petty, notwithstanding the close attention he paid to the quantitative requirements for money, believed that the value of money was simply a function of the production costs of precious metals, Montanari realised that the value of money was determined by the relationship between the amount of money in circulation and available commodities. He recognised that the value of money depended on the value of the precious metal itself only to the extent that the quantity of money was reduced by the melting down of coins when the metal content of the coins exceeded the nominal value of the currency and, conversely, the quantity of money was increased by the minting of new coins when the nominal value of the coin exceeded its value as a precious metal. This rather advanced quantity theory of money, which was adopted on the Continent by the Austrians Becher[21] and Hörnigk[22], found its first English proponent in the great philosopher John Locke (1632-1704).[23] While Locke's contributions to the theory of money were not nearly so original as Petty's, Locke's writings had a far greater immediate and decisive influence on monetary theory in the eighteenth century. Locke had only a casual interest in these questions and expressed his views on current monetary policy in part at the insistence of his powerful patron, yet his views carried the day in the controversy about coinage reform. His first contribution, "Consequences of the Lowering of Interest and Raising the Value of Money"[24] (1692), was an attack on measures lowering the maximum legally allowed interest rate as well as on the widely advocated reduction of the metal content of silver coins or, as it was called, the 'raising of its nominal value'. Although this publication contains Locke's most significant views on monetary theory, his

[19] [Geminiano Montanari, *Della Moneta*, reprinted in *Scrittori Classici Italiani di Economia Politica*, vol. 3 (Milan: G. G. Destefanis, 1804). Montanari's book was originally published in 1683 under the title *La Zecca in Consulta Di Stato*. -Ed.]

[20] [Bernardo Davanzati (1529-1606), merchant, economist, and historian; known as a translator of Tacitus. -Ed.]

[21] [Johann Joachim Becher (1635-1682), prominent Continental mercantilist. -Ed.]

[22] [Philipp Wilhelm von Hörnigk (1640-1714), Becher's son-in-law and author of *Österreich über alles* (Nuremberg: Erblanc Wolfahrt, 1684). -Ed.]

[23] [On Montanari's and Locke's versions of the quantity theory see Hugo Hegeland, *The Quantity Theory of Money* (Gothenburg: Elanders Boktryckeri Aktiebolag, 1951). -Ed.]

[24] [John Locke, *Some Considerations of the Consequences of the Lowering of Interest, and Raising the Value of Money* [1692], in *The Works of John Locke*, twelfth edition, vol. 4 (London: C. and J. Rivington et al., 1824). -Ed.]

contributions to this discussion in subsequent years were even more important in our opinion. There was first of all his reply[25] to an anonymous and long-forgotten pamphlet criticising the views expressed in Locke's previous publication. But his most crucial contribution is his famous *Further Considerations Concerning Raising the Value of Money*,[26] which appeared in 1695 as a reply to the report of the Secretary of the Treasury, William Lowndes, to which we shall return shortly. But first a few words about Locke's overall position about monetary theory.

A large part of Locke's doctrines consists of an elaboration of Petty's work with few original features. There is little new in his account of the variability in the value relation between the two precious metals and the resulting impossibility of establishing a fixed relationship between the values of the coins made from the two metals, as well as his case for using silver rather than gold as the basis for the currency. What is new in Locke is the idea that *the value of money should be as stable as possible in terms of commodities*, even though complete rigidity was unattainable, and that fluctuations could best be estimated from fluctuations in the price of wheat, where the relation between supply and demand was relatively steady.

As previously mentioned, Locke was the first to introduce to England the concept that the value of money was affected by fluctuations in the quantity of money. Silver, for instance, whose quantity had increased tenfold since the discovery of the West Indies, consequently was worth nine-tenths less now than prior to that time. Locke summarises this quantity theory of money by stating that the value of money in general is determined by the relation of the quantity of money worldwide to the global amount of commerce, and in each country the value of money is determined by the relation between the available money and the country's commerce. When Locke talks about the *quantity of money*, he always has in mind the quantity of *precious metals*, and he never tires of emphasising that changes in the nominal value of money, that is, changes in the metal content of a specific coin, are incapable of altering the value of its metal content. Locke adopted Petty's account of the circumstances determining monetary requirements,

---

[25] *Short Observations on a Printed Paper, Intituled, "For Encouraging the Coining of Silver Money in England", etc.* (London: Printed for A. & J. Churchill, 1695).

[26] [John Locke, *Further Considerations Concerning Raising the Value of Money* (London: Printed for A. & J. Churchill, 1695); reprinted in *The Works of John Locke*, op. cit. -Ed.]

elaborating the doctrine about money's 'quickness of circulation', a term that he was the first to use, and stressing the importance of customary methods of payment. It is therefore puzzling that Locke fails to make any attempt to use this concept in explaining either the value of money and its fluctuations or the fluctuations of exchange rates. Here he even disregards Petty's tentative explanations and falls back on prevailing mercantilist views about the status of the balance of trade. On the other hand, Locke's treatment of the question widely debated at that time regarding the consequences of allowing the circulation of coins with different weight but having the same face value represents decisive progress. He is probably the first to give a satisfactory explanation of Gresham's law, refusing to attribute the driving out of good money to mysterious and criminal manipulations of foreigners and recognising it instead as the necessary consequence of the action of all merchants pursuing the dictates of their self-interest.

His theory was to gain practical significance in 1695, when the newly appointed Secretary of the Treasury, William Lowndes, presented an officially mandated report[27] about the status of the coinage system. After giving a noteworthy account of its evolution, Lowndes offered a proposal for coinage reform, the gist of which was *that all silver money should be reminted as quickly as possible and the new coins reduced by one-fifth* below the currently mandated weight. This reasonable proposal, which was meant to recognise the existing debasement of money and to adapt the official minted weight of coins to the actual value of the old coins that were currently in circulation (and whose nominal value exceeded the value of their metal content), was motivated by the following argument: the *price* of the silver contained in the currently circulating coins had *gone up*, so that the amount of silver needed to stamp out coins with a face value of 5 shillings actually cost 6 shillings and 5 pence. For that reason it would be futile at this point to stamp new coins at the old weight, since they would immediately be melted down. Under these circumstances, he rightly concluded, the best solution was to follow the age-old custom and reduce the weight of the coins.

Lowndes's proposals created a great stir and were favourably received by many people, but not by the government, whose leading statesmen requested a reply from Locke.

---

[27] *A Report Containing an Essay for the Amendment of the Silver Coins* (London: Printed by C. Bill, 1695).

Lowndes himself had also solicited Locke's opinion by presenting him with the first copy. Within a month, Locke put together his above-mentioned *Further Considerations*, which immediately appeared in print, at the request of the government, at the end of December 1695. His main contention was that an ounce of silver, minted or unminted, must perforce always be equal in value and hence Lowndes's point of departure, namely, that the price of silver expressed in terms of silver coins had gone up, was an absurdity. This argument seemed irrefutable to Locke's contemporaries, and for many years it was believed that Lowndes had been thoroughly defeated. Locke had argued that the value of silver coins was always and exclusively determined by its silver content and a rise in the price of silver could only be explained by the fact that the silver content of the shillings in circulation had been reduced. This truism, which made such a big impression on his contemporaries, to wit, that an ounce of silver must always be worth the same as another ounce of silver, actually disregarded certain facts. Locke neglected to take into account that minting and melting down of silver coins was in effect not unrestricted as the truism presupposed, inasmuch as the actual value of the silver coins precluded their being minted at the legal weight, while melting down the coins was out of the question because their metal content was generally so low that the metal value of the coins was even lower than their face value. He overlooked the fact that the amount of silver on hand, which he had recognised as the determining factor in the value of silver, was simultaneously an independent determinant of the value of the coin, as long as coins and metal were not freely convertible. Locke applied his quantity theory exclusively to the value of silver and not to the value of the coins produced from this metal, which, as we know, was far lower than the value of their legally established silver content, though it was also far higher than that of the actual silver content.[28] This approach, in conjunction with his views about the impact of the balance of trade on the export of precious metals, led Locke to dispute Lowndes's undoubtedly accurate assertion that the minting of silver coins would become lucrative again once the

---

[28] [The silver content of individual shilling coins varied considerably, and the weight of coins varied throughout England. There is the tale quoted in Andréadès, of "the Lancashire Quaker, who during a journey to London, found to his amazement that the value of his money changed and increased as he drew nearer to the Capital. When he got there his wealth was half as great again as when he started" (op. cit., pp. 94-95). This phenomenon gives rise to the still unresolved question of what does constitute a monetary standard. -Ed.]

141

legal mint weight was lowered sufficiently to match the actual value of the circulating silver coins and that these newly minted coins would then remain in circulation for some time. Locke also overlooked the fact that his proposal to restore the old silver content of coins was tantamount to increasing the value of money, while he was under the impression that all he was doing was to attack a proposal to lower the value of money. The conflict between him and Lowndes was basically the same as the one that was fought out after periods of money debasement between the advocates of stabilisation, based on the lowered value to which money had in fact sunk, that is, so-called 'devaluation', and the proponents of restoration of the old value of money or 'deflation'. There was some justification to Locke's viewpoint, in that the marked devaluation of money was of relatively recent vintage and many money claims dated from a time when money had had a higher value, so that their owners would have suffered severely from stabilisation. On the other hand, the implementation of his proposal, which rested on his erroneous conception of the factors determining the value of money, would have done the greatest harm to all property owners.[29] It was Locke's conviction that further debasement of money by clipping of coins could be averted only by letting all silver coins circulate at the value corresponding to the ratio of their actual weight compared with the official mint weight. He failed to realise that while this made it possible for new and debased old coins to circulate simultaneously, the old coins would have to lose 30 to 40 per cent of

[29] [Who was harmed by the recoinage depended upon the ability to pass debased coins at face value before they were called in by the government. Before this deadline the government accepted clipped money in payment of debts and taxes. "Who then were the people who suffered? It is easy to be certain who were not. The landowners with land and property tax to pay, the merchants with customs and excise duties to pay, the tax-collectors, the bankers, the stock-jobbers, and the well-to-do middle-class people of the towns who could subscribe to loans and annuities—these had not only been able to unload upon the Exchequer any stock of bad money they possessed, but in many cases, no doubt, had made a nice profit by purchasing clipped money at a discount from less fortunate persons. The people who were left with it were the wage-earning and poorer classes, who found that the shopkeepers at an early stage refused to take it at par, and who had no chance of getting it into the Exchequer before the time" (Sir Albert Feavearyear, *The Pound Sterling: A History of English Money*, second edition, rev. E. Victor Morgan (Oxford: Clarendon Press, 1963), pp. 139-140). Compare the practice *circa* 1990 of the Argentine government which permits businesses to pay taxes with government bonds which can be bought in the market for considerably less than face value. -Ed.]

their value, the amount by which their value exceeded their silver content.[30]

VI

Locke's admirably clear and coherent presentation greatly impressed his contemporaries and remained unchallenged even with respect to certain points that are now recognised as flawed. It was probably in response to his most impressive and most justified argument, namely, that a lowering of the coinage standard would be damaging to England's credit, that the decision was reached to restore the old metal weight of the coins. In December 1695 (after parliamentary committees had deliberated the question for eight years), the coinage reform was formulated in such a way that coins that were clipped beyond a certain point, as well as coins that were counterfeit but not obviously recognisable as such, were to be withdrawn from circulation within about four months and restamped. The major stumbling block to this procedure was the great cost of the opera-

---

[30] We cannot discuss in detail the writings of the numerous other participants in the debate of 1695 and 1696 (there are known to exist around fifty pamphlets and treatises from these two years alone, largely cited in Kalkmann, Andréadès, and Richards. [Philipp Kalkmann, *Englands Übergang zur Goldwährung im Achtzehnten Jahrhundert* (Strasbourg: K. J. Trübner, 1895); Andreas M. Andréadès, *History of the Bank of England*, op. cit.; R. D. Richards, *The Early History of Banking in England*, op. cit. -Ed.] Many of the pamphlets were published anonymously, but among those whose authors are known, let us mention here the most important only: Simon Clement, Nicholas Barbon, John Cary, and John Pollexfen. [Simon Clement, *A Discourse on the General Notions of Money, Trade, & Exchanges* [anon.] (London: n. p., 1695); *Dialogue Between a Countrey Gentleman and a Merchant, Concerning the Falling of Guinea's* [anon.] (London: Printed by J. Astwood for S. Crouch, 1696); Nicholas Barbon, *A Discourse Concerning Coining the New Money Lighter* (London: Printed for R. Chiswell, 1696); John Cary, *An Essay on the Coyn and Credit of England: As They Stand with respect to its Trade* (Bristol: Printed by W. Bonny, 1696); *An Essay on the State of England, in relation to its Trade, its Poor, and its Taxes, for Carrying on the Present War against France* (Bristol: Printed by W. Bonny, 1695); *An Essay Towards the Settlement of National Credit, in the Kingdom of England* (London: Printed by F. Collins, 1696); John Pollexfen, *A Discourse of Trade, Coyn, and Paper Credit* [anon.] (London: Printed for Brabazon Aylmer, 1697 (actually printed 1696; the pamphlet is sometimes attributed incorrectly to Sir Henry Pollexfen, who contributed an appendix, "The Argument of a Learned Council, etc.")). -Ed.] An English translation of Davanzati was published in 1696. [Bernardo Davanzati, *A Discourse Upon Coins*, trans. John Toland (London: Printed by J. D. for A. & J. Churchill, 1696). -Ed.]

tion, but the Bank of England advanced the requisite sum.[31] Another problem was the extended transition period and the resulting severe shortage of money during that time. To increase the efficiency of the mint, the renowned natural scientist Sir Isaac Newton (1642-1727) was appointed Master of the Mint, as Locke had urged. In addition, a number of branches of the Mint were established outside London a few months later. These measures notwithstanding, money was very soon in extremely short supply, and a decisive collapse of stock speculation and of recently founded speculative enterprises ensued, as did a sharp drop in the price of commodities. In short a real economic crisis arose. The shortage of silver money had other peculiar effects as well, notably the rise in the value of silver money. The guinea's official rate of exchange, which had been set at 30 shillings the previous year, proved to be too high. Gold imports, which had begun to rise some months before, greatly increased and the minting of guineas proceeded at a much greater rate than before. It was feared that this might result in a displacement of silver coins as the currency of choice. Banning the import of gold had already been attempted in 1695, but the ineffectiveness of this measure led to the cancellation of the free minting of gold. In the first four months of 1696, the maximum rate for the guinea was set officially first at 28, then at 26, and finally at 22 shillings. Silver money had been maintained at 30 shillings during this period of scarcity and rising value of silver coins only because that was its official rate. The lower rate of the guinea therefore created no difficulties in the market.

The position of the Bank of England suffered a first blow at this time, and the value of its notes was undermined in part as a result of the reminting. As mentioned earlier, the Bank had been forced to make an advance to the state at the beginning of the reminting,

---

[31] [The first loan from the Bank of England to the government, to defray costs of the war with France, preceded the recoinage. "The Government in a leisurely manner commenced to prepare for the recoinage. It was decided to raise the necessary funds to pay the cost by means of a tax upon windows. The tax, however, would take some time to assess and collect, and for the general purposes of the year it would be necessary to borrow something like 2 millions. There were long debates regarding the method of doing this. It was decided not to ask the Bank of England to furnish the money. A state bank was suggested, but the proposal was put aside. Finally the famous scheme for the Land Bank was evolved, about which all that need be said here is that it was a plan to start a new corporation which was to lend money, in the form of inconvertible notes, to private persons upon mortgages, and at the same time to lend 2½ millions to the Government" (Feavearyear, op. cit., pp. 137-138). -Ed.]

and this advance was equivalent to its total capital. But this was not all: to alleviate the shortage of currency, the Bank had extended its notes in circulation far above the legal limit of 1,200,000 pounds, since it believed that this limitation applied only to its interest-bearing notes, not to the non-interest-bearing notes that it had issued in addition. The credit of the Bank was further undermined by the abortive establishment of a competing bank, the National Land Bank.[32] The new bank was founded on the visionary notion of issuing low-interest notes to agriculturalists, whose property and land was to serve as sole security. Since the requisite capital could not be raised, this government-supported project had to be abandoned.

The devaluation of notes in relation to metal currency soon manifested itself and increased markedly at the beginning of May, when the Bank of England could no longer keep up with claims against it and was obliged to put a partial stop to its payments in currency. This crisis was triggered by the fact that May 4 was the deadline for turning in all the bad coins and withdrawing them from circulation. Such was the shortage of silver money that in many cases even rich people were unable to pay for their daily purchases with coins of low denomination, so that everyone was trying to change bank notes into silver coins. But the fundamental reasons for the Bank's inability to meet its obligations lay elsewhere. The Bank's directors had failed to devise a policy for preserving the convertibility of bank notes and had rashly lent out nearly its entire stock of currency. Even slightly increased demands rapidly exhausted the wholly inadequate supply of currency. When the project to establish the National Land Bank, which was to raise money for the government, failed to materialise, the Bank of England once again had to bail out the government with substantial amounts of money. The unprecedented issuing of treasury notes to cover the government's pressing financial needs also contributed to the devaluation of all paper money in relation to metal currency. The Bank of England was forced to stop payment on its notes for a good part of the following year, until the Bank's problems—largely caused by government actions—had been resolved. Its privileges were then reinstated. Two somewhat earlier measures, dating back to 1696, should be mentioned in this context. The first was adopted by the Bank of England in the fall of that year, presumably to counteract the shortage of coins. It involved an entry of payments in the

---

[32] [For a full account of this episode see Andréadès, op. cit., pp. 103-113. -Ed.]

Bank's books, a practice taken over from the old banks in Italy and in Amsterdam. The second was the withdrawal of the entire remaining stock of old coins at the beginning of winter. The law specified only the withdrawal of 'hammered' coins, which pre-dated 1663, but such rolled coins had dropped out of circulation long before. Reversing the practice regarding debased coins that were turned in at the beginning of the year, the coins now withdrawn from circulation were redeemed by the government according to their weight, not their face value, so that their owners had to bear the brunt of the loss.

Once the Bank's position had been consolidated, a new law confirmed the expansion of its privilege in early 1697. One reason for the favourable response to the Bank's wishes was the government's need for a new loan. The Bank could agree to this request only if it was allowed to increase its capital, if its privilege was extended up to 1710, and if it received a monopoly position until the expiration of this privilege, which meant that parliament would not permit any other company of more than six persons to conduct a banking operation. The Bank was also entitled to issue notes up to the amount of its new capital, that is, 2,301,171 pounds. Since the raising of the new capital, which could be paid in as bank notes or as treasury notes of indebtedness, had had the effect of curtailing the amount of paper money in circulation, the irredeemability of the notes soon came to an end.[33] By the end of the year, after the conclusion of the Peace of Rijswijk and the resumption of dividend payments on the part of the Bank had re-established its reputation, the redemption of notes could be resumed.

By 1698 the recoinage had progressed to such an extent that the use of old coins even on the basis of their weight could be declared unlawful. By 1699, after a transition period of three and a half years and the enormous expenditure of nearly 3 million pounds (compared with regular annual government revenue of only about 2 million) the recoinage was completed. Only newly minted money remained in circulation, but even this failed to lead to a permanent

---

[33] [Hayek fails to emphasise the significance of this event. The original capital of the Bank was never fully paid in—a deficiency that contributed directly to the inflationary effect of the Bank's note issue. "Thus the king's immediate difficulties were surmounted by an inflation of credit of the simplest order. 'The Bank', said Michael Godfrey, the first Deputy Governor, 'have called in but £720,000. . . . They have paid into the Exchequer the whole of the £1,200,000 before the time. . . . The rest is left to circulate in trade.' Godfrey foresaw no ill effects" (Sir Albert Feavearyear, *The Pound Sterling*, second edition, op. cit., p. 127). -Ed.]

improvement in the condition of the coinage system. On the one hand, no effort was made to prevent a new debasement of silver money by setting a definite minimum weight, and on the other the relation of gold and silver coins in terms of weight and value did not match those prevailing on the world market. The guinea, which was now freely mintable again, continued to be overvalued, a situation that resulted in large imports of gold and equally substantial outflow of new silver coins. In part on the basis of the London Board of Trade's report, of which Locke was a co-signer and probably also the principal author, the guinea was lowered to 21½ shillings, the level recommended by the report as matching the two metals' relative market value, which it had calculated in detail. But since silver continued to be undervalued, the new level failed to stem its outflow, and in subsequent years the same cycle of erosion and debasement of silver money which had preceded the recoinage was set in motion.

VII

There is little of interest to report for the years around 1700 regarding monetary history. Discussion of the coinage reform was largely limited to a few scholarly studies, although various reports by Newton, who had become Master of the Mint, date from this time, notably his most important report, which belongs to the end of this period. A 1705 publication of the Scotsman John Law deserves to be mentioned here, but it will be discussed in the following chapter in connexion with his role in France. A book by Bishop Fleetwood, to whom we referred earlier, was published in 1707 and is of some interest.[34]

Bishop Fleetwood raises the question whether a stipulation of the founding document of his college, dating from the year 1400, to the effect that scholarship holders should have no more than 5 pounds of outside income, was intended to be applied literally to present conditions. This leads him to a careful investigation of the movement of prices of a number of commodities (cereals, meat, beverages, fabrics, fuel, books, and other necessities) and conveniences of life in the intervening centuries. He reaches the conclusion that the

---

[34] *Chronicon Preciosum: or, An Account of English Money, the Price of Corn, and other Commodities for the last 600 years* [anon.] (London: Printed for C. Harper, 1707): A second edition was published with the name of the author (London: T. Osborne, 1745).

same quantity of goods that had at one time cost 5 pounds would currently cost between 28 and 30 pounds, and hence the latter amount should replace the one mentioned by the founder. This work is of interest as a first attempt to construct price indexes, but its significance also lies in the fact that it convinced Adam Smith of the variability of the value of money, an insight that found a permanent niche in economic thought.

The consequences of the undervaluation of silver coins, which manifested themselves again soon after the exchange rate of the guinea had been lowered to 21½ shillings, became even more marked at the beginning of the eighteenth century, when the market value of silver in relation to gold began to climb again in the wake of the exploitation of Brazilian gold deposits which had been initiated in 1698. As practically no new silver was presented for minting and at the same time a large number of silver coins were exported, the amount of silver in circulation kept declining. By 1717 the situation had deteriorated to the point where government intervention was again unavoidable. Government action was taken on the basis of Newton's famous report, which he presented in September of that year.[35] In it he explained that while the gold and silver contents of English coins were priced at 15.57 to 1 at the prevailing exchange rate of the guinea of 21½ shillings, the exchange ratio between the two metals on the world market was 14.97 to 1. He therefore proposed (as he had already proposed unsuccessfully fifteen years earlier) that the guinea be lowered to 21 shillings, thereby reducing the incentive to export and melt down silver. Newton had envisaged this as a first step, which he realised would not suffice to encourage the minting of silver, which continued to be undervalued at the ratio of 15.21 to 1. It was not surprising that, after Newton's proposal had been embodied in a royal proclamation at the end of the year, nothing changed for the better. The value of silver in fact kept rising (or, to be precise, the value of gold kept declining), and a further lowering of the guinea below the

---

[35] "Sir Isaac Newton's State of the Gold and Silver Coin (25 Sept. 1717.)", reprinted in W. A. Shaw, *Select Tracts and Documents Illustrative of English Monetary History 1626-1730* (London: Clement Wilson, 1896); in German translation by Johann Philip Graumann, *Gesammelte Briefe von dem Gelde* [Collected Letters on Money] (Berlin: C. F. Boss, 1762). An earlier official report of Newton's, issued in 1712, appears in J. R. McCulloch's *Select Collection of Scarce and Valuable Tracts on Money* (London: Printed for the Political Economy Club, 1856), reprinted in 1933 by P. S. King & Son as *Old and Scarce Tracts on Money*. Reports dating from 1701 and 1702 appear in S. D. Horton, *The Silver Pound* (London: Macmillan, 1887).

21 shilling rate established in 1717 was precluded by the new law.[36]
As a result, the outflow of silver continued unabated, so that in the

[36] [The proclamation of 1717 forbade any person to pay or receive guineas at a
higher price than 21s. 0d. [21 shillings, 0 pence]. Thus a *maximum* value for guineas
was established in an attempt to reduce the import of gold and the export of silver.
"England did not establish the gold standard by any conscious and deliberate act,
and it is doubtful whether any one foresaw that it would establish itself. That Newton
in 1717 did not foresee it is clear from the following extract from his paper.

If things be let alone [he said] till silver money be a little scarcer the gold will fall
of itself. For people are already backward to give silver for gold and will in a
little time refuse to make payments in silver without a premium as they do in
Spain and this premium will be an abatement in the value of gold. And so the
question is whether gold shall be lowered by the Government or let alone till it
falls of itself by the want of silver money.

He realized that the two metals would not continue to circulate side by side at the
existing ratio, and that if both were to remain in circulation either gold must come
down or silver go up. But he did not realize that there was a vital difference
between these two contingencies. If, without any action on the part of the Government, guineas, by the ordinary working of supply and demand, came down, first to
21s. 0d., then to 20s. 6d., then to 20s. 0d. and perhaps lower, while shilling-pieces
contined to pass for 12d. the money was still based upon a silver standard. But if
guineas remained at 21s. 6d. while the shilling-pieces went to a premium and were
taken for 1s. 1d., 1s. 2d., or 1s. 3d., then the country had changed over to a gold
standard, and the value of 21s. 6d. in money was tied to the value of the gold in a
guinea and not to the value of the silver in twenty-one and a half shilling-pieces.

"It has never been satisfactorily explained why the latter contingency happened,
that is to say, why, after the last official reduction to 21s. 0d., guineas did not
continue to fall in price with the value of gold and so prevent the displacement of
silver.

". . . Thus by the time the recoinage had been completed the country was
prepared for using the guinea as the standard coin. 'This day', says Luttrell on 22
September 1698, 'the goldsmiths that went to receive money out of the Exchequer
were offered guineas at 22s. 6d. (by reason of the clerks of the customs and excise
yesterday would take them for no more) upon which they were told there was no
silver for them: so the goldsmiths went without their money.' They refused them at
22s. 0d., it should be noticed, not because they were not worth that, but because the
Government had taken them at 21s. 6d. In short the market was now ready to accept
the guinea as a standard coin at 22s. 0d., if the Government would permit it to do
so, to tie the value of the pound to the value of gold at that rate, and let silver
vanish if it would. There was no tendency whatever for the price to fall, in spite of
the fall in the value of gold. When the Government forced the price down to 21s. 6d.
there was considerable opposition, and when the proclamation making it 21s. 0d. was
issued there was so much general concern that the Commons forthwith passed a
resolution declaring that they would not alter further the standard of the gold and
silver coins 'in fineness, weight, or denomination'. The great volume of public
financial transactions which resulted from the enormous increase of the National Debt
as a result of the war with France compelled the market to follow the Government's
valuation of the coin. But a change in the denomination of gold was no longer the
trifling matter it was when silver was the standard, and although for some years after
1717 the mintings of gold continued heavy and silver still disappeared, no further
reduction was made" (Feavearyear, op. cit., pp. 154-157). -Ed.]

end all that was left in the country was a totally inadequate residue of the most heavily eroded silver coins, which at times even attained a value in excess of their face value as the sole available small change. Thus the last attempt to salvage a dual-metal currency in England had to be abandoned. As had actually been the case since recoining took place in 1695-6, gold coins were the only freely minted and full-weight coins in circulation, and they therefore determined the value of English money. The *de facto* shift to a gold currency had already taken place, at least until a decline in the value of silver again made the free minting of silver, which was still authorised by law, profitable again. Only at the turn of the nineteenth century, when this development again became a possibility, was the shift to the gold standard formalised. Until that time the status of the currency remained more or less what it had been prior to 1696. However, in contrast to that earlier period, whatever silver coins remained in circulation did not lose their value in terms of the gold coins, although their metal content had been greatly reduced though continued wear and tear. The value of the silver coins was not undermined by the rapid expansion of notes issued by the country banks after 1750, because an official exchange rate between the guinea and silver coins was now in force, as had not been true sixty years earlier, when the founding of the Bank of England had contributed to the devaluation of silver currency.

For the fifty- to sixty-year period after 1717, in which this development continued undisturbed, our focus of interest shifts to the scholarly treatment of the monetary system. Leaving aside Bishop George Berkeley's remarkable study[37] on monetary questions, we shall now turn to the third of the three great English empiricist philosophers, David Hume (1711-1776), whose *Political Discourses* (1752) made a decisive contribution to the understanding of monetary theory.[38] With an exposition of his doctrines, which undoubtedly constitute a first pinnacle in the development of monetary theory, we shall bring our study of the period in question to a close. The two major systematic analyses by Joseph Harris[39] and Sir

[37] *The Querist, containing several Queries, proposed to the Consideration of the Public* [anon.] (Dublin: J. Reilly, 1735-37). [See the edition edited by J. M. Hone (Dublin & Cork: Talbot Press, 1936). -Ed.]

[38] [On Hume's other contributions see this volume, chapter 7. -Ed.]

[39] *An Essay upon Money and Coins* [anon.] (London: G. Hawkins, 1757-58).

Steuart,[40] which appeared not long after Hume's work and served as basic 'textbooks' on the monetary system until the publication of Adam Smith's *Wealth of Nations*, and even beyond that time, failed to convey any significant new insights. They were strongly influenced, furthermore, by contemporary French studies, which we shall examine in the next chapter. Even in Hume's case the possibility cannot be excluded that he was influenced by Cantillon (c. 1680), who was his superior in many respects.[41] Although Cantillon's writings, which had been set down about twenty years before Hume's essays, were published only three years after the essays, there is evidence that they had been used in manuscript form by another English author before Hume began his work. Be that as it may, Hume's analysis had such a decisive influence on all subsequent developments that it deserves to be considered one of the lasting landmarks in the history of monetary theory. The three (1752) essays in question, entitled "Of Money", "Of Interest", and "Of the Balance of Trade",[42] short as they are, already offer important contributions to all the major problems of monetary theory. Hume prefaces his inquiry with the observation that "money is not, properly speaking, one of the subjects of commerce; but only the instrument which men have agreed upon to facilitate the exchange of one commodity for another". The significance of this remark lies in its repudiation of the mercantilists' excessive preoccupation with money. From Hume's perspective, it is therefore a matter of indifference how great a stock of money a country has, an idea which he first expresses in his famous (and later much abused and distorted) simile comparing money with "oil which renders the motion of the wheels more smooth and easy" (p. 33). In his eyes, "it seems a maxim almost self-evident" that "the prices of every thing depend on the proportion between commodities and money, and that any

---

[40] *An Inquiry into the Principles of Political Economy* (London: n. pub., 1767). [See the new edition, edited by Andrew S. Skinner (Chicago: University of Chicago Press, 1966). -Ed.]

[41] [See this volume, chapter 13. -Ed.]

[42] These have appeared in numerous editions in English as well as in German translation. For a convenient English edition, consult vol. 33 of *The World's Classics* in which they appear under the title *Essays Moral, Political and Literary* (London and Edinburgh: Henry Frowde, 1904; reprinted: London: Oxford University Press, 1963). The most recent German translation, by H. Niedermüller, bears the title *Nationalökonomische Abhandlungen von David Hume* (Leipzig: E. Koschny, 1877), which is the source of these quotations [in the German text of Hayek. Quotations in the present translation are from David Hume, *Writings on Economics*, edited and introduced by Eugene Rotwein (Madison, Wis.: University of Wisconsin Press, 1955). -Ed.]

considerable alteration on either has the same effect, either of heightening or lowering the price" (pp. 41-42), precisely the contention of the quantity theory of the value of money. But he recognises that while the size of a country's stock of money is a matter of indifference, the process of changing the supply of money will have a significant impact. Specifically, the fact that industry has been stimulated in all the nations of Europe since the discovery of mines in America can rightly be attributed to an increase in the supply of gold and silver. To explain this paradox, which seems to fly in the face of his original contention, he develops as a complementary hypothesis the important doctrine that an increase in the supply of money affects different prices in successive phases:

> Though the high price of commodities be a necessary consequence of the encrease of gold and silver, yet it follows not immediately upon that encrease; but some time is required before the money circulates through the whole state, and makes its effect be felt on all ranks of people. At first, no alteration is perceived; by degrees all price rises, first of one commodity, then of another; till the whole at last reaches a just proportion with the new quantity of specie which is in the kingdom. In my opinion, it is only in this interval or intermediate situation, between the acquisition of money and rise of prices, that the encreasing quantity of gold and silver is favourable to industry. When any quantity of money is imported into a nation, it is not at first dispersed into many hands, but is confined to the coffers of a few persons, who immediately seek to employ it to advantage. (p. 37)

Carrying his analysis one step further, Hume explores whether business activity for the very same reasons is dampened when the supply of money is reduced. Today we can no longer without qualifications accept his conclusions, which seem to support mercantilist doctrines. Hume suggests that a wise economic policy should aim to keep the supply of money constant or, better yet, increasing, thereby keeping alive "a spirit of industry in the nation" and increasing "the stock of labour, in which consists all real power and riches" (pp. 39-40). As is apparent from his determined opposition to the increase of the money supply by the issue of bank notes, whose inflationary effect he foresaw, what Hume had in mind, to be sure, was a stimulation of the natural growth in the nation's money supply, not an arbitrary (inflationist) increase in the supply of money. In fact, he questions the much-touted beneficial impact of banks and paper credit, preferring the Bank of Amsterdam's system of issuing only fully covered notes to the English system. He backs this argument in his essay on interest, which demonstrates with exemplary clarity that an increase in the supply of money can at best effect a temporary decline in the rate of interest, never a permanent reduction. He attributes the frequent coincidence of large money supplies and low interest rates in various countries to a common cause, namely, the countries' wealth, which would not be increased by an expansion of the money supply. Hume's second great and probably most significant contribution appears in his essay on the balance of trade, in which he anticipates most of the basic principles of the classical theory of international trade, which have maintained their validity up to the present time.[43] Though many of the points made by Hume were already raised in earlier works, it remains his enduring merit to have constructed a theoretical framework in which the quantity theory of the value of money, the movement of precious metals according to shifts in the balance of trade, the automatic distribution of the supply of precious metals among individual countries, and the influence of changes in exchange rates on prices could all be integrated into a coherent whole. It was the purpose of his doctrine to refute the view which even today has many adherents in the general public, though not among experts, to the effect that a country's economy is harmed by an outflow of money and that import barriers and similar measures should be imposed when a negative balance of trade threatens to lead to an outflow of money. In his counter-argument, Hume states:

> Suppose one-fifth of all the money in Great Britain to be annihilated in one night, . . . what would be the consequence? Must not the price of all labour and commodities sink in proportion, and everything be sold as cheap as they were in those ages? What nation could then dispute with us in any foreign market, or pretend to navigate or to sell manufactures at the same price, which to us would bring sufficient profit? In how little time, therefore, must this bring back the money which we had lost, and raise us to the level of all the neighbouring nations? Where, after we have arrived, we immediately lose the advantage of the cheapness of labour and commodities; and the farther flowing in of money is stopped by our fulness and repletion. (pp. 62-63)

To complete the argument, Hume then demonstrates that in the converse situation, if all the money in England increased fivefold overnight, the opposite mechanism would operate to correct this

---

[43] [Hume's contribution is known today as the 'price-specie-flow mechanism'. Discussions can be found in any modern international economics textbook. -Ed.]

unfair advantage. He concludes "that the same causes, which would correct these exorbitant inequalities, were they to happen miraculously, must prevent their happening in the common course of nature, and must for ever, in all neighbouring nations, preserve money nearly proportionable to the art and industry of each nation" (p. 63). In a footnote Hume suggests an additional more limited cause "which checks the wrong balance of trade, to every particular nation to which the kingdom trades. When we import more goods than we export, the exchange turns against us, and this becomes a new encouragement to export; as much as the charge of carriage and insurance of the money which becomes due would amount to. For the exchange can never rise but a little higher than that sum." Here Hume is giving a first if not altogether clear expression to the later 'gold point' doctrine, which states that the exchange rate between two countries on the gold standard can never rise or fall as long as payments can be made in gold. It was not until the beginning of the nineteenth century that this facet of Hume's doctrine of international trade and in fact his entire doctrine of international trade was to be fully elaborated. We shall present these developments in detail in chapter [11]. For now we shall turn to the French experiences of the eighteenth century and to the theories that they spawned. Their influence on nineteenth-century monetary theory was almost as significant as that of Hume and his forerunners.

TEN

FIRST PAPER MONEY IN 18th-CENTURY FRANCE

I

In the sixteenth century, France had been the country in which the most significant works on monetary theory in modern times had first appeared. After a century of relative stagnation, a revival took place somewhat later than in England, but within a few decades it culminated in a remarkably high level of achievement. While there were already some notable achievements around the turn of the eighteenth century, above all on the part of Pierre de Boisguilbert,[1] major progress was triggered only as a result of external influences, as had been the case in England. The famous 'system' of the Scotsman John Law had the same impact on scientific knowledge in France as the founding of the Bank of England and coin reform had had in England twenty years earlier.

Paper money, the tool used by Law in the implementation of his extraordinary financial plans, was hardly a novelty any more in Europe by that time (not to mention China, where it had already been permanently banned 300 years earlier after centuries of abuses). In addition to the notes issued by banks, established by that time in a number of states, various English colonies in America had issued paper money in large quantities by the end of the seventeenth century, with very unhappy results. France too had paper money since 1706 in the guise of 'billets de monnaie'. This paper money, which served to some extent as legal tender, had its origin in short-term government notes of indebtedness, which were converted to non-interest-paying legal tender when money for their redemption ran out. All these types of paper money, however, were the result of an organic evolution or of expediency in coping with financial stringencies. Law was the first to advocate the large-scale

---

[1] [Pierre le Pesant, Sieur de Boisguilbert (1645-1714), economist, lawyer, and liberal reformer. See Joseph J. Spengler, "Boisguilbert's Views vis-à-vis those of Contemporary Réformateurs", *History of Political Economy*, vol. 16, no. 1, Spring 1984, pp. 69-88. -Ed.]

introduction of paper money on the basis of theoretical considerations *and* the first to implement this scheme.

John Law (1671-1729) was one of the most unusual personalities and possibly the most famous one in financial history. The son of an Edinburgh goldsmith, that is, a banker of that period, John Law came to London at the age of twenty, in time to witness the founding of the Bank of England; Dr. Chamberlain's unsuccessful attempt to establish the Land Bank; and some of the final discussions on the impending coin reform.[2] Wealthy as he was and by family background well grounded in the banking business, brilliant and socially prominent, he soon immersed himself in financial questions in London. He was forced to flee from England after being sentenced for killing his opponent in a duel. He settled first in Holland, then in Italy, the country which had originated banking, extending his knowledge of banking there. At the beginning of the eighteenth century, his fortune made, he returned to Scotland in 1705 and presented parliament with his first proposal, entitled *Money and Trade Considered; with a proposal for supplying the nation with money*,[3] in connexion with discussions about the reform of the Bank of Scotland. This was Law's most important theoretical contribution. For this reason we shall examine his theoretical views at this point, drawing in addition on his later writings, particularly his memoranda on banking,[4] which were written in the years 1715 and 1716. In light of Law's highly practical objectives, the largely theoretical and systematic character of his works, composed in a remarkably clear style, deserves special mention. The general considerations that serve as his point of departure contain a wealth of insights that are a lasting contribution to monetary science. There are three questions concerning which Law shows great perspicacity. His enumeration of the characteristics making a substance well suited as money already contain just about all the qualities that are cited in subsequent

[2] [See this volume, chapter 9. -Ed.]

[3] *Money and Trade Considered, with a Proposal for Supplying the Nation with Money* (Edinburgh: A. Anderson, 1705; reprinted: New York: Augustus M. Kelley, 1966). Published in French as *Considérations sur le numéraire et le commerce*, reprinted in Eugène Daire, *Economistes-financiers du XVIIIe siècle* (Paris: Guillaumin, 1843), pp. 465-548. A poor German translation was issued under the title *Herrn Laws, Controlleur général der Financen in Franckreich Gedancken vom waaren- und Geld-Handel* (Leipzig: J. Schustern, 1720). A 1701 publication, previously ascribed to Law by most people, probably was not written by him. [Hayek refers to *Proposals & Reasons for Constituting a Council of Trade* (Edinburgh: n. p., 1701), now generally attributed to William Paterson (c. 1658-1719). -Ed.]

[4] *Mémoires sur les Banques*, reprinted in Daire, op. cit., pp. 549-618.

writings as being indispensable for this purpose. These are the requirements that he lists in various places, though not quite in these terms: homogeneity and divisibility, easy transportability and hence equal value in different localities, stability of value, durability, easy recognisability, and easy coinage. Far more important, however, are his views about the determinants of the value of money, which he derives from a general explanation of the value of commodities, anticipating many elements of the modern theory of subjective value. The first chapter of his 1705 publication begins with this sentence: "Commodities obtain their value from their utilisation, and this value is not determined by how highly this utilisation is esteemed or how necessary it is but by the relationship of its supply to its demand." Silver, which is the substance most commonly utilised as specie, derives its value as a metal like all other commodities. The fact that its value as metal and as money exceeds the value corresponding to the usefulness of silver as such is not attributable, as Locke believed, to an artificial convention. This higher value is not 'imaginary', but can be explained from the fact that the use of silver as money results in an additional demand for silver and thus raises its value. If silver were to be deprived of its utilisation as money, it would lose as much as half or even two-thirds of its value. This rejection of Locke's 'convention' theory of money value and the lucid distinction between the use value of money as a commodity and its functional value as money constitute some of Law's most important insights. He explains the instability of the value of silver by its inability to adapt to demand and unpredictable increases in its supply, which could depress its value, as happened on a large scale in the preceding century. As we shall see below, Law bases his reform proposal in part on this doctrine of the inadequate stability of the value of silver, though the proposal is a direct consequence of the third and critical basic idea of his doctrine.

His point of departure here is the traditional doctrine according to which the genesis of money could be traced to the difficulties encountered in barter. He refined this doctrine considerably, however, by replacing rationalist explanations with a historical account of the evolution of money, which induced Carl Menger to call him the "founder of the correct theory of the origin of money".[5] Recognising that many acts of exchange would never have materialised in the

---

[5] [Carl Menger, *Grundsätze der Volkswirtschaftslehre* [1871], translated by James Dingwall and Bert F. Hoselitz as *Principles of Economics* (New York and London: New York University Press, 1981), p. 318. -Ed.]

absence of money, Law infers that an increase in the supply of money would lead to a further intensification of exchanges. From this he draws conclusions that constitute the fundamental and fatal flaw of his doctrine: "The quantity of money in a state must be adjusted to the number of its inhabitants . . . . One million can create employment for only a limited number of persons, . . . a larger amount of money can create employment for more people than a smaller amount, and each reduction in the money supply lowers the employment level to the same extent." The reason for Scotland's having so little trade was attributed by Law to its having so little money. Here Law is carrying the mercantilists' characteristic views to extreme lengths. At the same time he rejects all proposals by contemporary writers advocating that the country's supply of money be increased by an improved balance of trade, turning silver vessels into coins, reducing the weight of coins, etc., and character-ises the issue of paper money as the only sensible way of increasing the money supply. Law contended that paper money had all the distinctive qualities of silver and in addition had several great advantages: the amount could be adjusted easily to the current demand for money and would be more *stable* in value than a metallic currency, since the supply and demand of money could always be kept in balance. Law proposed in his 1705 publication that this paper money be secured by land; in other words, that it be issued only as mortgage-backed loans. Since land, in contrast with metals, was bound to appreciate in value, the money would be more secure than metallic currency. It would have the added advantage that it could not be exported and its supply could not be diminished in this way. In later years he envisaged unsecured bank issues, the soundness of the paper money resting entirely on the credit of the issuing institution. His writings display an accurate knowledge of contemporary banking systems in other countries. He correctly distinguished two main types of banks: pure deposit banks, like the Bank of Amsterdam, which, according to its statutes, could only keep monies deposited with it in safe-keeping, without loaning it out to others (Law claims that this statute was not always ob-served), and issue and discount banks like the Bank of England, which retained only part of the money deposited with them as security and profitably invested the rest.[6] Law consistently supported

---

[6] Paul Jacob Marperger's work *Beschreibung der Banqven* (Halle and Leipzig: F. dv Serre, 1717), which appeared in 1717, concurrently with the flowering of Law's 'system', distinguishes between six types of banks: the land banks or land savings banks, pawn banks, exchange banks, deposit banks (which he designates as the only

the second type of banking, since it was the only kind that could be instrumental in increasing the quantity of money. He expected the greatest blessings to accrue for a country from their introduction; as a result of the paper money issued by them, "the inhabitants would gain employment, the soil would be better cultivated, manufacturing would be encouraged, internal and foreign trade would be stimulated, and the wealth and power of the country would be built on a solid foundation."

The individual components of Law's proposal were nothing new. The idea of basing paper money on land had been familiarised by Petty and Davenant and had become popular as a result of Dr. Chamberlain's project for the Land Bank.[7] (Law made a point of clearly differentiating his own project from Chamberlain's.) The notion that an increase in money would stimulate trade and exchange was more or less common property of all mercantilist writers. But these ideas had never been presented with equal brilliance and persuasiveness. Rejection of Law's ideas came almost entirely from those opposed to any kind of paper money. At that time nobody was capable of refuting the fatal fundamental error that was for the first time revealed with full clarity in his writings. This error, which became firmly embedded in writings about money and repeatedly played a nefarious role over the years, consisted in Law's notion that no harm could come of increasing the supply of money as long as the money supply was geared to the 'demand' for money.

II

Law received no positive response to his proposals in Scotland or in England, where he had also sent them. The response was equally negative in France, where he turned next. There too the plans offered in several additional papers were turned down at first. Until 1714, the year that he finally took up permanent residence in Paris, he was constantly on the move, pleading everywhere for his projects—in Italy, Holland, Germany and, incidentally, towards the end of 1714 in Vienna, where, after a first attempt had failed in 1707, the Vienna City Bank was successfully founded. This success-

full-fledged banks), note-emission banks (which he characterizes as 'pernicious' projects), and a kind of mixed-purpose bank, along with occasional 'financiers'.

[7] [See this volume, chapter 9, section VI. -Ed.]

ful example had its share in making French authorities take a favourable view of Law's projects at last. Although the death of Louis XIV in 1715 at first interfered with Law's favourable prospects, the financial situation in France after the king's death was so catastrophic that before long, after all other remedies had been exhausted, the Regent, Philip of Orléans, was compelled to consider Law's plans. His first suggestion was to establish a state bank, a project that had been under discussion in France for many years, but that now foundered on the opposition of the bankers, who had initially been favourable to it. Instead, the desperate plight of state finances prompted recourse to such old-fashioned remedies as the debasing of coinage, cancellation of part of the state debt, and other arbitrary measures. When these remedies secured only a transient improvement, Law, who had meanwhile worked out a new project, was finally authorised to establish a bank at his own risk. This bank was to be in the form of a stock company operating as a deposit and discount house. The major condition attached to this privilege was that three-quarters of the 6 million livres constituting the bank's initial capital be paid in the form of the devalued state notes. These notes were then retired, so that this part of the bank's capital was effectively turned over at once to the state as a liquidation of part of its debts. Only a part of the capital had to be paid in at once, furthermore, so that the bank started out on its operations with exceedingly scant resources. The two types of business to which, by statute, the bank was to devote itself and which at first constituted its entire operation brought it very rapid popularity and success. The deposits that it took in were expressed not in terms of the units of coins in current circulation but, following the model of the Bank of Amsterdam, as abstract units defined in terms of a specific quantity of silver. Deposits were thus protected against the frequent coin debasements and soon preferred to coins by the public. The interest rate was low (the bank discounted bills of exchange at 3 or even 2 per cent, while previously an interest rate of 3 per cent was nothing unusual) and this led to a rapid expansion of its credit. It had reached a circulation of 66 million livres in notes by the end of the first year (a livre was almost exactly equivalent to the later franc), without untoward effect on the value of money. In fact, the bank notes, which were redeemable in a fixed amount of metal, even attained an excess value compared with coins. This situation remained unchanged until Law began to use the bank as an instrument for his further plans.

He had set himself two further broad goals: the first was that the stimulation of the French economy, which was to be based on bank credit, should be further enhanced by the establishment of large trading companies; and the second was that the lowering of the interest rate, which had been achieved, as planned, by the founding of the bank, should ease the state's heavy burden of interest payments on the huge state debt. It was to be the bank's function to supply the requisite means for both goals.

There existed a number of overseas trading companies in France that had been established in the previous century, but that proved to be unsuccessful. In 1717 Law seized the chance to acquire the trade monopoly for the American colony Louisiana, which had been given up by a big merchant. He used this monopoly to found the Compagnie d'Occident, known by the name of "Mississippi Company", extending its monopoly to Canada. Shares in this company were issued like those for the bank itself, that is, against payment of devalued state notes that remained in circulation. The amount received had to be destroyed at once. Like the bank, this trading company immediately loaned out its entire capital to the state, as so frequently happened at that time. In exchange it received a 4 per cent return from the state. From the very start the company had to depend on bank credit on a large scale in order to finance its business. As a result, the bank notes in circulation increased rapidly, while the reputation of the bank grew at the same pace. Its bank notes were declared acceptable for tax payments. In 1718, the bank, which had meanwhile developed effectively into a depository for all state revenues, was officially converted from a private institution into a royal bank, owned exclusively by the state, in line with Law's original intention. This conversion did not prevent Law from using the bank to further his subsequent plans. When the Compagnie d'Occident a few months later took over several additional companies and under the new name of Compagnie des Indes combined the entire French maritime trade under its control, the new company found itself in need of additional capital for its giant undertakings. At this point Law resorted to a procedure for raising capital that was a peculiarity of his system and that eventually led to his downfall.

The bank was obliged to issue new notes to the public, so that the public in turn could acquire the new shares. In Law's view, the profits to be anticipated by the shareholders constituted an adequate security for these notes. More and more enterprises, such as running the Mint and collecting taxes, were taken over with the same procedures for raising capital. There are many fascinating details about the ensuing gigantic stock speculation, which already bore most of the distinctive features of modern stock market gambling, but they are beyond the scope of our study. Another of Law's ventures that deserves to be mentioned is his attempt to use bank credit to put state finances on a sound footing, an objective of Law's to which we referred earlier. His preliminary plan for reforming the entire system of state revenues is perhaps his most brilliant intellectual feat, though it was never implemented. As a final major step, Law undertook a conversion of the accumulated debt, whereby his Compagnie would assume the entire debt by paying off all other creditors and remain the sole state creditor. The state would then pay back the debt at a much lower interest rate than it was paying to its current debt holders. The money was to be raised partially by the issue of new bank notes and partially by the issuing of additional stock, which in turn required an increased issue of notes. Law had been named Controller General of State Finances at the beginning of the year 1720, reaching the pinnacle of his success and nearly unlimited power in its wake. However, just then the dire consequences of the proliferation of bank notes began to manifest themselves more and more ominously. When Law, to stem the devaluation of the notes by giving them greater scope, attacked metallic currency, progressively restricted and finally forbade its use altogether, declaring the notes to be the sole legal tender, he aroused violent suspicion against the bank notes. The ultimate collapse was triggered, however, by the high level of the stock prices which had been induced by speculation.

Stocks had attained such high levels that the company could no longer pay adequate returns on them, despite the large bank credit at its disposal. An extremely high dividend was declared, but even so it represented only a relatively small percentage in terms of the current price of the shares, which thereby triggered a decline in stock price.[8] Law fought to prevent this decline with all the means at his disposal, without being able to stem it, despite the fact that the bank issued further huge amounts of notes for the purchase of shares. Until August 1720 Law waged a desperate fight to maintain the price of the notes and shares. He resorted to every conceivable trick to accomplish this purpose. The Bank and the Compagnie were combined into a single enterprise, the shares were declared to be money, coins were debased to restore the equivalence of coins and notes. Finally Law was compelled gradually to lower the face value of the shares and bank notes. Though this measure was later

---

[8] [The manuscript is defective here. A definite percentage figure is indicated but not supplied. -Ed.]

rescinded, the announcement led to Law's temporary removal from his post and sealed the fate of his system. After his reappointment, he took steps in the right direction by trying to reduce the volume of notes in circulation and the number of shares being traded, but it was all in vain. By the end of August the notes which had already fallen in terms of their silver value crashed to a third of that value and the price of shares crumbled ineluctably. Law was permanently removed from his post and was forced to flee from the country to escape public outrage. The notes remaining in circulation were exchanged against government annuities and those that were not traded in within a short period of time were declared invalid; the bank itself was dissolved before the end of the year. All that was left of the entire system barely half a year after it had reached its pinnacle was a very prosperous but publicly discredited Compagnie, which was quickly destroyed by Law's enemies. The heavy losses suffered by all the persons who participated in the speculation and by the broad segments of the population that had held bank notes, as well as the violent crisis that engulfed the entire French economy in the wake of the 'system's' collapse, discredited Law's system to such an extent that it came to be regarded as a pure fraud. Such was the distrust generated by its failure that for several decades no new banks were permitted in France.

III

We have intentionally kept to a relatively succinct description of Law's French experiment, because the insights gained from this experience are far less valuable than Law's astonishing theoretical achievements. Had Law been deprived of the opportunity to put into practice his most flawed idea—though perhaps the part of his doctrine that he himself considered the most original—all his other accomplishments in the field of monetary theory would undoubtedly have earned him a place of honour in the history of monetary theory. It is reasonable to assume, furthermore, that his writing had as great a share in stimulating the substantial advances in monetary theory in the subsequent two decades as his 'system'. Most of the publications in question involve either critiques or defences of Law's doctrine, such as those of his most important and most dangerous opponent, Chancellor Henri d'Aguesseau, which however appeared only a half-century later.[9] Another critical work is that of Joseph Paris-Duverney,[10] a banker who took charge of the liquidation of Law's bank. Among works supporting Law are tracts by his former employees Jean-François Mélon[11] and Dutot[12]. But all these men and even Law himself were overshadowed by one contemporary, who was probably the most important political economist before Adam Smith and perhaps even the most important monetary theorist before Ricardo, namely, the Irish banker and trader Richard Cantillon. Little is known about his life.[13] We shall mention here only that at the time of Law's system he owned a banking concern in Paris, which he conducted sometimes personally and sometimes through a strawman, and that he had travelled widely in various countries. Rumour has it that he came into conflict with Law because of his stand on the Law system, whose collapse he had foreseen far in advance, and that he himself made huge profits from the speculations. In 1734 he was murdered at a relatively youthful age in his London home by his cook, in the course of an attempted robbery. Cantillon left behind a manuscript that has disappeared since then (it may already have been destroyed when his murderer burned down his house). Cantillon himself had already translated a large part of the manuscript into French for a friend. This French translation, after many vicissitudes, was published anonymously in 1755 and reprinted several times in the next few years.[14] Prior to its publication, it had been used and copied by various persons in France and England (where the original manuscript may still have survived). We must obviously focus here on the book's contribution

[9] "Considérations sur les monnaies", published 1777 in the chancellor's *Oeuvres* (Paris: Les Libraires associés, 1761-89), vol. 10.

[10] *Examen du livre intitulé Réflexions politiques sur les finances et le commerce* (La Haye: V. & N. Prevôt, 1740).

[11] *Essay politique sur le commerce* [1734], reprinted in Daire, op. cit., pp. 707-836.

[12] *Réflexions politiques sur les finances et le commerce* [1738], reprinted in Daire, op. cit., pp. 845-1008.

[13] [Much more has been learned about Cantillon's life and the publication of his *Essai sur la nature du commerce en général* since Hayek wrote this chapter. For an update see the text and footnotes in this volume, chapter 13, and especially Antoin E. Murphy, *Richard Cantillon: Entrepeneur and Economist* (Oxford: Clarendon Press, 1986), chapters 5, 8, and 9. -Ed.]

[14] [The 1755 edition of Cantillon's *Essai sur la nature du commerce en général* gave the publication information "A Londres, chez Fletcher Gyles, dans Holborn", which is now known to be incorrect. The standard modern edition of the *Essai* is the one edited by Henry Higgs and published with an English translation in 1931 (London: Royal Economic Society, Macmillan, 1931; reprinted New York: Augustus M. Kelley, 1964). -Ed.]

to monetary theory, but it is worth noting that this unusually interesting work exerted a great influence on political economists of the second part of the eighteenth century, both directly and through its various plagiarists. Strangely enough, it fell nearly completely into oblivion in the nineteenth century until it was rediscovered by W. S. Jevons in 1881.[15] Despite the author's eminently practical experiences, the work is strictly theoretical in character and emphasises the extent to which it builds on the work of its best forerunners, particularly Petty[16] and Locke[17]. Cantillon was the first author to present a coherent and systematic theory of value and also the first to distinguish between normal (or, as he calls it, 'intrinsic') value and market value, which fluctuates around it, a distinction that came to be widely adopted in later years.[18] He applied his cost theory, based on an ingenious balancing of labour and land input, to the determination of the value of precious metals. His distinction between intrinsic value and market value offers him a starting point for discussing—for the first time—the influence of costs on the one hand and the influence of supply and demand on the other on the equilibrium value of precious metals. "The market value of metals, as of other merchandise or produce, is sometimes above, sometimes below, the intrinsic value, and varies with their plenty or scarcity according to the demand."[19]

When consumption goes down, value will fall below costs and production will be cut back; the same thing will happen with mines that are currently being exploited when mines with lower costs are discovered. These relationships, which are valid for all metals, apply as well to gold and silver, which have demonstrated their special suitability as a common measure of value among all the commodities that mankind has used over millennia to avoid the problems of direct barter: their small volume, uniform quality, ease of transport,

---

[15] Wilhelm Roscher's *Geschichte der Nationalökonomie in Deutschland* (Munich: R. Oldenbourg, 1874), English translation by John J. Laler, *Principles of Political Economy* (New York: H. Holt, 1878), is an exception. [The reference to Jevons is to his "Richard Cantillon and the Nationality of Political Economy", *Contemporary Review*, vol. 39, January 1881, reprinted in W. Stanley Jevons, *The Principles of Economics: A Fragment of a Treatise on the Industrial Mechanism of Society and other Papers* (London: Macmillan, 1905), pp. 155-183, and in Higgs, op. cit., pp. 333-360. -Ed.]

[16] [Sir William Petty (1623-1687). On Petty's contributions see this volume, chapter 9, section IV. -Ed.]

[17] [John Locke (1632-1704). See this volume, chapter 9, section V. -Ed.]

[18] [Hayek may be too eager to accord 'first' priority to Cantillon. The distinction between 'market' and 'intrinsic' value also appears in Locke. See this volume, chapter 9. -Ed.]

[19] [Higgs's translation of Cantillon's *Essai*, op. cit., p. 97. -Ed.]

divisibility without loss, ease of safekeeping, all of these combined with beauty and brilliance and nearly infinite durability. By thus enumerating the properties of a commodity well suited to serve as money and by rejecting the theory whereby money originated from an arbitrary human decision to use a particular commodity, Cantillon largely sides with Law (but never refers to him specifically), and against Locke.[20] His own explanation of the value of money is incomparably more profound than Law's. Cantillon agrees with the basic idea of Locke's quantity theory of money, but he objects to the fact that this theory, like all other English theories of money, can explain only the current market value of money, not the determinants of the intrinsic value of precious metals, namely the cost of production and the subsistence costs of the workers required to produce them. He thereby derives the equilibrium value of money, but he goes even further.[21] In an analysis[22] that Jevons considers "one of the most marvelous things in the book", Cantillon explains the phased impact of a rising production of precious metals, whose sophistication was matched only 130 years later by Cairnes.[23] Cantillon points out that Locke had correctly recognised the fact that an overabundance of money made all prices rise, but had not investigated the mechanism involved. Cantillon emphasises that the major difficulty in such an investigation is to determine the mechan-

[20] [Hayek may be overemphasising Cantillon's difference with Locke. The passage from Cantillon reads as follows: "Mr. Locke says that the consent of mankind has given its value to gold and silver. This cannot be doubted since absolute Necessity had no share in it. It is the same consent which has given and does give every day a value to Lace, Linen, fine Cloths, Copper and other Metals" (Cantillon, ed. Higgs, op. cit., p. 113). In his German original, Hayek used the term *Konventionstheorie* to refer to Locke's account of the origins of the use of money. But the German term is not applicable to what Locke and his contemporaries would have understood as 'consent' or 'agreement'. See also Karen Iversen Vaughn, *John Locke* (Chicago and London: University of Chicago Press, 1980). -Ed.]

[21] [The weakness of Cantillon's theory of the value of money rests on his attempts to derive the 'intrinsic' or 'normal' value of precious metals from their costs of production, i.e., the cost of land and labour. Cantillon assumes as given the ownership of all land, whereas the influx of precious metals was largely from America where the ownership of land and the costs of production were indeterminate. Thus the supply of *money* was independent of the cost of land and labour, and no equilibrium value of money was possible. See part I, chapters 1 and 3 of Cantillon's *Essay on the Nature of Trade in General*, ed. H. Higgs, op. cit. -Ed.]

[22] [*Ibid.*, pp. 159-199. -Ed.]

[23] [John Elliott Cairnes (1823-1875), often described as 'the last of the classical economists'. Hayek refers to Cairnes's "Essays Towards a Solution of the Gold Question", in Cairnes, *Essays in Political Economy* (London: Macmillan, 1873), pp. 1-165. -Ed.]

ism of price increases and the varying proportions in which increases in the supply of money raise the prices of commodities. Cantillon begins his analysis exactly like the most modern writers by showing the effect of the consumption expenditures by the persons whose income increases as a result of the higher production of precious metals. The immediate impact of their higher income is a rise in the price of food, which they now consume in larger amounts, and a rise in the income of craftsmen, to whom they give greater employment. Even though this will induce an increased production of the commodities whose demand has gone up, their increased consumption, and the increased consumption of all the persons who first benefit from the higher demand for them, will be at the expense of those persons who will have to restrict their consumption when prices rise. Gradually all prices and wages will rise, though not always uniformly. On the one hand it will then become advantageous to import commodities from abroad into the state with the mines, and where the impact of the increased production first manifests itself, inasmuch as these goods can be produced elsewhere at a lower cost; on the other hand the situation of the craftsmen producing these commodities in the country with the mines and of all persons with a fixed money income will become so unfavourable that they will be forced to emigrate. The final outcome will be the impoverishment of the state with the mines: all its other industries will be ruined and the entire metal extracted from the mines will have to be used to pay for the products from other countries, where all the gold and silver will finally accumulate. This was the fate that Spain suffered after the discovery of the West Indies, and the same fate befell Portugal after the discovery of Brazil. Both Spain and Portugal had been the losers, while England and France, neither of which owned any mines, had been the winners.

Cantillon combines this analysis with considerations about the advantage of large quantities of money flowing into a state through trade, in which he remains reasonably faithful to the mercantilist tradition. He does distinguish himself from most contemporary writers by stressing not the absolute amount of money circulating in a country but its magnitude compared with that of other countries. A more important point than these considerations about economic policy is his treatment of two more strictly monetary questions, namely his investigation of the velocity of money circulation and his theory of exchange rates. We can touch on these two questions only briefly. Like Petty and Locke, on whose work he builds, he arrives at the conception of the velocity of circulation by trying to deter mine a country's requirement for money. Starting out from a presentation of the circulation of money, which was to a large extent a model for the Physiocrats' *Tableau économique*,[24] Cantillon proceeds to examine what determines the amount of money held by individuals (such as provision for unpredictable contingencies). He then looks at the whole question from a new perspective by making it clear that a change in the velocity of money would have the same impact as a change in the quantity of money. He was thus the first to demonstrate that the velocity of circulation and its fluctuations influence the value of money.[25] In his contributions to the theory of exchange rates, to which we can refer only in passing, Cantillon gives a more accurate formulation of the prevalent explanation based on the production and shipping costs of the various types of money, but his most original insight lies in his recognition that speculation is capable of smoothing out predictable fluctuations in the exchange rate but not of altering their natural level in the long run. Cantillon has a profound understanding of the working of bi-metallism and chides Newton[26] for his unworkable attempt to align the legal value relation between gold and silver coins with the constantly fluctuating market relations between gold and silver by lowering the exchange value of the guinea. A much more effective way to staunch the outflow of silver, Cantillon believes, is to mint silver coins at a correspondingly lighter weight.[27] As we stated, Cantillon was a banker, and so his comprehension of the banking system is hardly surprising. In connexion with his study of the velocity of money circulation, he is the first to point out the determinants for the proper ratio of currency backing and deposits for different kinds of banks. Interestingly enough, he gives the ratio of 1 to 10 as typical for the coverage ratio, a figure that has been consistently reaffirmed in the relevant literature.

[24] [François Quesnay, *Tableau économique*, published anonymously in Paris in three editions between 1758 and 1759. -Ed.]

[25] [Higgs's translation of Cantillon's *Essai*, op. cit., pp. 121-139. -Ed.]

[26] [Sir Isaac Newton (1642-1727) was Warden and later Master of the Mint in London from 1696 until his death. See this volume, chapter 9, section VII. -Ed.]

[27] It should be mentioned too in this connexion that Cantillon recognises the crucial role of credit and banking as accelerators of the velocity of a given money supply and that he uses this concept in a manner that remained unique until reintroduced only recently by Knut Wicksell. [See Wicksell's *Föreläsningar i nationalekonomi, Häft II: Om penningar och kredit* [1906]. The third edition was translated by E. Classen and edited by Lionel Robbins as *Lectures on Political Economy, Vol. 2: Money* (London: Routledge & Kegan Paul, 1935). -Ed.]

With the sole exception of Mirabeau the Elder,[28] of whom it is known that he had the manuscript of Cantillon's essay in his possession for sixteen years before its publication, Cantillon's impact in France could not be ascertained before the physiocrats. The latter, however, made no significant contributions in monetary theory, with the exception to some extent of A. R. J. Turgot, whose *Reflexions sur la formation et la distribution des richesses* was published in 1769 and 1770 and constituted a kind of textbook.[29] His treatment of monetary theory is terse but extremely clear and conveys important new insights on the closely related subject of interest theory. Turgot's letter on paper money[30] written in 1749 but published much later contains the often-quoted sentence "Tout crédit est un emprunt et a un rapport essential à son remboursement" (All credit represents a loan and has a vital relationship with its repayment).[31] A year prior to the composition of this letter, a work had appeared in France that was to influence the development of monetary theory more by its extremely wide dissemination than by its original contributions to the subject—Montesquieu's *Esprit des loix*.[32] This work was responsible for popularising the quantity theory of money in Davanzati's version.[33] At about the same time, another Italian author, Ferdinando Galiani, composed *Della Moneta*,[34] a work worthy of the tradition of Davanzati and Montanari. Galiani's work almost rivals the great achievements of Cantillon and Hume; he even surpasses them in his

[28] [Victor Riquetti, Marquis de Mirabeau (1715-1789). -Ed.]

[29] [The book, written in 1766, was originally published (with errata) in three parts in the journal *Ephémérides du Citoyen* in 1769 and 1770; a corrected edition was published in 1788. See the English translation by Peter Groenewegen in his *The Economics of A. R. J. Turgot* (The Hague: Martinus Nijhoff, 1977), pp. 43-95. -Ed.]

[30] "Lettre sur le papier suppléé à la monnaie" [1749], in Gustave Schelle, ed., *Oeuvres de Turgot et documents le concernant* (Paris: Félix Alcan, 1913-23; reprinted Glashütten im Taunus: Detlev Auvermann, 1972), vol. 1, pp. 143-152. [For an English translation see Groenewegen, op. cit., pp. 1-8. -Ed.]

[31] [Schelle, op. cit., p. 145; in Groenewegen's translation, op. cit., p. 3. -Ed.]

[32] [*De l'esprit des loix* [anon.] (Geneve: Barrillot, 1748); translated by Anne Cohler and Basia Miller as *The Spirit of Laws* (Cambridge: Cambridge University Press, 1989). -Ed.]

[33] [See Hugo Hegeland, *The Quantity Theory of Money* (Göteborg: Elanders Boktryckeri Aktiebolag, 1951), pp. 31-34. -Ed.]

[34] [*Della Moneta* [anon.] (Napoli: Presso G. Raimondo, 1750). See English translation by Peter R. Toscano, *On Money* (Ann Arbor, Mich.: Published for the Department of Economics, University of Chicago, by University Microfilms International, 1977). -Ed.]

basic approach to the theory of value, which brings him far closer even than Law to modern thinking on this subject.[35]

IV

While a fair number of works on monetary theory appeared in France in the middle of the eighteenth century, a certain quiescence set in once the physiocrats were in the ascendant. In the last decades of the century, however, developments in the monetary system, which was subjected to some wrenching changes during the great revolution, provided a multitude of instructive experiences.[36] The years from 1789 to 1797 were a time of colossal paper money inflation. This inflation differed markedly from the one generated by Law's system, but it offered a classic example for subsequent periods of paper money, which recurred several times in the following decades in the wake of wars and revolutions.

At the outbreak of the revolution in 1789, the financial problems of the French government had again become exacerbated; in fact, they had been among the immediate causes of the revolution. It was these difficulties that made it imperative to convoke the Estates General, which ended the dispensation of the clergy and the nobility from paying taxes. Since a number of oppressive taxes were lifted at the same time, however, and since all revolutionary governments have large expenditures, the chronic budget deficit, which began several decades earlier, became larger rather than smaller. The most pressing problem was the huge state debt, which came to 4½ billion livres and whose servicing alone absorbed a third of the total government expenditures. Reduction of these debts seemed to be the most urgent task in putting the government on a sound financial footing. All eyes turned to the one source from which the state could expect to raise such very large resources. Shortly after the

---

[35] Cantillon's expositions on this point are of particular importance, because they happened to be reprinted as early as 1762 in German translation in Johann Philip Graumann's *Gesammelte Briefe von dem Gelde* [Collected letters on money] (Berlin: C. F. Boss, 1762), the best and most popular German work of that period on the monetary system, and thus reached a larger audience.

[36] [On the history of this period see Ernest Labrousse, *La crise de l'économie française à la fin de l'Ancien Regime* (Paris: Presses Universitaires de France, 1943); *Histoire économique et sociale de la France* (Paris: Presses Universitaires de France, 1970-82), vol. 3:1, chapter 1; Florin Aftalion, *L'économie de la Révolution française* (Paris: Hachette/Pluriel, 1987); and Pierre Vilar, *A History of Gold and Money 1450-1920*, trans. Judith White (London: New Left Books, 1976), pp. 300-308. -Ed.]

revolution, the large estates of the Church and the Crown had been expropriated. The Church holdings were by far the more extensive and, together with the confiscated holdings of the Crown, were evaluated at 3½ billion livres. But how could these treasures be converted to liquid assets? Notwithstanding the bitter recollections of John Law and his 'system', proposals poured in from all sides to issue paper money backed by these national assets.

It should be mentioned that at the outbreak of the revolution there already existed a kind of paper money, the discount notes issued by the Caisse d'Escompte, which had been established by Turgot in 1776. The Caisse d'Escompte was the predecessor of the Banque de France, and in 1788 its notes had been designated as legal tender. As a result of secret loans to the state, these notes had already reached a sizable circulation at the time of the outbreak of the revolution. Perhaps because they had denominations of 200 livres and higher, and thus were ill-suited for ordinary transactions, their value was 2-5 per cent lower than that of metal money. This paper money constituted barely a twentieth of the metallic money in circulation at that time, estimated at more than 2 billion. The decision to increase the quantity of circulating paper money was not taken lightly. It was the general impression, on the contrary, that the discount notes, which were viewed with distrust, were being replaced by a sounder credit paper when the first 'assignats' (drafts) were issued in December 1789 to cover the most urgent financial requirements. After prolonged discussions, in which the outspoken opponents of paper money of any kind kept the upper hand for a long time, the decision was reached to use the Church property that had been confiscated a month earlier as security for the issue of 400 million livres' worth of interest-bearing assignats in large denominations of 1,000 livres each. The intention was to redeem them within five years from the proceeds of the sale of national property. They were also to be applicable directly to such a purchase, but for the time being they could not be used as legal tender. Four months later there followed an issue of an additional 400 million livres' worth of assignats. These no longer bore much resemblance to investment certificates, as their interest rate had been reduced from 5 to 3 per cent and at the same time denominations had been lowered to 200 livres. Furthermore they had been de-clared to be legal tender. In September 1790 a third issue took place, which doubled the total number of assignats and eliminated interest payments for all the notes issued. Within nine months, investment certificates had been transformed to pure paper money.

The change in character of the assignats is a clear expression of the fact that the initial opposition to the issue of paper money, notably on the part of Necker, the Minister of Finance, and particularly of the two political economists DuPont de Nemours[37] and Condorcet[38], had to give way when the financial needs of the revolution became more pressing. The various proposals for the direct issuing of paper money had been turned down initially and the assignats had won out because a connexion had been established between them and the treasures belonging to the state. Tenuous and theoretical in character as this connexion was, it sufficed to confirm the confidence of the large masses in the assignats. As mentioned before, the only connexion between the national property and the notes was that the owners of the latter were entitled to use them for the purchase of national property and that the cash proceeds obtained from the sale of national property would then be applied to the redemption of the assignats. Either way, the redeemed assignats were then to be destroyed and not reissued. From the very start there could be no real redemption of the assignats by a transfer of land, the only security backing their value, since their owners had no claim to any specific piece of land, nor had a price even been set for the sale of national property, so that its price kept rising as the assignats depreciated. Yet it might have been possible to avoid a large-scale depreciation of the assignats had their issue been kept within the bounds of the national property by which they were secured and the property systematically sold, and had the redeemed assignats all been burned, as was done initially.

At first, the assignats circulated alongside metal currency and their impact on the price of commodities remained imperceptible. They started out by displacing only an equivalent amount of metal currency. As they were first issued solely in large denominations of 1,000 and then 200 livres, there arose a distinct scarcity of small coins, as a result of which the negative premium that the assignats had inherited from the discount notes increased slightly. When the denomination of the notes was reduced first to 50 livres in September 1790 and then in May of the following year to 5 livres, the

---

[37] [Pierre Samuel DuPont de Nemours (1739-1817), historian of economics and editor of Quesnay and Turgot. In 1815 he settled in Delaware, where his son Irenée started the gunpowder factory that later evolved into the DuPont chemical conglomerate. -Ed.]

[38] [Marie Jean Antoine Nicolas Caritat, Marquis de Condorcet (1743-1794), mathematician and philosopher, known as a pioneer of the mathematical analysis of voting. -Ed.]

negative premium for these smaller notes was greatly reduced. The introduction of the small notes facilitated the total displacement of metal currency, however. When an additional issue of 600 million livres was implemented in July 1791 and the assignats issued totalled more than the previous amount of metallic currency in circulation, the latter disappeared completely from the money supply.

During these first two years already the issuance of assignats had taken care of three-quarters of the entire state expenditures. Notwithstanding, until that time their issuance had been envisaged as a temporary emergency measure. With each new issue, an upper limit had been set to the total quantity to be issued, which was not to be exceeded. The outbreak of the first war against the European Coalition, which embroiled France in conflicts along all its borders, drained the State Treasury and led to the accelerated issue of assignats. No reliable figures are available for the number of assignats issued during the subsequent four-year period, in which no restrictions on their issuance was maintained, nor can it be ascertained exactly how great a depreciation of the assignats ensued. Suffice it to say that each year between 1792 and 1795 the assignats in circulation nearly doubled, so that after another doubling during the first nine months of 1796 (in which we include the 'territorial mandates', about which more later) a total of about 40 billion livres was probably reached.[39]

The history of these inflationary years is particularly instructive because it manifests for the first time all the typical features of later inflationary periods and also because the revolutionary government in France was neither better nor worse equipped to cope with the problems that arose than the governments of our times that resorted to inflation as a means of deficit financing. The official stand on the causes of the depreciation was no different from the one taken over and over in subsequent years by those who had been the perpetrators of the inflation. While the logic of the quantity theory of money, which had been so successfully propagated by Montesquieu,[40] clearly blamed devaluation on the proliferation of money, this explanation was emphatically rejected. The blame was placed

[39] [There still do not exist reliable estimates of the total circulation and value of the assignats, partly because daily records of issues were lost when the Finance Ministry burned in 1879. For some rough estimates see the table in the *Histoire économique et sociale de la France*, op. cit., vol. 3:1, p. 26, and the simple econometric work in Aftalion, op. cit., pp. 256-260. -Ed.]

[40] [*De l'esprit des loix*, op. cit. -Ed.]

alternately on speculation, enemy propaganda, the counterfeiting of assignats, and the shortage of food. The obvious fact that devaluation did not run exactly parallel with the increase in the money supply and that at times the value of the assignats even rose in the face of this increase was eagerly seized upon by contemporaries and by later opponents of the quantity theory of money to demonstrate that inflation was not responsible for the devaluation. It is true that Montesquieu's formulation of the quantity theory of money, which until recently remained the generally accepted formulation, insisted on a strict parallelism between the movement of prices and increases in the money supply, so that these objections were partially justified. In all periods of serious inflation it can be observed that devaluation soon begins to outstrip the proliferation of paper money because further increases in prices are expected, while concurrent speculative interventions may temporarily secure short periods of respite. Cantillon's more sophisticated but less widely known analysis might have accounted for these phenomena, which Montesquieu's more simplistic but also more influential theory could not explain.[41] The same applies with respect to the observation that the livre's exchange rate in international markets dropped more rapidly than devaluation progressed in France in terms of prices.

The same parallelism holds for the attempts made by the French government to halt the depreciation and similar measures taken by later governments. Devaluation manifested itself most clearly in the rising prices of precious metals and gold and silver coins. Severe penalties were enacted against the sale of gold and silver as well as coins at a higher price than the face value of the assignats and against accepting such payments. At times the penalty for such a transgression was enforced with barbaric severity and even included the death penalty. The outcome was that precious metals were completely withdrawn from circulation and were converted to private hoards, whereupon penalties were imposed for their mere possession. When prices rose alarmingly, the revolutionary government tried to cope with this by setting maximum prices first for grain and eventually for all essential commodities. These measures were able to stem price rises at least for short periods of time, especially during the so-called reign of terror. But since farmers in the countryside refused to supply food at these prices, enforced food deliveries were the inevitable next step. Taxes were in part collected *in natura*. The attempt to enforce maximum prices proved

---

[41] [See Hegeland, op. cit., chapter 2. -Ed.]

to be so stultifying to all branches of trade that shortly after the collapse of Robespierre's reign of terror these maxima were lifted. But as the devaluation of money continued unabated even after the victorious conclusion of the war, the depreciation of the assignats became increasingly obvious. In October 1794, their value fell to one-fifth and in April 1795 to only one-tenth of their face value in relation to their metallic equivalent. While the National Convention conducted endless debates about the best way to counter the depreciation during the following spring and summer and various experiments were made with introducing and again outlawing dealings in metallic currency, depreciation accelerated to such an extent that by September the assignats had dropped to one-fiftieth and by November to one-hundredth of their original value. Regulations began to be widely ignored and assignats were increasingly accepted only at their exchange value with respect to coins.

The Directoire, which came to power at the end of 1795, made one last desperate attempt to stem the devaluation of paper money, but without simultaneously stopping its proliferation. Experience had shown that the theoretical mortgaging of national lands as security for the assignats had not been able to prevent their depreciation. It was now believed that by eliminating this particular procedural flaw, through the issue of new paper money entitling the owner to land at a specific price, one could prevent further depreciation. New notes, the so-called territorial mandates, were issued in March 1796. These were actually promissory notes for the final territorial mandates, which would entitle the holder to purchase national land at twenty-two times the income yielded in 1790. But since the supporters of the assignats, which had meanwhile dropped to one three-hundredth of their original value, had succeeded in imposing a 30 to 1 trade-off between the assignats and the territorial mandates, thereby raising the purchase price of the latter accordingly, the fate of the new notes was also sealed. The sale of national land, which had legally been set at ridiculously low prices, had to be abruptly halted and completed sales revoked. The mandates, which had started out at 20 per cent of face value, fell within four months to 4 per cent and to 1 per cent by the end of the year. A contributing factor in this rapid depreciation was the legalisation in July of that year of metallic currency and the permission to trade assignats at their exchange value, thereby increasing the reluctance of commerce to accept the mandates. Large quantities of metallic currency resurfaced with surprising speed for commercial use. The reappearance of hoarded coins accounted only partially for this resurgence. Large quantities also poured in from abroad in exchange for commodities offered at relatively low prices by the cash-starved French population. As the government began to collect part of its taxes and other sums due in the form of metal currency or paper money at its market rate of exchange, the expansion of paper money came to a halt in the second half of 1796. The financial situation of the government remained precarious for years, to be sure, and various promissory paper notes had to be issued at times, but these were never confirmed as legal tender and depreciated independently, without having any impact on the general value of the monetary unit, which had meanwhile reverted to its metallic base. At the beginning of 1797, both assignats and mandates ceased to function as legal tender, thereby consummating the complete return to a metallic currency, which was not abandoned throughout all the vicissitudes of the following decade.

One interesting point, the unusual way in which the government regulated the repayment of debts after the return to metallic currency, deserves mention here. The transition from paper money to metal currency having taken place at fluctuating daily rates of exchange, the face value of the newly reintroduced metal coins was the same as that of the paper money, which had dropped to a fraction of its value. It was therefore impossible to prescribe a uniform conversion rate or to enforce repayment of debts incurred in paper money with metallic currency having the same face value. In one instance the creditor, whose claims dated from a time in which devaluation had been less severe, would be robbed of a large part of his due. In the second instance, the debtors, who had assumed their obligations in terms of depreciated assignats, would be forced to pay a much greater amount. To avoid these injustices, official tabulations were prepared showing the depreciation of the assignats on a month-by-month basis, so that each debt could be recalculated according to the official value of the assignats at the time that the debt was incurred.

ELEVEN

THE PERIOD OF RESTRICTIONS, 1797-1821, AND THE BULLION DEBATE IN ENGLAND

I

The appearance around the middle of the eighteenth century of Cantillon's and Hume's ground-breaking works had prepared the soil for systematic expositions of economics and particularly monetary theory, thereby enabling broader circles in England and France to acquire a scientific grounding in these areas[1]. Besides Montesquieu's and Turgot's widely translated works, this role was played initially by Sir James Steuart's and J. Harris's writings. They were all overshadowed, however, by the publication in 1776-7 of Adam Smith's immensely successful *Wealth of Nations*. Harris's book,[2] which might be considered the first modern textbook on monetary science,

---

[1] [For additional reading on the Restriction Period and the 'bullion controversy' consult Frank W. Fetter, *Development of British Monetary Orthodoxy 1797-1875* (Cambridge, Mass.: Harvard University Press, 1965); Sir John Clapham, *The Bank of England: A History*, 2 vols (Cambridge: Cambridge University Press, 1945); Jacob Viner, *Studies in the Theory of International Trade* (New York and London: Harper, 1937), pp. 119-217; Edwin Cannan, *The Paper Pound of 1797-1821* (London: P. S. King, 1919), pp. vii-xlvi; E. Victor Morgan, *The Theory and Practice of Central Banking 1797-1913* (Cambridge: Cambridge University Press, 1943), pp. 23-48; Charles Rist, *History of Monetary and Credit Theory from John Law to the Present Day*, trans. Jane Degras (New York: Macmillan, 1940), pp. 131-201; Arthur D. Gayer, W. W. Rostow, and Anna Jacobson Schwartz, *The Growth and Fluctuation of the British Economy, 1790-1850*, 2 vols (Oxford: Clarendon Press, 1953); and Lionel Robbins, *Robert Torrens and the Evolution of Classical Economics* (London: Macmillan, 1958). -Ed.]

[2] Anon. [J. Harris], *An Essay upon Money and Coins* (London: G. Hawkins, 1757-8). It is highly likely and can be proved with considerable certainty that Harris, like most of his English contemporaries, had encountered Cantillon not in the original but through the intermediary of M. Postlethwayt. Large sections of Cantillon's theoretical expositions on monetary theory were reproduced, presumably from Cantillon's original English manuscript, which has since been lost, in Postlethwayt's *Universal Dictionary of Trade and Commerce*, whose first edition came out in 1751, that is, a year before Hume's treatises on monetary theory and four years prior to the original edition of Cantillon's essay. In fact, part of the material was first printed two years earlier in Postlethwayt's prospectus for his *Universal Dictionary*. Nowhere is Cantillon mentioned by name either in the prospectus or in the *Dictionary*.

contains a fine presentation of the entire current state of knowledge of monetary theory, which freely reproduces Hume's and Cantillon's arguments without acknowledging any intellectual debt to these authors. Steuart[3] for his part stands out primarily as a fanatical opponent of the quantity theory of money, which he attacks with a set of brilliant but often unclear and in some respects antiquated notions.

Adam Smith for his part contributes very few significant advances in the field of monetary theory.[4] While providing a far greater abundance of ideas and facts about the monetary system than any previous author, as he does on many other subjects, he nevertheless falls short of his predecessors Cantillon and Hume in terms of theoretical insights. Yet so great has his influence been down to the present that his views cannot be neglected.

Smith first broaches the problems of the monetary system in connexion with the question of determining a general standard of value. It is due to his skilful exposition that precious metals have generally been recognised ever since as useful instruments for the short-run transfer of value, but as themselves subjected to decades-long slowly progressing changes in value, so that grains actually represent a much better long-range standard of value. We owe to Adam Smith the first full account of how increases in the value of money place a burden on debtors and create an advantage for creditors, while declines in the value of money are damaging to creditors and beneficial to debtors.[5] We also find in his work a

---

[3] *An Inquiry into the Principles of Political Economy* (London: n. p., 1767). [See the new edition, edited by Andrew S. Skinner (Chicago: University of Chicago Press, 1966). -Ed.]

[4] [See this volume, chapter 9. -Ed.]

[5] [Adam Smith was not the first to address these effects. It is worthwhile to compare his account with John Locke's earlier argument:

The standard once settled by public authority, the quantity of silver established under the several denominations (I humbly conceive) should not be altered till there were an absolute necessity shown of such a change, which I think can never be.

The reason why it should not be changed is this; because the public authority is guarantee for the performance of all legal contracts. But men are absolved from the performance of their legal contracts, if the quantity of silver under settled and legal denominations be altered; as is evident, if borrowing 100 *l.* or 400 ounces of silver, to repay the same quantity of silver (for that is understood by the same sum, and so the law warrants it) or taking a lease of lands for years to come, at the like rent of 100 *l.* they shall pay both the one and the other, in money coined under the same denominations, with one fifth less silver in it, than at the time of the bargain; the landlord here and creditor are each defrauded of twenty per cent. of what they contracted for, and is their due. And I ask, how much juster it would be thus to dissolve the contracts they had made, than to make a law, that from henceforth all landlords and creditors should be paid their past debts, and the rents for leases already made, in clipped money, twenty per cent. lighter than it should be? Both ways they lose twenty per cent. of their due, and with equal justice.

The case would be the same, and legal contracts be avoided, if the standard should be altered, on the other side, and each species of our coin be made one fifth heavier; for then he that had borrowed, or contracted for any sum, could not be discharged, by paying the quantity he agreed for, but be liable to be forced to pay twenty per cent. more than he bargained for, that is, more than he ought.

On the other side: Whether the creditor be forced to receive less, or the debtor be forced to pay more than his contract, the damage and injury is the same, whenever a man is defrauded of his due; and whether this will not be a public failure of justice thus arbitrarily to give one man's right and possession to another, without any fault on the suffering man's side, and without any the least advantage to the public, I shall leave to be considered.

Raising of coin is but a specious word to deceive the unwary. (John Locke, *Further Considerations Concerning Raising the Value of Money* (London: Printed for A. & J. Churchill, 1695); reprinted in *The Works of John Locke*, twelfth edition, vol. 4 (London: Printed for C. and J. Rivington, et al., 1824), pp. 144ff.)

The raising of the denomination of the coin has been the most usual expedient by which a real publick bankruptcy has been disguised under the appearance of a pretended payment. If a sixpence, for example, should either by act of parliament or royal proclamation be raised to the denomination of a shilling, and twenty sixpences to that of a pound sterling; the person who under the old denomination had borrowed twenty shillings, or near four ounces of silver, would, under the new, pay with twenty sixpences, or with something less than two ounces. A national debt of about a hundred and twenty-eight millions, nearly the capital of the funded and unfunded debt of Great Britain, might in this manner be paid with about sixty-four millions of our present money. It would indeed be a pretended payment only, and the creditors of the publick would really be defrauded of ten shillings in the pound of what was due to them. The calamity too would extend much further than to the creditors of the publick, and those of every private person would suffer a proportionable loss; and this without any advantage, but in most cases with a great additional loss, to the creditors of the publick. If the creditors of the publick indeed were generally much in debt to other people, they might in some measure compensate their loss by paying their creditors in the same coin in which the publick had paid them. But in most countries the creditors of the publick are, the greater part of them, wealthy people, who stand more in the relation of creditors than in that of debtors towards the rest of their fellow-citizens. A pretended payment of this kind, therefore, instead of alleviating, aggravates in most cases the loss of the creditors of the publick; and without any advantage to the publick, extends the calamity to a great number of other innocent people. It occasions a general and most pernicious subversion of the fortunes of private people; enriching in most cases the idle and profuse debtor at the expence of the industrious and frugal creditor, and transporting a great part of the national capital from the hands which were likely to increase and improve it, to those which are likely to dissipate and

detailed historical survey on the great fluctuations over the preceding three centuries in the value of money, in the wake of changes in the circumstances under which precious metals were produced. He scores his most complete success in fulfilling his historic mission of gaining general acceptance for the major insights attained up to his time by his persuasive refutation of the mercantilist view that the accumulation of the largest possible amount of money inside a country constitutes the prime objective of the government's economic policy (he somewhat simplified this view by defining it as a confusion of money with wealth). Though from a broader perspective this part of Smith's work may be considered his greatest achievement, his remarks on paper money, whose formulation is truly classic, carry far greater weight in attempts to understand the next phase in the development of monetary theory.[6] Contrary to Hume, who greatly influenced him in most questions of monetary theory, Smith is rather favourable to paper money. While Hume was strongly affected by the bad experiences people had had with it in Scotland in his day, recollections thereof had dimmed by the time that the *Wealth of Nations* was composed. On the other hand, the French experiment with assignats[7] still lay far ahead, and the Bank of England, which had kept its notes redeemable for over eighty years, seemed to be, in Smith's eyes, as reliable as the English government itself. He therefore considered the replacement of metallic currency by bank notes as desirable because "it replaces a very expensive instrument of commerce with one much less costly, and sometimes equally convenient", or, as he expressed it by an often-quoted simile, "the gold and silver money which circulates in any country may very properly be compared to a highway, which, while it circulates and carries to market all the grass and corn of the country, produces itself not a single pile of either. The judicious operations of banking, by providing, if I may be allowed so violent a metaphor, a sort of waggon-way through the air, enable the country to convert, as it were, a great part of its highways into

destroy it. (Adam Smith, *An Inquiry into the Nature and Causes of the Wealth of Nations*, in Campbell, Skinner, and Todd's edition, *The Glasgow Edition of the Works and Correspondence of Adam Smith* (Oxford: Clarendon Press, 1976), vols 2:1 and 2:2; reprinted Indianapolis, Ind.: Liberty*Classics*, 1981), vol. 2, pp. 929f.) -Ed.]

[6] Cf. especially book II, chapter 2, of *An Inquiry into the Nature and Causes of the Wealth of Nations*. [See Campbell, Skinner, and Todd's edition, op. cit., pp. 286-329. -Ed.]

[7] [See this volume, chapter 10, section IV. -Ed.]

good pastures and corn-fields, and thereby to increase very considerably the annual produce of its land and labour."[8]

Smith's disquisitions on the process whereby paper money replaces metallic currency are fundamental for later discussions. He asserts that in a country with a circulation of a million pounds in metal coins, in which a bank issues 800,000 pounds in paper notes, there will be an overflow of money in circulation, since there had originally been an adequate supply of money and the additional amount served no useful purpose. Since the paper money could not flow off abroad, as much gold and silver as had been issued in new notes would move out of the country, so that in the end domestic money circulation would be at the original level, but it would consist of eight-tenths paper and only one-fifth metallic currency.[9] "The whole paper money of every kind which can easily circulate in any country never can exceed the value of the gold and silver, of which it supplies the place, or which (the commerce being supposed the same) would circulate there, if there was no paper money."[10] In their own interest banks will not issue too many notes—Smith is thinking here exclusively of redeemable notes—inasmuch as any excess amount of notes will immediately be presented to them for redemption, and they will therefore often be compelled to buy the requisite gold at a premium over the mint price and thus incur a sizable loss. He describes how the Bank of England was forced for years to buy on average 850,000 pounds of gold a year at about 3 per cent above the mint price, in order to redeem these excess notes, whereby they incurred a considerable loss, quite aside from the additional coinage costs incurred by the state.

II

In the two decades following the publication of the *Wealth of Nations*, during which the economy expanded in every respect, there was no further stimulus to monetary theory. These were the years when England underwent the most intensive phase of the industrial revolution, by which is meant the application of technical inventions to the production process, and a huge industrial expansion ensued.

[8] [*Ibid.*, p. 321. -Ed.]
[9] [*Ibid.*, pp. 292-294. -Ed.]
[10] [*Ibid.*, p. 300. -Ed.]

Important developments in the sphere of credit and finances were associated with this industrial expansion. Their significance came to be recognised only in the course of the discussions that took place during the restriction period to which we shall now turn. The rapid development of the so-called country banks is the most noteworthy event of that time. These were small banks with a maximum of six partners, which were exempt from the Bank Act of 1742 applicable in England (but not Scotland).[11] Larger banks fell under the Act's prohibition to issue any notes. Country banks proliferated during these years of great economic prosperity. These country banks were in many cases very small banking operations, conducted on the side by businessmen along with their other business activities. They therefore constituted a very weak link in the continuously expanding credit structure, and often could not cope with the strains caused by economic crises, which arose periodically during these years. Another significant development was the increased use of cheques, which became especially noticeable after the 1793 crisis when private London bankers gave up their established right to issue notes and which led to an orderly clearing system between the different banks. This innovation was facilitated by the fact that both the country banks and the London bankers relied on the Bank of England to back their notes and deposits respectively. The only coverage for their own deposits were Bank of England notes or deposits with the Bank of England,[12] as they counted on being able to supplement these assets with further discounting of their own notes by the Bank of England. The Bank of England imperceptibly changed from being just a bank (or rather, a large bank among many small banks) to serving as the Bankers' Bank, the first modern central bank, whose function as the last resort for credit and cash for all other banks became far more important than its direct dealings with the public at large.

It is surely no accident that this change in the structure of the credit system coincided with the recurrence of periodic economic crises, which arose in 1763, 1772, 1783, and particularly 1793.

---

[11] [On the history of Scottish banking see Sydney G. Checkland, *Scottish Banking: A History, 1695-1973* (Glasgow: Collins, 1975); Lawrence H. White, *Free Banking in Britain: Theory, Experience, and Debate, 1800-1845* (Cambridge: Cambridge University Press, 1984), pp. 23-49; and Murray N. Rothbard, "The Myth of Free Banking in Scotland", *The Review of Austrian Economics*, vol. 2, 1988, pp. 229-245. -Ed.]

[12] [This type of banking structure is known in the literature as the inverted pyramid. The Bank of England issues notes using specie as reserves, and the country and London banks issue their own notes using Bank of England notes as their reserves; that is, they 'pyramid' credit on top of the Bank of England. -Ed.]

These crises gradually made the Bank of England aware of its changed position. During each crisis the Bank was faced with very heavy demands. During the crisis of 1783 it established a systematic policy, which was summarised as follows under the so-called Bosanquet rule, named after the Bank Governor:[13]

That while a drain of specie is going on, their issues should be contracted as much as possible, but that as soon as the tide had given signs of ceasing, and turning the other way, it was then safe to extend their issues freely.

When the Bank of England reasserted this policy in 1793, at the time of a violent crisis that coincided with the outbreak of the war with France, there ensued an extremely tight money supply. A panic was imminent and was barely averted by the government's offering to issue up to 5 million pounds in Exchequer bills to the commercial community, which could in turn be used to secure specie from the Bank of England. In the wake of this incident, concern about tight money loomed larger than fear of excessive note issues. The literature began to draw a distinction between the implication of gold withdrawal from the Bank of England arising from a greater domestic need for metallic currency and of withdrawal resulting from the export of gold—between an 'internal drain' and an 'external drain' of gold.

Before turning to the next critical date, namely the year 1797, which actually initiates the period with which this chapter is concerned, we must briefly state certain facts about currency policy which are essential for an understanding of our subsequent discussion. As mentioned earlier,[14] England had effectively been using a gold currency ever since the guinea had been set at 21 shillings, inasmuch as there was not the least incentive to mint silver at such an undervalued level. In view of the deteriorated condition of the

---

[13] Cf. Henry Dunning Macleod, *Theory and Practice of Banking*, reprint of its sixth edition (London and New York: Longmans, Green, 1902-11), vol. 1, p. 508, from which the exact wording given in the text is taken. Speaking before the parliamentary investigating committee appointed in 1797 in conjunction with the stoppage of the Bank of England's cash payments, S. Bosanquet formulated the rule in these terms: "Whenever there is an influx of Bullion into the country, the Banks have nothing to fear; when a drain takes place from the country, is in general the period for them to be alarmed." (Cf. *Reports from the Committees of Secrecy, (1797) On the Outstanding Demands of the Bank of England*, p. 25. [Reprinted in the *Irish University Press Series of British Parliamentary Papers* (Shannon, Ireland: Irish University Press, 1968-71), Monetary Policy, General, vol. 1, pp. 23-142. -Ed.])

[14] [I.e., in this volume, chapter 9. -Ed.]

silver coins that remained in circulation, a further step was taken in 1774 in the direction of a legal gold currency: silver coins were accepted as legal tender for payments in excess of 25 pounds only on the basis of their weight. Bank notes were issued only at 10-pound denominations by the Bank of England and at 5-pound denominations by the country banks, so that gold coins, that is, guineas (21 shillings), half guineas, and 7-shilling pieces provided the main stock of circulating money. The export of these gold coins and of gold obtained by melting down gold coins was forbidden by law. This legal restriction could not prevent the export of gold, when this was profitable, nor a rise in the market value of gold in its unminted form ('bullion'), but it sufficed to keep the guinea on a par with the paper notes. To avoid interrupting our subsequent discussion, we mention at this point that a year after the Bank of England had stopped its cash payments and thereby contributed to a relative increase in the value of gold, silver in turn ceased to be undervalued in English coins and minting silver appeared to be profitable again. To prevent the ensuing oversupply of silver, the free minting of silver was abolished. This step laid the legal foundations for a gold currency, which had effectively prevailed for the previous eighty years and culminated eighteen years later in a full legal recognition of the gold standard.

III

The events to which we now turn are directly connected with the war against France, in which England had been embroiled since 1793. The huge expenditures that it entailed raised government expenditures in Great Britain from an annual level of 26-28 million pounds in the three years prior to the outbreak of war to 70 million pounds in 1797. Even in the years before the war, part of government expenses had been financed by borrowing, and now regular state revenues could not even remotely keep pace with mounting expenditures. The fraction of total expenses financed by loans increased from 12 million pounds in 1793 to 53 million in 1797, or from 34.4 per cent to 71.2 per cent. Since it proved impossible to place such large long-term loans in the general population, the part that had to be placed as a floating debt with the Bank of England increased steadily, from 31.5 per cent of total annual new indebtedness in 1793 to a maximum of 80 per cent in 1796 and 1797. The salutary regulations which had been imposed on the Bank of England to prevent it from lending the government large amounts without express parliamentary consent had fallen into complete oblivion in recent decades and Prime Minister Pitt had lifted the regulations completely in the first years of the war, thus eliminating any serious obstacles to financing military expenses largely through bank credit. It must be kept in mind that a large part of these military expenses had to be remitted abroad, since England was fighting on the continent, and cash was therefore required. Commanders of the expeditionary troops cavalierly signed Exchequer bills drawn on the Bank of England, which the bank was forced to pay out in gold, though no cover had been provided for them. The large subsidies and loans that England had furnished to its allies, among them two loans to Austria totalling 6½ million pounds, had a similar impact. To compensate for the transfer of these large sums, which had not been raised by taxes but had been largely borrowed directly from the Bank of England, a very energetic policy of credit restriction at home had to be applied, if the exchange rates were not to suffer unduly. There were additionally, we might almost say, all conceivable circumstances conspiring to have an unfavourable temporary impact on the country's balance of trade and exerting pressure on the exchange rate. A series of unusually bad harvests made large imports of grains to England unavoidable, since England had turned from a grain-exporting to a grain-importing country by 1780 in response to increasing industrialisation. At the same time the export of English goods was hampered by the war with France and later by a systematic blockade against English trade. A further factor was the above-mentioned shift in value relations between gold and silver, which may have been somehow associated with the strong demand for gold in France after the elimination of the assignats, thus enhancing the gold drain from England. Each of these factors taken individually would have demanded vigorous credit restrictions to lower prices in England, increase English exports and reduce English imports, thereby restoring equilibrium. The Bank of England was severely handicapped in imposing such measures, because it could not successfully resist the demands of its major borrower, the government. When gold outflow began to assume more and more alarming proportions and exchange rates kept becoming more unfavourable for England, the Bank finally resorted to the only weapon at its disposal and energetically restricted the discounting of bills. Since usury laws prohibited raising the discount rate above 5 per cent, the only remaining means at its disposal was the rationing of credit, as we would now call it: it announced in December 1795 that henceforth it would set a daily limit to the total amount of bills to be discounted and that this amount would be divided up among the individual claimants without regard to the creditworthiness of each person. Although this measure aroused much commotion and indignation, it allowed the bank in the course of the next months to diminish the amount of notes in circulation, stem the rise in prices of commodities, and even to reverse the unfavourable exchange rate and halt the export of gold. In view of the unusually difficult circumstances, it took several months of credit restriction to bring the 'external drain' to a standstill, but even so, the Bank of England's gold holdings had been so sharply reduced that any new claim on them would cause serious difficulties to the Bank. The claim that finally led to a halt in cash payments came in the guise of an 'internal drain', that is, an outflow of gold for domestic use.

As invariably happens, credit restrictions coming on the heels of a period of credit expansion triggered an economic crisis, which in the course of 1796 assumed very serious dimensions and was exacerbated particularly by the fact that the Bank of England persevered in its restrictive policy despite the return of a favourable exchange rate. Political uncertainty was one of the contributing factors in the collapse of an unusually large number of firms, amongst them many country banks. The resulting crisis of confidence reached its climax in February 1797, when a single French frigate landed troops in the Bay of Wales and the French invasion, which had long been feared, seemed imminent. As the Bank of England had already experienced a large gold drain in the first weeks of the year, this incident induced such a violent run on the Bank that its currency reserves, which had amounted to 2½ million pounds at the end of 1796, dwindled to half that amount in a matter of days. The directors of the Bank of England appealed to Prime Minister Pitt, who convoked a special Crown Council, in which it was decided by royal decree that the Bank would be prohibited from redeeming its notes and other obligations in gold. When the Bank opened its counters the following morning, February 27, this decree had already been posted, together with an explanation on the part of the Bank stating that its situation was altogether sound and that there was no occasion to doubt the security of its notes. The fact that this startling event failed to arouse greater concern is probably due not so much to the Bank's statement as to the resolution passed by a gathering of the most highly respected members of the London mercantile community, which was convoked at once, and in which it was solemnly declared that the undersigned were willing to accept bank notes for all kinds of payments. This resolution received the signature of 4,000 persons within a very short period of time.

After the Crown Council had formally transmitted the royal decree to parliament for a legislative ruling on the matter, parliament sanctioned the decree by passage of the Bank Restriction Act of May 3, 1797, after both Houses had appointed special investigating committees, in which quite intense debates had taken place.[15]

Although the new law was intended to remain in effect only until the 24th of June, or about seven weeks, it was actually in force for nearly a quarter-century. In addition to its prohibition of cash payments, from which, however, payments to the army and navy and repayment of money deposited after promulgation of the law were exempted, the Restriction Act contained a provision limiting advances to the government during the restriction period to 600,000 pounds. It also contained ambiguously worded provisions about the use of bank notes as a means of payment, which intentionally avoided assigning them a compulsory value, that is, giving them the status of legal tender. The same object was nearly achieved, however, by stating that the notes were to be accepted at face value for all payments to the state and by hindering the courts from enforcing payments in cash.

It is nearly impossible to judge today whether under the given circumstances, which had been caused by the government's requests from the Bank of England and, to some extent, to be sure, by the Bank's own misguided policy, it would have been possible to avert stoppage of cash payments and whether, as Ricardo[16] later claimed, the run on the Bank would have come to a halt before its cash reserve had been completely exhausted, had the Bank continued paying in gold. The desire to maintain a gold reserve for military needs undoubtedly contributed to the government's decision. But even if it were legitimate to lift the Bank's obligation to make cash payments temporarily, nothing justified keeping the Restriction Act in force beyond the next few weeks; all the more since the favourable exchange rate resulted in a large influx of gold to the Bank, so that its cash holdings exceeded 4 million in August and rose to as much as 7½ million pounds in the course of the first two years

---

[15] Cf. the text of the law in Johannes Wolter, *Das staatliche Geldwesen Englands zur Zeit der Bank-restriction (1797 bis 1821)* (Strasbourg: K. J. Trübner, 1917), vol. 33 of *Abhandlungen aus dem Staatswissenschaftlichen Seminar zu Straßburg*. [The text of the law is given in English. -Ed.]

[16] *Proposals for an Economical and Secure Currency* [1816], reprinted in J. R. McCulloch, *Works of David Ricardo* (London: John Murray, 1846), p. 406. [See also *The Works and Correspondence of David Ricardo*, in 11 vols, edited by Piero Sraffa, with the collaboration of M. H. Dobb (Cambridge: Cambridge University Press for the Royal Economic Society, 1951-73), vol. 4, p. 68. -Ed.]

after the passage of the Restriction Act. Notwithstanding, the Act was first prolonged to one month after the reopening of parliament. After a new investigation by a parliamentary committee[17] in the autumn, it was extended to a month after the conclusion of a peace treaty. One of the reasons that the Act was so readily accepted was that this measure, which had originally aroused such great misgivings, produced no clearly harmful effects in the first few years. But this in turn was due to the fact that during the first two years of restriction the government's requests from the Bank were fairly restrained and that during the prevailing economic depression there was no inducement for the Bank to overextend the circulation of its notes for the purpose of granting commercial credit.

IV

Around the beginning of 1800 this situation changed markedly. The unsatisfactory receipts from new taxes introduced to pay for war expenses, particularly the new income tax, forced Pitt to rely more heavily again on borrowings. As a first step in that direction, he allowed the Bank of England to purchase an extension of its privilege, which would have expired only in 1812, by a loan of 3 million pounds. He also drew on its credit in other ways. With a rapid increase of the notes in circulation, exchange rates seriously deteriorated in mid-1799 and a substantial increase in prices arose. What caused most concern, however, was the circumstance that concurrently, by the very nature of things, the price of unminted gold ('bullion') rose above the price of minted gold by a large margin and attained a premium of about 10 per cent in the fall of 1800. These signs of a rather large devaluation of the English currency, which actually—it should be mentioned at once— disappeared again to some extent in the next years, stimulated the first important discussions in print of the monetary problems connected with these phenomena. This discussion brought to the fore nearly all the doctrines which were widely disseminated only at a later stage of these deliberations, which culminated in the famous Bullion Report of 1810. Even today these doctrines are attributed almost exclusively to the participants in the later discussion, notably

---

[17] Cf. *Report from the Committee of Secrecy upon the Restriction of Payments in Cash by The Bank,* 1797. [Reprinted in the *Irish University Press Series of British Parliamentary Papers,* op. cit., Monetary Policy, General, vol. 1, pp. 141-142. -Ed.]

to Ricardo. The Restriction Act of 1797 had occasioned a flood of polemical publications, but the only work that possibly deserves to be mentioned is Sir Francis Baring's[18] presentation of the events leading up to the stoppage of cash payments, which, however, makes a rather poor case for the Bank of England's policy. Serious discussion of the issue was delayed until the beginning of 1801, when Walter Boyd's letter to Prime Minister Pitt,[19] which had already been sent off in early November of the previous year, was published two months later with an explanatory preface.

Boyd had been one of the most determined opponents of the continued policy of contraction by the Bank of England in the face of the recovery of exchange rates and had, in fact, experienced the failure of his own bank. He was now the first to attribute the generally recognised rise in prices to the over-issue of notes by the Bank of England. It had been reserved to him, he writes[20] "to assign, as the cause of the general rise, which almost all things have experienced, within the last two or three years (and which grain, as the article that comes most frequently in contact with money, feels the soonest and the most) to the existence of a great Bank, invested with the power of issuing paper, professing to be payable on demand, but which, in fact, the Bank which issues it, is not obliged to pay." Interestingly enough, when Boyd sent his letter to Pitt, the actual changes that had taken place in note circulation were not known, since at that time the Bank did not yet publish any reports; so that Boyd could only surmise the increased circulation of bank notes from circumstantial evidence. He based his contention on the general rise in the price level, which was too familiar to be in need of proof, and on the deterioration in the exchange rate of the pound in Hamburg, which had fallen from 35.20 in February 1797 to 31.1 in November 1800, as well as on the rise in the price of gold. He cleverly refuted the prevalent explanations which ascribed each of these phenomena to specific causes, such as the shortage of grain, speculation, population increase, or the war. All these causes might account for the price rise of specific commodities or a temporary deterioration of exchange rates, but they could not explain

---

[18] Sir Francis Baring, *Observations on the Establishment of the Bank of England and of the Paper Currency of the Country* (London: Sewell, Cornhill, and Debrett, 1797).

[19] *A Letter to the Right Honourable William Pitt, on the Influence of the Stoppage of Issues in Specie at the Bank of England: on the Prices of Provisions, and other Commodities* (London: Printed for J. Wright by T. Gillet, 1801; second edition, 1801; third edition, revised by the author: James Ridgway, 1811).

[20] [*Ibid.*, 1811 edition, p. 60. -Ed.]

their persistence and the continuing premium on gold. It was all too likely that the directors had succumbed to the temptation of expanding the notes in circulation, since this was a profitable operation for them. They were now no longer inhibited from the over-issue of notes, inasmuch as the mechanism which had kept them in check before the prohibition of cash payments, namely the presentation of excess notes for redemption in gold for export, had been dismantled.

The over-issue of notes could therefore be blamed only on the Bank of England, not, as was commonly assumed, on provincial banks, since only the former had been liberated from the obligation to redeem notes, while the latter were obliged to redeem their notes in notes of the Bank of England. In this context Boyd makes a particularly interesting observation, to which due attention was not paid again until many years later, in the recent period of great inflation.[21]

It lies in Boyd's recognition that the devaluation of money at home proceeds more gradually than does that of the country's exchange rate, so that there may be a transient boost to the country's exports while its money deteriorates.

Boyd had the satisfaction of seeing his contention impressively confirmed by newly publicised information even before his letter to Pitt appeared in print. A report drawn up by the Bank of England in response to a parliamentary request showed that the circulation of its notes had increased between the time that cash payments were stopped and the 6th of December 1800 from 8.6 to 15.5 million pounds. Additional evidence, which Boyd mentions in his preface, is the pound's further decline in Hamburg from 9 per cent to 14 per cent in the two months between the writing of his letter and its publication, as well as a further small increase in the price of bullion. Under these circumstances, Boyd's assertions could not fail to make a strong impression. The publication of the letter stimulated a lively discussion in print, with Sir Francis Baring as one of the participants reiterating his defence of the Bank of England in rather awkward terms.[22] Among these publications there is one work of such disproportionate merit that it deserves to be discussed in greater detail—Henry Thornton's *An Enquiry into the Nature and*

---

[21] [E.g., the German hyperinflation of 1922-3, in which the value of the deutsche mark fell from 275 marks to the dollar in May 1922 to 16,667 in June 1923. -Ed.]

[22] Sir Francis Baring, *Observations on the Publication of Walter Boyd* (London: J. Sewell, 1801).

of the Paper Credit of Great Britain.[23] Henry Thornton,[24] one of the most highly respected personalities in the City and a member of parliament, was equipped not only with unusually solid knowledge but also with a rare theoretical talent in his work. His book deserves to be ranked as one of the few outstanding achievements in the development of monetary theory. Its only flaw, a flaw that often mars theoretical investigations by practical men, is its unsystematic and incoherent structure, which makes it hard reading. For that reason its great and speedy impact was attributable less to the immediate popularity of the book than to the excellent restatement of its contents in Francis Horner's detailed review, published at the beginning of the following year in the new *Edinburgh Review.*[25] Since Horner, Thornton, and a third author jointly drew up the Bullion Report, we shall refer interchangeably to Thornton's book and Horner's review thereof in our comments.

Thornton's book is outstanding both as the first careful description of the entire credit structure that had developed in England in the previous decades and as a theoretical analysis of the relations between the quantity of money, prices, and exchange rates. Discussion at this juncture was increasingly concentrated on the determinants of the latter. Controversy centred on a question that was to be the subject of repeated debate in similar situations, particularly in the inflationary years after 1918, though on a far less sophisticated theoretical level, to wit, whether the fall in the exchange rate and the related increase in the price of gold bullion should be ascribed to a deterioration in the balance of payments or to an excessive expansion of paper money circulation. Let it be clarified at once that in these early years the discussion was hampered by the fact that the drop in the value of the pound was linked only to an

[23] Henry Thornton, *An Enquiry into the Nature and Effects of the Paper Credit of Great Britain* [1802], reprinted in J. R. McCulloch, *A Select Collection of Scarce and Valuable Tracts and other Publications, on Paper, Currency and Banking* (London: n. p., 1857) [reprinted Fairfield, N.J.: Augustus M. Kelley, 1978. See also Hayek's edition of Thornton's *Paper Credit* (London: Allen & Unwin, 1939), the introduction to which is reprinted in this volume as chapter 14. -Ed.]

[24] Not to be confused with his brother Samuel Thornton, who was at that time Governor of the Bank of England, and who was well known as a witness at the various parliamentary investigations of that period. [See this volume, chapter 14. -Ed.]

[25] *The Edinburgh Review or Critical Journal,* vol. 1, no. 1, October 1802, Art. XXV, pp. 172-201 [reprinted in Frank W. Fetter, ed., *The Economic Writings of Francis Horner in the Edinburgh Review 1802-6* (New York: Kelley & Millman, 1957), pp. 28-56. -Ed.]. Horner's reviews of books by Thornton and King appeared in a German translation by Adam Müller in the collection *Die Fortschritte der nationalökonomischen Wissenschaft in England während des laufenden Jahrhunderts* (Leipzig and Oltenburg: Brockhaus, 1817).

absolute increase in the amount of money in circulation. Nobody had as yet asserted that in the face of a deteriorating balance of payments, such as the one which had undoubtedly been caused by the circumstances we mentioned earlier, the exchange rates could only have maintained their stability if the domestic money in circulation had been reduced and the price level lowered, a mechanism that would have been triggered automatically under the gold standard by the outflow of gold.[26] Thornton, however, vigorously upheld the policy of the Bank of England on this score and believed that he could refute the claim that there had been an over-issue of notes by showing that the increased circulation of notes compared with the pre-war average was barely sufficient to replace the gold coins that had disappeared from circulation. Although he was mistaken in this respect, his stand is plausible to the extent that, at the time that he was writing, the bank had once more reduced its notes in circulation compared with the temporary maximum reached in 1800 and that the exchange rate of the pound had consequently improved again and remained relatively stable for the next seven years.

Irrespective of his evaluation of the current situation, Thornton shows a most unusual grasp of the determinants of exchange rates and is the first to describe the mechanism whereby the equilibrium of the exchange rate is restored in the face of a deterioration of the balance of payments resulting from increased demand for grain after bad harvests, large payments abroad, etc. He builds the foundations of this theory by starting out with an extension of Boyd's doctrine that the country banks could not possibly have indulged in an over-issue of notes. He goes much further than Boyd, who only pointed out that the country banks for their part were not exempt from the obligation to redeem their notes, like the Bank of England, and were compelled to redeem their own notes at any time against those of the Bank of England. Thornton proceeds to elucidate the mechanism whereby any excess in the quantity of notes issued immediately flows back to the country banks. The local price rise instigated by the increase in the country bank's notes must in due course lead to the inflow of commodities from other places and to what one might call a deterioration of the balance of payments of this locality. As a result the country bank will be obliged to turn over larger sums in notes of the Bank of England

---

[26] [The automatic mechanism referred to is Hume's price-specie-flow mechanism, discussed in this volume, chapter 9, section VII. -Ed.]

or in gold to pay for these commodities, or it will be presented with large numbers of notes by the sellers of these commodities, which it will have to exchange against gold or notes of the Bank of England. Thornton then extends the same mechanism to relations between two countries with differing monetary systems and links this analysis to a criticism of Adam Smith's earlier mentioned doctrine that an overabundant amount of money in circulation will create an 'overflow'. He rightly takes exception to this concept because it fails to give any explanation of the way in which this overflow comes about. Money as such would never become unutilisable just because of its quantity; rather, the quantity of money can affect the outflow or inflow of gold only through the intermediary of commodity prices. An increase in the quantity of money would first raise prices and thereby hamper the export of commodities, stimulate imports, and hence induce a temporary deterioration of the balance of payments, which would necessitate an export of gold. The fact is that gold will remain the cheapest commodity to export until the point is reached when gold is reduced to such a small amount in the country that its price rises again, which means that the price of all other commodities, expressed in gold, has become lower again, whereby the equilibrium between import and export will be restored.

The same mechanism will operate in reverse when there initially occurs a reduction in the amount of money in circulation and prices fall domestically. In contrast to the views later presented by Ricardo, Thornton makes it clear in his theoretical analyses that such gold movements can be set in motion not only by prior changes in prices but also by independent changes in the balance of payments, such as the particularly relevant case of having to make large payments abroad in the form of subsidies, for the upkeep of expeditionary troops or unusual grain imports. Thornton demonstrates how the exchange rates of the country that must make such payments will deteriorate at first; subsequently gold exports will occur, until finally the resulting reduction in the money supply induces the requisite increase in the export of commodities and decrease in imported commodities, which will allow the payments to be made in kind rather than in gold. Although Thornton correctly assessed this sequence of events in theoretical terms, he fails to realise that the only way the pound's rate of exchange could have been kept from sinking below the gold point and the rise in the price of gold bullion could have been prevented would have been to produce such a reduction of the money in circulation in England. Despite this flaw in the application of his analysis, Thornton must be recognised as the first to formulate the so-called classical theory of exchange rates. It gained wide acceptance when it was later adopted by John Stuart Mill and has survived in the current literature under the name of purchasing power parity theory without significant changes.[27] Its originator was certainly not Ricardo, who in fact opposed it in some respects, as we already mentioned. We shall come back to this point more fully.

Thornton criticises Adam Smith on another point, which is highly important for his approach and which helps him develop his own doctrine. Smith had claimed that the issue of paper money displaced an exactly equivalent amount of gold from circulation. Thornton denies this claim by stating that the velocity of circulation of paper money is much slower than that of gold coins. He uses this occasion to explore more fully than any previous author or any author many decades after him, what circumstances determine the differences in velocity of circulation of the various types of money and the fluctuations therein. He shows how fear of progressive devaluation of money accelerates this velocity, but he is even more concerned about the fact that conversely, in times of crisis, when everyone attempts to hoard cash, the velocity of circulation is reduced and may trigger a serious shortage of money. The major part of the first half of Thornton's book is devoted to a detailed presentation of the dangers of such a scarcity of money. Suffice it to recognise here its major contribution to economic science: gaining acceptance for the principle that in the face of gold withdrawals caused by such a domestic shortage of money, that is, an 'internal drain', the correct response for a note-issuing bank is to maintain the level of circulating money rather than decrease it, if a panic is to be avoided. We shall now turn to Thornton's final and perhaps most significant contribution, which has been nearly neglected until now. It concerns the foundations of the discount policy pursued by note-issuing banks.[28]

Thornton raises the question whether there exists a natural tendency to keep note circulation within limits that exclude a dangerous devaluation of notes. In answering this question he first demonstrates that neither reliance on the wealth of the borrower nor limitation to genuine commodity-backed notes can offer assurance against this danger. Even if these two aspects are taken into account, it would not prevent an unreasonable increase in the

---

[27] [See, for example, Viner, op. cit., pp. 379-387. -Ed.]

[28] Chapter X, especially pp. 283-290 of the original edition and pp. 399-410 of the German translation. [Pp. 251-256 in the Hayek edition, op. cit. -Ed.]

number of borrowers nor an unwarranted proliferation of commodity-based notes. Thornton reiterates emphatically that every time the prevailing profit rate in business exceeded the interest rate of the bank, there would be a tendency to over-issue notes. The bank should therefore attempt to adjust its interest rate to the market rate. Thornton thereby not only resolved in advance a controversy that was to rage in the middle of the nineteenth century between the currency and the banking schools,[29] but even anticipated by nearly a century K. Wicksell's theory[30] about the significance of the 'money interest rate' falling behind the 'natural' interest rate.[31]

At the time that Thornton's book was published, the peace treaty concluded with France in April 1802 created a new situation, which led to new discussions about lifting or maintaining the Restriction Act. In view of the improvements in the exchange rate and the consolidated position of the Bank of England, it would undoubtedly have been feasible not to renew the provision exempting the Bank of England from making cash payments, and to let the law expire, as planned, one month after peace had been concluded. In the face of a vigorous opposition, the government nevertheless obtained another year's extension and, when, a year later, a new war with France seemed imminent, the restriction remained in force. Among the opponents of the extension Lord Peter King, to whom we shall come back later in another context, played a prominent role. His speech against the extension of the Restriction Act in parliament in

---

[29] [See this volume, chapter 12. -Ed.]

[30] [See Knut Wicksell, *Geldzins und Güterpreise bestimmenden Uraschen* [1898], translated by R. F. Kahn as *Interest and Prices* (London: Macmillan, 1936; reprinted New York: Augustus M. Kelley, 1965). See also Thomas M. Humphrey, "Cumulative Process Models from Thornton to Wicksell", Federal Reserve Bank of Richmond *Economic Review*, vol. 72, no. 3, May-June 1986, pp. 18-25. -Ed.]

[31] [This is a key reference in the development of Hayek's theoretical work in economics. He combined the concept of a difference in the 'money interest rate' and the 'natural' interest rate with insights gained from statistical investigations of the US economy by the then newly established Federal Reserve Banks to produce the ideas found in *Monetary Theory and the Trade Cycle* (*Geldtheorie und Konjunkturtheorie*, Beitrage zur Konjunkturforschung, herausgegeben vom Österreichisches Institut für Konjunturforschung, no. 1, Vienna, 1929; translated and reprinted as *Monetary Theory and the Trade Cycle* (Clifton, N.J.: Augustus M. Kelley, 1966)). The product of Hayek's early visit to the United States in 1922 was "Die Wahrungspolitik der Vereinigten Staaten seit der Überwindung der Krise von 1920" published in *Zeitschrift für Volkswirtschaft und Sozialpolitik*, N.S. 5, 1925. A section of this work was translated and published as "The Monetary Policy of the United States After the Recovery from the 1920 Crisis", in *Money, Capital and Fluctuations, Early Essays*, ed. Roy McCloughry (London: Routledge & Kegan Paul, 1984), p. 5. The complete translation appears in vol. 6 of *The Collected Works of F.A. Hayek*. -Ed.]

1803 was published as a pamphlet,[32] and ranks with Boyd's and Thornton's works among the best publications of that year.

Although the pamphlet contains no theoretical innovations, it applies the ideas of the two other authors so lucidly to the current situation that it quickly overshadowed their writings in the public mind. King points with such great firmness to the rise in the market price of gold bullion and the fall of the exchange rate and the evidence and degree of devaluation of paper money that H. D. Macleod referred to this insight straightforwardly as King's law.[33]

King is the first, moreover, to have supplemented his theoretical arguments with comprehensive statistical data on the movement of the exchange rates, prices, circulation of precious metal and notes in the preceding years, so that his pamphlet serves even today as an important source of information about the actual situation at the time.

When King's pamphlet appeared, a new currency question was coming to the attention of wider circles. Its exploration was to prove particularly instructive for the English in the years that followed, during which little changed in the situation of the English currency. This new question therefore contributed greatly to a clarification of opinions. In 1797 the Bank of Ireland had been exempted from the obligation to make cash payments, together with the Bank of England, 'for the sake of uniformity', although it was in a much more favourable position than the Bank of England, and the Irish exchange rates were favourable as well. The directors of the Bank of Ireland exploited their freedom to expand their note circulation without penalty to an even greater extent than did those of the Bank of England; the amount of notes outstanding had quadrupled between February 1797 and February 1803 and the self-evident consequence was that the Irish exchange rate, which was generally above par in England until 1797, fell to about 20 per cent below par. It was particularly striking that this deterioration applied only to bills of exchange drawn in those areas in which the notes of the Bank of Ireland circulated, whereas there had been practically

---

[32] *Thoughts on the Restriction of Payments in Specie at the Banks of England and Ireland* (London: Cadell & Davies, 1803); second edition entitled *Thoughts on the Effects of the Bank Restrictions* (London: Cadell & Davies, 1804). The pamphlet was fully reviewed by F. Horner in the *Edinburgh Review*, vol. 2, no. 4, July 1803, Art. XI, pp. 402-421 [reprinted in Fetter, *Writings of Francis Horner*, op. cit., pp. 77-95. -Ed.] and Lord King's reply thereto appears in an appendix to the second edition of the pamphlet.

[33] *The Theory and Practice of Banking* (London: Longman, Brown, Green, & Longmans, 1855 and later). Cf. vol. 1, pp. 387ff. of the 1925 edition.

no decline for the notes drawn on Belfast, which continued to use metallic currency and notes of local banks. As a result of these conditions, the value of money varied within Ireland, and notes against Dublin were accepted at a discount in Belfast just as they were in London. These phenomena could not but make it obvious even to the less discerning that the deterioration of the Irish notes was attributable to an over-issue of notes by the Bank of Ireland.

Discussion concerning this Irish currency problem spawned a whole set of critical treatises, some of them outstanding.[34] It also led the English parliament to appoint its first special committee on paper currency. At the hearings of this committee and in its report[35] the confrontation between the so-called 'Bullionist' group, who held the same views as Boyd, Thornton, Horner, and King, and the supporters of the policy of the Bank of England and the Bank of Ireland manifested itself clearly for the first time. Although it received relatively little notice and was soon nearly forgotten, the committee report already contains nearly all the ideas of the famous 'Bullion Report' of 1810, which will have to be discussed in greater detail because of its wider influence. A single point will be men-

---

[34] The most notable among them are: Henry Parnell, *Observations upon the State of Currency in Ireland, and upon the Course of Exchange between Dublin and London* (Dublin: Printed for M. N. Mahon, 1804); John Leslie Foster, *An Essay upon the Principles of Commercial Exchanges* (London: J. Hatchard, 1804); Lord Lauderdale, *Thoughts on the Alarming State of the Circulation, and on the Means of Redressing the Pecuniary Grievances in Ireland* (Edinburgh: A. Constable, 1805). [See also the bibliography in Frank W. Fetter, *The Irish Pound 1797-1826* (London: Allen & Unwin, 1955), pp. 125-128. -Ed.] Of special importance are the ambitious but largely neglected works by John Wheatley, *Remarks on Currency and Commerce* (London: Cadell & Davies, 1803), and *An Essay on the Theory of Money and Principles of Commerce* (London: Printed for T. Cadell & W. Davies, by W. Bulmer and Co., 1807; vol. 2, 1822). The only completely systematic monograph about monetary science originating during the bullion controversy is Charles Jenkinson, Earl of Liverpool's history of the English coinage system, which is noteworthy for its clear presentation and further elaboration of the modern interpretation of exchange rates initiated by Thornton (*A Treatise on the Coins of the Realm; in a Letter to the King* (Oxford: At the University Press, for Cadell and Davies, London, 1805; reissued 1880 by the Bank of England)). This work constitutes the most important source on its subject even today. It also developed the proposals that led to the coinage reform of 1816, in which the gold standard was finally adopted and silver coins were relegated to the role of small change.

[35] *Report, Minutes of evidence, and Appendix, from the Committee on the Circulating Paper, the Species and the Current Coin of Ireland; and also on the Exchange between that Part of the United Kingdom and Great Britain*, May and June 1804, reprinted 1826. [Also reprinted, with an introduction by Frank W. Fetter, as *The Irish Pound 1797-1826*, op. cit. -Ed.] This committee was formed on the motion of J. L. Foster (mentioned in the above footnote). Both Foster and Sheridan were members of this committee, as well as of the subsequent 'Bullion Committee'.

tioned about this earlier and in some respects more interesting report. It concerns the defence of the directors of the Bank of Ireland against the reproach that they had overextended their notes in circulation. The argument that they presented was later adopted by the Bank of England and the government, but it was stated more frankly and less ambiguously than was done six years later by their English colleagues. On one score, however, they merely needed to apply the arguments used earlier by the Bank of England to their special situation. They too asserted that the unfavourable state of the exchange rate was due exclusively to the large payments abroad, in their case payments of the Irish leaseholders to the landowners, who mostly lived in England (the much discussed 'absentee owners'). To this was added the later much-favoured assertion that it was not their notes that had in any way depreciated, but the rise in the price of gold which had caused a premium. In conclusion they stated explicitly that, since the obligation to make cash payments had been lifted, they no longer felt that it was their duty to regulate circulation along the same principles as when notes had to be redeemed in cash. They now regulated circulation on 'entirely different principles', namely according to the need for credit. They completely ignored the fact that Thornton had already totally refuted their claim that they could avert the devaluation of the bank notes in this manner. The committee's recommendation that the Bank of Ireland be obliged to redeem its notes at all times at least with notes of the Bank of England, which was meant to prevent it from over-issuing notes, did not prevail. However, under the impact of the committee's investigation, apparently, the Bank of Ireland attempted and largely succeeded in reducing the circulation of its notes to a more modest amount.

V

The currency situation in England from 1803 to 1808 had offered little incentive to continue discussions on the subject, but in the fall of 1808 there occurred a new rise in the price of gold and in the foreign exchange rate. The intensification of the struggle against Napoleon was accompanied by a large increase in government expenditures, which had to be covered once more by notes issued by the Bank of England. The pressure exerted directly on the exchange rate by increased payments to the expeditionary force and imposition of the continental blockade accelerated the inflationary tendency that had been fanned by demands for credit on the part of the business community. It so happened that in 1808 and 1809 new opportunities for English overseas trade presented themselves with the re-opening of communications with Portuguese and Spanish possessions in Central and South America, after several years of severe constraints due to the military situation. The credit offered by the Bank of England at the extremely low rate of 5 per cent was therefore exploited to the fullest and triggered a period of extremely lively speculation, which ended in a serious crisis in 1810. Critical observers began to express concern at the rise in prices, which came in response to the recent increases to about 20 per cent above par both of the bullion price of gold and of the foreign exchange rates.

As it happened, the first important publication to fall within this time interval was David Ricardo's initial literary manifestation. An unsigned communication by him was printed in the London daily, *The Morning Chronicle*, in late August 1809, in which Ricardo attacked the progressive devaluation of bank notes with the same line of arguments that had been presented in earlier writings by Boyd, Thornton, and King. He refuted the contention that it was not the notes that had fallen in value but gold that had increased in value. He also recommended that parliament request a gradual reduction of the note circulation of the Bank of England and predicted that the price of gold would thereby be lowered to its mint price and that the exchange rates would come back to par.[36] Ricardo objects with special vehemence against the often repeated argument that stoppage of cash payment should remain in effect as long as the exchange rates are unfavourable and counters it with the statement that the resumption of cash payments would be the surest means of raising the exchange rate of the pound to parity. Ricardo published two additional anonymous communications in *The Morning Chronicle* in response to various replies in this and other newspapers. At the end of the year he published his extremely well-known pamphlet *The High Price of Bullion, a Proof of the Depreciation of Bank Notes*.[37]

---

[36] Ricardo's communication was published in *The Morning Chronicle* of August 29, 1809, and further communications appeared in its issues for September 20 and November 23 of the same year. All three communications were reprinted by J. H. Hollander as *Three Letters on the Price of Gold* (Baltimore, Md.: The Johns Hopkins University Press, 1903). [Also reprinted in the Sraffa edition of Ricardo's *Works*, op. cit., vol. 3, pp. 13-46. -Ed.]

[37] London: John Murray, 1810. Two additional and partially supplemented editions appeared within a few months. A fourth edition was published in 1811, with a voluminous appendix, which will be discussed more fully later. The latter edition is reprinted in *The Works of David Ricardo*, ed. J. R. McCulloch, op. cit., and in *Economic Essays, by David Ricardo*, ed. E. C. K. Gonner (London: Frank Cass, 1923). A partially

This work was probably largely composed several years earlier, but is incorrectly considered by most people as the cradle of 'Bullionist' doctrine. The fact of the matter is that none of Ricardo's early publications contain any essential new insights, as he himself emphasises at the end of his pamphlet, though they are as impressive in their lucidity and sharpness as Lord King's earlier pamphlet. Ricardo's tendency towards simplification and polemical exaggeration may even have led him to sacrifice certain insights that had already been gained, particularly with respect to one point, where he criticises Thornton, with whom he otherwise largely agrees. While Ricardo incorporates unaltered the main features of Hume's, Smith's, and Thornton's analysis—that is, their doctrine about the international distribution of precious metals, the mechanism of bimetallism, the relation between the Bank of England and the country banks, and the purely temporary lowering of the interest rate through the increase in money supply[38]—he challenges Thornton's contention that a temporarily unfavourable balance of payments—occasioned by a poor harvest—could lead to an outflow of gold without any prior deterioration of the currency. He rightly objects to Thornton's recommendation that the Bank replenish the vacuum created in the money supply by this outflow of gold by increasing its issue of notes. He is mistaken, however, when he questions Thornton's assertion that an unfavourable balance of payments could cause an outflow of gold on the ground that it would first have to be explained why other countries were unwilling to accept the deficit in commodities rather than exclusively in gold. In his view, this could be accounted for only by the fact that the money supply had become excessive.

Thornton is completely right, however, when he shows that the only way payment for the extra imports can lead to an increase in exports is through the outflow of gold, which eventually produces a lowering of the domestic commodity prices.[39] As mentioned earlier,

---

flawed translation of excerpts can be found in *Ausgewählte Lesestücke zum Studium der politischen Ökonomie*, ed. K. Diehl and P. Mombert, vol. 1, *Zur Lehre vom Gelde* (Karlsruhe: G. Braun, 1911). [See the Sraffa edition of Ricardo's *Works*, op. cit., vol. 3, pp. 47-127. -Ed.]

[38] The later well-known distinction between 'natural interest rates' and 'money interest rates' introduced by Wicksell already appears almost exactly in this formulation in Ricardo, who states that as long as the increase in note circulation has not yet had its full impact on prices, interest will remain "under its natural level" (Gonner edition, p. 35). [See the Sraffa edition, op. cit., vol. 3, p. 91. -Ed.]

[39] Cf. p. 9 of the fourth edition; pp. 9-12 and 22 of Gonner's edition; pp. 267-269 of McCulloch's edition. [Vol. 3, pp. 59-63 of Sraffa's edition, op. cit. -Ed.]

the classical theory of exchange rates later generally attributed to Ricardo actually represented Thornton's rather than Ricardo's views.

Ricardo's work was largely responsible for the fact that parliament again took up the question of currency devaluation in early 1810. On a motion by Francis Horner, whose name was mentioned earlier, the House of Commons appointed a committee "to enquire into the Cause of the High Price of Gold Bullion, and to take into consideration the State of the Circulating Medium and of the Exchanges between Great Britain and Foreign Parts". This 'Bullion Committee', of which Thornton, but not, as is often claimed, Ricardo, was a member, was chaired by Horner. In the following three months the committee examined thirty witnesses, who represented the London financial community. With only two exceptions,[40] these witnesses supported the Bank's point of view and defended its policy. The declarations of the representatives of the Bank of England are of special interest, as they most clearly reflect the contemporary view of things; these declarations have meanwhile—at least in England—become "almost classical by their nonsense".[41]

The governor of the Bank of England and his deputy, while adamantly rejecting the idea that they had officially taken cognizance of the committee report on the Irish currency issued in 1804,[42] expressly stated that in determining how large an amount of notes to discount, they considered nothing but the quality of the promissory note, that is, its rating as a commercial paper, without taking the current price of gold or the level of exchange rates into account. According to Vice Governor Pearse,

[40] Namely Sir Francis Baring, who now firmly condemned the bank's policy, and an unidentified "continental merchant", whose testimony demonstrated an unusually good grasp of the situation.

[41] As stated by W. Bagehot, *Lombard Street*, new edition by H. Withers (London: Smith, Elder, 1910), p. 177. In German translation edited by Plenge/Staatswissenschaftliche Musterbücher, no. 4, Essen, 1920, p. 111. [See Norman St. John-Stevas's edition, in *The Collected Works of Walter Bagehot*, vol. 9 (London: The Economist, 1978), p. 136. -Ed.]

[42] The minutes of the depositions are reproduced in the appendix to the report of the Bullion Committee, *Report, together with the Minutes of Evidence, and Accounts, from the Select Committee on the High Price of Gold Bullion*, Ordered by the House of Commons to be printed, 8 June 1810. There are two contemporary editions, an official *in folio* edition and a privately printed *in octavo* edition dating from the same year. [The *folio* edition is reprinted in the *Irish University Press Series of British Parliamentary Papers*, op. cit., Monetary Policy, General, vol. 1, pp. 187-418. -Ed.] The depositions discussed below are reproduced on pp. 96ff. of the *folio* edition and pp. 125ff. of the *octavo* edition. The text of the report, without appendix, has been newly edited with an introduction by Edwin Cannan under the title *The Paper Pound of 1797-1821* (London: P. S. King, 1919); [reprinted New York: Augustus M. Kelley, 1969. -Ed.]

> I am individually of the opinion that the price of Bullion, or the state of the exchanges, can never be a reason for lessening the amount of bank notes to be issued.

and the governor confirmed this assertion emphatically, stating:

> I am so much of the same opinion, that I never think it necessary to advert to the price of Gold or the state of the exchange, on the days on which we make our advances.

In reply to a question about the Bank's criterion for keeping its note circulation within the requisite limits, he continued:

> [W]e never forced a Bank note into circulation, and the criterion by which I judge of the exact proportion to be maintained is, by avoiding as much as possible to discount what does not appear to be legitimate mercantile paper. The Bank notes would revert to us if there was a redundancy in circulation, as no one would pay interest for a bank note that he did not want to make use of.

Mr. Pearse, who strongly agreed with this declaration, ventured so far as to express the opinion that even if the discount rate were lowered from 5 to 4 or even 3 per cent, there would be no greater danger of issuing too many notes as long as the principle prevailed that only reliable commercial papers should be discounted. Here again the governor voiced his support. It goes without saying that in their testimony on this occasion they emphatically defended the view that the bank notes had not depreciated, but rather that gold had gone up in price.

The committee's report to the House of Commons was drawn up by Horner, Thornton and W. Huskisson. The latter was to demonstrate his expertise in the field by publishing a few months after the report a first-rate pamphlet, which was intended as a justification of the stand taken by the report.[43] As was true of Ricardo's first publications, the report added nothing crucial to the arguments pres-

---

[43] William Huskisson, *The Question concerning the Depreciation of our Currency Stated and Examined* (London: John Murray, 1810), reprinted also in McCulloch, *Tracts on Paper Currency*, op. cit. This treatise is a masterly popular presentation of the subject and was among the most widely read works of the period. Within a year it reached seven editions. Among the host of other, mostly antagonistic tracts, issued in the wake of the Bullion Report, a single work along these lines by another committee member will be mentioned, D. Giddy (who later went by the name of Davies Gilbert), *A Plain Statement of the Bullion Question* (London: J. Stockdale, 1811).

ented eight years earlier in the previously mentioned publications and in the Irish currency report of 1804. It earned the unusual reputation that it achieved under the name of 'Bullion Report' in part by the excellence of its formulation. In the main, however, it owes its great fame to the fact that it came to serve to some extent as the bible of the 'Bullionist' party in the course of the debate sparked by its publication and continuing uninterrupted even beyond the resumption of cash payments, so that it reached a far wider audience in the process than was originally the case. It contained a clear presentation of the arguments showing that the over-issue of bank notes in recent years had led to a devaluation of the pound, with supporting data about notes in circulation, exchange rates, gold prices, etc.

Starting out from the undisputed facts that the price of gold bullion had risen to 15½ per cent above that of the mint price and that the exchange rate of the pound had fallen between 7 and 14 per cent on the major foreign exchanges and that nearly all old coins had disappeared from circulation, the report emphasised that these manifestations all pointed to the condition of the internal money circulation as the most probable cause. Symptoms of this kind had surfaced in the past only in times of deteriorating coinage, not in wartime and the kind of trade disruptions currently in effect. No evidence could be found for an increase in the value of gold, to which witnesses had repeatedly referred, since there was no sign of it in other countries. But even if the assertion were correct, this would not account for the below par value of the notes, since England was legally on a gold currency, which meant that with convertibility of notes the value of the pound should always be equal to the value of a certain amount of gold. Wartime conditions might possibly be responsible for a shift in the gold points, as a result of which gold export might be profitable only if notes depreciated more than in normal times, but they could not possibly account for the fact that foreign exchange rates persistently stayed at a level above the gold point or that the price of gold bullion maintained itself above the mint price for longer periods. Inasmuch as the automatic mechanism preventing a depreciation of the notes by over-issue had not been in force ever since the stoppage of cash payments, it was now most urgent to take the state of the exchanges and the market price of gold into consideration in regulating the circulation of notes. The depositions of the Bank directors had demonstrated, however, that the directors laboured under the great practical misapprehension that the size of the note issue had no influence on exchange rates and the gold price. The report emphasises, on the contrary, not only the principle that the over-issue of notes will perforce raise foreign exchange rates and the price of gold, but also will find its confirmation in the history of almost all states that resorted to paper money in modern times. Aside from the familiar occurrences in the American colonies and the French assignats,[44] the report drew attention to Austria's very recent experience with paper money, about which the unidentified "continental merchant" had informed the committee.[45] The report is therefore highly critical of the Bank directors' views and expresses its conviction that the over-issue of notes is responsible for their devaluation. The resumption of cash payments is recommended as the only way to avert further devaluation and to maintain permanently the parity of notes with gold. It therefore is of the opinion that a law should set a two-year deadline after the expiration of which the Bank would resume cash payments under all circumstances. In the interim it would be left to the Bank directors' discretion to take all necessary steps for the resumption of cash payments.

VI

The committee report, which was presented to parliament in June 1810, led to no further parliamentary action for almost a year, but it aroused great public response. In the two years following the publication of the report, a host of treatises on monetary problems burst forth, the like of which had never been seen in such a short time span before and perhaps was never again to be seen thereafter. We can single out only a few of these works, notably the ones by R. Mushet,[46] W. Blake,[47] Charles Bosanquet,[48] and Ricardo's reply

---

[44] [See this volume, chapter 10, section IV. -Ed.]

[45] Cf. on this subject J. C. L. Simonde de Sismondi, *Du papier-monnaie dans les Etats austrichiens et des moyens de le supprimer* (Weimar: Landes-industrie-comptoir, 1810), and Heinrich J. Watteroth, *Politische Vorlesungen über Papiergeld* (Vienna: Kupffer und Wimmer, 1811).

[46] Robert Mushet, *An Enquiry into the Effects Produced on the National Currency, and Rates of Exchange, by the Bank Restriction Bill; Explaining the Cause of the High Price of Bullion, with Plans for Maintaining the National Coins in a State of Uniformity and Perfection* (London: Printed for C. and R. Baldwin, 1810).

[47] William Blake, *Observations on the Principles which Regulate the Course of Exchange; and on the Present Depreciated State of the Currency* (London: Printed for Edmund Lloyd, 1810). Also in McCulloch, *Tracts on Paper Currency*, op. cit.

[48] Charles Bosanquet, *Practical Observations on the Report of the Bullion-Committee* (London: Printed for J. M. Richardson, 1810).

to the arguments of the latter.[49] These works, together with Ricardo's first publication and the previously mentioned study by Huskisson, were selected by their contemporary, T. R. Malthus, as the best contributions and reviewed jointly in a noteworthy article in the *Edinburgh Review*.[50] A few words about Mushet and Blake, who both belong to the 'Bullionist' group. Mushet, an official in the Royal Mint, on the whole shares Ricardo's views. His pamphlet deserves mention, however, because its abundant and cleverly interpreted statistics are particularly useful for any investigation about the currency policies of the period and not superseded even by the material contained in the Bullion Report. Blake's work on the other hand has independent theoretical value and was for nearly five decades regarded as the best presentation of the theory of exchange rates. While it follows in the main Thornton's approach, its major merit was considered to be its distinction between 'real exchanges', which are determined by the relationship between supply and demand for foreign exchange, that is, subject to fluctuations in the relationship between the payments that a country makes and the payments it receives and which are independent of the value of its money, and 'nominal exchanges', whose fluctuations are determined by changes in the value of money. The third author that we mentioned, Bank Governor Bosanquet, is an opponent of the opinions expressed in the Bullion Report. His weakly argued "Practical Observations on the Report of the Bullion Committee" actually owes its reputation mainly to its being the subject of a masterly refutation by Ricardo.[51] His way of countering the typical objections of the

---

[49] David Ricardo, *Reply to Mr. Bosanquet's 'Practical Observations on the Report of the Bullion Committee'* (London: John Murray, 1811). [In the Sraffa edition of Ricardo's *Works*, op. cit., vol. 3, pp. 155-256. -Ed.]

[50] "Publications on the Depreciation of the Paper Currency", *The Edinburgh Review*, vol. 18, no. 34, February 1811. This book review, like all the other reviews in this journal, appeared anonymously. The fact that it was written by Malthus is conclusively shown in Ricardo's letters to Malthus (cf. *Letters of David Ricardo to Thomas Robert Malthus 1810-1823*, ed. James Bonar (Oxford: Clarendon Press, 1887), p. 10), which are of the greatest importance for understanding their respective points of view on the problems under discussion here. [Hayek refers to the letter of June 18, 1811. See the Sraffa edition of Ricardo's *Works*, vol. 6, p. 25. -Ed.]

[51] Among the numerous writings by opponents of the Bullion Report, let us still mention here Sir John Sinclair's *Remarks on a pamphlet intituled, "The Question concerning the Depreciation of the Currency stated and examined." By William Huskisson, Esq., M. P.* (London: Cadell & Davies, 1810) and Robert Torrens, *An Essay on Money and Paper Currency* (London: J. Johnson, 1812), as the best works along these lines. [On Torrens's role as an anti-bullionist see Lionel Robbins, *Robert Torrens and the Evolution of Classical Economics*, op. cit., pp. 74-80. -Ed.]

practical man to the principles of the Bullion Report probably contributed more to his becoming the recognised leader of the Bullionist group than any of his earlier publications. But even though his earlier ideas are expressed here with extraordinary rigour and thoroughness and applied to every facet of the concrete situation and to important historical stages of the evolution of the English currency, there are scarcely any new theoretical insights even in this work. Of far greater importance is the short appendix that he added in the same year to the fourth edition of his pamphlet on the high price of gold bullion.[52]

In the above-mentioned collective review, Malthus had firmly sided with Thornton on the point where Ricardo's theory of exchange rates deviated from Thornton's. We already referred to Ricardo's rejecting the idea that a deterioration of the balance of payments could constitute an independent factor in the outflow of gold (or, to put it differently, that there could be a sequence: deterioration of the balance of payments, deterioration of the exchange rates, gold outflow, lower prices, and restoration of the balance of payments) and his insistence that only a prior deterioration of the domestic value of a currency could result in an outflow of gold. The Bullion Report had already espoused Thornton's views on this point.[53] Malthus now turned to Ricardo with the question why a country that had just been the recipient of a subsidy, for instance, would simultaneously be prepared to purchase a large quantity of commodities from the other country at the same price as before. Ricardo devoted a voluminous appendix at the end of the fourth edition of his first independent publication[54] to countering

---

of Classical Economics, op. cit., pp. 74-80. -Ed.]

[52] [See footnote 37 above. -Ed.]

[53] It is true that in some respects the Bullion Report represents a decisive advance, as when it approvingly quotes the remarks of the anonymous "continental merchant", which in fact go to the heart of the matter. The "continental merchant" had stated that the exchange rates had originally deteriorated because of various circumstances that had had an unfavourable influence on the balance of payments, notably Napoleon's blockade, and that the exchanges had failed to recover because the bank notes were not redeemed in specie (i.e., because the contraction of the note circulation required to restore equilibrium did not take place). Cf. pp. 8-9 and p. 73 of the folio edition and p. 21 and p. 90 in the octavo edition. [Pp. 19-21 in Cannan's edition, op. cit. -Ed.]

[54] "Observation on Some Passages in an article in the Edinburgh Review, on the Depreciation of Paper Currency; also Suggestions for Securing to the Public a Currency as Invariable as Gold, with a Very Moderate Supply of That Metal." Appendix to the fourth edition of The High Price of Bullion (London: John Murray, 1811). [In the Sraffa edition of Ricardo's Works, op. cit., vol. 3, pp. 99-127. -Ed.]

objections brought forward, he proposed in addition for the first time a novel and highly significant idea, the notion of a gold standard without circulating gold specie, a 'gold exchange standard' as it is now called. As Ricardo developed this idea more fully five years later in a special work on the subject, which was to constitute the basis for implementing the proposal, we shall take it up at a later point. We will concern ourselves instead with another very significant idea that was raised for the first time in the discussion between Malthus and Ricardo. In his review Malthus had made the point that an increase in paper money might also have a favourable impact by shifting the relationship between capital and income in favour of the former. It could be said to help increase capital, a theory that was to be the subject of lively debate a hundred years later under the heading of 'forced savings'.[55] According to Malthus, "on every fresh issue of notes, not only is the quantity of the circulating medium increased, but the distribution of the whole mass is altered. A larger proportion falls into the hands of those who consume and produce, and a smaller proportion into the hands of those who only consume. And as we have always considered capital as that portion of the national accumulations and annual produce, which is at the command of those who mean to employ it with a view to reproduction, we are bound to acknowledge, that an increased issue of notes tends·to increase the national capital, and by an almost, though not strictly necessary consequence, to lower the rate of interest."[56] Ricardo admitted that the distribution of the money supply might indeed be relevant in this respect and could have such consequences. He challenged the assumption underlying Malthus's argument that the recipients of fixed incomes, at whose expense the new capital would be formed, would react only by restricting their consumption. "Do not the stockholders give as great a stimulus to the growth of the national wealth by saving half their incomes and investing it in the stocks, thereby liberating a capital which will ultimately be employed by those who consume and

---

[55] [See Hayek's "A Note on the Development of the Doctrine of 'Forced Saving'", *Quarterly Journal of Economics*, vol. 47, no. 1, November 1932, pp. 123-133, reprinted in *Profits, Interest and Investment; and Other Essays on the Theory of Industrial Fluctuations* (London: Routledge & Kegan Paul, 1939; reprinted New York: Augustus M. Kelley, 1969 and 1975) and Fritz Machlup, "Forced or Induced Saving: An Exploration into its Synonyms and Homonyms", *Review of Economic Statistics*, vol. 25, no. 1, February 1943, pp. 26-39. -Ed.]

[56] *The Edinburgh Review*, vol. 17, no. 34, 1811, p. 364.

produce, as would be done if their incomes were depreciated 50 per cent by the issues of bank-notes, and the power of saving were in consequence entirely taken from them, although the Bank should lend to an industrious man an amount of notes equal in value to the diminished income of the stockholder? The difference, and the only difference appears to me to be this, that in the one case the interest on the money lent would be paid to the real owner of the property, in the other it would ultimately be paid in the shape of increased dividends or bonuses to the bank proprietors, who had been enabled unjustly to possess themselves of it."[57] Although Ricardo failed to pursue these conjectures at greater length, they deserve special attention as the initial approach to a topic that is increasingly becoming the central concern of monetary theory.

VII

Although the discussion about the Bullion Report greatly enhanced scientific knowledge and was increasing recognition for Bullionist views, the Bullionists nevertheless were thwarted in their efforts to influence English currency policy. When in May 1811 Horner finally motioned to discuss the committee report in parliament, a large majority of the members of parliament demonstrated their opposition to the views defended in the report.[58] Sixteen resolutions summarising the basic ideas of the report were submitted by him and were voted down, whereupon seventeen resolutions in opposition were submitted by Vansittart, the later Chancellor of the Exchequer, and approved by parliament. Vansittart's resolutions denied the conclusions of the report point by point. One of the resolutions has become a classic in that it boldly asserted that the bank notes had hitherto been and were currently "held in public estimation to be equivalent to the legal coin of the realm".[59] The last of the seventeen resolutions approved by parliament stated that setting a definite deadline for repealing the Restriction Act earlier than six months before the conclusion of peace would be highly

---

[57] Cf. *The Works of David Ricardo*, ed. McCulloch, op. cit, pp. 299f., and *Economic Essays, by David Ricardo*, ed. Gonner, op. cit., pp. 56f. [In the Sraffa edition of Ricardo's *Works*, op. cit., vol. 3, p. 122. -Ed.]

[58] [See *Hansard's Parliamentary Debates*, 1st series, vol. 19, pp. 798-1128 and 1151-1169; vol. 20, pp. 1-128, 134-146, and 150-176, covering May 6 to May 15, 1811. -Ed.]

[59] [Resolution 3, in *ibid.*, vol. 20, p. 70. -Ed.]

ineffectual as well as dangerous, thus turning down the proposals of the Bullion Committee for the time being.

The parliament's contention that the bank notes had not depreciated was speedily disproved by Lord King by a practical demonstration. When the next quarterly rent payments were due, he addressed a circular to the numerous tenants on his large estate, informing them that in view of the depreciation of the bank notes he was no longer able to accept these notes—which had not been specifically designated as legal tender—at their face value and expressed his willingness to accept, in the place of the legal gold coins, which had disappeared from circulation, either foreign gold coins of equal weight or an amount of bank notes which would be adequate for purchasing the number of guineas required to pay the rent at market value. This was by no means an unreasonable request, since the tenants were receiving higher prices for their products, while they were paying their lease in depreciated paper money, but it was greeted with great alarm by the government party. The very same persons who had just denied the depreciation of the notes were reporting innumerable instances where as much as 27 shillings had been paid for a guinea and drew a gloomy picture of what would inevitably happen if two sorts of prices generally prevailed, one for paying in notes and another for paying in gold. After another extensive discussion of the whole currency question, a law was finally approved which declared it a delict to refuse to accept paper money at the same rate as gold coins. The wording thus avoided designating the bank notes as legal tender, but it served the same purpose.[60]

The last major and finally successful efforts to defeat Napoleon in the years that followed were accompanied by an accelerated increase in notes, caused by the rapidly mounting advances the Bank had to make to the government. A further devaluation of the pound both in terms of foreign currencies and on the domestic market ensued. In late summer and fall of 1813, the market price of gold bullion climbed to 5 pounds 10 shillings per ounce, that is, over 40 per cent above the mint price, the highest price it was to reach. The Allies' victory over Napoleon and the first Treaty of Paris of May 1814 triggered a rapid rise in the value of the pound, which promptly dropped again sharply after Napoleon's return from Elba and during the Hundred Days, yet during the entire period

---

[60] Cf. text of the law in Wolter, op. cit., p. 189. [The text is given in English. -Ed.]

there was no let-up in the increase of notes in circulation. This divergence between the fluctuations in the value of the pound and changes in note circulation was regarded as a refutation of the quantity theory of money underlying the Bullion Report. The above contention by the opponents of the Bullion Report then and later ignored the fact that the report had in mind only a long-term linkage between the increase in notes and the devaluation of money, as Ricardo had made clear. With the conclusion of the second Treaty of Paris in November 1815 the pound appreciated again, in part because the Bank of England, which had to be prepared to resume cash payments in July 1816 (the date through which restriction had been extended after the first Treaty of Paris), was endeavouring to reduce its notes in circulation. This sparked a new public discussion about the definitive return to the gold standard. The significant feature of this discussion lies in the fact that by then the views of the Bullion Report had become widely accepted and the government's efforts to keep extending the Restriction Act encountered mounting resistance.

It was Ricardo who made the most important contribution to this discussion with his *Proposals for an Economical and Secure Currency*,[61] in which he proposed a gold exchange standard, to which we referred earlier. This proposal was finally implemented at least temporarily when the gold standard was restored and put into full effect a hundred years later.[62] Even aside from this proposal, this work, which is less famous than Ricardo's 1809 and 1811 publications, contains in some respects his most original and most valuable contributions to monetary theory. His *Principles of Political Economy*,[63] which were published a year later, offered no significant additional insights in the relevant chapters. The work is composed as a pamphlet in connexion with the pending parliamentary negotiations about the resumption of cash payments and other questions affecting relations between the government and the Bank of England. We

---

[61] *Proposals for an Economical and Secure Currency* [1816]. Reprinted in *Works of David Ricardo*, ed. McCulloch, op. cit., and *Economic Essays, by David Ricardo*, ed. Gonner, op. cit. A partial translation by W. Fromowitz and F. Machlup can be found in the appendix to F. Machlup, *Die Goldkernwährung* (Halberstadt: H. Meyer, 1925), and later also in a special edition with an introduction by Machlup (Halberstadt: H. Meyer, 1927). [See the Sraffa edition of Ricardo's *Works*, op. cit., vol. 4, pp. 43-141. -Ed.]

[62] [A gold exchange standard was also the central feature of the international Bretton Woods system of 1945-71. -Ed.]

[63] [*On the Principles of Political Economy and Taxation* (London: John Murray, 1817), reprinted as vol. 1 of the Sraffa edition of Ricardo's *Works*, op. cit. -Ed.]

shall not dwell on the extensive sections of the pamphlet concerned with the unduly high profits derived by the Bank from its services to the government. The main question that Ricardo set out to answer here was whether the return to the gold standard would necessitate the reintroduction of a large circulation of gold coins or whether there was not some way of combining the advantages of circulating paper money, recognised since the time of Adam Smith, and the security of a currency based on metal. Paper money in circulation would have among its advantages "the facility with which it may be altered in quantity, as the wants of commerce and temporary circumstances may require", while there might be a considerably greater time lag between an increase in the value of money and an increase in the amount of money when only metallic currency was used. There was too great a risk, however, with a completely unrestricted paper currency that it would lead to an oversupply of money. Ricardo considers a commonly offered suggestion that commodities generally "become a standard to regulate the quantity and value of money" as impossible to implement in practice. Although at that time the method of index numbers had not yet been developed,[64] Ricardo already offers the major objections to its basic concept in this context.[65] In his view, precious metals remain the best available foundation for the currency, notwithstanding their undeniable fluctuations in value. Ricardo proposes to secure agreement between the value of the circulating paper money with the value of the precious metal, whether gold or silver, serving as the basis of the currency by obliging the Bank of England to redeem its notes not in guineas but in gold or silver bullion and, conversely, to issue notes in exchange for bullion of these precious metals. The Bank would be spared excessive importunities by limiting its gold transactions to amounts exceeding 20 ounces (which would correspond to 77 pounds). The purchase price of bullion would be kept

---

[64] [For an introduction to modern index number theory see Franklin M. Fisher and Karl Shell, *The Economic Theory of Price Indices* (New York: Academic Press, 1972). See also Ludwig von Mises, *Theory of Money and Credit*, new edition (Indianapolis, Ind.: Liberty*Classics*, 1981), pp. 215-223. -Ed.]

[65] [Hayek was not entirely persuaded by Ricardo's argument. In 1943 he published in the *Economic Journal* a proposal for a commodity reserve currency. Drawn largely from two other works, *Storage and Stability* by Benjamin Graham (New York: McGraw-Hill, 1937) and *Social Goals and Economic Institutions* by Frank D. Graham (Princeton, N.J.: Princeton University Press, 1942), the proposal was submitted to the international conference at Bretton Woods in 1944 for consideration as the basis for a new international monetary standard to replace or supplement the defunct gold standard. See *Money and Nations*, vol. 6 of *The Collected Works*. -Ed.]

slightly lower than the sales price, but this difference should always remain sufficiently small that it would be in the interest of the gold seller to sell it to the Bank rather than to coin it. Agreement between the value of bank notes and the metallic currency standard would thus be fully guaranteed, since any drop in the value of bank notes would inevitably trigger requests for redemption and lead to the export of gold (Ricardo was consistent enough to demand unrestricted export of gold). Thus every drop in the value of money would induce a decrease in the money supply and every rise in the value of notes would lead to an increased trading in of bullion for notes. "Under such a system, and with a currency so regulated, the Bank would never be liable to any embarrassments whatever, excepting on those extraordinary occasions, when a general panic seizes the country, and when every one is desirous of possessing the precious metals as the most convenient mode of realising or concealing his property . . . . A panic of this kind was the cause of the crisis in 1797; and not, as has been supposed, the large advances which the Bank had then made to government . . . . If the Bank had continued paying in cash, probably the panic would have subsided before their coin had been exhausted."[66]

At the time that Ricardo's *Proposals* were published, the resumption of cash payments seemed imminent, since the deadline for rescinding the Act expired in July 1816. The price of gold had fallen nearly to the mint price in response to the Bank's prudent policy and it was reasonable to assume that the resumption of cash payments would quickly eliminate the remaining difference. The government nevertheless asked for an additional two-year extension of the Restriction Act and its request was granted. Shortly thereafter another important law was promulgated, which put the finishing touch on the century-long transition to the gold standard. Preliminary steps had been taken by overvaluing silver in setting the value relation between the coins in 1717, then by limiting silver coins as legal tender to amounts of less than 25 pounds, and finally by ending the free minting of silver in 1798. Nevertheless, the ultimate step, the formal debasement of silver coins to small change, still remained to be completed. This step was in part the outcome of the recent period of money depreciation. Although some of the silver coins—in contrast to gold coins—had remained in circulation, particularly coins that were already heavily degraded, the rest of the silver coins had been temporarily replaced by all sorts of token

---

[66] [*Proposals*, in Sraffa, op. cit., vol. 4, p. 68. -Ed.]

money rather than by notes, and the situation was in urgent need of remedial action. Prime Minister Lord Liverpool,[67] the son of the author of a previously mentioned work, in which the theoretical foundations for this coin reform had been laid, proposed that new, undervalued silver coins be issued to supply this need, with face values not to exceed 40 shillings and with the express declaration that gold constituted the only currency standard. These measures were laid down in the coinage law of June 22, 1816, and have remained valid until this day.[68] A year later the guinea, the gold coin equivalent to 21 shillings, which had been introduced, one might say, fortuitously, was eliminated; it was replaced by a new currency unit, the sovereign, a gold coin equivalent to 20 shillings.

There was to be a delay of several years, however, before the return to a genuine, legally backed gold currency was to be completed. As it happened, when in 1818 the extended deadline for the resumption of cash payments by the Bank of England was about to expire, a rise in the price of gold and in foreign exchange rates again occurred when the Bank exacerbated a temporary deterioration in the balance of payments, triggered by large foreign loans, by making large advances to the government, instead of counteracting the deterioration by reducing its circulation of notes. The deadline was once more extended by a year. A year later, the government not only failed to rescind the Restriction Act but instead enacted an ordinance enjoining the Bank from continuing the redemption of certain categories of notes (those issued prior to a certain date), as it had been doing voluntarily for the last three years on an experimental basis. This renewed postponement of the deadline aroused such general indignation, however, that the government was forced to accede to repeated demands and appoint new parliamentary investigating committees in both Houses, which were to examine the possibility of resuming cash payments. Both committees again interrogated numerous witnesses, among them Ricardo. The reports of these committees and the appended protocols of these interrogations[69] are of nearly as much interest as those issued by the commit-

---

[67] [Robert Banks Jenkinson, second Earl of Liverpool (1770-1828), son of Charles Jenkinson, first Earl of Liverpool, who is cited in footnote 34 above. -Ed.]

[68] Cf. the text of the law in Wolter, op. cit., pp. 194ff. [The text is given in English. -Ed.]

[69] [These reports of 1819 are reprinted as *Reports from Secret Committees of the House of Commons and the House of Lords on the Expediency of the Resumption of Cash Payments with Minutes of Evidence and Appendices*, in the *Irish University Press Series of British Parliamentary Papers*, op. cit., Monetary Policy, General, vol. 2. -Ed.]

tees in 1797, 1804, and 1810. It is particularly striking to note that in the course of the previous nine years general opinion had completely adopted the principles of the Bullion Report, which had originally been ridiculed. Even the representatives of the Bank of England questioned at the hearings had to recognise the correctness of its major principles, and Robert Peel, who chaired the committee in the House of Commons and was later to play a decisive role in the legal organisation of the English banking system, admitted that in the course of the hearings he had become completely convinced of the soundness of the principles that he had hitherto opposed. Despite the concessions of most of its individual members, however, the directorate of the Bank as a closed body retained its old views and restated officially in its resolution, in response to the opinion expressed by some persons "that the bank has only to reduce its issues to obtain a favourable turn in the exchanges, and a consequent influx of the precious metals", that the bank itself "is unable to discover any solid foundation for such a sentiment." This time, however, legislation could no longer be deterred. In line with the recommendations of both committees, the motion of Robert Peel was approved (against the vote of his father) and the law of July 2, 1819,[70] often called the first Peel Act, was passed. The law stipulated that May 1, 1823, be set as the final deadline for reactivating the Bank of England's obligation to redeem its notes in gold coins. The Act also ordered the Bank to begin on the 1st of February 1820 to redeem its notes at a rate gradually reaching coin parity, although, in line with Ricardo's proposal, the redemption was to be in gold bullion. At the same time, the prohibitions against melting down and exporting gold coins, which for years had been the object of attacks by monetary theorists, were rescinded.

The only sizable opposition to these measures was directed not against the principle of resuming cash payments but against the return to the former coinage rate. Lord Lauderdale proposed, for instance, that the stabilisation of the pound at its current level should be achieved by reducing the gold content of the pound sufficiently to match its actual value rather than by a reduction in the note circulation that would gradually restore the former value of the pound. Even Ricardo, who happened to give his brilliant maiden speech in the House of Commons on the subject of this law, recognised that the choice between devaluation and the return to

[70] Cf. the text of the law in Wolter, op. cit., p. 208. [The text is given in English. -Ed.]

the original value of the gold coin presented serious problems, for which no generally valid solution existed. We already encountered this conflict between the exponents of the two approaches in the debate between Lowndes and Locke,[71] and further controversy was to break out repeatedly in later years. As Ricardo later expressly stated in a letter, he would never urge a government to restore a currency that had suffered a 30 per cent depreciation to par; he would recommend instead that the currency be set to match its reduced value by lowering the metallic content of the coin.[72] The reason that he favoured returning to the old coinage rate, as did the majority in parliament, was that in 1819 the devaluation of the pound was so slight that the small increase in value required to restore the pre-war rate seemed like a lesser evil, compared with the erosion of confidence that England would suffer in the eyes of the world by diminishing the gold content of the pound. Interestingly enough, the very persons (with the single exception of Lauderdale) who demanded the devaluation of the pound, arguing that a return to the old coinage rate would mean a huge rise in value, were the very same persons who had only recently denied that the bank notes had depreciated in terms of gold.

The actual return to the gold standard was implemented more rapidly and easily than expected. The Bank of England, having been forced to adopt a cautious policy after the introduction of a limited convertibility to gold, experienced almost no loss in gold and soon witnessed an inflow of gold. After operating just over a year according to Ricardo's 'Bullion Plan', the Bank reached an agreement with the government on the 1st of May, 1821, to resume unlimited payment in gold coins. The restriction period was thereby finally closed.

---

[71] [See this volume, chapter 9, section V. -Ed.]

[72] In a letter to John Wheatley of September 18, 1821, published in *Letters of David Ricardo to Hutches Trower and others 1811-1823*, ed. James Bonar and J. H. Hollander (Oxford: Clarendon Press, 1899), pp. 159f. [See the Sraffa edition of Ricardo's *Works*, op. cit., vol. 9, pp. 71-74. This letter came to occupy an extraordinary place in Hayek's later writings, since he included it in evidence to support his charge that John Maynard Keynes had but a "limited knowledge of economic theory". In 1975 Hayek wrote, "I ask myself often how different the economic history of the world might have been if in the discussion of the years preceding 1925 one English economist had remembered and pointed out this long-before published passage in one of Ricardo's letters". See. p. 199 and pp. 229-231 in *New Studies in Philosophy, Politics, Economics and the History of Ideas* (Chicago: University of Chicago Press; London: Routledge & Kegan Paul, 1978), as well as vol. 6 of *The Collected Works of F. A. Hayek*. -Ed.]

TWELVE

THE DISPUTE BETWEEN THE CURRENCY SCHOOL
AND THE BANKING SCHOOL, 1821-1848

I

Basic knowledge about monetary matters had been consolidated, enhanced, and spread more widely in England through the discussions about problems created by the Bank of England's stoppage of cash payments. For roughly another three decades, the growth of monetary theory was largely confined to England. The policy of the Bank of England, which had been a centre of public attention during the restriction period, remained an object of general concern and criticism, stimulating various parliamentary investigations and regulations, which finally culminated in a completely new organisation of the Bank with the passage of the famous Peel's Act of 1844, whose purpose it was to make the Bank comply with a specific policy. These first attempts to place the policies of the note-issuing bank under legislative control and the heated scientific debates surrounding these efforts eventually drew attention to these problems even on the Continent and in the United States, where, by the middle of the nineteenth century, such concerns had also become relevant in the wake of economic development. From that time on, the discussion assumed an international character and the topic remained the focal point of scientific exchanges throughout the third quarter of the century. In 1873, however, interest shifted to more urgent questions about the currency standard and to the controversy between supporters of the gold standard and bimetallists.

The period between 1821 and 1849, with which this chapter is concerned, is more or less self-contained not only with respect to the main topic of the discussion on monetary policy, but also with respect to the trends in the production of precious metals and price movements. The period covered in the previous chapter, 1797-1821, happened to be equally self-contained in these respects. Beginning with 1821, gold production gradually climbed and reached a substantial volume even prior to the discovery of the gold fields in California, which drastically altered the production level. The downward tendency in the international price level initiated in 1815 continued until 1849, probably as a result of the low silver production between 1811 and 1831 and the related shift to gold currency in countries with a bimetallic standard, in response to the relative increase in the value of silver.

In the first years after the resumption of cash payments in England the drop in the price level was exacerbated by the Bank of England's credit policy. The Bank continued to restrict credit for a considerable length of time even in the face of favourable exchange rates and persistent influx of gold, although this policy had been required only in the preceding years, when the value of the bank notes had to be adjusted to the value of gold and when a gold hoard had to be accumulated for the resumption of cash payments. With the ensuing shrinkage of its profit-bearing investments—the more its gold hoard increased, the smaller the amount of securities it could hold as cover for its notes and deposits—the Bank was induced in 1822 to lower its discount rate, which had been maintained steadily at 5 per cent for over a hundred years, to 4 per cent. When even this measure was ineffective, the Bank attempted to dispose of some of its gold by purchasing large amounts of government bonds and by extending its lending business to commodity-backed and mortgage loans. Like all steps taken by the Bank of England in the next years, this step came far too late, at a point when the influx of gold would have come to a halt in any case, because the low interest rate had already had the effect of stimulating business activity as a whole, first stock market speculation in particular, but soon commodity trading as well. Two factors combined in 1824 to set off an economic boom and a wave of mad speculation on the stock exchange: the opening up of Central and South America to English trade and investments and the associated potential for large new profits, which occurred in this period, and the favourable money situation, which was prolonged artificially by the Bank's policy. But neither the speculative boom nor the gradual decline of the exchange rates, which first manifested itself at the end of 1823 and which resulted in large outflows of gold in the following year, initially incited the Bank to restrict its credit. By summer 1825, however, after gold holdings, which had reached a maximum of 14.2 million pounds in the previous year and had already dropped below 12 million pounds meanwhile, the gold supply started on a precipitous decline. The Bank became nervous, stopped its advances based on securities, raised its terms for discounting bills, though the interest rate was not raised above the 4 per cent level, and sold part of its government treasury notes to be able to keep up with increasing demands for discounting notes. By these steps the Bank with one hand deprived the money market of the very sums that it was anxious to supply in the form of discounts with the other. By the time this credit reduction made itself felt, however, the stock exchange and commodity trade had already reached a plateau, which presaged an imminent reversal. The shortage of money accelerated the decline in the price of securities and goods. Since only the most reliable firms were able to obtain credit, a substantial number of provincial banks and trading companies found themselves in trouble. When one of the larger banking firms was unable to meet its payments, all banks became an object of suspicion and there was a run on provincial banks for the redemption of notes. These banks in turn were forced to get cash at all costs from the London banks with which they had regular dealings (the problem was mainly the redemption of 1 and 2 pound notes, which were issued by country banks, but which the Bank of England no longer supplied, and which could therefore be redeemed only in gold). The general panic came to a climax in early December 1825, when two respected London banks proved incapable in turn of satisfying these requests. Up to that time, the Bank of England had failed to act on the widely accepted principles formulated by Henry Thornton[1] and the Bullion Report[2]. Just as it had first neglected to counteract the 'external drain' by a restriction of its credit, now that the shortage of money had improved the exchange rates and the 'external drain' had consequently been stopped, the Bank exacerbated the current 'internal drain' by its restrictive credit policy. At the height of the panic, when everyone was intent on maintaining their capacity for making cash payments at all costs, the Bank abruptly, a day after its directors had rejected any increase in the note issue, in agreement with the views of the entire business press,[3] reversed its stand, apparently upon instructions from the government. While the discount rate was raised back to the 5 per cent level, the Bank agreed to discount all sound bills at that rate and to resume commodity loans and the purchase of treasury bills. An enormous expansion of the Bank's note circulation ensued at once and its gold hoard declined so precipitously that the Bank inquired about government permission to stop cash payments.

---

[1] [See this volume, chapter 14. -Ed.]

[2] [See this volume, chapter 11. -Ed.]

[3] Thomas Joplin's articles in the *Courier* constituted the only exception. Joplin for this reason claimed credit for the reversal of the Bank's policy. Cf. also his *Analysis and History of the Currency Question* cited below. Joplin's contributions are discussed further on in the chapter.

Although the government denied permission, the panic soon subsided and gave way to a severe economic depression.

II

These developments were ample fodder for the critics of the Bank of England and of the whole English banking system. New minds largely played the leading role in the increasingly heated discussion, but one of the basic ideas that gained prominence in the process had already been expressed by Ricardo in his *Plan for the Establishment of a National Bank*,[4] which was published in 1824 shortly after his death and constituted a sort of legacy on his part. Ricardo had from the very start emphasised in this work that the Bank of England conducted two entirely different and not necessarily related businesses, which might just as well be handled by two separate agencies: the issue of paper money to replace metallic currency and the granting of loans. Ricardo was less motivated, to be sure, by theoretical views on currency policy than by his mistrust towards the Bank and the desire to save the state its annual bank payments in offering the practical recommendation that the right to issue notes be transferred from the Bank of England to a national bank, i.e., a note-issuing authority under the direction of five permanently appointed government commissioners, whose only function would be to keep the price of gold stable by the purchase and sale of gold against notes. This idea of separating note issue from the remaining banking functions presented here was taken over a little later by the so-called Currency School and urged as a solution for problems of banking policy which Ricardo had hardly anticipated and which became obvious only during the 1825 crisis. It is true that a year before Ricardo, Thomas Joplin had already stated the fundamental idea of the Currency School that note issue should be proportional

---

[4] David Ricardo, *Plan for the Establishment of a National Bank* [1824], reprinted in *Works of David Ricardo*, ed. J. R. McCulloch (London: John Murray, 1846), and as an appendix to A. Andréadès, *History of the Bank of England 1640 to 1903* (London: P. S. King, 1909 and later editions). [Also reprinted in *The Works and Correspondence of David Ricardo*, in 11 vols, edited by Piero Sraffa, with the collaboration of M. H. Dobb (Cambridge: Cambridge University Press for the Royal Economic Society, 1951-73), vol. 4, pp. 171-300. -Ed.]

to the inflow or outflow of gold from the bank, in a work that received very little attention at that time.[5]

This work, however, had less impact than a study published by Joplin a year earlier, in which he was the first to draw attention to the previously neglected Scottish banking system and to point out that a loophole existed in the privileges granted the Bank of England making it legally permissible, contrary to general opinion, to establish joint-stock banks in England as well as in Scotland.[6] While "in the part of Great Britain called England" the Bank of England had been reserved the exclusive right to issue notes (which at the time was considered the major function of a bank) as the only such company with more than six partners by the privileges of 1709 and 1742, vigorous joint-stock banks had been founded in Scotland, which had consistently weathered crises under which small English country banks invariably foundered.[7] Joplin not only demonstrated the advantages of the Scottish system, but also stressed that while joint-stock banks in England were excluded from note-issuing, they could serve the more important function of facilitating the placement of capital. While this possibility was not exploited immediately and the only step taken initially in 1826 was to restrict the Bank's monopoly to London and a sixty-five-mile radius, it was surely the result of Joplin's discovery that ten years later, in 1832, the renewal of the Bank's privilege included an explicit reference to this legal situation, whereupon the first large joint-stock bank was founded in London.

---

[5] Thomas Joplin, *Outlines of a System of Political Economy; written with a view to prove . . . that the cause of the present agricultural distress is entirely artificial; and to suggest a plan for the management of the currency* (London: Baldwin, Cradock, and Joy, 1823). The author, who became one of the most indefatigable participants in the Bank discussion and published more than a dozen works on the subject in the next twenty years, reports fully on this very rare 1823 publication in his *An Analysis and History of the Currency Question* (London: J. Ridgway, 1832), esp. pp. 141ff. On Joplin, cf. also Maberly Phillips, *A History of Banks, Bankers, and Banking in Northumberland, etc.* (London: E. Wilson, 1849), pp. 88-108, and Hartley Withers, *The National Provincial Bank, 1833-1933* (London: Waterlow, 1933).

[6] *An Essay on the General Principles and Present Practice of Banking in England and Scotland* (Newcastle-upon-Tyne: E. Walker, 1822), especially in the "Supplementary observations" appended in the same year to the third edition of this publication. A fourth edition appeared as an appendix to the above-mentioned *Outlines of a System of Political Economy*, 1823.

[7] [On the history of Scottish banking see Sydney G. Checkland, *Scottish Banking: A History, 1695-1973* (Glasgow: Collins, 1975), and Lawrence H. White, *Free Banking in Britain: Theory, Experience, and Debate, 1800-1845* (Cambridge: Cambridge University Press, 1984), pp. 23-49; and Murray N. Rothbard, "The Myth of Free Banking in Scotland", *The Review of Austrian Economics*, vol. 2, 1988, pp. 229-245. -Ed.]

Another author whose first publication dated from the 1820s was to gain greater prominence than Joplin: Thomas Tooke, who had already gained a reputation as one of the leaders of the free trade movement.[8] These early and probably best works by Tooke, notably, his *Considerations* (1826), are of special interest, because Tooke at that point still sided completely with the Bullionists and in particular Ricardo, while he later became one of the major opponents of the Currency School, which continued this doctrine. His early writings not only have the merit of presenting with unusual lucidity the Bullionist views, which he was later to challenge, but also expand this doctrine significantly, for instance by analysing the effects of increases in credit. Tooke clarifies the relationship between increases in note issue, a lowering of the interest rate, and price rises, thereby extending the views expressed by Thornton and Ricardo that we discussed earlier. He uses these theoretical insights to explain the 1825 crisis, giving one of the best early explanations of business cycles.[9] Tooke attributes the intensity of the 1825 crisis to the over-issue of notes by the Bank of England. In his eyes the large amount of notes in circulation compared with the total money supply in circulation constitutes a serious danger, which the relative cheapness of circulating notes does not counterbalance. It is a true irony of history that for this reason Tooke actually opposed Ricardo's proposal to use a gold exchange standard, relying exclusively on paper money as the circulating medium. He was especially outspoken in his opposition to the argument occasionally introduced by Ricardo in favour of this system, namely "the facility

---

[8] Thomas Tooke, *Thoughts and Details on the High and Low Prices of the Last Thirty Years*, parts I-IV (London: John Murray, 1823) (there also exists an expanded, undated, and probably later edition of part II); *Considerations on the State of the Currency* (London: John Murray, 1826). For the first-mentioned work, cf. the detailed (anonymous) review by T. H. Malthus, *Quarterly Review*, vol. 29, London, 1823. [Hayek's later chair at the London School of Economics was named for Tooke. -Ed.]

[9] Cf. chapter I of *Considerations*, especially pp. 21ff., the footnotes on p. 21-22, and pp. 75-78. Detailed explanations about the former topic also appear in the appendix to Tooke's most famous work, his *A History of Prices, and of the State of the Circulation, from 1793 to 1837* (London: Longman, Brown, Green, & Longmans, 1838), vol. 1, pp. 355ff.; German translation, *Die Geschichte und Bestimmung der Preise während der Jahre 1793-1857*, by C. W. Asher (Dresden: R. Kuntze, 1858-9), but it is revealing that important parts of the above-mentioned footnotes are omitted. For the development of the theory regarding interactions between the quantity of money, the interest rate, and business fluctuations, Robert Torrens's *An Essay on the Production of Wealth* (London: Longman, Hurst, Rees, Orme, & Brown, 1821), which pre-dates Tooke, and Sir Henry Brooke Parnell [Congleton]'s *Observations on Paper Money, Banking and Overtrading* (London: Printed for J. Ridgway and E. Wilson, 1827; second edition, 1829), which appeared shortly after Tooke's work, are important contributions.

with which it may be altered in quantity, as the wants of commerce and temporary circumstances may require".[10] Tooke offers three proposals to stave off these dangers: (1) obligating the Bank of England to publish periodic reports about its status, to make its policies subject to control; (2) restricting the Bank of England's monopoly position, which was responsible for the fact that only weak country banks could issue notes in addition to itself, and (3) forbidding the issue of small notes (under 5 pounds) in order to increase the amount of gold in circulation and reduce the contribution of notes to the total amount of money in circulation. While his first proposal was not immediately accepted, a second law was passed in 1826 which did partial justice to his second proposal by limiting the monopoly of the Bank of England to an area within a sixty-five-mile radius of London and to his third proposal by eliminating the issue of notes with a face value of less than 5 pounds, which had been introduced at the beginning of the restriction period.

The best evidence for the fact that in the 1820s the doctrines of the Bullionists had gained general acceptance is the fact that in 1827 even the Bank of England thought it proper to repudiate the formally approved 1819 resolution, in which the Bank had taken a stand against the 'unfounded opinion' that it might induce an improvement in the exchange rates and an influx of gold by reducing its note circulation. The only remaining opponents to Ricardo's now-prevalent doctrine were agriculturalists, who blamed persistently low prices and the consequent plight of agriculture on the policy of the Bank of England during and after the resumption of cash payments; beginning with demands for price stabilisation, they became more and more explicit about promoting a new inflation. This movement, which later joined forces with the Chartist movement, whose main focus was on electoral reform, found many supporters in the Birmingham textile industry, a classic instance of recurring inflationist pressures. At least its leaders, W. Cobbett[11] and particularly C. C. Western (who repeatedly brought forward in parlia-

---

[10] *Considerations* etc., pp. 97ff. The above-mentioned comment by Ricardo appears in his *Proposals for an Economical and Secure Currency* (London: John Murray, 1816), p. 8 (in *Economic Essays, by David Ricardo*, ed. E. C. K. Gonner (London: Frank Cass, 1923), p. 158; in the special edition of the German translation by Wilhelm Fromowitz and Fritz Machlup, *Die Goldkernwährung* (Halberstadt: H. Meyer's buchdr., 1925), p. 11). [In the Sraffa edition of Ricardo's *Works*, op. cit., vol. 4, p. 55. -Ed.]

[11] [William Cobbett (1763-1835), author of the anti-industrial and anti-commercial *Twopenny Register* newspaper, which ran from October 1816 until July 1820. -Ed.]

ment motions along these lines, stimulating interesting debates, in some of which Ricardo still participated), as well as T. Attwood[12] and the authors (T. B. Wright and J. Harlow) of the "Gemini Letters" published anonymously in 1844, deserve to be mentioned.

We must not forget to mention here an absolutely first-rate contribution to monetary science dating from this period, although it had little direct bearing on the currently relevant problems. We have in mind a series of lectures on monetary theory held by Nassau William Senior in 1828-9. Senior had just been appointed to Oxford University's first professorship for political economy, and his lectures—which were published only in bits and pieces, in small editions, some of them after years of delay[13]—must be ranked among the most impressive and brilliant achievements, worthy of mention along with the writings of Cantillon and Hume, Thornton and Ricardo. In these lectures, Senior concentrates on showing the weaknesses of the oversimplified mechanistic quantity theory of money, into which James Mill had barbarously distorted Ricardo's doctrine in Mill's *Elements of Political Economy*, published in 1826.[14] It is erroneously asserted that Senior countered the quantity theory by attempting to derive the value of money purely from the cost of production of precious metals. Far from offering a one-sided view, Senior offers a multifaceted analysis of the reciprocal relationships between costs of production and the monetary and industrial de-

[12] [Thomas Attwood (1783-1856), founder of the Birmingham Political Union and leader of the inflationist 'Birmingham School' of economics. On Attwood see Sydney G. Checkland, "The Birmingham Economists 1815-1850", *Economic History Review*, 2nd series, vol. 1, no. 1, 1948, pp. 1-19. -Ed.]

[13] Nassau W. Senior, *Three Lectures on the Transmission of the Precious Metal from Country to Country, and the Mercantile Theory of Wealth* (London: John Murray, 1828; second edition, 1830; reprinted London: The London School of Economics and Political Science, 1931); *Three Lectures on the Cost of Obtaining Money, and on some Effects of Private and Government Paper Money* (London: John Murray, 1830; reprinted London: The London School of Economics and Political Science, 1931); *Three Lectures on the Value of Money* (London: B. Fellowes, 1840; reprinted London: The London School of Economics and Political Science, 1931); the latter in German translation in Karl Diehl and Paul Mombert, *Ausgewählte Lesestücke zum Studium der politischen ökonomie*, vol. 1, *Zur Lehre vom Geld* (Karlsruhe: G. Braun, 1920). Cf. also a collection of various comments by Senior on questions of monetary theory in S. L. Levi's rather ill-assorted compilation, Nassau W. Senior, *Industrial Efficiency and Social Economy* (London: P. S. King, 1929). [On Senior see Marian Bowley, *Nassau Senior and Classical Economics* (London: George Allen & Unwin, 1937; reprinted New York: Octagon Books, 1967). -Ed.]

[14] [James Mill, *Elements of Political Economy* (London: Baldwin, Craddock, and Joy, 1826). Reprinted in Donald Winch, ed., *James Mill: Selected Economic Writings* (Edinburgh: Oliver & Boyd for the Scottish Economic Society, 1966). -Ed.]

mands for precious metals; to explain the demand for money, he carefully investigates "the causes which determine what proportion of the value of his income each individual habitually keeps by him in money" and shows how a state of equilibrium is reached once the money spent on the production of precious metals exactly equals the amount of precious metals secured thereby and, finally, how industrial demand for precious metals (using the numerical assumptions of his example) hinges on "the existence of persons able and willing to give for 16 ounces of plate, the commodities produced by the labour of one man for a year, his wages having been advanced for a year, and the power of people to raise, without payment of rent, 16 ounces of silver by a year's labour" and constitutes the pivotal point for all monetary transactions.[15] Even today his exposition, to which we can refer here only in passing, remains eminently worth reading as the classic exploration of this subject.[16]

I am forced to resist the temptation here to provide all the missing information for the as yet unwritten history of monetary controversy and must therefore limit myself to the most important publications. With this in mind, I would just mention in passing two 1829 publications by Tooke, were it not for the fact that in the appendix to the first of these publications an author who until very recently had received scant notice, James Pennington, first stated a doctrine which in its final formulation became very important in the banking controversy and constitutes the only contribution of lasting value made by the 'Banking School'. It was Pennington's object to show that "the book credits of a London banker, and the promissory notes of a country banker are essentially the same thing, that they are different forms of the same kind of credit; and that they are employed to perform the same function . . . . Both the one and the other are substitutes for a metallic currency, and are susceptible of a considerable increase or diminution, without a corresponding enlargement or contraction of the basis on which they rest."[17] This assertion about the equivalence of bank notes and cheque deposits later served as the crucial point of departure for the Banking School's criticism of Peel's Act.

---

[15] *Three Lectures on the Value of Money*, op. cit., p. 40; Diehl-Mombert, *Lesestücke*, vol. 1, op. cit., p. 155.

[16] [On Senior's theory of the value of money see Bowley, op. cit., pp. 201-234, and Hugo Hegeland, *The Quantity Theory of Money* (Gothenburg: Elanders Boktryckeri Aktiebolag, 1951), pp. 63-66. -Ed.]

[17] In the appendix to Tooke's *History of Prices*, op. cit., vol. 2, pp. 369 and 374.

In his 1840 publication Pennington explained at length that such deposits arose not only by the depositing of cash, but also through the advancing of credit by the banks themselves. The banks, therefore, even when they did not issue notes, were in a position to 'create' means of exchange in the form of such check deposits by advancing credit. The term 'create' that he used to describe this activity remains hotly disputed even now.[18]

III

The approaching expiration of the Bank of England's privilege gave rise to the appointment in 1832 of another parliamentary investigating committee, which was mainly expected to clarify the questions relating to the conditions for an extension of the privilege, that is, the questions about the maintenance or elimination of the Bank's monopoly, centralisation of the issue of notes and control of its administration.[19] The interrogation of the Bank directors on the guidelines for their credit policy focused general attention on these problems. In contrast to similar inquiries during the restriction period,[20] the experts who were called in for questioning, notably the Bank representatives, proved to be far more knowledgeable during this and subsequent investigations than the members of the parliamentary committee.[21] The Bank Governor, J. Horsley Palmer, in particular, was successful in his attempts to clarify the Bank's special position and its responsibility as the keeper of cash reserves for all the other banks. In the light of this position, it was the opinion of its directors that the Bank should not compete with other banks in normal times in discounting commercial bills, and that its usefulness

---

[18] [This essay was written in 1929. -Ed.]

[19] [This committee is sometimes referred to as the Althorp Committee after Lord Althorp, leader of the House of Commons in Lord Grey's Whig government, who proposed the investigation. -Ed.]

[20] [See this volume, chapter 11. -Ed.]

[21] *Report of the committee of Secrecy on the Bank of England Charter*, 1832, House of Commons Reports and Papers 722. A digest of the evidence on the bank charter taken before the committee of 1832 . . . was published in London in 1833. The most significant parts of the hearings are reprinted in T. E. Gregory, *Select Statutes Documents and Reports Relating to British Banking* (London: Oxford University Press, 1929), vol. 1, pp. 1-18. [The full report, including the minutes of evidence, is reprinted in the *Irish University Press Series of British Parliamentary Papers* (Shannon, Ireland: Irish University Press, 1968-71), Monetary Policy, General, vol. 4. -Ed.]

as an institution of last resort in times of difficulty would be hampered by altering its form of government.

Since their conversion to Bullionist doctrine, the directors had agreed to regulate note circulation on the basis of fixed rules, which they expounded for the first time in their statements before this parliamentary committee. These rules often served in later years as the foundation for the legal regulation of note issue; the rule of one-third coverage was not, to be sure, interpreted as rigorously as in later years, to the effect that the ratio of notes in circulation to specie reserve should be three to one, but rather, as a rule of thumb for periods of tranquillity, with the guiding principle that the uncovered fraction should remain as stable as possible. Palmer explained this principle to the committee in these terms: "The principle, with reference to the period of a full currency, and consequently a par of exchange, by which the Bank is guided in the regulation of their issues (excepting under special circumstances) is to invest and retain in securities, bearing interest, a given proportion of the deposits, and the value received for the notes in circulation, the remainder being held in coin and bullion . . . . [T]he circulation of the country, so far as the same may depend on the Bank, being subsequently regulated by the action of the Foreign Exchanges."[22] In subsequent testimonies, Palmer and G. W. Norman, another Bank director testifying before the Committee, emphasised that this coverage rule applied not only to notes but to all liabilities payable upon request, notably deposits (a form of coverage by fixed proportion that became more common again after the war). The directors clearly stated that the Bank did not forcibly regulate the amount of notes in circulation; it left it up to the public to act upon the Bank. The exchange rates would be automatically regulated, since a lowering of the pound's exchange rate would lead to an exchange of notes into gold for export. The notes in circulation would be progressively reduced until exchange rates were back to par. The magnitude of the requisite reserves was a function not only of the Bank's own notes but of the total note circulation in England. To keep fluctuations in the total amount of notes and deposits in line with the inflow and outflow of gold, the total amount of investment in securities should remain as steady as possible, given the one-third coverage ratio as a starting point. It was admitted that the principle was set aside from time to time

---

[22] [Question 79, p. 11 of the original Report; p. 3 of Gregory's edition, op. cit; p. 11 of the Irish University Press reprint, op. cit. -Ed.]

when the gold reserve became particularly large, in order to maintain the Bank's profitability. In such a case, Palmer conceded, the Bank might get rid of part of the gold in exchange for securities.

It is very interesting to note the views of the Bank directors about the type of securities that were considered desirable. In contrast to the views that were to predominate in subsequent years and that still predominate today, the Bank directors believed that discounting commercial bills was not desirable in normal periods. Exchequer bills were considered preferable because, as Palmer explained, competition by the Bank on the discount market with other banks would conjure up the threat of overexpansion of credit. It was only in times of crisis, when money was scarce and confidence low, that the Bank felt itself responsible for satisfying the increased demand for money by discounting commercial bills. It had in recent years been performing the same function with respect to the increased demand that regularly arose at the end of each quarterly period. The Bank's hands were tied in setting a policy for periods of crisis because of the usury laws, which prohibited raising the discount rate above 5 per cent, as this forced the Bank to maintain rigid maxima for the granting of credit instead of raising the discount rate.

The Bank Charter Act of 1833,[23] which was enacted right after the hearings, eliminated interest rate restrictions affecting the Bank's discount activity at the same time that it extended the Bank's privilege. The Act included a provision permitting the establishment of non-note-issuing joint-stock banks in every part of England. It also, for the first time, formally designated the Bank of England notes as legal tender and imposed a new obligation on the Bank, which Tooke had already demanded in 1826: the quarterly publication of accounts about the Bank's specie reserve, its notes in circulation, and its deposits.[24]

---

[23] Reprinted in Gregory, op. cit., vol. 1, pp. 19-27.

[24] [Hayek does not mention in this account the Act of 1834, which in retrospect deserves notice, particularly in view of Hayek's later work on the de-nationalisation of money (see *Money and Nations*, vol. 6 of *The Collected Works*). Much of the original capital of the Bank of England had come from abroad; there were over a thousand Dutch stockholders in the mid-eighteenth century. But "the Bank, rechartered in 1833, was now [in 1833] as thoroughly English in proprietary as in policy and name". What the Act of 1834 did was to transfer all remaining functions of the government's Exchequer to the Bank and "but this was not in the Act, nor was it in essence new—the Bank could use this consolidated government balance like the rest of its deposits, lending out some two-thirds and keeping the remainder in hand. So in the United Kingdom, and in this the United Kingdom was unique, all the money

IV

The disclosure by the Bank of England of the guidelines underlying its note issue stimulated a prolonged discussion, which eventually led to Peel's Act and the sharp clash of opinions between the 'Currency School' and the 'Banking School'. Right after the publication of the Althorp Committee's report—in the autumn of 1832—G. W. Norman drafted a pamphlet that was first published for private circulation in the following year.[25] In it Norman supported Ricardo's and Joplin's earlier views that the issue of notes be separated from regular banking activity and that it would automatically adapt to the movement of gold. This work, which became widely known in its final published version five years later, served in its original form as the true platform of the Currency School.

A few years later, in 1836, England was again plagued by a violent crisis. At that time the 1833 discussions were the point of departure for a new and sharp criticism of the Bank's policy, which led directly to its reorganisation under Peel's Act. The Bank was—justifiably—blamed for violating its self-imposed principles. Prior to the 1836 crisis, whose course mirrored the 1825 crisis, the Bank was accused of contributing to the crisis by its overly liberal granting of credit and of waiting until the brink of the crisis to raise the discount rate from 4 to 4½ to 5 per cent, when its specie reserve had shrunk to hardly more than one-fifth of its liabilities.[26]

---

that for the moment a government did not want was available for use by the business community". See Sir John Clapham, *The Bank of England, A History* (Cambridge: Cambridge University Press, 1944), vol. 2, pp. 132-133. -Ed.]

[25] *Remarks upon some Prevalent Errors, with respect to Currency and Banking, and suggestions to the legislature as to the renewal of the Bank Charter* (London: R. Hunter, 1833). In the enlarged 1838 publication, the end of the title was changed to "as to the improvement of the monetary system".

[26] [The crisis of 1836, both in England and the United States, has not received sufficient attention from economists. England's ability to remain on a gold standard lasted only as long as much of the rest of the world was *not* on a gold standard. "'The Bank,' Thomas Tooke wrote rather unkindly in 1838, 'having scrambled through its difficulties into a position of safety may naturally claim merit from the event.' But, he added, with truth, had the harvest of 1836 been bad, and had the American banks resolutely contracted their liabilities and called in every dollar due to them, *instead of suspending payment*, its last £4,000,000 of treasure might not have seen it through the spring of 1837" (Sir John Clapham, *The Bank of England, A History*, op. cit., p. 161; emphasis added). -Ed.]

The first effective criticism of the Bank's policy came out during these years in the form of an open letter to Lord Melbourne[27] by Robert Torrens[28] (whose many-sided accomplishments as an economist are insufficiently recognised even today).[28] Torrens—in a misinterpretation of Pennington's doctrine, although Pennington had contributed an appendix to the letter—reproached the Bank for not making a sharp enough distinction between 'circulating currency' and 'deposits'. He therefore urged that two separate departments be put in charge of creating deposits and issuing notes in order to be sure that the Bank followed what he considered an appropriate policy.

These proposals became more widely known when, that very same year, they were also espoused by the respected banker S. J. Loyd (later Lord Overstone), the future leader of the 'Currency School', in his detailed reply[29] to Horsley Palmer's defence of the Bank. Palmer's pamphlet[30] attempted to make other banks shoulder the blame for the crisis. He singled out the newly established joint-stock banks, which were particularly objectionable to the Bank of England. Interestingly enough, the pamphlet also reveals that Palmer himself had doubts about the appropriateness of the Bank's policy. He admits that the question might be raised seriously whether the Bank should not have increased the discount rate somewhat earlier, but such an intervention would have been in conflict with the stated principle of the Bank not to interfere with the course of

---

[27] [William Lamb, second Viscount Melbourne (1779-1848). -Ed.]

[28] Robert Torrens, *A Letter to the Right Honourable Lord Viscount Melbourne, on the Causes of the Recent Derangement in the Money Market, and on Bank Reform* (London: Longman, Rees, Orme, Brown, & Green, 1837). Cf. by the same author, *A Letter to Thomas Tooke, Esq. In Reply to his Objections against the Business of the Bank into a Department of Issue, and a Department of Deposit and Discount: With a Plan of Bank Reform* (London: Longman, Hurst, Orme, & Brown, 1840).

[28] [See now Lionel Robbins, *Robert Torrens and the Evolution of Classical Economics* (London: Macmillan, 1958). -Ed.]

[29] Samuel Jones Loyd [Overstone], *Reflections Suggested by a Perusal of Mr. J. Horsley Palmer's Pamphlet on the Causes and Consequences of the Pressure on the Money Market* (London: P. Richardson, 1837), reprinted in *Tracts and Other Publications on Metallic and Paper Currency, by the Right Hon. Lord Overstone*, ed. J. R. McCulloch, (London: Printed by Harrison and Sons, 1857). Cf. also Loyd's *Further Reflections on the State of the Currency and the Action of the Bank of England* (London: P. Richardson, 1837) (not in *Tracts, etc.*).

[30] John Horsley Palmer, *The Causes and Consequences of the Pressure upon the Money-Market; with a statement of the action of the Bank of England from 1st October 1833 to the 27th December 1836* (London: P. Richardson, 1837). Cf. also Palmer's *Reply to the Reflections, etc. etc. of Mr. Samuel Jones Loyd on the Pamphlet Entitled "Causes and Consequences of the Pressure on the Money-Market"* (London: P. Richardson, 1837).

events, but rather to maintain a passive stance towards them, a policy that had been tacitly accepted by parliament in 1832. Palmer emphasises the willingness of the Bank to alter these principles, if parliament felt that this would be advantageous. In his reply, Loyd showed, however, that the Bank had not adhered to its principle of keeping its total revenue-producing investments fixed and allowing the public to determine fluctuations in its note and deposit liabilities by the deposit and withdrawal of gold. The principle of keeping the sum of notes and deposits steady was observed only if one disregarded certain deposits that the Bank viewed as 'extraordinary'. The fluctuations in circulating notes, which Loyd considered crucial, did not visibly reflect changes in specie reserve; at times note circulation had even gone up when specie reserves had declined. Loyd considered this situation to be the inevitable consequence of the objectionable interconnexion between note issue and deposit activities on the part of the Bank and relentlessly repeated his demand that these two functions be separated. Only thus could one expect that a currency consisting of both notes and gold coins would function exactly like a purely metallic currency, that is, would keep perfectly adjusted to the amount of gold moving into and out of the country.

With publications by Norman,[31] Torrens, and Loyd, among whom Loyd was the recognised leader and the most brilliant writer, while Torrens was probably the best theoretician, the 'Currency School'—the name under which it soon became known—stepped forward with a well-defined programme, which was to be implemented as early as 1844. The opposing doctrine of the 'Banking School' developed only gradually and never attained a coherent set of ideas.

Divergent views about crucial questions surfaced first at the hearings of the investigating committee in 1840-1. By that time criticism of the Bank of England's policy had become widespread, sparked by the fact that two years after the 1837 crisis a serious shortage of money had developed, again because of the Bank's overly liberal credit policy. Specie reserves fell to such a low level that the Bank of France had to come to the rescue. Not only Currency School supporters, but also men like Thomas Tooke and

---

[31] George Warde Norman, *Remarks upon some Prevalent Errors, with respect to Currency and Banking, and Suggestions to the Legislature and the Public as to the Improvement in the Monetary System* (London: P. Richardson, 1838).

J. W. Gilbart,[32] two of the later leaders of the Banking School, participated in this criticism. Their objections focused particularly on the belated raising of discount rates, which stemmed from the Bank's principle not to intervene in the course of events. As late as 1840 Tooke spoke up vigorously against the Bank's alleged responsibility to accommodate itself to business needs. His critical views still relied fully on Ricardo's doctrine, from which he differed only in his greater emphasis on non-monetary causes of price fluctuations, such as good or bad harvests etc. He expounded similar views in the first two volumes of his major work on the history of prices[33] and even in the third volume, which was published in 1840. In 1840 his opinions underwent a change, however, as can be seen from his testimony before the investigating committee that year. His change of mind had a fateful effect, as his new and in many ways quite mistaken viewpoint attained wide circulation, together with the doctrines of his fellow combatants of the Banking School. This turning away from Ricardo's doctrine was highly deleterious for the development of monetary theory and even today some of its unhappy consequences linger on. Undoubtedly this reaction was set in motion by the unwavering support given to Peel's Act by Ricardo's strictest disciples, despite the fact that the Act certainly had its flaws and was not necessarily an outgrowth of Ricardo's doctrine.

The immediate cause for the appointment of the investigating committee in 1840 was the circumstance that the government had reserved the option of terminating the Bank's privilege in its previous extension of the privilege, which was to expire in 1844. The

---

[32] James William Gilbart had acquired an outstanding practical reputation as founder of the first London joint-stock bank, the London and Westminster Bank, which was established in 1833, and as author of textbooks on banking which were for decades the most widely used on the subject. He himself denied that he favoured any definite theory. His most relevant works on these questions are *An Inquiry into the Causes of the Pressure on the Money Market during the year 1839* (London: Longman, Orme, Brown, Green & Longmans, 1840) and *Currency and Banking: A Review of Some of the Principles and Plans that have Recently Engaged Public Attention* (London: H. Hooper, 1841); among his textbooks on the subject are *A Practical Treatise on Banking* (London: E. Wilson, 1827, and later editions) and *The History and Principles of Banking* (London: Longman, Rees, Orme, Brown, Green, & Longmans, 1834, and a 1907 edition revised by E. Sykes).

[33] Thomas Tooke, *A History of Prices and of the State of Circulation from 1793 to 1837*, op. cit. (German edition, with comments, by C. W. Asher, op. cit.). Four additional volumes continuing the first two were published in 1840, 1848, and 1857, the 1848 and 1857 volumes written in collaboration with William Newmarch. A new edition of the whole work appeared, with an introduction by T. E. Gregory, under the joint authorship of Tooke and Newmarch, *A History of Prices and of the State of Circulation from 1792 to 1856* (London: P. S. King, 1928).

opportunity therefore existed to introduce some changes in the Bank's status. The committee had been instructed to concentrate on the question whether the existence of a specially privileged bank was warranted in any case and whether a completely free banking system was not preferable. Though the investigation was indeed very comprehensive, it effectively concerned itself primarily with principles that should guide the Bank of England's note-issuing policy and gave its critics an opportunity to expound their objections and reform proposals. On this occasion the leading role was played by S. J. Loyd (Lord Overstone), who justified his stand with great lucidity by pointing out that the Bill of 1819 had restored the convertibility of notes into gold in order to guarantee the constant equality of value between paper currency and coins, so that in effect the currency functioned like a metallic currency, but this hope was not borne out by subsequent developments. "Since that period, a close investigation of the events which have occurred has led observant and reflecting minds to perceive, that the constant right of converting your paper into gold does not secure with sufficient efficiency those which are really the ultimate ends and objects for which that convertibility was established. They have found, or conceived that they have found, evidence that an extent of transactions and a range of prices may be maintained for limited periods under a convertible paper currency, which would not be maintained if that currency was really a metallic currency; and that, to obviate that evil, a further regulation is necessary, which shall be sufficient to preserve the notes at all times precisely at that amount which the metallic currency would be, and that, consequently, a depreciation in a certain sense of the word, of a temporary nature, may take place and be compatible with convertibility."[34] What Loyd had in mind was the fact that bank note circulation could continue to increase even after gold inflow had come to a halt, while domestic prices have not risen sufficiently to induce an outflow of gold. He rightly envisaged this credit expansion as a source of danger and blamed it for the violence of the ensuing crisis. He maintained that implementation of his proposal to tie changes in the circulation of notes completely to the inflow and outflow of gold would replace

---

[34] *Report from Select Committee on Banks of Issue*, 1840, House of Commons Reports and Papers 602, Question 2932. This testimony also appears under Loyd in McCulloch, ed., *Tracts, etc., by Lord Overstone*, op. cit., p. 428, and in Gregory, *Select Statutes, etc.*, op. cit., vol. 1, p. 53. [The report is reprinted in the *Irish University Press Series of British Parliamentary Papers*, op. cit., Monetary Policy, General, vol. 5; the quotation is on p. 257 of the minutes of evidence. -Ed.]

the sudden, belated restriction of credit by a more timely restriction. "It would have produced a regulation that depended upon principle instead of a regulation that depended upon panic, and therefore was incapable of being measured or regulated by any fixed rule. The contraction, upon that supposition, would have commenced in the early stage of the drain, before speculation and the rise of prices had reached its full height; and it would also have commenced before the internal drain had sprung up. Now, it is a very remarkable and very important phenomenon attending these drains, that the drain always goes on for some length of time, before prices, and speculation, and over-trading, and over-banking have reached their maximum point; and that the last stage of the drain is always characterised by the springing up of internal alarm, which gives rise to an internal drain. Now, an internal drain is clearly one that can be met by no principle; there is no method of meeting it but by paying out gold, till the drain ceases. It appears to me that contraction applied in the early stages would be applied when it could be borne without inconvenience to the community, and that it would necessarily tend to counteract and check in their early growth these tendencies, viz. to speculation, over-trading, excessive rise of prices, which by their undue expansion under our present system, and the consequent violence of the subsequent collapse, produce the extreme intensity which characterises the commercial crisis of this country."[35] So far as it goes, Loyd's justification for his proposal is hardly contestable. The weak point of his argument, on which a large part of the questions focused, was that his proposal failed to prevent an excessive expansion of cheque deposits, which also served as circulating media, and that on the other hand the sharp limitation on the issue of notes might hamper the convertibility of existing cheque holdings into notes. Loyd as well as the other supporters of the Currency School fell back on an artificial and meaningless distinction, namely that deposits simply did not count as 'money'.

Both Tooke and Gilbart[36] were summoned to the hearings to state the case for the opponents of the Currency School's reform proposals. Tooke, for his part, asserted that it was impossible in

---

[35] *Ibid.*, Question 2726; in McCulloch, *Tracts*, op. cit., p. 368; in Gregory, *Select Statutes, etc.*, op. cit., vol. 1, pp. 35-36. [In the Irish University Press reprint, op. cit., pp. 222-223. -Ed.]

[36] The importance of Gilbart's testimony before this committee in 1841 lies mainly in the elaboration of the theory of seasonal fluctuations in money requirements, which Horsley Palmer had first presented to the 1832 investigating committee.

principle for an excessive amount of redeemable notes to be issued and went so far as to affirm that in his opinion "the amount of the circulating medium is the effect and not the cause of the variations in prices" and that "no alteration in the prices can be traced in any way to the amount of the circulation".[37] His reform proposals were basically limited to insisting on a larger cash reserve on the part of the Bank. In his opinion, the reserve should have been double the amount actually held by the Bank.

V

The investigating committee appointed in 1840 reached no definite conclusions, even after its hearings were extended to 1841; it was not even prepared to issue a report. The committee's importance, however, lay in the fact that Robert Peel, as one of its members, had been converted to the principles of the Currency School and—after he became prime minister in 1841—was determined to implement them.[38] Even before the expiration of the Bank's privilege, he questioned the Bank in the spring of 1844 about its reaction to the various proposed changes in its privilege. After several exchanges of letters[39] had produced an agreement, Peel introduced a proposal for a new law, which he justified in two famous speeches, which identified him as a firm supporter of the Currency School doctrines.[40] The law was passed with only slight opposition in the House of Commons and accepted almost unanimously in the House of Lords.[41] In view of the law's overwhelming importance—it

[37] *Ibid.*, Questions 3299 and 3621; reprinted in Tooke's *History of Prices*, op. cit., vol. 4, pp. 461ff. [In the Irish University reprint, op. cit., pp. 299 and 340. -Ed.]

[38] [On Peel (1788-1850) see *Memoirs by the Right Honourable Sir Robert Peel* (London: John Murray, 1856-7; reprinted: New York: Kraus Reprint Co., 1969); Norman Gash, *Mr. Secretary Peel: The Life of Sir Robert Peel to 1830*, second edition (London and New York: Longman, 1985); Gash, *Sir Robert Peel: The Life of Sir Robert Peel after 1830* (London: Longman, 1972); and Donald Reed, *Peel and the Victorians* (Oxford: Basil Blackwell, 1987). -Ed.]

[39] This correspondence is reprinted in Gregory, *Select Statutes, etc.*, op. cit., vol. 1, pp. 117ff.

[40] Both of Peel's speeches and the ensuing debates appear in *Hansard's Parliamentary Debates* as well as in a special edition under the title *Debates in the House of Commons on Sir Robert Peel's Bank Bills of 1844 and 1845* (London: C. Buck, 1875).

[41] *An Act to regulate the Issue of Bank Notes, and for giving to the Governor and Company of the Bank of England certain Privileges for a limited Period*, July 19, 1844 (7 and 8 Vit.c. 32). The text of the law or at least extensive descriptions of the content can be found in most of the works listed in the bibliography for this chapter, notably

remains in effect even today with only minor modifications—we shall examine its contents at some length.

Peel's Act of 1844 (in contrast to the Act of 1819) is viewed as the most famous and controversial attempt to regulate the bank note system by law. Its most significant provisions are contained in the first two paragraphs, which state that the Bank's note-issuing activity is to be carried on exclusively by a specially created Issue Department and separated from all other activities carried on in the Banking Department. Specific rules for the issue of notes are laid down as well. On the day of its establishment the Issue Department was to take over the Bank's entire gold holdings with the exception of small sums needed for its daily business, together with the rigidly limited amount of 14 million pounds in securities, including the irredeemable government debt to the Bank amounting to about 11 million pounds in exchange for an equal amount of notes. From that point on, notes could be issued only against gold coins and gold bullion (and to a very small extent silver bullion as well).

The sum total of notes issued not on the basis of gold but of securities was not to be increased, except in specified exceptional situations. It might be diminished, if the Bank felt that it would be more appropriate to have a larger gold coverage. On the other hand, the Issue Department was obligated to issue notes in exchange for a given amount of gold and of course to redeem in gold coins all notes presented to it. It was believed that the 14 million pounds, which were not required to be covered by gold, represented the minimum amount of notes that were assumed to be needed in circulation, so that redemption would never be demanded. If circumstances should change in such a way, however, that this might be in the realm of possibility, the Bank would be free to reduce the securities in the Issue Department and to reduce in this fashion that fraction of the notes in circulation not covered by gold. An increase in the uncovered portion of the notes would take place only to the extent that other banks lost their right to issue notes (under provisions spelled out below), but not exceeding two-thirds of the amount of the notes issued by these banks. A final important provision concerned the Bank's obligation to publish weekly statements about the position of both the Issue and the Banking Departments. Peel's Act contained no provisions about the way in which the Banking Department was to conduct its affairs.

in Gregory, *Select Statutes, etc.*, op. cit., vol. 1, pp. 129-147.

We can best grasp the peculiar situation in which the Bank was placed by having its two business activities regulated in such different ways if we examine one of these statements. This is how N. G. Pierson,[42] whose masterly presentation of the effects of Peel's Act we shall follow very closely, characterises this situation: "The Bank issues notes, and it does other banking business as well. In respect to the former, it has no freedom of action whatever; in respect to the latter its freedom of action is complete. In other words, the Bank is a bank of issue and also a bank of deposit. In the former capacity it is bound by strict rules; in the latter it may do as it pleases." As mentioned earlier, the Issue Department has the right to issue any amount of notes it pleases, as long as it does so in exchange for gold; but its fiduciary issue is limited to a certain maximum amount. This maximum was originally set at 14 million pounds, but it was to be raised each time a bank in England or Wales gave up or lost its right to issue notes, up to two-thirds of the amount of that bank's uncovered notes. When the Bank of England increased its fiduciary issue, up to the maximum allowable, the Issue Department would invest in any kind of securities that it would receive from the Banking Department for that part of the issue not based on the permanently irredeemable government debt. These securities appear on the Issue Department's statement under the heading of 'other securities', right below the item for 'government debt'. The Banking Department for its part receives notes, which it can use in its business in the same way as any other deposit bank which has borrowed from another institution. As long as the notes have not been spent or to the extent that they are retained in any case as a cash reserve, they will appear once more on the credit side of its statement. Part of the notes issued by the Issue Department will therefore appear a second time on the Bank's statement, namely as the Banking Department's cash on hand, next to its specie holdings.

Over and above these notes the Banking Department of course also has notes that it receives from its regular business, through deposits by private individuals and particularly by the government, whose till it manages, as well as through repayment of loans. The size of this 'reserve' held by the Banking Department, consisting of both coins and notes, represents the crucial item for the expansion or contraction of its activities, as is true of any other bank. It is

---

[42] Nikolaas Gerard Pierson, *Principles of Economics*, translated from the Dutch by A. A. Wotzel, vol. 1 (London: Macmillan, 1902), pp. 461ff.

therefore the item which has always been watched most attentively in the Bank's statements—particularly its magnitude relative to the deposits. Once the Issue Department has taken over securities up to the legal maximum—which has in fact always been the case—this reserve is the only fund from which the Banking Department can make payments to private or government depositors. It cannot rely on the Issue Department to supply any funds.

The first Bank of England statement after the separation of the two departments is reproduced below. The format of the statements has remained unaltered and is still in use in 1929. It should be noted that, contrary to continental usage, the debits appear on the left and the credits on the right side of the balance sheet.

Weekly Report of the Bank of England for the Week ending 7 September 1844
Issue Department

Notes issued	£28.351.295	Government Debt	£11.015.100
		Other securities	2.984.900
		Gold Coin and Bullion	12.657.208
		Silver Bullion	1.694.087
	£28.351.295		£28.351.295

Banking Department

Proprietors' Capital	£14.553.000	Government Securities	£14.554.834
Rest	3.564.729	Other Securities	7.835.616
Public Deposits	3.630.809	Notes	8.175.025
Other Deposits	8.644.348	Gold and Silver Coin	857.765
Seven-day and other Bills	1.030.354		£31.423.240
	£31.423.240		

The only way to see how effectively the ideal of the Currency School was implemented by this method of dealing with note issue is by examining the way the Act of 1844 as well as a law passed in the following year dealt with the note issue of provincial banks. In view of his desire to respect existing rights, Peel could not immediately carry out the ideal of complete centralisation that he envisioned (the same kind of considerations probably also led him to establish the Issue Department within the framework of the Bank of England and not, as had often been considered, as an independent government authority). Nevertheless, his measure clearly aimed for a gradual approximation of this goal (which has meanwhile actually been attained). As a first step, provincial banks were prevented from increasing their note circulation by limiting the right to issue notes to those banks that were entitled to do so before the Act of 1844, and for them the maximum issue was set at the level of their average note circulation during a specified four-week period prior to the passage of the Act. There were additional provisions tending to reduce note issue by other banks: in case of bankruptcy of a bank and in case of a merger of several banks, resulting in the new firm's having more than six partners, the right to issue notes was transferred from these banks to the Bank of England. The process set in motion by the Act concentrated the issue of notes in the hands of the Bank of England at a slow but steady pace. After a period of about sixty years, the process was fully completed.

VI

Peel's Act received speedy approval by parliament, with relatively little opposition demonstrated in the debates, but already during the deliberations and right after the passage of the law the literature contained strong criticism, which swelled in subsequent years. Some misgivings surfaced already at the time that the proposed law was first made public, as can be seen in a banker's petition. Contrary to what people had been led to believe from a misinterpreted remark made by Peel, the government did not reserve the right, under unusual circumstances, such as a very serious crisis, to allow the Bank to issue more notes than the gold coverage ratio permitted. Despite these misgivings, Peel resolutely refused to consider adding a provision to that effect. In his tract defending the Bank Act, Loyd rightly pointed out that "any special provision, introduced into the Bill itself, for suspending its application at critical periods, must prove mischievous, by weakening the conviction that the measure will be adhered to, and thus checking the growth of the feelings and habits which are intimately connected with its success".[43] A better solution would be to let government leaders then in power decide what emergency measures were best suited to meet the

---

[43] S. J. Loyd, *Thoughts on the Separation of the Departments of the Bank of England* (London: Marchant, 1844), p. 55, reprinted in McCulloch, ed., *Tracts, etc. by Lord Overstone*, op. cit., p. 283. In German translation in Diehl-Mombert, *Lesestücke*, op. cit., vol. 10 (*Zur Lehre vom Geld* II).

special situation, as Huskisson had already recommended in 1810. These leaders would then, according to Loyd, have to take responsibility for their actions, subject to parliamentary approval.

Tooke was again the first to present an impressive criticism in his pamphlet about the Currency Principle,[44] which was published at the time of the parliamentary debates. Tooke's views had moved even further from his original position. He not only asserted now that prices were completely independent of the quantity of money in circulation,[45] but also claimed that "a reduced rate of interest has no necessary tendency to raise the price of commodities. On the contrary, it is a cause of diminished cost of production, and consequently of cheapness",[46] thus completely contradicting his earlier analysis. Tooke's total reversal of his earlier opinion, which manifested itself most clearly in the fourth volume of his history of prices, took place under the influence of his fellow combatant John Fullarton.[47] Fullarton was the most persuasive author among the supporters of the Banking School and published his widely circulated book *On the Regulation of Currencies*[48] right after the passage of Peel's Act. This work continued to exert a far-reaching and calamitous influence for over half a century. Since Fullarton starts out from Tooke's doctrines and builds on them, we shall discuss the two books, which were both published in 1844, in conjunction with each other.

Fullarton bases his criticism of Peel's Act primarily on an extension of the Pennington-Tooke doctrine that bank notes represent only one of many guises in which credit can substitute for money and that it is therefore absurd to limit the quantity of bank notes and nothing else. By emphasising that not only deposits but also promissory notes being passed along from hand to hand could serve

---

[44] Thomas Tooke, *An Inquiry into the Currency Principle: the Connection of the Currency with Prices and the Expediency of a Separation of Issue from Banking* (London: Longman, Brown, Green, & Longmans, 1844).

[45] *Ibid.*, p. 123.

[46] *Ibid.*, pp. 77, 81, 124.

[47] [John Fullarton (c. 1780-1849), surgeon, editor, traveller, and banker. On Fullarton's influence on such diverse writers as Marx, Keynes, and Rudolf Hilferding, see Roy Green's brief essay on Fullarton in *The New Palgrave: A Dictionary of Economics*, op. cit, vol. 2, pp. 433-434. -Ed.]

[48] John Fullarton, *On the Regulation of Currencies, being an Examination of the Principles on which it is Proposed to Restrict, within certain Fixed Limits, the Future Issues on Credit of the Bank of England and of the Other Banking Establishments throughout the Country* (London: J. Murray, 1844, second edition, revised 1845). The two most important chapters are available in German translation in Diehl-Mombert, *Lesestücke*, op. cit., vol. 10 (*Zur Lehre vom Geld* II).

as means of exchange, he could legitimately argue that it would do no good to restrict the expansion of just one form of circulating credit and not even the most important form. Fullarton carried the argument considerably further, however; not only did he object to this particular form of credit restriction, but he denied the effectiveness of any kind of restriction. Like Tooke before him, he believed that he could prove that it was not in the power of the Bank of England and the other banks to increase their note circulation at will. His argument was that bank notes, in contrast to government-issued paper money, come into circulation as loans rather than as payments. When the economy needed less money, it would flow back to the bank. The idea that under these conditions an over-issue of notes could be averted can be understood only in conjunction with Tooke's doctrine that prices are not affected by the level of the interest rate. In actuality it is beyond doubt that a lowering of the interest rate will increase the demand for loans in the economy and that banks can increase the amount of money in circulation by lowering the interest rate. Fullarton for his part disregarded or denied these interconnexions, which had been correctly understood for a number of years already. His doctrine became known as 'Fullarton's theory of the reflux' and reaped undeserved fame, although it merely reaffirmed the seemingly ineradicable error of the directors of the note-issuing banks, which can be found even in Adam Smith and later in the testimony given in 1804 and 1810 by the directors of the Bank of Ireland and the Bank of England. The error consists in the mistaken belief that banks are incapable of issuing too many notes as long as they meet business needs. This explicit resurrection of an error that had luckily been surmounted already (Fullarton indignantly related that one could not refer to 'needs' or 'legitimate needs' in this connexion in parliament without becoming the object of ridicule[49]) as a scientific principle is only one of several areas in which Fullarton's success constituted a definite retrogression. The same could be said of his doctrines regarding the effects of international gold movements and the determinants of exchange rates. In his 1844 publication,[50] Tooke had already argued that the movement of precious metals between two countries did not necessarily affect the actual quantity of money in circulation even under a purely metallic currency, since imported and exported metals were usually drawn from reserves rather than from circulating

[49] *Ibid.*, p. 206.
[50] *Ibid.*, pp. 6ff.

metal. In Fullarton's work, this view was elaborated into his notorious theory of hoards,[51] which functions as a "regular deus ex machina"[52] in his struggle against the quantity theory of money. The hoards presumably sop up excess quantities of money and release them again into circulation when demand for money increases. Fullarton's peculiar theory probably stemmed from his banking experiences in India, whose population has always been inclined to put aside large stores of precious metals for times of emergency and to return them to circulation after bad harvests etc. But even here price rises do not cause the increase in circulating money; the larger quantity of money does not, as Fullarton asserts, merely satisfy the greater need for money without influencing prices. Here too, the increase in prices, which had been triggered by the shortage of certain commodities, is reinforced and becomes generalised because of the fact that money shifts from hoards into circulation. However, there is no reason to think that hoards in Europe played the same role.

The impact of Fullarton's above-mentioned doctrine was especially pernicious in connexion with his explanation of exchange rate fluctuations as a function of variations in the balance of trade.

Since he misconstrued the mechanism of gold movements and believed that the current balance of trade was not responsive to monetary factors, he considered it harmless and even desirable for the Bank to expand its note circulation when there was a gold drain, to compensate for the money that had left the country. Natural fluctuations in the balance of trade would assure that the gold which had left the country would flow back on its own before long.

It is difficult enough to understand that a book in which all the insights gained at such great cost during the Restriction period were thrown overboard could meet with such an enthusiastic reception and be regarded as the most articulate work of the increasingly prominent Banking School, but it is nearly incomprehensible that its influence has been so persistent and must be reckoned with even today. A factor in the book's success was John Stuart Mill's adopting a large part of Fullarton's theories, as we mentioned earlier. Fullarton's influence was even stronger in Germany than in England,

---

[51] *Ibid.*, second edition, pp. 68ff., 138f.

[52] In Ludwig von Mises, *Theorie des Geldes und der Umlaufsmittel*, second edition (Munich: Duncker & Humblot, 1924), p. 127. [See the new English edition, translated by H. E. Batson (Indianapolis, Ind.: Liberty*Classics*, 1981), p. 169. -Ed.]

largely as a result of Adolf Wagner's[53] propagation of Fullarton's views. The main explanation of this success, however, is the fact that the reform of the Bank of England in line with the principles of the Currency School failed to have the desired effect, inasmuch as it failed to prevent the outbreak of panics on the money market especially in the first years after the passage of the new law. The real causes for this failure were not to be found where the Banking School claimed, however.

VII

There was one respect in which events quickly confirmed Fullarton's predictions. On the basis of the Banking School's doctrine that notes and deposits were interchangeable, he had drawn attention to the dangers inherent in relieving the Bank's Banking Department of all sense of special responsibility after its separation from the Issue Department and allowing it to subordinate all other considerations to profitability, just like any other bank. This was the conclusion that supporters of the Currency School had actually drawn from their unfortunate distinction, according to which only bank notes but not deposits based on cheques should be counted as 'money'. The idea that the Banking Department, although it no longer functioned as a note-issuing bank, had a special responsibility as the safekeeper of the reserves of all other banks, or—as we would say today—in its role as a central bank—gained acceptance only gradually. According to the Currency School, the Banking Department was to be operated exactly like any deposit bank. Although this conclusion did not necessarily follow from the Currency School's correct basic ideas, the Bank directors adopted the goal of profitability and immediately after the reorganisation of the Bank the discount rate was set first at 2½ per cent and later at 3½ per cent, so that they could compete with other banks. As its discount rate was at times even below the market rate, the Bank's discount business expanded significantly. The Bank nevertheless maintained this rate for about two years, though beginning with March 1845 it was considered a minimum rate, and it remained in force even after substantial gold exports began to occur. These two years following

---

[53] [Adolf H. G. Wagner (1835-1917), Professor of Political Economy at the University of Berlin, author of a book on the money and credit theory of Peel's Act, *Die Geld- und Credittheorie der Peel'schen Bankacte* (Vienna: Braumüller, 1862). -Ed.]

the passage of Peel's Act were a time of great prosperity, which was strongly stimulated by the favourable credit situation created by the Bank's artificially low discount rate. Railroad development and the founding of numerous railroad companies in England and elsewhere culminated in a wave of intense stock market speculation. By 1846, the credit expansion began to manifest itself in a marked rise in commodity prices. Around the middle of the year, gold withdrawals began to mount, but they did not induce the Bank to reverse its policy until the beginning of the following year. When it finally decided in April 1847 to raise its discount rate to 5 per cent and this still did not sufficiently reduce discount requests, the Bank thereupon proceeded to limit each prospective creditor to a certain amount. This action provoked so much pressure on the money market that market interest rates rose to more than 10 per cent. Many people wrongly attributed this strain on the money market to the limitations imposed by Peel's Act and demanded that the government invalidate these provisions of the Act. In reality the strain on the money market had on the contrary been produced by the prior over-expansion of credit. At last gold exports stopped and soon things quieted down. The ensuing collapse of the stock market speculation and the drop in commodity prices led to a large number of failures on the part of large firms and banks and gave rise to a serious crisis in confidence. The Bank of England could no longer meet the demands for cash generated by this crisis, since its gold reserve was already alarmingly low. Sharp credit limitations, which the Bank had to impose in October, actually increased demands for paying out their deposits, as it was generally feared that the Banking Department had exhausted its reserves and would have to stop payments. Panic was so severe on the money market that the government was finally forced to notify the Bank that it would request an *ex post* approval by parliament allowing the Bank to exceed the maximum note issue permitted by Peel's Act. Disclosure of this measure, which would enable the Bank to pay out all deposits in notes, sufficed to bring the run on the Bank to a halt and to bring back into circulation the notes that had been widely hoarded for fear that payments would be stopped. The Bank did not even need to make use of the government's permission to issue more notes, a permission that was, to be sure, tied to the condition that the Bank raise its discount rate to 8 per cent and return to the state coffers all proceeds from the additional note issue. The panic subsided and the transition to a period of depression proceeded smoothly.

This first 'suspension' of Peel's Bank Act a mere three years after its passage later recurred in the 1857 and 1866 crises. These incidents could not fail to reinforce criticism of Peel's Act. The investigating committees appointed in both houses of parliament to determine the causes of the crises have much valuable material in their protocols. The principle of Peel's Act was vindicated by the committees, but the policy of the Bank, which had shared the blame for speculative excesses by its underbidding of the market interest rate, was rightly criticised. The currency principle nevertheless came increasingly into disfavour. An influential factor in this respect was the publication between 1845 and 1847 of a collection of articles by the editor of the *Economist*, James Wilson, in which he propagated the doctrines of the Banking School. These articles constitute one of the most important works of the Banking School, together with Tooke's and Fullarton's writings, although they hardly add anything essential to the ideas developed by these two men.[54] The biggest success for the Banking School, however, was the incorporation of their major doctrines in John Stuart Mill's 1848 *Principles of Political Economy*,[55] which became the economists' bible in the following decades. Their errors became so firmly embedded that they could only be dislodged again by the lessons of the great inflation following the First World War. As to the problems that the Banking School had broached but had not been able to solve, that is, the significance of credit in general as substitute money, no deeper insight was gained until very recently. The essence of the Banking School's criticism of the prevailing doctrine, little as they themselves realised it, consisted in their showing that the deposit bank system depended on a variable note issue and was therefore incompatible with a purely metallic currency. This criticism at least made people pay greater attention to the influence of credit expansion by note-issuing banks and made the Bank of England realise that it could not rely on exchange rates alone to guide its discount policy, but rather that it must slow down excessive credit expansion by raising the discount rate even before a gold drain sets in.

---

[54] James Wilson, *Capital, Currency, and Banking* (London: The Economist, 1847).

[55] John Stuart Mill, *Principles of Political Economy with some of their Applications to Social Philosophy* (London: J. W. Parker, 1848 and later). Various German translations.

THIRTEEN

RICHARD CANTILLON (c. 1680-1734)[1]

I

In economics no less than in other sciences, it not infrequently happens that shortly after a 'new' doctrine has become accepted the

[1] [The present translation is by Dr. Grete Heinz. An earlier English translation by Micheál O Súilleabháin which appeared in *The Journal of Libertarian Studies*, vol. 7, Fall 1985, pp. 217-247, was consulted, as was the earlier French translation by Moïse Moisseev (that is, F. A. Hayek, "Richard Cantillon, sa vie, son oeuvre", *Revue des Sciences economiques*, Liège, April, June, October 1936). Hayek had made several revisions, improvements, and additions to the French translation, and these have for the most part been incorporated here. Numerous errors both from and to the French have been corrected. Professor Ralph Raico is also thanked for his generous advice and assistance with the translation.

This essay, together with textual comments on Cantillon's *Essai sur la nature du commerce en général*, was written by Hayek in German in 1931 as an introduction to Hella von Hayek's German translation of the French edition of 1755 of Cantillon's essay: Richard Cantillon, *Abhandlung über die Natur des Handels im Allgemeinen* (Jena: Verlag von Gustav Fischer, 1931), pp. v-lxvi. Page numbers cited here are however to the original French edition. For also in 1931, shortly after the appearance of Hayek's edition, the original French version of Cantillon's essay was republished, simultaneously with an English translation by Henry Higgs, by the Royal Economic Society (*Essai sur la nature du commerce en général by Richard Cantillon*, edited with an English translation and other material by Henry Higgs, C.B. (London: Royal Economic Society, Macmillan, 1931; reprinted New York: Augustus M. Kelley, 1964).

Appending a footnote to the French translation of his own essay, Hayek wrote of the Royal Economic Society edition: "This magnificently presented volume contains, apart from the reproduction of Jevons's celebrated article on Cantillon, an account of the results of Higgs's recent investigations, as well as a reproduction of portraits of the wife and daughter of Cantillon. For the English translation, use was made, to the extent possible, of Postlethwayt's text. As we shall see later, it probably ought to be regarded as the first version of the *Essai*. Higgs has given some complementary information about Cantillon in a note published in *The Economic Journal* in June 1932." The reference is to Malachy Postlethwayt, *A Dissertation on the Plan, Use, and Importance of the Universal Dictionary of Trade and Commerce; translated from the French of the late celebrated Mons. Savery...* (London: J. & P. Knapton, 1749), pp. 41ff., which was thought to have reproduced substantial parts of the 'original' version of Cantillon's *Essai*. See also F. A. Hayek, "Review of Richard Cantillon, *Essai sur la nature du commerce en général*, edited, with an English translation and other material, by Henry Higgs", *Economic Journal*, vol. 42, 1932, pp. 61-63, now republished as an Addendum to this essay.

There is some doubt about Cantillon's date of birth. Although it is often given either as 1680 or 1697, according to Antoin E. Murphy, *Richard Cantillon: Entrepreneur and Economist* (Oxford: Clarendon Press 1986), it can only be placed between 1680 and 1690. -Ed.]

discovery is made that some earlier, long-forgotten thinkers had genially anticipated in their own days the very ideas that have just gained sway.[2] In our own field, names such as Oresmius,[3] Montchrétien,[4] Barbon,[5] Rae,[6] W. F. Lloyd,[7] Cournot,[8] Jennings,[9] Longfield,[10] and Gossen[11] are among the most notable that come to mind. There can hardly be any scientific field, however, that can possibly duplicate the fate suffered by Cantillon's *Essai sur la nature du commerce en général.*[12] Here was a work that had exerted the very greatest influence on the initial stages of a science and that had given the first coherent survey of this new science, only to disappear completely from view for nearly a century, so that its purely accidental rediscovery was in the nature of a revelation. Investigations stimulated by this rediscovery produced equally startling results. It was learned that even contemporaries who had witnessed the publication of this book in 1755 had only a vague and partially misleading idea of its author, who had died twenty-one years earlier. It was also discovered that the work had already exerted a subterranean influence long before its publication, an influence whose strength we can only now begin to appreciate properly.

Even on its own merit, as the achievement of Richard Cantillon (deceased in 1734)—a fact that has now been fully ascertained—this work is of most unusual interest, quite aside from its history, odd as it is in all its particulars. Its rediscoverer, W. Stanley Jevons,[13] was hardly overstating the case when he acclaimed it as the cradle of economics, a science that could thus celebrate at the present time the bicentenary of its birth as an independent discipline.[14] In coun-

---

[2] The author is especially indebted to Professor Henry Higgs, London, Professor Dr. Fritz Karl Mann, Cologne, and Sektionsrat Dr. Ewald Schams, Vienna, who took the trouble to read through the manuscript of this [essay] and whose numerous comments led to the correction of some mistakes and to the filling of many omissions.

[3] [Nicholas Oresme (1335-1382). -Ed.]

[4] [Antoine de Montchrétien (c. 1575-1621). -Ed.]

[5] [Nicholas Barbon (c. 1640-1698). -Ed.]

[6] [John Rae (1796-1872). See this volume, chapter 16. -Ed.]

[7] [William F. Lloyd (1795-1852). -Ed.]

[8] [Antoine Augustine Cournot (1801-1877). -Ed.]

[9] [Richard Jennings (1814-1891). -Ed.]

[10] [Samuel Mountifort Longfield (1802-1844). -Ed.]

[11] [Hermann Heinrich Gossen (1810-1858). See this volume, chapter 15. -Ed.]

[12] Richard Cantillon, *Essai sur la nature du commerce en général*, traduit de l'anglais (London: chez Fletcher Gyles, 1755). [See the discussion of Cantillon in this volume, chapter 11. -Ed.]

[13] [William Stanley Jevons (1835-1882). -Ed.]

[14] [Hayek's essay was first published in 1931. -Ed.]

246

tries other than Germany, hardly anyone would contest that the book has this significance. The fact that it has remained quite unfamiliar here[15] until the present and that the publication of a German translation undoubtedly still needs justifying is, once again, due to a particular piece of bad luck that is quite in keeping with the whole history of the book, to which we shall come back when we give the full acccount of this story.

The rediscovery of Cantillon's *Essai* stems from its being among the very few works cited by Adam Smith. In the eighth chapter of the first book of the *Wealth of Nations*,[16] he mentions, unexpectedly and without further preliminaries, Mr. Cantillon's views on the wage level—apparently presuming him to be familiar to the reader. Cantillon, he writes, seems, upon this account,

> to suppose that the lowest species of common labourers must every where earn at least double their own maintenance, in order that one with another they may be enabled to bring up two children; the labour of the wife, on account of her necessary attendance on the children, being supposed no more than sufficient to provide for herself. But one-half the children born, it is computed, die before the age of manhood. The poorest labourers, therefore, according to this account, must, one with another, attempt to rear at least four children, in order that two may have an equal chance of living to that age. But the necessary maintenance of four children, it is supposed, may be nearly equal to that of one man. The labour of an able-bodied slave, the same author adds, is computed to be worth double his maintenance; and that of the meanest labourer, he thinks, cannot be worth less than that of an able-bodied slave. Thus far [it] at least seems certain that, in order to bring up a family, the labour of the husband and wife together must, even in the lowest species of common labour, be able to earn something more than what is precisely necessary for their own maintenance; but in what proportion, whether in that above mentioned, or in any other, I shall not take upon me to determine.

---

[15] [I.e., in Germany. -Ed.]

[16] [See Cannan's edition (London: Methuen, 1904 and later editions), vol. I, p. 70. See now also R. H. Campbell and A. S. Skinner's edition: Adam Smith, *An Inquiry into the Nature and Causes of the Wealth of Nations* (Indianapolis, Ind.: LibertyClassics, 1981), pp. 85-86. See now also Edwin G. West, *Adam Smith: The Man and His Works* (New Rochelle, N.Y.: Arlington House, 1969); Edwin G. West, "Richard Cantillon and Adam Smith: A Reappraisal", Carletown University Economics Working Paper 80-12, August 1980, and Roger W. Garrison, "West's 'Cantillon and Adam Smith': A Comment", *Journal of Libertarian Studies*, vol. 7, no. 2, Fall 1985, pp. 287-294. See also Hayek's essays on Smith, in this volume, chapter 8. -Ed.]

The only economic work that had appeared under the name Cantillon at that time, and to which one hence might initially connect this passage, was an extremely mediocre publication whose full title reads as follows:

> An Analysis of Trade, Commerce, Coin, Bullion, Banks, and Foreign Exchange, Wherein the true Principles of this useful Knowledge are fully but briefly laid down and explained, to give a clear idea of their happy consequences to Society when well regulated. Taken chiefly from a Manuscript of a very ingenious Gentleman deceas'd, and adapted to the present situation of our trade. By Philip Cantillon, Late of the City of London, Merchant. London, Printed for the Author and sold by . . . . MDCCLIX.

In this book, however, there are to be found no discussions to which Smith could have been referring by the passage quoted. On the other hand, French literature of the same period, particularly the writings of most of the physiocrats, shows that another work that had appeared anonymously in French was generally attributed by contemporaries to a "de Cantillon"—namely, the *Essai sur la nature du commerce en général*, published in 1755 with the incorrect information, "translated from the English" and the equally incorrect place of publication, "A Londres, chez Fletcher Gyles, dans Holborn".[17] And in it are actually to be found (p. 43) the arguments that Smith had reported (albeit quite inexactly).[18]

This work enjoyed wide circulation in its own time. So much may be shown—quite apart from the numerous references to it in the French literature of the second half of the eighteenth century—above all from the fact that, besides the edition of 1755, two other editions appeared during the following year. The first of these likewise was published as a separate book and differs from the first edition, apart from the date, only in its slightly smaller typeface, so that it contains only 432 pages (427 of them paginated) instead of 436 pages (430 respectively). The second is a reprint that appears in the third volume of a collection edited by Eleazar Mauvillon, father

---

[17] The same fictitious printing location is borne also by the French translation (published under the title *Questions importantes sur le commerce*) of Tucker's *Reflections on the Expediency of a Law for the Naturalization of Foreign Protestants*, which Turgot, probably at the suggestion of Gournay, took in hand. Both books were probably printed in Paris. In 1755 there had been no bookseller by name of Fletcher Gyles for many years.

[18] [Compare p. 43 of the original with p. 22 of Hella von Hayek's translation into German, op. cit. -Ed.]

of the German physiocrat Jakob Mauvillon,[19] a collection which in some sets bears the overall heading *Discours Politiques*, after the translation of Hume's *Political Discourses* contained in the first volume, and which in other sets is entitled *Les Intérêts de la France*, after the essay by Goudar contained in volumes four and five.[20] In addition, an Italian translation by F. Scottoni appeared in 1767.[21]

It is this French *Essai*—which later authors, prior to Jevons's investigations, continued wrongly to attribute to a Philip Cantillon—that enjoyed high esteem among the physiocrats and with which Adam Smith probably became acquainted when he was introduced to this circle in 1765.[22] The first member of this group to mention Cantillon was Victor de Riquetti, Marquis de Mirabeau,[23] not to be confused with his famous son, Count Honoré Gabriel Mirabeau,[24] generally known simply as the Marquis Mirabeau. The reference to Cantillon occurs in his *L'Ami des Hommes*, published in 1757, that is, two years after Cantillon's *Essai*.[25] This constitutes one of the most important biographical sources for Cantillon, to which a peculiar story is attached and to which we shall later return in detail. We might mention here only one of Mirabeau's later remarks concerning Cantillon, which also bears on Cantillon's relation with the other members of the physiocratic school. In a letter to Rousseau of July 30, 1767, while stating his views on questions of population, the chief subject of his *L'Ami des Hommes*, Mirabeau writes as follows:

---

[19] [Jakob Mauvillon (1743-1794). -Ed.]

[20] [*Discours Politiques*, trans. Eleazar Mauvillon (Amsterdam: n.p., 1754); *Les Intérêts de la France mal entendus dans les branches de l'agriculture, des finances, et du commerce* (Amsterdam: Jacques Coeur, 1756). -Ed.] This edition, which obviously owes the varied form in which it appeared to the business acumen of a book dealer who hoped to further sales by altering the title page, is supposed also to occur with the dates 1755-61.

[21] *Saggio sulla natura de commercio*. Autore Inglese, with a Foreword by F. Scottoni (Venice: n.p., 1767).

[22] Cf. *Lectures on Justice, Police, Revenue and Arms, delivered in the University of Glasgow by Adam Smith reported by a Student in 1763*, edited with an introduction and notes by Edwin Cannan (Oxford: Clarendon Press, 1896), pp. 157, 164, 172, particularly p. 174 and the footnote at the bottom of this page.

[23] [Victor Riquetti, Marquis de Mirabeau (1715-1789). -Ed.]

[24] [Honoré Gabriel Riquetti, Comte de Mirabeau (1749-1791). -Ed.]

[25] The first edition of the work, although dated on the title page as Paris 1756, was however actually published only in 1757. See G. Weulersse, *Les Manuscrits Economiques de François Quesnay et du Marquis de Mirabeau aux Archives Nationales* (Paris: P. Geuthner, 1910), pp. 19ff.

I drew my first and only views on this subject from Cantillon's "Essai sur la nature du commerce", which I possessed in manuscript for more than sixteen years. . . . Goliath strode into battle with a confidence which surely was no greater than mine at the moment on finding a man who, as someone said to me, wrote on the margin of my book daring words such as these: *The child has been nourished with bad milk: the strength of his temperament often helps him to arrive at good results, but he understands nothing of the principles.*

My critic did not spare me and told me frankly that I had put the cart before the ox and that Cantillon, so far from being [a] founder of political science, was but an idiot. This calumny led me to regard the man who uttered it as a fool; nonetheless reflection, which attends all controversy, forced me to check myself, I broke off the conversation and took up the question again in the evening with a rested mind. Then it happened that Goliath's head was cleaved.[26]

When Mirabeau wrote this he had, as we shall see, completely altered his earlier views and had been converted from an admirer of Cantillon into an equally enthusiastic follower of Quesnay[27] without ever having wholly understood either one or the other. Indeed, in the continuation of the passage cited, he succeeded in turning the views of Cantillon into their exact opposite. Even Quesnay's assessment of Cantillon that is mentioned in the above passage (for Quesnay is obviously the person he has in mind from the passage that followed) is surely due only to the garbled rendering of Cantillon's views in Mirabeau's book, and the strong expressions he attributes to Quesnay doubtless stemmed not from the latter but rather from Mirabeau himself.[28] In any case, this report

[26] Cf. *J.-J. Rousseau, ses Amis et ses Ennemis*, correspondence published by M. G. Streckeisen-Moultou (with an introduction by J. Levallois) (Paris: Callman-Lévy, 1865), vol. II, pp. 365f. The passage is rendered more completely in the *Oeuvres économiques et philosophiques de F. Quesnay*, ed. A. Oncken (Frankfurt and Paris: J. Baer, 1888), pp. 4f., note, and in the German translation of the same work by A. Oncken, *Entstehung und Werden der physiokratischen Theorie*, in *Vierteljahrsschrift für Staats- und Volkswirtschaft*, ed. K. Frankenstein, vol. 5, 1895, pp. 275f., as well as in the same author's *Geschichte der Nationalökonomie*, part I (Leipzig: C. L. Hirschfield, 1902 and later editions), pp. 318f. In the article by Oncken mentioned first there is also reproduced a report of the conversation which is essentially in the same tenor, one which Mirabeau gave in another letter at the end of the 1870s, and which is taken from the well-known work of L. de Loménie, *Les Mirabeau, nouvelles études sur la société française au XVIIIᵉ siècle* (Paris: E. Dentu, 1879), vol. II, pp. 170f.

[27] [François Quesnay (1694-1774). -Ed.]

[28] See Oncken, *Entstehung und Werden*, op. cit., p. 279. How little Mirabeau's report of the course of the conversation is to be believed can also be seen from the fact that, in a letter to his brother written immediately after the conversation, he

shows that the relationship around which the physiocratic school eventually developed—Mirabeau's acquaintance with Quesnay—came about through the book that Mirabeau had written under the stimulation of Cantillon.

As it happened, a year earlier (the discussion is supposed to have taken place in 1757, about four months after the appearance of *L'Ami des Hommes*), in the article "Grains" in the first edition of the *Encyclopédie Methodique* of d'Alembert and Diderot,[29] Quesnay had already approvingly cited passages from Cantillon's essay, remarking that this author had correctly realised the fundamental truths.[30] Quesnay was one of the two recognised masters of the physiocrats; from the other, J. C. V. de Gournay,[31] who never published any independent work, we know that he recommended "above all the careful reading of Cantillon's *Essai*, an excellent work that is being neglected".[32]

In the twenty years from 1756 to 1776, the period when the physiocratic school blossomed, we find Cantillon mentioned again and again. Turgot[33] named him with Montesquieu, Hume, Quesnay, and Gournay as one of the great men who had surpassed their predecessor Mélon.[34] DuPont de Nemours,[35] Morellet,[36] Mably,[37] Graslin,[38] and Savary[39] all knew the *Essai*.[40] Already in 1762, in his

described himself as the victor. Cf. Oncken, op. cit., p. 275, and Loménie, op. cit., vol. 2, p. 196.

[29] [*Encyclopédie Méthodique*, ou par ordre de matièrs; par une société de gens de lettres, de savans et d'artistes; précédée d'un vocabulaire universel, servant de table pour tout l'ouvrage, ornée des portraits de Mrs. Diderot & d'Alembert, premiers editeurs de l'Encyclopédie (Paris: Chez Panckoucke, 1782-1832). -Ed.]

[30] See the 1757 edition, vol. 7, p. 821, reprinted in A. Oncken, ed., *Oeuvres économiques et philosophiques de F. Quesnay*, op. cit., p. 218.

[31] [Jacques Claude Vincent de Gournay (1712-1759). -Ed.]

[32] See *Mémoires inédits de l'Abbé Morellet* (Paris: Baudouin Frères, 1823), vol. 1, pp. 37f.

[33] See E. Daire's edition of Turgot's works (Paris: Guillaumin, 1848), vol. 2, p. 819.

[34] J. F. Mélon, *Essai politique sur le Commerce* (Rouen or Bordeaux: n.p., 1734). In fact Mélon was thus not a predecessor of Cantillon, who died in the year in which Mélon's writings appeared.

[35] [Pierre Samuel DuPont de Nemours (1739-1817). -Ed.]

[36] [André Morellet (1727-1819). -Ed.]

[37] [Gabriel Bonnot de Mably (1709-1785). -Ed.]

[38] [Jean J. L. Graslin (1727-1790). -Ed.]

[39] [Jacques Savary (1622-1690). -Ed.]

[40] See "Notice abrégée des différents écrits modernes qui ont concouru en France à former la science de l'Economie politique" in *Oeuvres économiques et philosophiques de F. Quesnay*, ed. A. Oncken, op. cit., under "Années 1754 et 1755", p. 148. Compare on this matter the more precise information of H. Higgs, *Economic Journal*,

Gesammelte Briefe vom Gelde, the German Johann Philip Graumann reproduces a great part of the essay's argument about the relationship of gold and silver;[41] James Steuart[42] cites Cantillon with reference to Philip Cantillon's garbled English *Analysis of Trade*.[43] And finally—in his much too little appreciated work *Du Commerce et du Gouvernement*, which appeared in the same year as Adam Smith's *Wealth of Nations*—even Condillac[44] heaped high praise on the *Essai* as one of the best books on the circulation of money of which he knew and which he had taken as the foundation of his own analysis.[45] Finally, we find some information on Cantillon in Arthur Young's *Political Arithmetic*[46] and in J. C. Büsch's preface to the first volume of his *Abhandlung von dem Geldumlauf*.[47]

But then, virtually all at once, the name of Cantillon disappeared completely from economic literature.[48] The later classical writers, for whom it was natural to suppose that Adam Smith's reference was to the quite mediocre English publication of Philip Cantillon, seem (with the possible exception of Malthus) not to have known him, although doubtless a large part of his arguments were passed on to them by various plagiarists whom we shall become acquainted with later. Already in Blanqui's *Nationalökonomische Dogmengeschichte* one seeks in vain for Cantillon's name, and until 1870 his name turns up only in quite isolated cases, as in Ganilh,[49] in scattered footnotes

---

vol. 1, 1891, pp. 262-291.

[41] [Johann Philip Graumann, *Gesammelte Briefe von dem Gelde usw.* (Berlin: C. F. Boss, 1762), pp. 114ff. Compare pp. 371-381 of the original edition with pp. 178-183 of the Hayek translation. -Ed.]

[42] Sir James Steuart, *An Inquiry into the Principles of Political Economy*, book III, II/3, *Collection des sciences sociales*, vol. 15, p. 284 (reprinted Chicago: University of Chicago Press, 1966).

[43] See discussion above.

[44] [Etienne Bonnot de Condillac (1714-1780). -Ed.]

[45] See E. B. de Condillac, *Du Commerce et du Gouvernement, considerés relativement l'un à l'autre* (Amsterdam and Paris: Chez Jombert & Cellot, 1776), chapter 16, p. 143; *Oeuvres Complètes* (Paris: Dufart, 1803), vol. 6, p. 141. Compare with this also A. Lebeau, *Condillac économiste* (Paris: Guillaumin, 1903), pp. 11, 350, 412.

[46] Arthur Young, *Political Arithmétic* (London: T. Cadell, 1779), part I, p. 29.

[47] J. G. Büsch, *Abhandlung von dem Geldumlauf*, second edition (Hamburg: C. E. Bohn, 1800).

[48] Some further information about the effect of Cantillon on writers of this time is presented at the end of this essay.

[49] Charles Ganilh, *Des systèmes d'économie politique*, second edition, 1821, vol. 1, pp. xv, 134; vol. 2, p. 107.

in Eugène Daire's edition of the physiocrats,[50] in 1834 in John Rae's brilliant *New Principles*,[51] and finally in 1860 in Julius Kautz's account of the *Geschichtliche Entwicklung der National-Ökonomik und ihrer Literatur*, where Cantillon is, for the first time, again quite aptly "considered as a transitional figure between mercantilists, physiocrats, and Smithians, ranked among the real founders of economics, however, especially on account of his originality and the independence of his conception and treatment".[52] Above all, however, there must be mentioned here something that has been forgotten since the rediscovery of Cantillon: namely, that Wilhelm Roscher[53] always emphasised Cantillon's significance, mentioned him in his *Grundlagen der Nationalökonomie* as frequently as only a few other early authors, and in his *Geschichte der Nationalökonomie* says of Cantillon's essay that it "already contains in great perfection many of the main features and chief merits of the physiocrats".[54] It may also be due to Roscher's influence that in 1874, in his essay on "Turgot's Place in the History of Economics",[55] Friedrich von Sivers gives Cantillon his full

[50] Eugène Daire, *Physiocrates. Quesnay, Dupont de Nemours, Mercier de la Rivière, l'Abbé Baudeau, Le Trosne, avec une Introduction sur la doctrine des Physiocrates, des Commentaires et des Notices historiques* (Paris: Guillaumin, 1846), part I, pp. 74, 82, 274. It is hard to understand, and certainly contributed much to Cantillon's becoming forgotten, that Daire did not include the "Essai" that he had so highly esteemed in the fifteen-volume *Collection des principaux économistes* (1843-8) which he edited, a collection whose second volume the aforementioned physiocrats comprise.

[51] John Rae, *Statement of some new principles on the subject of Political Economy* (Boston: Hilliard, Gray, 1834), republished by C. W. Mixter under the title *The Sociological Theory of Capital* (New York: Macmillan, 1905), p. 450 of Mixter's edition. [See the discussion of Rae in this volume, chapter 16, on John Stuart Mill. -Ed.]

[52] Dr. Julius Kautz, *Theorie und Geschichte der Nationalökonomik, Propyläen zum Volks- und staatswirtschaftlichen Studium*, part II, *Literatur-Geschichte der National-Ökonomik* (Vienna: C. Gerold's Sohn, 1860), pp. 320f.

[53] [Wilhelm Georg Friedrich Roscher (1817-1894). -Ed.]

[54] W. Roscher, *Geschichte der Nationalökonomie in Deutschland* (Munich: R. Oldenbourg, 1874), p. 481.

[55] "Turgots Stellung in der Geschichte der Nationalökonomie", *Jahrbücher für Nationalökonomie und Statistik*, vol. 23, Jena, 1874. On pp. 158-162, which are completely devoted to Cantillon, he writes: "In the 'Essai sur la nature du commerce en général', Cantillon justifies more deeply than by superficial opinion the idea of the dependence of the entire population on landlords. Observing more incisively, and making finer distinctions, he sees that value cannot be explained by supply and demand alone, and recognises that the market price formed by supply and demand oscillates around a pivotal point which is determined by other causes. . . ." This is sufficient proof that the three-fold division of society later attributed to Quesnay first appeared in Cantillon. Farm workers produce the wealth, landlords alone are independent, artists and merchants live from the net income of landlords. The division of rent is the same as in the "Analyse du tableau économique"; the only difference consists in that there the division is made in the proportions of 2.1.3.5.,

due, and finds words of the highest praise for his doctrines, which he quotes at length. Already four years earlier, however, in France, Léonce de Lavergne, that fine historian of eighteenth-century economics, in the introduction to his account of the physiocratic school, had treated Cantillon and Gournay as its two precursors and had said of the *Essai* that "in the book all theories of the Economistes are anticipated, albeit it is scarcely the size of a duodecimo volume".[56]

Notwithstanding these increasingly frequent references to Cantillon in the 1870s, the honour of having recognised the true significance of Cantillon and of having given him his deserved place in the history of economic thought must be reserved for W. Stanley Jevons. Jevons's essay on "Richard Cantillon and the Nationality of Political Economy", published in 1881 in the *Contemporary Review*,[57] not only won general recognition for Cantillon at least in the English- and French-speaking countries, but also first presented a clear picture of the author and provided leads for subsequent research concerning him. Practically everything that we know about Cantillon is due either directly to Jevons or to the researches by Higgs that he inspired. Suffice it to recall here his summing up of Cantillon's achievement:

> The *Essai* is far more than a mere essay or even collection of disconnected essays like those of Hume. It is a systematic and connected treatise, going over in a concise manner nearly the whole field of economics, with the exception of taxation. It is thus, more than any other book I know, *the first treatise on economics*. Sir William Petty's *Political Arithmetic* and his *Treatise of Taxes and Contributions* are wonderful books in their way, and at their time, but, compared with Cantillon's *Essai*, they are merely collections of casual hints. There were earlier English works of great merit, such as those of Vaughan, Locke, Child, Mun, etc., but these were either occasional essays and pamphlets, or else fragmentary treatises. Cantillon's essay

whereas here the division is into sixths.

[56] Léonce de Lavergne, *Les économistes français du dix-huitième siècle* (Paris: Guillaumin, 1870), p. 167. The quotation cited in the text goes on: "Property in general and landed property in particular is presented there as the basis of society. Cantillon derives almost all his conclusions from this principle, particularly freedom of commerce in all its forms. Had he lived longer, he would have become one of the leaders of the school of the Economistes."

[57] "Richard Cantillon and the Nationality of Political Economy", *Contemporary Review*, vol. 39, January 1881, reprinted in W. Stanley Jevons, *The Principles of Economics: A Fragment of a Treatise on the Industrial Mechanism of Society and other Papers*, with a preface by Henry Higgs (London: Macmillan, 1905), pp. 155-183.

is, more emphatically than any other single work, "the Cradle of Political Economy".[58]

Jevons's essay opened the way for a torrent of writing on Cantillon. The *Dictionary of National Biography*,[59] *Palgrave's Dictionary of Political Economy*,[60] and a supplementary volume of the *Nouveau Dictionnaire d'Economie Politique*[61] devoted space to him. In the years that followed, J. K. Ingram,[62] R. Zuckerkandl,[63] and especially A. Espinas[64] discussed him in their doctrinal histories. And in the first edition of his *Principles of Economics* Alfred Marshall made a widely noted remark about Cantillon to the effect that he "was very acute and in some respects much ahead of his time. But he seems to me wanting in solidity."[65] More important than the above named, however, are the researches by Stephen Bauer and, above all, by Henry Higgs, who, following clues which Jevons uncovered but was unable to pursue because of his sudden death,[66] brought to light some very interesting details about the story of Cantillon and his work. These he published in 1891 in the second number of the *Economic Journal*, at that time a new publication.[67]

A year later there also appeared, by arrangement with Harvard University, a new printing of the *Essai*, a work which, as Palgrave's Dictionary states, had become "one of the rarest works of economic

---

[58] W. Stanley Jevons, *Principles of Economics*, op. cit., p. 164.

[59] Article, "Cantillon", by H. R. Tedder in the *Dictionary of National Biography*, ed. L. Stephen and Sidney Lee (London: Smith, Elder, 1886), vol. 8, p. 455.

[60] Article "Cantillon" by Higgs, F. Y. Edgeworth, and Stephen Bauer in the *Dictionary of Political Economy*, ed. R. H. Inglis Palgrave (London: Macmillan, 1894).

[61] Article "Cantillon", by Castelot in *Nouveau Dictionnaire d'Economie Politique*, ed. Leon Say, Supplement (Paris: Guillaumin, 1897).

[62] J. K. Ingram, *A History of Political Economy* (Edinburgh: A. & C. Black, 1888), pp. 60ff.

[63] R. Zuckerkandl, *Zur Theorie des Preises mit besonderer Berücksichigung der geschichtlichen Entwicklung der Lehre* (Leipzig: Duncker & Humblot, 1889).

[64] A. Espinas, *Histoire des Doctrines Economiques* (Paris: A. Colin, 1891), pp. 179-197.

[65] A. Marshall, *Principles of Economics* (London: Macmillan, 1891), p. 53. In later editions, however, Marshall altered his judgement, and remarks (in a footnote to the passage wherein he characterises the physiocrats as having made the first attempt at a systematic elaboration of the material (seventh edition, London, 1916, Appendix B2, p. 756)) that Cantillon's *Essai* would already have a certain claim to be regarded as systematic.

[66] See William Stanley Jevons, *Letters and Journal*, edited by his wife (London: Macmillan, 1886), p. 425.

[67] H. Higgs, "Richard Cantillon", *The Economic Journal*, vol. 1, 1891, pp. 262-291.

literature".[68] This edition, not quite a facsimile but as close to the original as could be achieved without creating a special type for this purpose, has also been out of print for years, and not many copies seem to have reached Germany.

High esteem and admiration of Cantillon's *Essai* was by no means restricted in England and France to the small circle of his discoverers and biographers, and his position as, at the least, one of the founders of our science is, as already mentioned, more or less uncontested in these countries. One could adduce many testimonies from English scholars to prove this point: suffice it, however, to mention as an example that H. S. Foxwell claims to see in Petty,[69] Cantillon, Ricardo, and Jevons the main stages in the development of political economy.[70] Moreover, Edwin Cannan has very recently confirmed that Jevons's enthusiastic words about Cantillon were not in the least exaggerated.[71] But in France too Cantillon's importance is recognised almost to the same extent as it is in England despite some initial prejudice against him[72] roused perhaps by Jevons's attempt to use his rediscovery of Cantillon to shift back credit for the founding of economics from France to England. Charles Gide is a case in point. In his article on French economics in the second volume of Palgrave's *Dictionary*, Gide expressly declares Cantillon's *Essai* to be the first systematic treatment of political economy and adds: "In this work practically the entire subject matter of modern political economy is treated in the clearest and most exact manner." This is the very same Charles Gide who in his *Histoire des doctrines économiques*[73]—which he co-authored with Charles Rist and which, to be sure, begins with the physiocrats—barely mentioned Cantillon, adding in a footnote that "This Cantillon, whom no one has mentioned for more than a century, has during the past few years become very fashionable again, like all precursors who are discov-

---

[68] Cantillon, *Essai sur le Commerce*, reprinted for Harvard University (Boston: George H. Ellis; London: Macmillan, 1892), with a foreword by Henry Higgs.

[69] [Sir William Petty (1623-1687). -Ed.]

[70] See his Introduction to W. Stanley Jevons, *Investigations in Currency and Finance* (London: Macmillan, 1884), p. xlii.

[71] See E. Cannan, *A Review of Economic Theory* (London: P. S. King, 1929), p. 20, footnote. This fascinating book, which finally led me to my own close concern with Cantillon, has the most comprehensive view of Cantillon's significance for the development of economics as a whole.

[72] See on the other hand the excellent appreciation in the *Histoire des Doctrines Economiques* by A. Espinas, which appeared already in 1891, pp. 179-197.

[73] [Hayek refers here to the German edition, *Geschichte der volkswirtschaftlichen Lehrmeinungen*, second edition (Jena: G. Fischer, 1921), p. 52. -Ed.]

ered afresh. The influence on the physiocrats which is being attributed to him is probably overstated."

In Germany, as stated, special circumstances prevented equally rapid recognition. At the time when the rediscovered *Essai* was being discussed in England and France, the leading German authority on French economics of the period in question, August Oncken,[74] was a particularly keen admirer of and expert on the physiocratic school. We owe him exceedingly important conclusions about this doctrine. But just as a good biographer always has to have a somewhat exaggerated liking for his subject, so Oncken's admiration for the physiocrats also seems to have led to his forming a certain bias against the man who was presented to him, quite accurately, as the actual founder of the physiocratic doctrine. As a result of this bias, and perhaps also under the influence of his particular perspective as to the main tasks of economics, Oncken first firmly rejected the claim that Cantillon was the real founder of the physiocratic doctrine[75] and later, in his popular *Geschichte der Nationalökonomie*,[76] the standard German work on the history of our science prior to Adam Smith, passed such an unfavourable verdict on Cantillon that serious interest in our author could hardly any longer arise in Germany. The statement in which Oncken summarises his judgement on Cantillon and which largely discredited Cantillon in Germany is so characteristic both of Oncken's viewpoint and of the overall conception of economics which led to Cantillon's being ignored in Germany that it deserves to be quoted here. Oncken writes:

> All this goes to show while some common points exist between the two doctrines [i.e., between Cantillon's and the physiocrats], this is a long way from justifying the conclusion that Cantillon could be envisioned as "the father of Physiocracy"[77] and hence as the originator of economics as a science. The latter claim cannot be sustained, as the great moral and philosophical underpinning inherent in Quesnay's system as well as in that of Adam Smith is lacking in the *Essai*. Cantillon was an acute thinker and unusually well educated for his time; for all that, he was nothing more than(!) a merchant,

---

[74] [August Oncken (1844-1911). -Ed.]

[75] See A. Oncken, *Entstehung und Werden der physiokratischen Theorie*, in *Vierteljahrsschrift für Staats- und Volkswirtschaft*, ed. K. Frankenstein, vol. 5, 1897, especially the footnote on pp. 280ff.

[76] A. Oncken, *Geschichte der Nationalökonomie*, part I, *Die Zeit vor Adam Smith* (Leipzig: C. L. Hirschfeld, 1902), esp. p. 279.

[77] [The phrase is given thus in English in the original. -Ed.]

as were North, Child and later on Ricardo(!). He was not the founder of a science.

Perhaps even Cantillon could, elsewhere, have been satisfied with a verdict putting him on the same footing as Ricardo, but, given the views then prevailing in German economics, the verdict sufficed to perpetuate Cantillon's complete neglect, as illustrated by the following remark, made by a certain Herr Oberfohren in line with Oncken's judgement, to the effect that it was

> really incomprehensible how this rather mediocre and disconnected piece of writing could be branded as one of the most influential works of the pre-physiocrats.[78]

In the face of such adverse judgements, it has hardly made any difference so far that individual researchers such as W. Lexis,[79] F. J. Neumann,[80] and (presumably subsequent to the latter) O. von Zwiedineck-Südenhorst[81] have fully acknowledged the value of specific doctrines of Cantillon or that Joseph Schumpeter, in his brilliant treatment of the *Epochen der Dogmen- und Methodengeschichte*, summed up the matter aptly with this verdict:[82]

> It is Cantillon, however, who deserves the palm. . . . His *Essai* . . . can be regarded as the first systematic penetration of the field of economics. It bears the stamp of a scientific spirit. Individual

---

[78] Ernst Oberfohren, *Die Idee der Universalökonomie in der französischen wirtschaftswissenschaftlichen Literatur bis auf Turgot* (Probleme der Weltwirtschaft, Schriften des kgl. Institutes für Seeverkehr und Weltwirtschaften der Universität Kiel, no. 23), Jena, 1915, p. 124.

[79] See W. Lexis's article, "Physiokratisches System" in *Handwörterbuch der Staatswissenschaften*, third edition, vol. 6 (Jena: G. Fischer, 1913), p. 1039: "In particular, however, we see . . . what are really essential points of physiocratic theory anticipated . . . in Cantillon's *Essai* . . . even if Quesnay did not recognise this and indeed spoke disparagingly about Cantillon in a letter (?) to Mirabeau.—In any case Cantillon is less one-sided than the physiocrats." See also the same author's *Allgemeine Volkswirtschaftslehre* (Leipzig: B. G. Teubner, 1913), p. 239, where Cantillon's *Essai* is also described as "the first attempt at a comprehensive theory of economics".

[80] Friedrich Julius Neumann, "Zur Geschichte der Lehre von der Gravitation der Löhne nach gewissen Kostenbeträgen", *Jahrbücher für Nationalökonomie und Statistik*, III, F., vol. 17, Jena, 1899, pp. 147ff.

[81] See O. von Zwiedineck-Südenhorst, "Die Lohnpreisbildung", *Grundriß der Sozialökonomik*, vol. 4/1, p. 320, where it is said of Cantillon: "all essential arguments of what is usually regarded as the framework of classical theory are to be found articulated in this Irish pioneer of physiocratic ideas".

[82] See J. Schumpeter, *Epochen der Dogmen- und Methodengeschichte, Grundriß der Sozialökonomik*, vol. I, part 1, first edition, p. 143 (Tübingen: J. C. B. Mohr, 1914).

problems are presented in the light of unified explanatory principles and form part of a boldly designed comprehensive analysis. The narrowness of earlier trains of thought is transcended. Primitive mistakes are avoided—those arising from deficient analytic training no less than those for which the influence of philosophy must shoulder the blame.

Nonetheless, it is certainly no exaggeration even today to describe Cantillon as an author known to most German economists only by name. The astonishment that my desire to bring out a German edition of his work generally evoked bears eloquent testimony to this state of affairs.

II

Although we do not intend to present here a detailed exposition of the contents of the *Essai* which, apart from the original text, is now translated into both English and German,[83] we may point out here, in order to give the reader some initial orientation, that the three independent but not specifically identified parts into which the book falls may be informally entitled "On Wealth or Production", "On Exchange", and "On International Trade" respectively. We shall go one step further, though without any attempt to reproduce Cantillon's train of thought coherently, by drawing the reader's attention to certain idiosyncrasies of his method and to particular theories in the book that are especially noteworthy.

The first point to emphasise is the very specific meaning that our author attaches to the words 'nature' and 'natural'. The former term, in fact, occurs in the title itself, which, incidentally, just like

---

[83] R. Legrand, *Richard Cantillon, un mercantiliste précurseur des physiocrates* (Paris: V. Giard & E. Brière, 1900) provides the most detailed monographic study of the contents of the *Essai* and its connexions to predecessors and successors. Like most investigations of Cantillon, this too nonetheless suffers in being less interested in the original achievement of Cantillon than in the question whether Cantillon is to be regarded more as a mercantilist or already as a physiocrat. More detailed accounts of the contents, apart from the already mentioned works by Jevons, Espinas, Higgs (*Quarterly Journal of Economics*, vol. 6, 1892, pp. 436-456), are: W. Rouxel, "Un Precurseur des physiocrates: Cantillon", *Journal des Economistes*, 1891; Wilhelm Kretzschmer, *Über den Richard Cantillon zugeschriebenen Essai sur la nature du commerce en général mit besonderer Berücksichtigung der Lehren von Otto Effertz* (University of Basel dissertation) (Liestal: Buchdruckerei Gebrüder Lüdin, 1899). A number of special investigations into individual theories of Cantillon will be cited at the appropriate places.

the selection of subjects treated, has much in common[84] with other works that appeared around 1735, such as those of Mélon[85] and Dutot[86]. Cantillon uses the expression 'natural' in an entirely consistent way, in the sense of a connexion between cause and effect, that is, as a causal scientific explanation, and the word appears in this sense some thirty times in the *Essai*. Closely related to this is his pursuit of 'methodological purity'—quite especially remarkable for a writer of his time. By this is meant his deliberately and consistently limiting himself to the *explanation* of relationships, to the exclusion of all value judgements. Hence he frequently breaks off the discussion of a subject with the remark that "but this no longer pertains to my subject"; for example, when he mentions the possibility that even the entrepreneur's attempt to cheat his customers could influence prices,[87] or when he declines to judge whether it is better for a state to have a small but well-fed population or a large but badly fed one,[88] when he excludes from discussion the motives that induce ministers to debase the currency.[89] It is especially characteristic for him and quite contrary to the views of his contemporaries, though quite in line with modern views, that he regards even investigations into the expediency of particular taxes as no longer belonging to his subject.[90] But the fact that Cantillon aspired only to understand relationships, tying his exposition neither to proposals for reform nor to ethical considerations, and seeking merely to explain the way things are in the most dispassionate way, free of all metaphysical speculation—this very fact, together with his somewhat ponderous French, has been the chief reason why his *Essai* was able to influence only a small select circle.

But even within theoretical analysis, Cantillon wields its most important tool, the method of 'isolating abstraction' as one would say today, with true virtuosity. Not only does he freely make use of the assumption of *ceteris paribus*, which can already be found in earlier writers,[91] but he also resorts frequently to the fiction of an

---

[84] See notably *An Essay on Trade in general, and on that of Ireland in particular*, by the author of *Seasonable Remarks* (Sir John Browne) (Dublin: Printed by S. Powell for George Ewing, 1728).

[85] J. F. Mélon, *Essai politique sur le commerce* (Rouen or Bordeaux: n.p., 1734).

[86] [n.n.] Dutot, *Réflexions politiques sur les finances et le commerce* (La Haye: Les Frères Valliant & N. Prevost, 1738) [See also n 11, this volume, p. 164. -Ed.]

[87] P. 70 of the original; p. 36 of Hella von Hayek's translation.

[88] Respectively pp. 113 and 56.

[89] Respectively pp. 392 and 188.

[90] Respectively pp. 210 and 102.

[91] Respectively pp. 60 and 61.

isolated state,[92] and to the step by step explanation of price formation from the simplest case of monopoly to more complicated
cases.[93] He also repeatedly leaves aside incidental effects to avoid
needlessly complicating an already complex subject.[94]

The best known part of the whole *Essai* is undoubtedly the
sentence with which the first chapter opens and in which Cantillon's
basic conception is concentrated into its most concise expression.
This concerns the relationship of labour and land, as the two
equally important sources of wealth, to wealth itself, which "is
nothing other than food, the comforts, and the amenities of life".
This entirely psychological concept of wealth, by far the most
important part of the famous sentence, though it is generally overlooked, is an extraordinary achievement on Cantillon's part, and so
decisive for his whole perspective that a modern French scholar
could describe Cantillon, not entirely unjustly, as a precursor of the
modern hedonists.[95] Even without adopting this perhaps somewhat
daring verdict on Cantillon, it is wise to bear this definition in mind
in considering Cantillon's later statements on value and price.

Nothing further need be said here about the introductory
chapters, 2-6 of Part I, which deal with the development and
grouping of human society and the emergence of private property.[96] All the more attention must be drawn to the ensuing chapters,
7 and 8, which, together with chapter 15 of Part I, contain Cantillon's exceptionally interesting population and wage theories, which
have repeatedly become the subject of special studies.[97] His population theory is interesting because, as Jevons pointed out, it antici-

---

[92] Pp. 59 and 31 respectively.
[93] Pp. 76 and 131 and pp. 39 and 64 respectively.
[94] Pp. 112 and 350 and pp. 56 and 168 respectively.
[95] A. Huart, "Cantillon, précurseur des Hedonistes", *Monde économique*, 17, May
31, June 7, 21, 28, July 29, 1913. Information about the content of this essay, which
was available neither in the Vienna nor in the Berlin libraries, was obtained from
Herr Sektionsrat Dr. Ewald Schams, of Vienna.
[96] On the fourth and fifth chapters on the rise of the cities see also R. Meunier,
"Théories de la formation des villes", *Revue d'Économie politique*, Paris, 1910.
[97] See especially, in addition to the above-mentioned works by Jevons, Higgs,
and Neumann, A. Landry, "Une théorie négligée. De l'influence de la direction de la
demande sur la productivité du travail, les salaires et la population", *Revue d'Economie
Politique*, vol. 24, Paris, 1910, as well as the same author's "Les idées de Quesnay sur
la population", *Revue d'histoire des doctrines économiques et sociales*, vol. 2, 1909, esp. pp.
83ff.; see also R. Picard, "Etude sur quelques théories du salaire au XVIIIᵉ siècle",
ibid., vol. 3, 1910, pp. 153ff., and R. Gonnard, *Histoire des doctrines de la population*
(Paris: Nouvelle Librairie Nationale, 1923), pp. 142 and 173f., and the same author's
essay, "Les doctrines de la population avant Malthus", *Revue d'histoire économique et
sociale*, vol. 17, Paris, 1929, esp. p. 223.

pates in a few brief sentences the core ideas of Malthusian population theory, but doubtless there is an even closer link involved here.
The passages in Smith through which Malthus is supposed to have
been led to his own investigations exhibit, even in wording, a strong
correspondence with Cantillon's arguments.[98] Higgs recalls in this
connexion,[99] to show how far with a bit of imagination Cantillon's
influence can be traced, that Darwin was in turn inspired by Malthus in his own revolutionary work.[100]

Cantillon's wage theory is very closely linked with his theory of
value, which builds on the wage theory. The latter, to characterise it
briefly, is a standard-of-living theory, which, as such, is a direct
outgrowth of the population theory. That so relatively much space is
nonetheless devoted to it owes to the fact that it provides Cantillon
with the key to the question identified by Petty as the most important problem of political arithmetic, namely the problem of 'pari'
(par value) or of the equation between work and land, which forms
the basis of Cantillon's cost theory of value. As to this theory of
value, the comprehensive assessment of G. Pirou may be quoted:[101]

> With Cantillon we find ourselves for the first time in the history of
> economic doctrine in the presence of a clear, coherent, theory. If
> one wishes to appreciate the measure of originality, of novelty, that
> this theory offers compared to earlier views, and to Petty's in par-

[98] One may compare the well-known statement at the beginning of the first
section of the eleventh chapter in the first book of *Wealth of Nations*, "As men, like all
other animals, naturally multiply in proportion to the means of their subsistence,
food is always, more or less, in demand", with the arguments in the fifteenth chapter
of the first part of Cantillon's *Essai*, especially with the sentence (pp. 110 and 54
respectively), "Men multiply like mice in a barn when they have unlimited means to
maintain their life". Huart, op. cit., feels justified in the belief that Malthus was
directly influenced by Cantillon.

[99] *Quarterly Journal*, vol. 6, 1892, p. 455.

[100] [See Hayek's treatment of Adam Smith as a precursor of Darwin in "Diskus-
sion [Leitung: Franz Kreuzer]", in *Evolution und Menschenbild*, ed. Rupert J. Riedl and
Frank Kreuzer (Hamburg: Hoffmann & Campe, 1983), pp. 225-241. See also F. A.
Hayek, *The Fatal Conceit*, op. cit., p. 24 and note. -Ed.]

[101] Gaëtan Pirou, "La théorie de la valeur et des prix, chez W. Petty et chez R.
Cantillon", *Revue d'Histoire des Doctrines Economiques et Sociales*, vol. 4, Paris, 1911, p.
271. Other studies on the place of Cantillon's value and price theories in the history
of economic doctrines are to be found in the well-known works by R. Zuckerkandl
and R. Legrand already cited and in R. Kaulla, *Die geschichtliche Entwicklung der
modernen Werttheorien* (Tübingen: H. Laupp, 1906), pp. 92ff., and H. R. Sewall, "The
Theory of Value before Adam Smith", *Publications of the American Economic Association*,
3rd series, vol. 2, no. 3 (New York: Macmillan, 1901). See also A. Dubois, "Les
théories psychologiques de la valeur au XVIIIᵉ siècle", *Revue d'Économie politique*, Paris,
1897, pp. 849ff.

ticular, one must consider it from three points of view: 1. So far as the problem of *normal value* is concerned, Cantillon no longer limits himself to vague and casual remarks; he raises the question directly and openly and attempts to give it a satisfactory answer. 2. His analysis of the perturbing influences which prevent the *market price* from coinciding with normal value is extremely thorough and penetrating and endeavours to deal with the concepts of supply and demand in a rigorously scientific way, showing by what mechanism variations in the quantity of money influence prices. 3. Finally and most importantly, Cantillon welds together the two theories he has just developed by attempting to show that, despite the impact of all the factors operating against coincidence, the market price never deviates far from normal value, because a powerful economic force tends unceasingly to re-establish coincidence. And this view of Cantillon is all the more remarkable in that it is completely free of all providentialist or teleological character. It is no exaggeration to say that Cantillon anticipates the theorists of *economic equilibrium* on this score.

Pirou's concluding remark, though fully justified, calls for a brief clarification, lest it be misleading in one respect. What is most significant about Cantillon's achievement in the field of value and price theory is his down-playing the quest for rules and formulae that might account for the 'normal' relationship between the value or price of various goods and concentrating instead on the forces and mechanisms that are consistently at work in restoring these normal relationships. As an example, refer especially to the model of market price formation in Part II, chapter 2,[102] which clearly anticipates Böhm-Bawerk's famous horse-market example.

However, before we go on to the remaining parts of the book, we must emphasise one point from the first part, which is significant both as an example of the strictly scientific way in which Cantillon forms concepts, and as the earliest elaboration of a central economic phenomenon: namely, his doctrine of the entrepreneur (chapter 13).[103] For Cantillon, an entrepreneur is, quite in the modern sense, anyone who is a risk-taker and whose income is derived from profits instead of land rent or wages. Not only in this contrast, but also in many other points, Cantillon anticipates classifications of income types that later became conventional. Thus there is, especially, the recurring distinction, drawn from English

---

[102] See p. 155 of the original, p. 76 of the German translation.

[103] On Cantillon's doctrine of the entrepreneur see especially E. Cannan, *A Review of Economic Theory*, op. cit., pp. 285f. and 303f.

usage, between the three kinds of rents that the leaseholder has to realise: true land rent, which he pays to the owner; wages covering his own maintenance and that of his workers; and finally his entrepreneurial profit, to which Cantillon explicitly adds the interest from money lent out, as a further possible source of income.[104]

The closing chapter of Part I, with its investigation of the value of precious metals and the emergence of coinage, forms the basis for the discussion of monetary theory that occupies most of the second and also of the third parts of the book. This theory undeniably constitutes Cantillon's greatest achievement. At least in this field, he was doubtless the greatest pre-classical figure, and in many respects the classical writers not only failed to overtake him but did not even measure up to him. Here too we can only draw attention to the main points. For a detailed assessment the reader can consult P. Harsin's excellent history of monetary and financial theory in France from the sixteenth to the eighteenth century, as well as several other discussions.[105] In his monetary theory Cantillon was obviously influenced on many points by John Law,[106] although he never mentions him. This is especially clear in his position on John Locke, with whom he often has differences of opinion, for example with respect to Locke's convention theory of the origin of money which he, like Law, expressly rejects, just as he rejects Locke's explanation of the value of precious metals as having been determined by an agreement among men.[107] In other respects, however, Cantillon far surpasses Law, whose importance as a monetary theorist is largely overlooked today—as a consequence, to be sure, of his errors (which Cantillon in no point shares). Cantillon's achievements rival those of all the other pioneers in monetary theory. Among them is his critique of Locke's naive quantity theory, and its replacement by a detailed account of how an increase in

---

[104] See also the passage cited above from Sivers's work.

[105] P. Harsin, *Les doctrines monétaires et financières en France, du XVIᵉ au XVIIIᵉ siècle* (Paris: F. Alcan, 1928), pp. 227-236. See also, in addition to the works already cited by Jevons and Legrand, A. E. Monroe, *Monetary Theory before Adam Smith* (Cambridge, Mass.: Harvard University Press, 1923), J. W. Angell, *The Theory of International Prices* (Cambridge, Mass.: Harvard University Press, 1926), esp. pp. 207ff., and F. Hoffmann, *Kritische Dogmengeschichte der Geldwerttheorien* (Leipzig: Hirschfeld, 1907), esp. pp. 56-64.

[106] [John Law (1671-1729). -Ed.]

[107] [Hayek's statement of Cantillon's differences with Locke on this point is not entirely accurate. See this volume, chapter 10, note 20. See also Karen Iversen Vaughn, *John Locke: Economist and Social Scientist* (Chicago and London: University of Chicago Press, 1980), p. 33 and n. 44. -Ed.]

money progressively affects the various prices. This account, which appears in the splendid sixth chapter of Part II, has been rightly described by Jevons as one of the most wonderful things in the book. There is also his account of the factors determining the velocity of money, which elaborates considerably Petty's initial ideas on the subject and "where, for the first time, it is unequivocally stated that the velocity of money circulation is as important as its quantity in determining its value".[108] Also to be mentioned are his description of the functioning of a bimetallic currency, and the related critique of the actions taken by Newton[109] after the passage of the English coinage reform in 1717,[110] and finally his doctrine of exchange rates,[111] which, in Jevons's opinion, has never, not even in Goschen's well-known book,[112] been treated with more insight and scientific accuracy than in Cantillon's *Essai*.

It should also be mentioned that Cantillon, in the final two chapters of the *Essai*, provides a relatively elaborate theory of interest (one that even Böhm-Bawerk overlooked, remarkably enough). It contains not only a clear refutation of the view that the quantity of money determines interest (an achievement usually attributed to Hume), but also an accurate description of the effects

---

[108] M. W. Holtrop, *De Omloopsnelheid van het Geld* (Amsterdam: H. J. Paris, 1928), p. 9.

[109] Concerning this point, see in addition to the work mentioned by Jevons, S. D. Horton, *Sir Isaac Newton and England's Prohibitive Tariff upon Silver Money* (Cincinnati, Ohio: R. Clarke, 1881), reprinted in the same author's *Silver and Gold and their Relation to the Problem of Resumption* (Cincinnati, Ohio: R. Clarke, 1895), as well as W. Stanley Jevons's uncompleted reply, "Sir Isaac Newton and Bimetallism", printed in his *Investigations in Currency and Finance*, ed. H. S. Foxwell (London: Macmillan, 1884), pp. 330ff.

[110] Cantillon himself writes in error "1728" instead of "1717" (p. 373 of the original, p. 179 of the Hayek translation). It is difficult to understand how this error arose; since the number is given in words and not in numerals it can hardly be a writing or printing error. Moreover Cantillon not only himself witnessed the event mentioned, but seems to have been in direct contact with Newton. The mistake has for all that made the rounds in the literature and is to be found in Steuart (*Inquiry into the Principles of Political Economy*, book III, chapter 7, iii, p. 47 of the Basel edition of 1796 and vol. 2, p. 135 of the *Collected Works* (London: T. Cadell & W. Davies, 1805)) and again in J. G. Hoffmann, *Die Lehre vom Gelde* (Berlin: Nicolai, 1838), p. 104. The mistake is corrected in J. H. Graumann, who, as mentioned, reproduces these passages of the *Essai* in detail (*Gesammelte Brief vom Gelde*, etc. (Berlin: C. F. Boss, 1762)). See also P. Kalkmann, *Englands Übergang zur Goldwährung im achtzehnten Jahrhundert* (Strasbourg: K. J. Trübner, 1895), p. 127.

[111] On Cantillon's theory of exchange rates see A. M. de Jong, "Bijdrage tot de geschiedenis van de theorie der wisselkoersen voor Adam Smith", *De Economist*, vol. 74, nos. 5-8, The Hague, May-August 1925.

[112] [*Theory of the Foreign Exchanges* (London: E. Wilson, 1861). -Ed.]

---

of a temporary reduction in the rate of interest caused by an increase in the quantity of money. In the third part (after his treatment of exchange rates and bimetallic currency), Cantillon comes at last to a detailed account of banking in which, for example, he already investigates what particular circumstances can force a banker to hold a cash reserve greater or less than the customary 10 per cent of his liabilities. Having mentioned all these achievements, we have essentially accomplished our only objective here, which was to draw the reader's attention to the main points [of Cantillon's work].

One further point, however, needs to be stressed. In the first quarter of the *Essai*, Cantillon repeatedly refers (pages 9, 19, 25, 46, 50, 56, and 59) to an appendix containing calculations whose results he uses in the text. This appendix, which allegedly was seen with the manuscript, is contained in none of the printed versions, and thus is lost. Its loss is particularly regrettable, for the appendix must have contained unique statistical material collected by Cantillon himself. It is, of course, not improbable that Cantillon himself was never able to complete this appendix, which he mentions only in Part I of the *Essai*, and indeed just on this account did not publish the work himself.

Only one more brief remark about Cantillon's place in the history of economic thought may be added here. My purpose in doing so is not to shed further light on the relatively unimportant question whether Cantillon should be viewed chiefly as a mercantilist still or as the first of the physiocrats. The almost obsessive preoccupation with this question has contributed greatly to the fact that even among the authors who have treated Cantillon many have misunderstood his real significance.

No reader of the *Essai* will fail to see that the basic ideas of the physiocrats are to be found in Cantillon (see especially pages 9, 29ff., 37ff., and 78ff.). And Quesnay himself has attested that he is indebted to Cantillon for the most fertile ideas. Anyone who wishes to learn more about the connexions between specific theories of Cantillon and those of both the mercantilists and the physiocrats will find a point by point comparison in Legrand's book, which has already been cited repeatedly.[113] The significance of Cantillon seems to me to lie precisely in the fact that he kept aloof from any

---

[113] See also S. Weulersse, *Le mouvement physiocratique en France* (Paris: F. Alcan, 1910), 2 vols, and the same author's [recently published] work "Les physiocrates", *Encyclopédie Scientifique* (Paris: G. Doin, 1931) and G. Schelle, *Le Docteur Quesnay* (Paris: F. Alcan, 1907), pp. 131-184.

schools. As an outsider of genius, yet placed most advantageously 'in the midst of the action', he tried, quite independently, rather like Petty before him, to organise systematically the phenomena that came to his attention with the eyes of a born theoretician. Thereby he became the first person to succeed in penetrating and surveying nearly the entire range of what today we call economics. Thus Cantillon seems to me to represent a highly important and perhaps in many respects the first rung of that straight line of intellectual development, from which members of 'schools' always deviated one way or the other. The physiocrats, like at least some of the later classical thinkers, were therefore more likely to hinder than to further progress, while the great strides always came from out-side—and for the most part in opposition to—the schools. As far as really new knowledge—knowledge which represented a lasting gain for science—is concerned, we doubtless find more in Cantillon than in any other author prior to 1776, the year when the works of Adam Smith and Condillac were published, certainly more than in the physiocrats, even if their characterisation of economic cy-cles—which might quite well be described as a schematisation of Cantillon's ideas—was easier to grasp and hence for the moment more influential. Whether on this basis Cantillon should be called *the* founder of scientific economics is of little consequence. What marks the beginning of a science is always in large measure an arbitrary matter. After the reader has read his work, it is to be hoped that he will be convinced to rank Cantillon among the very great minds of our science. The actual influence that his achieve-ment exerted on the development of our science is of course a different matter. We shall set aside this very difficult question until we have told what little we know about the life of Cantillon and the history of the manuscript from his death until its publication.

III

That we know only very little about the circumstances of Cantillon's life is by no means the major obstacle in attempting to give an impression of the personality of the author of the *Essai*. Far more frustrating is the fact that a very large number of the reports handed down about him are demonstrably false. Moreover, up until now almost all literary efforts devoted to him have been ill-fated. Even otherwise scrupulously meticulous writers were led, the mo-ment they came to write about Cantillon, into error and misstatement, until finally several mutually exclusive accounts were put forward on virtually every point.[114]

The fact of the matter is that only Higgs's findings are truly trustworthy, and even the earlier reports can be regarded as reliable only to the extent that they were confirmed by his investigations. The fact that even today Cantillon's life still remains largely shrouded in mystery may in part be due to Cantillon's anxiousness—not unusual even today among successors in his own profession—to avoid publicity. What we do know about Cantillon at any rate supports this hypothesis. It is certainly odd that Higgs has to report that a search of many hundred volumes of contemporary memoirs and diaries yielded not a single mention of Cantillon's name and that—of the many writers who had, according to his own research, concerned themselves with Cantillon—not one contributed anything at all to our knowledge of the facts of his life.[115] Moreover, one of the best specialists in French financial history of that period, P. Harsin, has very recently emphasised how astonishing it is that

---

[114] As illustration of the above, a few of these quite unjustified statements from the later literature may be cited here. (The early sources will be examined in detail later.) The list begins with G. Kellner (*Zur Geschichte des Physiokratismus. Quesnay-Gournay-Turgot* (Göttingen: Druck und Verlag der Dieterischen Buchhandlung, 1847), p. 93), who says of Gournay that he had prevailed upon Cantillon (who died in 1734!) to translate his *Essai*. Similarly, J. W. Angell, a recent author (*The Theory of International Prices* (Cambridge, Mass.: Harvard University Press, 1926), p. 213, footnote) remarks patronisingly that it was not unlikely that Cantillon had borrowed his ideas from the economic treatises of David Hume (published in 1752), whose year of publication he set back to 1741 (*ibid.*, p. 24). The report by Grimm (which is still to be mentioned) explains why many French authors even today still usually give 1733 as Cantillon's year of death, but does not explain why, according to R. Gonnard (*Histoire des doctrines de la population* (Paris: Nouvelle Librairie Nationale, 1923), p. 142), it is 1735. Even the year of publication of the *Essai* is arbitrarily shifted to 1752 by J. Bonar (*Philosophy and Political Economy* (London: Macmillan, 1893), p. 106), and even to 1736 by E. S. Furniss (*The Position of the Laborer in a System of Nationalism* (Boston and New York: Houghton Mifflin, 1920), pp. 162ff). P. Harsin (*Les doctrines monétaires et financières en France du XVIᵉ au XVIIIᵉ siècle* (Paris: F. Alcan, 1928), p. 228) solves the riddle of who is responsible for the final publication of the *Essai* with an offhand attribution to Eleazar Mauvillon, of whom one knows only that he took the *Essai* that appeared in 1755 and reprinted it a year later together with his translation of Hume's *Political Discourses*, which of course only speaks against the assumption that he also had been the editor of the original edition. No more justified is the claim of H. R. Sewall (*The Theory of Value before Adam Smith* (New York: Macmillan, 1901), p. 80) that Cantillon was of French descent, or R. Legrand's assertion (in the book mentioned numerous times, p. 4) that Cantillon himself had visited all the countries of which he speaks in the *Essai*.

[115] See Higgs's Preface to W. Stanley Jevons's posthumous *Principles of Economics*, op. cit., pp. xi and xiii.

French sources offer nothing at all on the matter.[116] Under these circumstances, it need hardly be emphasised that what follows below on the whole only recapitulates known facts.[117]

There is unfortunately no space here to portray in detail the milieu in which Cantillon lived. (References are given in the footnote to some really informative and little-known works on these matters.[118]) The circumstances we have just mentioned serve to justify the form of our presentation, whose aim it is to piece together all leads by sifting through the most important available material. These leads can then serve as a basis for further research.

The earliest account of the book is to be found in the well-known literary correspondence—published only later—carried on by Baron Friedrich Melchior von Grimm,[119] together with Diderot and others, with German princely houses. Grimm wrote on July 1, 1755:[120]

> For a month we have had a new work on commerce, presented in a suitably large volume, entitled *Essai sur la nature du commerce en général, traduit de l'anglais*. The book is not translated from English as its title leads one to believe. The original work was written in French by an Englishman named Cantillon, a man of standing who ended his days in Languedoc, where he had retired and had lived for several years.

Grimm proceeds to provide a detailed account of the contents, one which in modern type comprises nearly six pages. In his next letter, written fourteen days later, Grimm enlarges on his communication as follows:

---

[116] *Les doctrines monétaires*, op. cit., p. 228, footnote. Huart (op. cit., 17/V) reports that even the "Procès-verbaux du Conseil de Commerce et du bureau du Commerce 1700-1791", published by Bonnastieux and Lelong, contain nothing about Cantillon, a fact that he considers extremely peculiar.

[117] It may be noted here for the convenience of specialists in the Cantillon literature that the data hitherto available concerning Cantillon's life and work are supplemented here only with respect to the earliest plagiarism by Postlethwayt and the plagiarism by Serionne as well as by our reference to the connexions with Montesquieu.

[118] H. Thirion, *La vie privée des financiers au XVIIIᵉ siècle* (Paris: E. Plon, Nourrit, 1885), Cornélis de Witt, *La Société française et la Société anglaise au XVIIIᵉ siècle* (Paris: Lévy Frères, 1864), J. H. Jesse, *Memories of the Pretenders and their Adherents* (London: R. Bentley, 1845).

[119] [Friedrich Melchior von Grimm (1773-1809). -Ed.]

[120] See pp. 43ff. (respectively pp. 52 and 71) of the third volume of the most complete edition of the *Correspondance littéraire, philosophique et critique par Grimm, Diderot, Reynal, Meister, etc.*, ed. by Maurice Tourneux (Paris: Garnier Frères, 1878).

M. de Cantillon, about whom I had the honour of communicating with you in my last letter, often refers in his work on the nature of commerce to another book, which he considers a complement to the first and which contains chiefly some very ingenious and interesting calculations. This work has, one is assured, been lost, and all the trouble that one has taken to recover it has not been crowned by success. The admiration merited by the first volume only increases one's regret on the loss of the other.

After a further space of two weeks, on August 1, Grimm has to amend his information about Cantillon the man:

I was falsely informed about the person of M. de Cantillon when I had the honour of speaking on the subject of his excellent work. Cantillon, an Englishman and a man of intellect, as his book sufficiently proves, was a banker in Paris during the Regency period, and enjoyed extraordinary credit. In the beginnings of the System, John Law summoned him and said to him: "If we were in England we would have to negotiate and reach an agreement; but in France, as you know, I could tell you that you will be in the Bastille this evening if you do not give me your promise to leave the kingdom within forty-eight hours." Cantillon thought it over for a moment and then replied: "Very well. I shall not go, instead, I shall contribute to the success of your system", and to do this he took over a considerable quantity of securities, which he immediately placed on the market with all the exchange brokers, and which, thanks to his credit, were brought into circulation. Several days later he departed for Holland with several millions. It is claimed that he was on very good terms with the Princess of Auvergne. It is usually said that he died in 1733 when his house in London caught fire. The fact is that the fire was quickly extinguished, but that Cantillon was found stabbed. The fire had obviously been set in order to conceal the crime, and this event gave rise at the time to considerable gossip.

This communication is supplemented by the second contemporary account of the publication of the book, the review contained in the 1755 volume of Fréron's *Année littéraire*.[121] As with Grimm, the detailed review of the book (in the third letter of the fifth volume, dated August 4, 1755), begins with the declaration that the *Essai* is not a true translation:

---

[121] Elie Catherine Fréron, ed., *L'année littéraire*, Amsterdam, 1755, vol. 5, p. 67.

It was conceived in French and the English have translated it into their tongue from Cantillon's original. He (Cantillon) was Irish, had lived for a long time as a banker in Paris and died accidentally in a fire. He was a man of great intellect, who had contacts with persons of the highest social standing, counting among them as a special friend Lord Bolingbroke. It is not known through whose efforts and under what circumstances the manuscript was published, nor why its publication was delayed by twenty years. Nor is it known why, when it was printed, the very interesting calculations which several persons have testified to me that they had seen in the manuscript were omitted.

Fréron, in turn, later corrected his report about Cantillon. In the table of contents to the volume, the reference to the book by the late "famous banker" Cantillon contains the following comment:

It was in error that it was said that he died in a fire in Paris. In 1733 or 1734 he had returned to his homeland, England. Shortly thereafter he was burgled by a servant, who set fire to the house in order to conceal his deed, but was nonetheless discovered, arrested, and executed in London. Cantillon had married his daughter to Lord Bulkeley, Lieutenant-General in the service of France, Chevalier des Ordres du Roi, brother of Madame la Maréchale Berwick. Madame Bulkeley died in Paris six or seven years ago.

These partly contradictory biographical statements, with their equally inaccurate corrections, comprised practically everything known about Cantillon up to the time of Higgs's research.[122] Even the two great

---

[122] [See now also Antoin E. Murphy, *Richard Cantillon: Entrepreneur and Economist* (Oxford: Clarendon Press, 1986), and especially the genealogical tables contained therein. On Murphy's book, see Peter Groenewegen's review in *Journal of Economic Literature*, vol. 26, December 1988, pp. 1743-1744, and D. P. O'Brien's review in *Economic Journal*, vol. 97, December 1987, pp. 1035-1036. See also G. Antonetti, "Autour de Cantillon", Monograph 29 (1968-9, *Mémoires de la Société pour l'Histoire du Droit et des Institutions des Anciens pays Bourguignons, Comtois et Romands*, Faculty of Law and Political Science, Dijon; Richard Hayes, *Biographical Dictionary of Irishmen in France*, *Studies* (June 1942), p. 242; R. F. Hébert, "Richard Cantillon's Early Contributions to Spatial Economics", *Economica*, vol. 48, February 1981, pp. 71-77; Joseph Hone, "Richard Cantillon, Economist—Biographical Note", *Economic Journal*, vol. 54, no. 213, April 1944, pp. 96-100; Leonard P. Liggio, "Richard Cantillon and the French Economists: Distinctive French Contributions to J. B. Say", *Journal of Libertarian Studies*, vol. 7, no. 2, Fall 1985, pp. 295-304; John Nagle, *Richard Cantillon of Ballyheigue*, *Studies* (Dublin: Educational Company of Ireland, March 1932); *Notice Historique*, "Généalogique et Bibliographique de la Familie De Cantillon Par le Chevalier O'S. . .*, Gentilhomme Irlandais, Benard et Companie" (Paris: Gauthier-Villars, 1844); Joseph J. Spengler, "Richard Cantillon: First of the Moderns", *Journal of Political Economy*, vol. 62, August-October 1954, pp. 281-295, 406-424, reprinted in Joseph J. Spengler and

French biographical dictionaries, the *Biographie Universelle*[123] and the *Nouvelle Biographie Générale*[124] simply reproduce the content of these reports. A reader conversant with the gossip of the time might nonetheless have recalled a passage in the letters of Horace Walpole[125] in which, under the date April 25, 1743, he relates:[126]

> Lord Stafford is come over to marry Miss Cantillon, a vast fortune, of his own religion. She is the daughter of the Cantillon who was robbed and murdered, and had his house burned by his cook a few years ago. She is as ugly as he; but when she comes to Paris, and wears a good deal of rouge, and a separate apartment, who knows but she may be a beauty!

The editor adds in a footnote that Cantillon had been a Parisian wine merchant and banker, who had worked with Law in the Mississippi Company and later brought his wealth to England and settled there. In May 1734 (on May 14, to be exact), a number of his servants, led by the cook, plotted to murder him, knowing that he had substantial sums of money in the house. They killed him and set the house afire, but the flames were easily extinguished and the body with the wounds they had inflicted was found. The cook fled abroad, while three of his accomplices were charged with murder but later acquitted. These reports were apparently taken from contemporary weekly newspapers, which Jevons later tracked down, and with which they tally.[127] The marriage mentioned by

William R. Allen, eds, *Essays in Economic Thought: Aristotle to Marshall* (Chicago: Rand McNally, 1960), pp. 105-140; Takumi Tsuda, "Etude Bibliographique sur l'Essai de Cantillon" in *Richard Cantillon: Essai de la Nature du Commerce en Général* (Tokyo: Kinokuniya, 1979), pp. 416ff. -Ed.]

[123] *Biographie Universelle Ancienne et Moderne* . . . . New edition published under the direction of J. F. & M. G. Michaud, vol. 6 (Paris: A. T. Displaces, 1843), [article] under the false name of Philippe de Cantillon. The author of the article was allegedly named Weiß.

[124] *Nouvelle Biographie Générale depuis les temps les plus reculés jusqu'à nos jours*, published by Messrs. Firmin Didot Brothers under the direction of Dr. Hoefer, vol. 8 (Paris: Firmin Didot Frères, 1855), likewise entered under the name "Philippe Cantillon".

[125] [Horace Walpole (1717-1797). -Ed.]

[126] *The Letters of Horace Walpole Earl of Oxford* (London: R. Bentley, 1840), vol. 1, pp. 274 and 295. See also *The Works of Jonathan Swift*, ed. Walter Scott (Edinburgh: A. Constable, 1814), vol. 16, pp. 262ff., which affirms Cantillon's presence in Paris in 1716.

[127] *The Country Journal*, or *The Craftsman*, May 18 and June 15, 1734, *Reads Weekly Journal*, or *British Gazette*, June 1, 1734, and *Gentleman's Magazine*, May and December 7, 1734.

Walpole is recorded in genealogical reference books, which report that on July 8 or 26, 1743, Henrietta, the daughter of Richard (or Philip) Cantillon, a banker from Paris, married William Mathias, Earl of Stafford. Following his premature death seven years later, she married Robert (Maxwell), Baron (later Earl) of Farnham, on October 11, 1759, and she died on August 30, 1761, at about 34 years of age.[128]

The third contemporary source on Cantillon is the elder Mirabeau's remarks, mentioned at the outset, contained in his famous *L'Ami des Hommes*, published in 1757, two years after Cantillon's *Essai*. Mirabeau's work, as it later turned out, was far more closely connected to Cantillon's *Essai* than one could gather from Mirabeau's own assertions. Already in the preface Mirabeau refers to Cantillon's *Essai* but not explicitly. In order to excuse the rather unsystematic construction of the book, he mentions a change of plan that became necessary in the course of his work:[129]

> I began it in the form of a free commentary on an outstanding work which I then possessed in manuscript and which I would have liked to publish. The work appeared, however, before I had commenced the third section; this led me to modify the form of my project and to bring together under my own name the scattered and neglected fragments which I had allowed to flow from my pen.

From subsequent remarks by Mirabeau in the text of his book it transpires that he was referring to Cantillon's *Essai*. After quoting from the fifteenth chapter of Part I of the *Essai*, Mirabeau continues:[130]

---

[128] See *Complete Peerage of England, Scotland, Ireland, Great Britain and the United Kingdom, extant extinct or dormant, alphabetically arranged*, ed. George Edward Cockayne, vol. 7 (London: St. Catherine Press, 1896), p. 217 (Stafford) and vol. 3 (London: St. Catherine Press, 1890), p. 319 (Farnham), and also Higgs, *Economic Journal*, vol. 1, 1891, p. 288, who reports that Lady Henrietta Farnham, the only surviving child of the second marriage of Cantillon's daughter, died in 1852, and that from her marriage with the Rt. Hon. Dennis Daly the first Lord Dunsandle was born, whose offspring are therefore direct descendants of Cantillon. I mention this here because this trail can perhaps one day still help us increase the meagre information now available concerning Cantillon.

[129] Victor de Riquetti, Marquis de Mirabeau, *L'Ami des Hommes ou Traité de la population*, part I (Avignon: n.p., 1756 (actually 1757)), p. vi. See also the note at the bottom of page 18 of chapter 2.

[130] *Ibid.*, p. 85 (beginning of the seventh chapter). The quotation from Cantillon to which these remarks are joined is from p. 107 of the original edition (p. 53 of the Hayek translation), beginning with "le nombre des habitants" to the end of the passage on the following page.

These words are taken from the work of Cantillon which was printed last year. He was uncontestedly the most competent man ever known in this field. This fragment, which disappeared in the throng of things of that sort which fashion produces today, is only a hundredth part of the work of this illustrious man, which perished with him in a catastrophe that was as singular as it was deadly. This particular item itself is truncated, for it lacks the supplement to which he often referred and where he had set up all the calculations. He had translated the first part of it himself for the benefit of one of his friends; and it is on the basis of this manuscript that it has been printed more than twenty years after the death of the author. The principle which he establishes here is only a succession of inductions, demonstrated and in such a manner connected one with the other that it is impossible to escape them. I refer to it those who will deny the principles to me. I would have been able to repeat or to make extracts from them; but on the one hand the role of plagiarist does not suit me; on the other hand, everything is so interconnected in this work that there is not a single thought that can be extracted from its place. Besides, one can only wonder whether the dryness of this work was not the cause of the indifference with which so incomparable a work was allowed to disappear in the crowd.

Mirabeau had every reason to stress that he was not inclined to plagiarise Cantillon. At the very least the rightful owners of Cantillon's manuscript might well have had good reason to suspect that that was for a time precisely his intention. As emerges from the letter from Mirabeau to Rousseau that was mentioned earlier, he had the manuscript in his possession for no less than sixteen years. This remark, to which Alfred Stern drew attention in his work on *Das Leben Mirabeaus*,[131] prompted Stephen Bauer to become interested in the manuscripts of Mirabeau mentioned by Stern, which are in the National Archives in Paris, and there he found what he took to be a copy of the manuscript of the *Essai*.[132] Only when Henry Higgs[133] undertook a closer examination of the manuscripts

---

[131] Alfred Stern, *Das Leben Mirabeaus* (Berlin: S. Cronbach, 1889), vol. I, p. 26, who already remarked there: "Of great influence on the development of his ideas was Cantillon's work, *Essai sur la nature du commerce en général*, which he knew in manuscript already long before its publication."

[132] See Stephen Bauer, "Studies on the Origin of the French Economists", *Quarterly Journal of Economics*, vol. 5, 1891, p. 101.

[133] See the essay in the *Economic Journal*, vol. 1, 1891, already cited repeatedly, as well as the description of the manuscript in G. Weulersse, *Les Manuscrits Economiques de François Quesnay et du Marquis de Mirabeau aux Archives Nationales* (Paris: P. Geuth-

relating to Cantillon did it turn out that the apparent copy was no faithful copy but rather an abbreviated version of the *Essai*. Not only had various alterations been made with the obvious aim of deceiving the reader as to its true authorship, but a preface had been added to it as well, probably addressed, to judge by the initials in its heading, to the Duke of Noailles, and which in Higgs's view showed all the characteristics of Mirabeau's style. From the complete text published by Higgs only the following passage need be reproduced here, one that characterises the work, purporting to be his own, in terms rather similar to those Mirabeau employed with regard to Cantillon in the passage cited from *L'Ami des Hommes*.

> May the dryness of the style of the *Essai* be excused; persuaded that in such a subject it is difficult to subdue the imagination, and not having confidence in my own, I fell into the opposite extreme. The main thing is that it is an abridged sketch of a complete account. To get it ready, I have set aside the longer part of it, which must be damaging to its continuity. But the present piece cannot be long; and in case any point whatsoever interests you sufficiently to undertake a more detailed study of the subject, you know then who is its author.

In the text of the *Essai* that followed, the passages which were altered or eliminated were mainly those which would have betrayed a detailed knowledge not to be expected from Mirabeau. In addition, explanations are occasionally added as to how the author acquired his information, as if to justify his possessing it. Whether and how Mirabeau made use of this reworked text is not known. That his motives, as Higgs suggests, were thoroughly dishonourable can scarcely be doubted.

The second manuscript is perhaps even more interesting. It is a somewhat truer copy of the first half of the *Essai* (up until the beginning of the sixth chapter of the second Part), which apparently originated from one of Mirabeau's secretaries, but which contains a running commentary by Mirabeau himself in the form of marginal notes in the first part. It is from these notes that *L'Ami des Hommes* eventually was developed.

The appeal to Epicureans, which appears in the preface to *L'Ami des Hommes*, where it is followed by the brief allusion to Cantillon's work we mentioned earlier, is associated here, in addition, with a recognition and assessment of Cantillon in which, oddly enough, the

ner, 1910), pp. 2f.

name "Cantillon", as originally given, is stricken out and replaced by the simple expression "this man". The following is a translation of excerpts from this extensive passage, which is reproduced more fully by Higgs.[134]

But it is time to render justice to whom it is due. In the numerous publications on commerce and trade that have recently appeared, and which I have read on the whole with interest, among many useful notions I came upon little underlying precision of principle. Finally a rare manuscript fell into my hands, the sole remains of the immense work of one of the ablest men that Europe has ever produced. I should have named this man with pleasure [Originally, "Cet homme est M. Cantillon"], and I owe him too much not to feel myself obliged on his behalf to hand over to posterity his name and some details of his hard-working life, at the very least those which could bestow on his work all the authenticity that it merits. Yet only the reading of the work will provide that. Moreover, I have been assured that I would annoy his family [by publishing it]. On the basis of this simple claim, without wanting either to verify or even to assume a fact which might in my opinion be perceived as a reproach by those persons which it concerns, there was enough uncertainty that I might shock someone or other to restrain my pen, holy instrument in honest hands, poisoned dagger in those of someone foolish or corrupt at heart.

Hence I say only that it is the work of one of the premier geniuses of commerce of our century. His profound erudition embraces everything with an exorbitant diligence, and always connects what he has to say with various points of view. He anticipated the complete course of Law's system.[135] Forced by certain circumstances to participate in it, he quitted the theatre of this astonishing revolution, while nevertheless, prior to departing, leaving behind for his associate directions on the subject of each of the steps according to which this catastrophe would have to unfold. This fact is not mentioned here at all lightly, its details have been debated before the assizes of the greatest tribunal of Europe. One does not forget that men like him knew how to keep clear of the crash of this colossal and frail edifice and to make good pickings from its ruins. It was thus easy for them to profit during the crisis which gripped state securities in virtually all of Europe, Venice, Amsterdam and England. But this man, a true genius in heart as well as in mind, considered gold as a slave and, surveying at a

---

[134] *Economic Journal*, vol. 1, 1891, pp. 262-291, esp. pp. 267-268.

[135] [I.e., the famous Mississippi Bubble in Paris in 1719-20, set in motion by John Law, who established and controlled the nationalised Banque Royale. See below. -Ed.]

glance all the commerce and wealth of the whole world, he made these serve his own tastes and curiosity without ever thinking of acquiring any of it unless, at some moment, he might unexpectedly happen on something, whether a new fantasy or some occasion to follow his penchant for generosity. Like all energetic men subject at times to passions, his principle was nonetheless always independence and liberty. Cosmopolitan or, rather, a citizen of the world, he possessed houses in seven of the chief cities of Europe, and the least matter of acquiring knowledge or of verifying a prediction would send him from one place to another. One of my friends has told me of having one day found him at his house in Paris, in his dressing gown, having Titus Livius[136] on his desk. "I am going to make a little trip", he said to him. "One is always deceived by the value in legal tender of the coins with which the Romans ransomed their city from the hand of the Gauls. Whatever the facts, interpreters are asses, and I want to be certain about my own ideas about the matter. One of the coins of the time is among the medals of the grand duke, and I am going there to verify the weight and the alloy." While he spoke the horses arrived and he took leave of his friend to mount his seat. During these trips he would question everything, would descend from his carriage and go to interrogate a worker in his field, would consider the quality of the soil, would taste it, would make notes, and an accountant whom he always took along would work over these for him the whole of the evening at their lodgings. Many precious writings perished with him in a singular and deplorable catastrophe. Of them there remains only this sketch which makes one regret the loss of the rest all the more. This piece fell into my hands by a sort of theft since confessed by the person for whom this translation was made.

Mirabeau then goes on to relate that he hesitated to publish the work because the supplement was missing and also because it was somewhat ponderous in expression—since "the author" (originally: "M. Cantillon") had first written it in his native language and then had translated it for the use of a friend without exercising particular care. He had originally planned to revise the text but finally however er convinced himself that it is impossible "to touch the works of great men if one is not at least their equal". Not wanting to confine himself to commenting on the text, he had included it in his own work and, in so doing, altered the title, since one was already overwhelmed with "Essais sur le commerce".

---

[136] [(59 BC-AD 17), the Roman historian. -Ed.]

As we know from the passage already cited from the preface to *L'Ami des Hommes*, this plan ran aground in that the *Essai* was published elsewhere before Mirabeau had brought his planned work to a close. However, even the version of *L'Ami des Hommes* that was eventually published as Mirabeau's exclusive work still amply demonstrates the influence of Cantillon; and Higgs reports that still further proof for the influence could be adduced from the unpublished manuscripts.[137]

Mirabeau was not the only person, however, who sought to appropriate the manuscript prior to the publication of the *Essai*. As already pointed out by Jevons, two English authors—M. Postlethwayt[138] and the distinguished monetary theorist J. Harris[139]—ruthlessly plagiarised Cantillon soon after the publication of the French edition.[140] Somewhat later however E. Cannan[141] discovered that the same Postlethwayt had copied long extracts from it verbatim already in the first volume of his *Universal Dictionary of Trade and Commerce*,[142]

---

[137] In view of these documents it is especially amusing that L. Brocard in his book on Mirabeau's *L'Ami des Hommes (Les doctrines économiques et sociales du Marquis de Mirabeau dans l'Ami des Hommes* (Paris: V. Giard & E. Brière, 1902), p. 48) turns angrily against R. Legrand for cautiously observing, on the strength of Higgs's research (*Richard Cantillon, un mercantiliste précurseur des physiocrates* (Paris: V. Giard & E. Brière, 1900), p. 8): "It is safe to assume that the Marquis de Mirabeau intended to help himself to Cantillon's manuscript and to publish it under his own signature with some small changes." (R. Legrand obviously was unfamiliar with Higgs's work.)

[138] *Great Britain's True System* (London: A. Millar, 1757).

[139] *An Essay upon Money and Coins* (anon.) (London: A. Hawkins, 1757-8).

[140] Even in France there was to be found at least one plagiarist soon after the publication of the *Essai*, namely Accarias de Serionne, who in his work *Les Intérêts des Nations de l'Europe dévelopés relativement au Commerce* (Leiden: Chez les Herit. De Weidmann et Reich, 1766; second edition, Paris: E. Luzac, 1767) copied a number of passages from Cantillon: that is, in the second volume (of the second edition), on p. 127, in a footnote the report, verbatim, on the living conditions of the Chinese from pp. 50f. of the *Essai* (p. 26 of the Hayek translation), on pp. 135f. the argument on the various value relationships between gold and silver in various lands from pp. 364-366 of the *Essai* (p. 175 of the Hayek translation) and on p. 148 the story about Newton's attitude toward the English coinage reform from p. 377 of the *Essai* (p. 178 of the Hayek translation) even including the misdating of this occurrence by Cantillon.

[141] See the editorial report in the *Economic Journal*, vol. 6, 1896, p. 165.

[142] *The Universal Dictionary of Trade and Commerce, translated from the French of the Celebrated Monsieur Savary . . . with large additions and Improvements incorporated throughout the Whole Work which more particularly accommodate the same to the Trade and Navigations of the Kingdoms . . . By Malachy Postlethwayt* (London: J. & P. Knapton), vol. 1, 1751, vol. 2, 1755. See especially the articles Arbitration, Balance of Trade, Banks, Barter, Britain, Cash Circulation, Coin, Exchange and Interest in the first volume and the articles Labour, Manure, Mines and Money in the second volume. The article Labour reproduces verbatim almost the entire contents of chapters 2 and 7-11 of the first

published in 1751, that is, four years prior to the publication of the French *Essai*. In fact, a prospectus[143] ·for this Dictionary that was published two years earlier contains passages which are undoubtedly taken from Cantillon's *Essai*. It cannot be said with certainty whether Postlethwayt had the French translation at his disposal or even the original English manuscript, which contemporaries assumed to have perished in the flames at the time of Cantillon's death.[144] Probability speaks for the latter, because it is known that the French manuscript had for a long time been in Mirabeau's hands and second because certain errors in the French text[145] do not appear here. A final clue that speaks in favour of the English manuscript is the fact that the "papers of a highly ingenious deceased gentleman", from which the greater part of Philip Cantillon's earlier mentioned *Analysis of Trade* was admittedly taken, can hardly be anything other than the original English manuscript of the *Essai*, thus still in existence in 1759, even though that publication contains only a mutilated version of Richard Cantillon's thoughts.

The manuscript of the *Essai* was probably known by far more persons than those who have been named and who can be proved today to have known it. It may indeed also have been available in several copies. In favour of this there speaks at least the passage quoted earlier from Fréron, who knew of several persons who claimed to have seen the appendix. On the basis of what little we know about the set of persons among whom Cantillon moved, we can only speculate what became of the manuscript after Cantillon's death.

part of the *Essai*.

[143] *A Dissertation on the Plan, Use, and Importance of The Universal Dictionary of Trade and Commerce, Translated from the French . . . . Addressed to the Nobility, Gentry, Merchants and Great Britain* (London: J. & P. Knapton, 1749).

[144] [It is now widely believed that there never was an English original; the French version was designed to appear as a translation to avoid French censorship laws. See Murphy, op. cit., pp. 299-321. -Ed.]

[145] Thus the example of the respective share of labour and material in the value of a watch spring, obviously erroneously given in the French text as "one to one", is given correctly as "one to a million" (see p. 35 of the French text and p. 18 of the Hayek translation). The fact that Postlethwayt in his earlier mentioned work, *Great Britain's True System*, op. cit., p. 154, gave the relationship more exactly as 1 to 1,538,460 led Cannan to the question (see the report cited above in the *Economic Journal*, vol. 6) whether Postlethwayt might not even have possessed the lost appendix to the *Essai* as well, a question which cannot be answered, however.

IV

The origins and person of Cantillon are hardly less shrouded in mystery than the fate of his writings. It is true that Jevons found the above-mentioned notices about his family in genealogical publications. Yet on closer inspection their contents prove to be so much at odds with what we do know for certain about Cantillon that it is wiser to do without them. All that can be taken as certain is that the Cantillons were settled in Ireland for centuries and that several members of the family emigrated to France no later than the end of the seventeenth century, on the occasion of the expulsion of the Stuarts from England with James II. A certain Richard Cantillon, clearly not the economist and, according to the unreliable family trees, his cousin, a veteran wounded in 1690 in the Battle of the Boyne between the followers of James II and those of William of Orange, was a banker in Paris as early as 1705 and as such apparently the confidant of the large group of English Catholics who had gathered there around the son of James II, the 'Old Pretender'. Details of various business dealings of this Richard Cantillon have been reported by Higgs, in particular about a troublesome lottery, run for the benefit of the Benedictines who had emigrated from Ireland to France.[146] The first reference however to our own Richard Cantillon turns up after the death of his cousin on August 5, 1717. The latter had contracted debts far in excess of his means, so that some of his creditors had to be satisfied initially with 25 per cent of their claims. But in March 1720, "M. Cantillon, who in the lifetime of the chevalier Cantillon was known by the name of Richard Cantillon junior, volunteered to pay all creditors of the deceased the missing three-quarters to their full satisfaction, although he was himself a creditor for a large amount . . . and he made his offer . . . although he was driven to do so by no reasons known to us, apart from that of doing honour to a person whose name he bore."[147] It is however likely that, even before 1717, the real owner of the bank was not the invalid veteran but rather our own Richard Cantillon. As to reasons for this suggestion, we know from other sources that Cantillon himself stated in 1719 that he had

---

[146] *Economic Journal*, vol. 1, 1891, pp. 270-275.

[147] The above passage is cited by H. Higgs (*Economic Journal*, vol. 1, 1891, p. 284) from a character reference which is found in the records of the trial, to be mentioned below, "Carol vs. Cantillon" (Bibliothèque Nationale, Fm. 2740, 2838). The details mentioned in the following are also taken from Higgs's essay.

been engaged in banking in Paris for many years, and in another source it is said of him that he established himself as a banker in Paris in 1716. It is unlikely, however, that two firms of the same name would have co-existed here without some sort of distinction being made between them in the available references. Moreover, as we shall also see, Cantillon later set up a relative by the same name as a straw man in a firm which actually belonged entirely to him. It is certain, at any rate, that after the death of the elder Richard Cantillon, the Cantillon banking company maintained its clientele.

As early as 1715 it was said of "the banker Cantillon in Paris", without any more specific designation being given, that he had for years been the banker with whom the English there regularly dealt. The number of English residents in Paris at this time was exceptionally large. The majority of them were Catholic emigrants, many of them, like Cantillon, being Irish. Some had come to Paris with the expelled Stuarts, others independently. With the most famous among these, such as the statesman and philosopher Henry St. John Bolingbroke (1678-1751), who had also joined the 'Old Pretender', and with James Fitzjames, Duke of Berwick (1670-1734), natural son of James II, and Marshall in the service of the French, Cantillon was intimately connected. In Bolingbroke's published correspondence we find confirmation of the contact already referred to by Fréron in the passage cited earlier.[148] As for Marshall Berwick, Cantillon became related to him through his marriage, apparently in London, in 1722 (the deeds of marriage from there are dated February 16, 1722) with Mary Anne Mahony. Mary Anne was the daughter of Daniel Mahony (or O'Mahony, hence also written as 'Ommani' by the French), a rich Irish merchant from Paris, from his marriage with the widowed Lady Clare, née Charlotte Bulkeley,[149] whose sister Anne Bulkeley was the wife of Marshall Berwick. Her brother, Francis Bulkeley, married Cantillon's widow, his own niece, in either 1736 or 1737, following Cantillon's death.[150]

---

[148] *Lettres Historiques, Politiques, Philosophiques et Particulières de Henri Saint John Bolingbroke depuis 1710 jusqu'en 1736*, ed. Grimoard (Paris: Dentu, 1808), vol. 2, pp. 452 and 455; Letters to the Abbé Alari of February 2 and 3, 1718.

[149] This information comes partly from Higgs and partly from the articles on "Bulkeley" and "Clare" in the *Dictionnaire généalogique, chronologique et historique . . . par M. D. L. C. D. B.* (François Alexandre Aubert de la Chesnay-des-Bois) (Paris: Duchesne, 1757), vol. 1. According to the latter source, Daniel Mahoni was "titular count of Castille, by grant of King Philippe V lieutenant general of his armies".

[150] If the information mentioned from the *Dictionnaire généalogique* is correct. Higgs supposes that the Francis Bulkeley who married Cantillon's widow was her cousin. Since we shall refer again to the text concerning Bulkeley, let me provide

These family relationships are of particular interest because both Berwick and Bulkeley had been close friends of Montesquieu[151] since 1717 (or, in the case of the latter, at least since 1723) and hence it is at least very probable that Cantillon also knew Montesquieu.

But even if Montesquieu should not have known Cantillon personally, it still can scarcely be doubted that he was familiar with his manuscript, for, as various letters show, he was on most friendly terms with Cantillon's widow (who herself died in 1749 or 1750) between 1736 and 1749 or 1750, she by then being the wife of Bulkeley.[152] It might also be noted that it is very likely, after all that has gone before, that it was also this Bulkeley who, after the death of his wife, published the work of her first husband. He may have delayed this step until then out of consideration for the attitude of Cantillon's family, to which Mirabeau alluded. Moreover, his own death following immediately afterwards (January 14, 1756) would also explain why his contemporaries failed to discover who was responsible for publishing the work.

We have already spoken of Cantillon's participation in the Mississippi speculations.[153] Professor Einaudi has pointed out[154] quite

here the particulars which I was able to obtain about his life: Born in London on September 11, 1686, as the son of Henry Bulkeley, Chamberlain to Charles II and James II, and the brother of the second Viscount Bulkeley; he came to France in 1700, served here under Marshall Berwick to the rank of lieutenant general, took part in the abortive expedition to Scotland in 1715-16 of the 'Old Pretender', to whom he, together with Berwick's son, was supposed to deliver a large sum of gold; he died on January 14, 1756, after he had been permitted to hand over his Irish infantry regiment to his son. (According to the *Mémoires du Maréchal de Berwick, écrits par lui même* (Switzerland, 1778), vol. 2, pp. 169, 172, and *Lettres historiques, politiques et particulières de Henri Saint-John, Lord Vicomte Bolingbroke, depuis 1710 jusqu'en 1736*, vol. 3 (Paris: Grimoard, 1808), p. 132n.

[151] [Charles de Secondat, Baron de la Brède et de Montesquieu (1689-1755). -Ed.]

[152] See *Correspondance de Montesquieu, publiée par François Gebelin et André Morize* (Paris: H. Champion, 1914), 2 vols. Bulkeley's first letter to Montesquieu is dated September 10, 1723, the last, September 20, 1751. Madame Bulkeley was mentioned for the first time by Montesquieu in a letter of May or June 1740 and for the last time on July 22, 1749, in a letter to Bulkeley in which Montesquieu reported that he had spoken with Madame Bulkeley. Already on July 18, 1736, Montesquieu wrote to Bulkeley: "Faites ma cour à Mme de Cantillon."

[153] [That is, the great Mississippi Bubble of 1719-20 in Paris, in which the stock of John Law's Compagnie des Indes (including the former East India Company) was eventually bid from £500 to £18,000 before the bubble burst in January 1720. Law formed the Compagnie d'Occident, with monopolies on Louisiana and the Canadian fur trade in 1717; by 1719 the company had acquired the East India Company, the tobacco monopoly, and trading monopolies with Africa and China, and Law changed its name to the Companie des Indes. -Ed.]

recently an interesting communication made in a contemporaneous work which gives an idea of the probable extent of this activity. In this work, du Hauchamps[155] gives a complete list of those who, after the suspension of September 15, 1722, had been subjected to a special tax. One finds our Richard Cantillon among the first forty-six of the largest shareholders, with a presumed balance of 20,000,000 pounds assigned to Law and a corresponding tax of 2,400,000 pounds. One does not know whether Cantillon paid this tax. Even du Hauchamps confines himself, in his notes, to the remark "unknown".[156]

Only for the time from 1720 on do we know somewhat more about the life of Cantillon, who spent this year for the most part not in Paris but rather in London, to which he returned around this time, and in travelling. This information we owe to those court cases to which Mirabeau alluded, the records of which Higgs tracked down, following a clue discovered by Jevons.[157] From these it appears that Cantillon had at the beginning of 1720 changed his Paris bank into a limited partnership under the name "Cantillon & Hughes", which partners did not include him but were rather his four-year-old nephew of the same name and a certain John Hughes, although to be sure Cantillon senior supplied, as limited partner, the entire capital of the company and was also supposed to receive two-thirds of the profit, while Hughes received a third in his capacity as manager as it were, and the nephew emerged with nothing at all. Shortly afterwards—it was right at the peak of the Mississippi speculation[158]—the firm engaged in those transactions which became the subject of the court cases. That is, it advanced some 40,000 pounds for the purchase of these shares to a number of people, mostly members of the English nobility, who were still counting on a further increase of the price level of the Mississippi shares. Cantillon, who foresaw the imminent collapse of Law's system, advised Hughes immediately to sell the shares received as security, to convert the proceeds into sterling credits and actually to hold only as many shares as necessary in order to be able immediately to

---

[154] "A forgotten quotation about Cantillon's life", *Economic Journal*, vol. 43, no. 3, September 1933, pp. 534-537.

[155] *Histoire générale et particulière du visa fait en France pour la réduction et l'extinction de tous les papiers royaux et des actions de la Compagnie des Indes, que le système des finances avoit enfautez* (The Hague: F. H. Schuerleer, 1743), vol. 2, p. 170.

[156] [This paragraph was added to the French translation of 1936. -Ed.]

[157] See the essay in the *Economic Journal*, 1891, pp. 277ff.

[158] [January 1720. -Ed.]

comply with possible demands for handing over the stocks. His point of view was, as he later explained, that the shares given to him, since their numbers had not been registered, were not a genuine deposit, but rather—as one would say today—a block deposit so that none of his customers had claim to specific securities. The firm actually made an extraordinary profit in this way, since it could buy back at reduced prices the shares sold at high prices, and meanwhile the capital, for which they were charging high interest, lost nothing at all but rather was safely invested in pounds. When Cantillon, who had partially made these advances in his own name, asked for repayments of the loans from the speculators, who had suffered great losses, and finally took them to court, the latter demanded that the profits obtained by Cantillon and the firm from their shares be credited against these advances. They in turn took Cantillon to court in London and Paris, charging fraud and usury. By presenting to the courts correspondence between Cantillon and the firm, they averred that the entire transaction was carried out under Cantillon's immediate direction and that he therefore bore personal responsibility. When Hughes died in 1723 and Cantillon liquidated the firm, Hughes's widow also joined Cantillon's opponents and made claims on the grounds that Hughes was not just a fictitious but a genuine co-owner, and as such entitled to a share of the net proceeds from the liquidation. After some years Cantillon emerged victorious from one part of this litigation, but another part was still going on at the time of his death in 1734. A whole series of interesting documents has survived this litigation, above all letters from Cantillon to Hughes and to his attorney. Higgs unearthed these in the London Public Records Office and in the Bibliothèque Nationale in Paris, although probably a larger part is still untapped for lack of indexing of the archives.[159]

From these it emerges, in addition to some of the biographical information already mentioned, that Cantillon, having departed from Paris in June 1720 not to return for almost six years, lived first in Amsterdam, then for some years in his house in London, but nonetheless frequently travelling on the continent. Thus in the spring of 1724 he declared to the court that he wished to travel on business with his wife to Naples and other Italian cities, but would, as always, return to London, "where he had his house and his family and, in the neighbourhood, his son (who must have died young) in the care of a nurse". In 1726 he actually departed with

---

[159] See Higgs, *Economic Journal*, vol. 1, 1891, pp. 276, 284.

his wife, writing in April from Nampon near Abbeville, in May from Paris, in June from Rotterdam, and in December from Brussels and Cologne. He seems also to have spent the following year in travelling, and in April and May he wrote from Verona, visiting Genoa between writing these two letters. On the basis of reports about the trial in Paris, he feels obliged to return there. Between 1729 and 1733 he was often in Paris, in 1733 in Utrecht and Brussels as well, and in 1734 again in London, where he became victim of the crime mentioned earlier. Here Higgs's description may be reproduced verbatim:[160]

> On Monday, May 14, 1734, Richard Cantillon was driving about London to his friend Garvan's in the Middle Temple, and to a house at Queen Square, Westminster, where he supped, and was set down at his door at ten at night. According to the evidence of a servant the next day,[161] "for about three weeks last past his Master had taken the key of the Street-Door up into his Bed-Chamber; and [the Examinant] believes his reason for so doing was upon some Distaste he took to a servant discharg'd three weeks ago; but that last Night he left the key, together with his Watch, below in the Parlour; and believes it was on account of this Examinant's being [ordered] to go early in the morning to take a Box for him in the Opera; because that he gave him Directions for that purpose . . . his Master last Night . . . undrest himself in the Parlour as usual; took his Candle and Book, and went up to Bed soon after; and told this Examinant he would read." This, it seems, was his usual practice.
>
> It was at first supposed that Cantillon fell asleep with his candle burning, and set fire to the house by accident. But facts soon transpired which left little doubt that the dismissed servant, Joseph Denier, *alias* Le Blanc, entered the house in the night with the complicity of the other servants (three men and two maids), and, having murdered and robbed his former master, set fire to the house.

Cantillon bequeathed a considerable fortune to his wife and daughter, who at the time of his death were in Paris, as is only to be expected of a man of whom his cashier reported that within a short interval he had withdrawn two and a half million (Livres Tournois?[162]) from his business. An inventory of his fortune drafted by

---

[160] Henry Higgs, "Richard Cantillon", *Economic Journal*, vol. 1, June 1891, pp. 262-291, esp. p. 287.

[161] *Old Bailey Sessions Papers*, 1734.

[162] [The question mark is Hayek's. -Ed.]

him shortly before his death shows in addition to cash with bankers in London, Amsterdam, Vienna, Cadiz, and Brussels, land and houses in England, Paris, Asnières, and Louisiana, and various annuities and claims. He seemed in his final years to have been engaged primarily in trade, as was also true to some extent earlier. He is occasionally described as a silk trader and wine merchant, and we know that he was involved in the copper business. Some employees referred to his being a tyrant, but generally he appears to have enjoyed great trust, and to have been very popular with his friends. His great outspokenness seems to have brought him into conflict with Law, who took offence at his frank criticism. According to Higgs, his letters show "Cantillon to have been a person of extreme ability and very great energy, as a writer possessed of great lucidity and quick grasp, quick to penetrate ambiguity or weakness of argument, able at combination and calculation, and so thorough a master of the foreign exchanges that his speculations exhibit a scientific prevision amounting almost to certainty".[163] Besides the letters, a memorandum by Cantillon (or almost certainly by him) has also been preserved. It was printed along with the records of his Paris trials[164] and spelled out to his lawyer the distinction between usury and a profit arising from a difference of exchange rates. His explanation of their nature follows the same line as in the *Essai* and refers to Dupuy and Savary in addition to the authors mentioned in the *Essai*.

V

While the magnitude of Cantillon's scientific accomplishment can scarcely be disputed, it is extraordinarily difficult to assess his actual influence on the development of economic thought. From the cases already mentioned, in which such an influence can be demonstrated

---

[163] [Two separate passages from Higgs (*Economic Journal*, vol. 1, 1891) are woven together here without change of meaning. The first is: "The lengthy English correspondence shows Cantillon to have been a person of extreme ability and very great energy" (p. 285), and the second is: "The impression left on the mind by a perusal of Cantillon's letters is that the writer was possessed of great clearness and grasp, quick to penetrate ambiguity or weakness of argument, able at combination and calculation, and so thorough a master of the foreign exchanges that his speculations exhibit a scientific prevision amounting almost to certainty" (p. 289). -Ed.]

[164] See the two folio volumes in the Bibliothèque Nationale, Paris, Fm. 2740 and 2838, printed by André Knapen, Paris, 1730. See Higgs, *Economic Journal*, vol. 1, 1891, pp. 284-285 and *Quarterly Journal of Economics*, vol. 6, 1892, p. 438.

both for the period prior to the publication of the *Essai* and for later writers who do not actually name Cantillon, it is reasonable to infer that numerous others also knew and used his work. Little effort has been made to explore the exceedingly rich literature of the mid-eighteenth century from this angle. The period and milieu in which Cantillon wrote was in any event exceptionally propitious for achieving a large impact through personal communication. After all, the intellectual revolution taking place in English-French society in the second quarter of that century laid the foundations both for ensuing political revolution and for the rapid progress of the political sciences. Voltaire and Rousseau as well as Montesquieu resided in England around this time, and were in close contact with those circles in which Cantillon also moved. Nor was the movement all in one direction: David Hume and Adam Smith found crucial stimulation in France. Adam Smith's acquaintance with Cantillon has already been mentioned. It is more difficult, but especially interesting, to ascertain this point with respect to Hume, whose *Political Discourses*, which contained his economic papers, were published three years prior to Cantillon's *Essai*. When one compares Hume's views on monetary theory with those of Cantillon, the impression is inescapable that Hume must in fact have known Cantillon.[165] Some of Cantillon's relevant arguments had already, to be sure, appeared in Postlethwayt's *Dictionary* in 1751, a year before Hume's *Essay* appeared, so that an influence would already be likely through this modality. The similarities are by no means confined to the arguments reproduced by Postlethwayt, however. On several points, such as Hume's explanation of the effects of an increase in the money supply, or his refutation of the idea that an increase in the money supply could lower the rate of interest, only the circumstance that Hume remained far behind Cantillon in the depth of his knowledge

---

[165] Even A. Huart (op. cit., in the essay of 26 July) finds that Cantillon's influence on Hume was very large. On the other hand, A. E. Monroe (op. cit., p. 228) believes that there is no reason to suppose that Hume knew Cantillon's manuscript, although it is known that it passed through several hands. [See Hayek's comments on the connexion between Hume and Cantillon in *Prices and Production* (London: Routledge, second edition, 1935), p. 9, and the remarks by Antoin E. Murphy in "Richard Cantillon—Banker and Economist", *Journal of Libertarian Studies*, vol. 7, no. 2, Fall 1985, p. 203, and Robert F. Hebert's review of Antoin E. Murphy, *Richard Cantillon: Entrepreneur and Economist*, in *Austrian Economics Newsletter*, vol. 10, no. 1, Fall 1988, pp. 7-8. See also Robert F. Hebert, "Was Richard Cantillon an Austrian Economist?", *Journal of Libertarian Studies*, vol. 7, no. 2, Fall 1985, pp. 269-280. -Ed.]

raises some doubts that the former knew the latter.[166] Hume doubtless had an opportunity to become acquainted with the manuscript of the *Essai*, having lived for three years in France, beginning in 1734, and also having in later years corresponded regularly with French scholars, notably after 1749 with Montesquieu. The surmise is reinforced by the fact that Hume's economics notes, which are supposed to date mainly from the years 1740 and 1741, contain an entry to the effect that a pound of steel, when processed, can be worth 10,000 pounds, which is strongly reminiscent of Cantillon's example of the watch spring (p. 18 of the Hayek translation).[167] If it could be ascertained that not only Smith but also Hume and perhaps even Malthus—as appears quite likely from several passages of his *Essay on the Principle of Population*—knew Cantillon and relied on this work, this would certainly suffice to guarantee his enduring influence on all later economists.[168]

In conjunction with the evidence given earlier as to the effect which the *Essai* had in France, the peculiar fact might be added here that its year of publication, 1755, was repeatedly identified by contemporary writers as the year in which the new economic school emerged. Later Germain Garnier,[169] the first proponent of the abstinence theory,[170] relied extensively on Cantillon's ideas, but again without mentioning his name, in his *Abrégé élémentaire des principes de l'économie politique* (Paris: H. Agasse, 1796) and sought to reconcile them with the views of Adam Smith, whom he had translated into

---

[166] See also L. Cossa, *An Introduction to the Study of Political Economy* (London and New York: Macmillan, 1893), p. 255. "Hume's *Political Discourses* . . . will not bear comparison on the score of coherence and unity with Cantillon's brief, systematic, and thoroughgoing performance."

[167] J. Hill Burton, *Life and Correspondence of David Hume* (Edinburgh: W. Tait, 1846), p. 367. Only excerpts from Hume's entries on economics are reproduced there. J. Y. T. Greig, of Newcastle-upon-Tyne, who is at the moment preparing a more complete edition of Hume's literary estate, was exceptionally kind in providing me with a complete copy; however it contained no further evidence of Cantillon's direct influence on Hume. [See now J. Y. T. Greig, ed., *The Letters of David Hume* (Oxford: Clarendon Press, 1932). -Ed.]

[168] Huart cites the English writer William Paley (*Principles of Moral and Political Philosophy* (London: R. Faulder, 1785), VI, II) as a further example of Cantillon's influence.

[169] [Germain Garnier (1754-1821). -Ed.]

[170] See W. Hasbach, "Germain Garnier als erster Aufsteller der Abstinenztheorie", *Jahrbuch für Gesetzgebung*, usw., 1905.

French, and the views of the physiocrats.[171] In places Garnier borrowed not only Cantillon's examples but even his wording.[172]

Only with the dismissal of all predecessors of Adam Smith, which began with J. B. Say,[173] was Cantillon forgotten even in France. But even in Germany and in Italy the *Essai* seems to have enjoyed a certain dissemination. In Italy the impact of the Italian translation can be observed at least in G. Filangieri,[174] and in Germany, in addition to Graumann, mentioned earlier, the 'German physiocrat' Jakob Mauvillon must have known the *Essai* reprinted by his father. It can certainly be proved that J. F. von Pfeifer was acquainted with Cantillon's work.[175] Without naming Cantillon, to be sure, but clearly referring to him, von Pfeifer said that "the physiocratic system was produced in England, was only propagated from there to France, and finally was passed on to Germany". The acquaintance of G. A. Will with Cantillon's work can also be demonstrated. In 1782, in his *Versuch über die Physiokratie*,[176] he quoted this remark of Pfeifer's, adding: "It is also correct that among others the Englishman Cantillon—in his fine essay on commerce—delineated already many years ago the theory of the physiocrats concerning the structure of the state, both in its most important principles and in its main conclusion."

---

[171] See E. Allix, "L'oeuvre économique de Germain Garnier traducteur d'Adam Smith et disciple de Cantillon", *Revue d'histoire des doctrines économiques et sociales*, vol. 5, Paris, 1912.

[172] Op. cit., p. 333.

[173] [Jean-Baptiste Say (1767-1832), known for 'Say's Law' of markets, the proposition that 'supply creates its own demand'. -Ed.]

[174] *Delle leggi politiche e economiche* (Scienza della legislazione II) (Naples: Cavilier Filangieri, 1780), reprinted in *Scrittori classici italiani di economia politica*, ed. Custodi, Parte moderna, vol. 32. See chapter 4.

[175] J. F. von Pfeifer, *Natürliche, aus dem Endzweck der Gesellschaft entstehende allgemeine Polizeiwissenschaft*, part II (Frankfurt: In der Esslinger Buchhandlung, 1779), p. 62.

[176] G. A. Will, *Versuch über die Physiokratie, deren Geschichte, Literatur, Inhalt und Werth* (Nuremberg: G. N. Raspe, 1782), p. 4.

Addenda: On Higgs

Higgs's Edition of Cantillon[177]

When a book of great importance has once fallen into undeserved oblivion for a long period, it seems to be very difficult to revive lasting interest in it, even though its rediscovery may, at first, have been greeted with considerable enthusiasm. If, in the case of Cantillon, the recognition of the importance of Jevons's was not so general and lasting as might have been expected, this was probably due to the fact that Jevons, in the brilliant article (now reprinted)[178] in which he proclaimed his discovery and called the *Essai* "the cradle of Political Economy", coupled the question of the importance of Cantillon with the problem of the "nationality of Political Economy". This immediately aroused the antagonism of all the admirers of the physiocrats, inside and outside France; and since the physiocrats, with their strong philosophical leanings, appeal more than does Cantillon to those who are not specialists in economic theory (and historians of economics usually are not), Cantillon has never achieved their popularity. Even in England he is certainly not as well known as he deserves to be—at least, not outside the sphere of influence of a few ardent admirers, of whom the editor of the present edition is one.

The need for a new edition of the *Essai* has long been felt, for the three contemporary editions are now very rare, and even the reprint published by Harvard University ten years after Jevons's discovery has long been out of print and difficult to obtain. We have every reason to be grateful to the editor and to the Royal Economic Society for the excellence of the present edition. It would, indeed, have been impossible to find anyone better qualified for the task of editing the *Essai* than Mr. Henry Higgs; for it was he who followed up certain clues about Cantillon which Jevons had been prevented from investigating owing to his death—which occurred only a year after his article was published. Practically all additions to

---

[177] [This notice was first published by Hayek in *Economic Journal*, vol. 42, March 1932, pp. 61-63, as a review of Richard Cantillon, *Essai sur la nature du commerce en général*, edited, with an English translation and other material, by Henry Higgs (London: Macmillan, for the Royal Economic Society, 1931; reprinted New York: Augustus M. Kelley, 1964). -Ed.]

[178] [Jevons's article is reprinted in Higgs's edition of Cantillon's *Essai*, op. cit. -Ed.]

the store of information discovered by Jevons are due to Mr. Higgs's painstaking and scholarly research.

The complete mystery which enshrouded the person of Cantillon and the manuscript of the *Essai*, and which could not be penetrated even at the time when the *Essai* was published twenty years after his death, has at last been sufficiently dissipated to reveal one of the most fascinating stories in the literature of economics. However, while sympathising with Mr. Higgs's point of view, I feel that he might have made the biographical account even more interesting if, instead of religiously preserving Jevons's article and supplementing it by a statement of what he himself has since discovered, he had given us a connected account of all that is known about Cantillon.

It is characteristic of the curious history of the *Essai* that neither of the two versions—the French and the English—which are printed in this volume, can truly be called the original.[179] The French text, which is often regarded as the original, is probably a translation, made by the author himself, of the lost English original. But, while part of the English text is a retranslation by Mr. Higgs of the French edition published in 1755, Mr. Higgs has been able to incorporate a very considerable part of what is, probably, the true original. For the preservation of these parts we are indebted to the industrious M. Postlethwayt, who seems to have been in possession of the original for several years prior to the publication of the French edition, and who printed long extracts from it in his *Universal Dictionary of Trade and Commerce* (1751-5). It is, in some measure, to be regretted that Mr. Higgs did not indicate in somewhat greater detail which passages are taken from this contemporary text (and which may, therefore, be regarded as the original) and which parts constitute the new translation. It even appears that, in some places, Mr. Higgs has adapted the Postlethwayt text by eliminating what are probably editorial changes, so as to make it correspond more closely to the French text. While, on the one hand, the effect of this revision being to produce an English version which is as close to the original as it is possible to make it, and the continuity of which is not interrupted by numerous footnotes, yet it still remains necessary, for purposes of serious research, to use the two original bulky volumes of Postlethwayt.

---

[179] [But see now Murphy, op. cit., esp. pp. 299-321, who argues that the French version is in fact the original, intended to appear as a translation to circumvent French censorship laws. Compare also Vivian Walsh, "Cantillon, Richard", in *The New Palgrave: A Dictionary of Economics*, ed. Eatwell, Milgate, and Newman (London: Macmillan, 1987), vol. 1, pp. 317-320. -Ed.]

However, this slight blemish is insignificant compared with the great importance of at last having available for the general student of economics a really good and convenient edition of this gem of economic literature. It is to be hoped that Cantillon will now assume the position in the history of economics which he rightly deserves. But, unlike so many of the early writers on this subject, Cantillon's claim on our attention is not primarily due to his position in the history of economics. In fact, the *Essai* is one of the six or eight works on our science, written in the period prior to modern developments (i.e., before about 1870), with which every economist should be familiar. Its truly scientific method of approach and the detached spirit of its analysis can still teach a great deal even to the modern student. If the only fact which emerged from a study of this *Essai* was that a keen scientific mind, 200 years ago, was led, by the study of the economic life of his time, to use essentially the same concepts and, in many cases, to draw the same conclusions as we do, then we should have an effective demonstration of the fact that the truth of the fundamental ideas of economic science is not dependent on the circumstances of the particular historical situation with which we are familiar; such a demonstration would be not a little valuable.

The attraction of this book for the theorist rests, however, almost entirely on its inherent merits and not on the role which it played in the history of economics. Adam Smith and Condillac are known to have been influenced by Cantillon, but after the year of the publication of their great works, his name is scarcely mentioned for a century. To what extent later writers have been influenced by him—directly or indirectly—and what the effect on the history of our science would have been had he been better known, are matters for interesting, but idle, speculation. Malthus is the only later author of the Classical period who is likely to have been influenced by Cantillon. Roscher seems to have been the first to rediscover his importance. Practically all the occasional references which occur before the publication of Jevons's article can probably be traced to Roscher's influence. Since that time he has been frequently quoted, but has probably not been so widely read as those references might lead one to suppose. If the present edition induces more economists to do so, then I have no doubt that they will feel that it has been well worth their while.

I must not fail to mention that this volume is not only well produced as regards typography and binding, but also that it is adorned with portraits of Cantillon's wife and daughter. Since we do not know what Cantillon himself was like, and since the daughter looks so much more intelligent than her mother, these pictures form a rather unusual but interesting substitute for the portrait of the author himself.

Higgs's Bibliography of Economics[180]

About the need for competent bibliographies as the basis of any work on the history of a science there can be no reasonable doubt. There could hardly have been a better foundation for such a work than the extraordinary wealth of material contained in the catalogues of the successive libraries accumulated (and of books not obtained) by Professor Foxwell during more than half a century of book-collecting. But the editing of the material thus gradually accumulated as a card catalogue is a monumental task if it is to be done with the care necessary in order that it may be done once and for all and that the result may be trusted implicitly. There can be no doubt about the exceptional competence of the editor and of the distinguished scholars whose help he acknowledges. And so far as completeness is concerned the editor and his collaborators seem to have done what is humanly possible. The 6,741 items which they list for the twenty-five year period covered by the volume seem to include practically everything which appeared during the period, not only in English, but also in French, German, Spanish, or Italian, and which is of immediate interest to the economist. The boundaries drawn for the material to be included are if anything rather too wide than too narrow, and the arrangement of the titles under each year in eleven different groups is convenient. Mr. Higgs mentioned in his Introduction that it is proposed to continue this first section of the bibliography backward and forward.[181] All economists must wish that he will succeed in carrying out this plan in the not too distant future.

Yet, without being ungrateful and without underrating the enormous burden which such a work imposes on the editor, some doubts must be expressed whether in the present case too much of the work of checking the individual items has not been left to subordinate assistants. I may have been particularly unfortunate, but the first half-hour spent with the volume had revealed a surprising number of inaccuracies and slips and closer examination has not

---

[180] [First published by Hayek in *Economica*, February 1936, pp. 99-100, as a review of *Bibliography of Economics*, 1751-75. Prepared for the British Academy by Henry Higgs, C.B. (Cambridge: Cambridge University Press, 1935). -Ed.]

[181] [The project was never completed. -Ed.]

completely dispelled that impression. Hardly sufficient pains seem to have been taken in identifying the authors of anonymous works, or at any rate, an explanation ought to have been given if the attribution of an anonymous work to a particular author, e.g., in the British Museum Catalogue, was deliberately not accepted. Several times one and the same work appears twice only because one of the entries is inaccurate, for example Joseph Harris's *Essay upon Money and Coins*, one under the year 1757 (No. 1516) as if it had appeared with the author's full name, and a second time under the year 1758 (No. 1759) with the author's name correctly in square brackets. (The two parts of the work were actually published in the successive years, but the title given in the second year is again that of Part I.) Similarly Matthew Raper's *Inquiry into the Nature of the Ancient Greek and Roman Money* is once given (No. 5267) under the year 1771 and a second time (No. 5519) with the author's name spelt "Roper" under the year 1772. (The alphabetical Index gives references to both items.) That "4273. Ferguson, A. *Versuch über die Geschichte der bürgerlichen Gesellschaft*. Leipzig 1768" is explained as a "translation of Anderon's History of Civil Society" is evidently just a misprint. Somewhat puzzling is the following item: "5847. Bentham, Jeremy. Introduction to Moral Philosophy, 2nd edn. 1773.8°." Is this a new discovery? But the most surprising item to encounter among the publications of the year 1769 is undoubtedly the following:

"4627. Schmoller, G. und Hintze, O. Die preussische Seidenindustrie 18. Jahrhundert und ihre Begründrung des (sic) Friedrich der (sic) Grossen. *Bd. I, Akten bis* 1768; *Bd. II, Akten seit* 1769; *Bd. III, Darstellung*, 1892. 3 vols. 8°."

The inclusion of this item can hardly be justified on the ground that in a few instances but by no means consistently (Adam Smith's Glasgow Lectures, F. Galiani's Correspondence, but none of the modern editions of David Hume's Correspondence) writings of economists have been included under the date when they were written, although they were only published much later. But to include modern publications of documents from official archives which illustrate the economic conditions of the period can hardly have been intended and would certainly mean that many more similar items should have been included.

FOURTEEN

HENRY THORNTON (1760-1815)[1]

I

To most of the contemporaries of Henry Thornton his authorship of *An Enquiry into the Nature and Effects of the Paper Credit of Great Britain (1802)*[2] would by no means have been regarded as his major title to fame. To them the fact that he was a successful banker and a great expert on finance probably appeared as the indispensable but comparatively uninteresting background which put him in the position to be a great philanthropist and the effective advocate of every good cause; certainly it enabled him to provide at his comfortable Clapham home the meeting place for the active and influential group of Evangelicals, who, quite apart from the great role they played in their own time, were probably one of the most profound influences which fashioned the outlook and character that was

---

[1] [Published as "Introduction" to Henry Thornton, *An Enquiry into the Nature and Effects of the Paper Credit of Great Britain [1802]*, edited with an Introduction by F. A. Hayek (London: Allen & Unwin, 1939), pp. 11-63. See Sir John Clapham's review of Thornton's book, and of Hayek's introduction, in *Economica*, N.S., vol. 8, no. 30, 1941, pp. 210-211; the review by Frank Whitson Fetter in *Journal of Political Economy*, vol. 5, 1940, pp. 766-767, and Fetter's later "The Bullion Report Reexamined" in *Quarterly Journal of Economics*, vol. 56, 1942, pp. 655-665, and *The Development of the British Monetary Orthodoxy* (Cambridge, Mass.: Harvard University Press, 1965). See also Sir John Hicks's review in *The Economic History Review*, vol. 10, 1940, p. 182, and his later treatment of Thornton and Hayek in "Thornton's *Paper Credit* (1802)", in John Hicks, *Critical Essays in Monetary Theory* (Oxford: Clarendon Press, 1967), pp. 174-188. The authoritative biography of Henry Thornton is Standish Meacham's *Henry Thornton of Clapham* (Cambridge, Mass.: Harvard University Press, 1964); other biographical information may be found in E. M. Forster, *Marianne Thornton: A Domestic Biography* (New York: Harcourt, Brace, 1956), in "Battersea Rise", *Abinger Harvest* (London: Edward Arnold, 1936) and "Henry Thornton" [1939] in his *Two Cheers for Democracy*, Abinger edition (London: Edward Arnold, 1972), pp. 185-189, and in the materials on the Clapham sect cited below. -Ed.]

[2] Now (1939) reprinted after 136 years. [Also reprinted by Augustus M. Kelley (New York) in 1962, and again in 1978. -Ed.]

typical of the English upper middle class of the nineteenth century.[3] It would be an interesting and instructive task to attempt a full-length Life of Henry Thornton, and, considering how many minor figures of the circle of which he and William Wilberforce were the centre have been honoured with biographies,[4] it is surprising that it has never been accomplished.[5] But the men who became the historians of the late eighteenth and early nineteenth century were on the whole not too sympathetic towards that austere view of life, which in many instances must have overshadowed their own youth, and which perhaps found its most perfect embodiment in the person of Henry Thornton. It may well be, however, that a more detached future historian will recognise that in their immediate influence the 'party of saints', of which Thornton may be regarded as the prototype, at least rival their better-known contemporaries, the Philosophical Radicals.[6] But even if such a complete biography

---

[3] The influence of the Clapham Sect in this respect is well brought out in E. Halévy's *History of the English People in 1815* (London: Penguin Books, 1937). [See also John A. Patten, *These Remarkable Men: The Beginnings of a World Enterprise* (London: Lutterworth Press, 1945); Ernest M. Howse, *Saints in Politics: The 'Clapham Sect' and the Growth of Freedom* (London: Allen & Unwin, 1953; reprinted 1960); L. E. Elliott-Binns, *The Early Evangelicals* (London: Lutterworth Press, 1953); Ford K. Brown, *Fathers of the Victorians* (Cambridge: Cambridge University Press, 1961); and David Spring, "The Clapham Sect: Some Social and Political Aspects", *Victorian Studies*, vol. 5, 1961-2, pp. 35-48. On some of the major figures of the Clapham Sect mentioned in the text see Oliver Warner, *William Wilberforce and His Times* (London: B. T. Batsford, 1962); R. Furneaux, *William Wilberforce* (London: Hamish Hamilton, 1974); Michael Hennell, *John Venn and the Clapham Sect* (London: Lutterworth Press, 1958); Bernard Martin, *John Newton: A Biography* (London: Heinemann, 1950); and M. G. Jones, *Hannah More* (Cambridge: Cambridge University Press, 1952). -Ed.]

[4] See bibliographical notes at the end of this chapter.

[5] W. Wilberforce at one time intended to write a biography of his friend Thornton, but never completed it. See on this *Life of Wilberforce* (London: John Murray, 1838) by his sons, vol. 2, p. 329; the *Correspondence of William Wilberforce* (London: John Murray, 1840), edited by the same, vol. 2, p. 422; and the Preface to Henry Thornton's *Family Prayers* (London: Hatchard, 1844) by R. H. Inglis.

[6] [The term 'Philosophical Radicals' is used loosely to denote Jeremy Bentham (1748-1832) and the two Mills and their political associates. More precisely, the philosophical radicals were a group of utilitarian political reformers of the 1820s and 1830s centring on the elder Mill (1773-1836) and, later, his son John Stuart Mill. The radicals included John Austin (1790-1858) and his brother Charles (1791-1874), George Grote (1794-1871), Charles Buller (1806-1848) and William Molesworth (1810-1885). The radicals, along with the Evangelicals, were early advocates of the abolition of slavery as well as of prison reform. See Leslie Stephen, *The English Utilitarians* (London: Duckworth Press, 1900); Frank J. Klingberg, *The Anti-Slavery Movement in England* (New Haven, Conn.: Yale University Press, 1926), pp. 51-53 and p. 130; and Elie Halévy, *The Growth of Philosophical Radicalism*, trans. Mary Morris (London: Faber, 1972). -Ed.]

of Henry Thornton would, as seems likely, contribute a great deal to our understanding of the social and economic views, the *Wirtschaftsgesinnung*,[7] that dominated the nineteenth century, it can certainly not be attempted here. In this essay we can do no more than give an outline of those sides of Henry Thornton's life which throw light on the circumstances in which the *Paper Credit of Great Britain* was written, and on the influence which the views of its author exerted on contemporary thought.

"We are all City people and connected with merchants, and nothing but merchants on every side" was Henry Thornton's own comment on the ambitions of his brothers to become members of high Society.[8] Although descended from a succession of Yorkshire clergymen, John Thornton, the common ancestor of the London Thorntons, was a merchant in Hull in the late seventeenth and early eighteenth century.[9] His two sons, Godfrey and Robert, the latter the grandfather of Henry, both went to London and appear to have engaged in the trade with Russia and the Baltic. Both were directors of the Bank of England, as was also the son of the former, the younger Godfrey, in whose counting-house his cousin's son Henry, the subject of this memoir, was to serve his apprenticeship, "chiefly employed in carrying out bills to be accepted and taking the weight of Hemp, Flax, etc., at the Custome House"[10]. Robert's son,

---

[7] [I.e., the 'economic-mindedness'. -Ed.]

[8] *MS. Recollections of Marianne Thornton* [Henry's daughter] (1857), unpublished first vellum book, papers held by E. M. Forster, pp. 1-434 (see the bibliographical notes at the end of this chapter). [In 1956 Forster published a biography of Marianne Thornton: *Marianne Thornton: A Domestic Biography*, op. cit. -Ed.]

[9] *The Genealogical and Heraldic History of the Landed Gentry* (London: Harrison, 1871), by the late Sir J. Bernard Burke; and P. M. Thornton, *Some Things We Remember* (London: Longmans, Green, 1912).

[10] *MS. Diary of Henry Thornton* (see bibliographical notes at the end of this chapter), first vellum book, papers held by E. M. Forster. The author wishes here to express his gratitude to three descendants of Henry Thornton, Mrs. P. M. Thornton, Mrs. D. Demarest, and Mr. E. M. Forster, for the loan of this and other documents and for permission to quote from them. [Among the Hayek papers at the Hoover Institution, Stanford University, there are to be found two sets of correspondence between Hayek and the descendants and other connexions of Henry Thornton, one dating from 1932, the second from 1938. It appears that on his arrival in Britain in 1931, Hayek was still intending to complete his book on the history of monetary theory (for which see chapters 9-12), of which an examination of Thornton's work was to be an important part. In January 1932 he began to contact the surviving Thornton grandchildren, as well as the descendants of Thornton's associates, such as William Wilberforce and Zachary Macaulay, in search of letters and papers concerning Henry Thornton, and they readily provided him with information, manuscripts, and books. After these initial contacts, Hayek prepared a draft of his article, which he then circulated amongst these and other relatives, including E. M. Forster, and also

another John and the father of Henry, was also a "Russian mer-chant" in the firm of Thornton, Cornwall & Co. He is known as the friend and benefactor of the poet William Cowper[11] and as a mem-ber of the first generation of Evangelicals—that Wesleyan wing within the Established Church who, just because they remained within the Church, probably did more to impress the stamp of Puritanism on nineteenth-century English society than Nonconform-ism.[12] His father, Robert, had already settled in Clapham, then the country residence of numerous City magnates, and here this branch of the Thornton family resided for another four generations. It was probably the then curate of Clapham, Henry Venn, who in the 1750s won John Thornton over to the tenets of Evangelicalism. But it was not until many years later, when their sons John Venn and

with G. M. Trevelyan, a descendant of Thornton's associate Zachary Macaulay, beginning in 1938. Forster called on Hayek at the Reform Club in July, carrying the Thornton manuscripts with him; later he arranged for Hayek to examine these at length at Forster's flat in London. And he and the other relatives provided him with further assistance, critical comments, books, and manuscripts throughout the summer of 1938. In the light of these the essay was revised and sent to the printers for publication in 1939. -Ed.]

[11] The connexion with Cowper came about through John Newton (1725-1807), one of the many clergymen whom John Thornton supported. Newton had, after a youth spent in the slave trade, become parson of Olney and when he took Cowper into his house Thornton gave him an extra allowance to support the poet. See the *Correspondence of W. Cowper*, ed. T. Wright (London, Hodder & Stoughton, 1904), and T. Wright, *The Life of William Cowper* (London: C. J. Farncombe, 1921); also *Memorials of the Rev. William Bull of Newport Pagnell* (London: J. Nisbet, 1865), compiled chiefly from his own letters and those of his friends Newton, Cowper, and Thornton, 1783-1814, by his grandson the Rev. Josiah Bull, M.A. (London, 1864). [The best modern biography of William Cowper (1731-1800) is James King, *William Cowper* (Durham, N.C.: Duke University Press, 1986). An excellent bibliography of secondary literature is contained in William Free's *William Cowper* (New York: Twayne Publish-ing, 1970). See also Charles Ryskamp, *William Cowper of the Inner Temple, Esq.* (Cambridge: Cambridge University Press, 1959). For Cowper's correspondence see *The Letters and Prose Writings of William Cowper*, in five volumes, ed. James King and Charles Rykamp (Oxford: Clarendon Press, 1979). Cowper was active in the abolition-ist movement, contributing *The Negro's Complaint* and two other anti-slavery poems in 1788 at Newton's request. See H. S. Milford, ed., *The Complete Poetical Works of William Cowper* (London and New York: Oxford University Press, 1913, pp. 371-375. On Newton see Bernard Martin, *John Newton: A Biography*, op. cit. -Ed.]

[12] [In fact, a noted historian of the Evangelicals says of John Thornton that he "has more claim than any other to be thought of as the founder of the Evangelical Revolution" (Ford K. Brown, *Fathers of the Victorians: The Age of Wilberforce*, op. cit., p. 78). See also L. E. Elliott-Binns, *The Early Evangelicals*, op. cit. -Ed.]

Henry Thornton lived at Clapham, that their circle became known as the 'Clapham Sect'.[13]

John Thornton, 'the Great and the Good', as he was called, was celebrated for his magnificent generosity, and he is reputed to have spent on charity in the course of his life the sum of 100,000 pounds or even 150,000 pounds.[14] His charity and his deep piety were fully inherited by his son, and the lines which in an elegy on his death in 1790 Cowper wrote of John Thornton

> Thou hadst an industry in doing good,
> Restless as his who toils and sweats for food[15]

---

[13] The term 'Clapham Sect' was apparently first used by [the Reverend] Sydney Smith in an article in the *Edinburgh Review*. [It is now thought, however, that it was not Sydney Smith but Sir James Stephen in the *Edinburgh Review* (1844) who coined the term. See Ernest M. Howse, *Saints in Politics: The 'Clapham Sect' and the Growth of Freedom*, op. cit., pp. 187-189. -Ed.]

[14] According to John Newton and Henry Venn respectively. See John Telford, *A Sect that Moved the World* (London: C. H. Kelly, 1907), p. 71; also R. de M. Rudolf's article on the Clapham Sect in *Clapham and the Clapham Sect* (Clapham: Clapham Antiquarian Society, 1927), and [Henry Venn], *The Love of Christ the Source of Genuine Philanthropy* (Providence, R.I.: Carter & Wilkinson, 1794), *A discourse on II Cor. chap. 5, ver. 14, 15, occasioned by the death of John Thornton, Esq., containing observations on his Character and Principles* (London: Printed for J. Johnson and sold by J. Matthews and C. Dilly, 1791), and Thos. Scott, *Discourses Occasioned by the Death of John Thornton, Esq.* (London: Printed for J. Johnson and sold by J. Matthews and C. Dilly, 1791). John Thornton also adapted in 1775 for English use an earlier translation of C. H. von Bogatsky's *Güldenes Schatzkästlein der Kinder Gottes* (Philadelphia: Gedruckt bey Conrad Zentler, für Georg W. Mentz, No. 71, in der Rehsstrasse, Zwischen der Zweyten und Dritten Strasse, 1811), as the *Golden Treasury Interleaved*, and it is reported that "he employed the extensive commerce in which he was engaged as a powerful instrument for conveying immense quantities of Bibles, Prayer Books, and the most useful publications, to every place visited by our trade. He printed, at his own sole expense, large editions of the latter for that purpose and it may safely be affirmed that there is scarcely a part of the known world, where such books could be introduced, which did not feel the salutary influence of this single individual" (*Life of John Newton* (Edinburgh: Johnstone & Hunter, 1853), written by himself, with a continuation by R. Cecil, Edinburgh, n.d.). [John Thornton's influence also extended to America, where he helped found Dartmouth College; Thornton Hall, named after him, still stands on the Dartmouth campus. See Frank W. Fetter, "John Thornton of Clapham", *Dartmouth Alumni Magazine*, October 1968, pp. 25-28; Frederick Chase, *A History of Dartmouth College* (Brattleboro, Vt.: Vermont Printing Co., 1928); and James D. McCallum, *Eleazar Wheelock: Founder of Dartmouth College* (Hanover, N.H.: Dartmouth College Publications, 1939), pp. 165-166 and p. 195. -Ed.]

[15] [William Cowper, "In Memory of the Late John Thornton, Esq." [Nov. 1790], in H. S. Milford, ed., *The Complete Poetical Works of William Cowper*, op. cit., pp. 399-400. -Ed.]

were equally true of Henry, who also succeeded his father to the friendship with Cowper. But in other respects the simple, passionate and occasionally even violent older man must have presented a curious contrast to his highly intellectual and disciplined son, who regarded enthusiasm and eagerness as grave sins. And although John, in spite of his princely munificence, succeeded in passing on to his children much increased the considerable fortune he had inherited,[16] his sterner son regarded him as a Jack of all trades who never thrives and as being somewhat too impulsive and unmethodical in his generosity.

Of John's three sons,[17] Samuel (1755-1838), the eldest, became like his father a 'Russian merchant', was M.P. for Hull and later for Surrey; and as a director and, from 1799 to 1801, Governor of the Bank of England, he was a figure of considerable importance in the City.[18] As he outlived his younger brother Henry by twenty-three years and after the latter's death gave important evidence on monetary problems to the Commons Committee on the Resumption of Specie Payments in 1819, he seems to have been the more familiar figure to the economists of the 1920s and 1930s. It must be due to a confusion with him that J. R. MacCulloch started the legend, since copied by practically everyone who ever mentioned Henry Thornton, that the latter was a director and Governor of the Bank of England.[19]

---

[16] According to an evidently exaggerated statement in the obituary notice in the *Gentleman's Magazine* (November 1790), "He began the world with £100,000 and left it with £600,000. His gains as a merchant were immense. He was the greatest merchant in Europe, except Mr. Hope, of Amsterdam; and generally one-half of his profits were dedicated to the poor."

[17] Of the two daughters, Jane married Lord Balgonie, later Earl of Leven, and the other died as a child.

[18] See the *Book of Yearly Recollections of Samuel Thornton, Esq.*, edited for private circulation with a Preface and Introduction by his grandson John Thornton (London: W. Clowes & Sons, 1891).

[19] J. R. MacCulloch, *The Literature of Political Economy* (London: Longman, Brown, Green, & Longmans, 1845), p. 169, who already suggests that Henry Thornton was in consequence unduly partial to the Bank of England. The error has entered even Leslie Stephen's article on Henry Thornton in the *Dictionary of National Biography* and has since again and again been made the basis of unfounded accusations of bias on the part of Thornton, especially by J. W. Angell, *The Theory of International Prices* (Cambridge, Mass.: Harvard University Press, 1926), p. 46. That Henry Thornton was never a director of the Bank of England is apparent from the complete list of directors given by W. M. Acres, *The Bank of England from Within, 1694-1900* (London: Printed for the Governor and the Company of the Bank of England by the Oxford University Press, 1931), vol. 2, pp. 613-630, and has been confirmed on enquiry by the Secretary of the Bank of England. The falsity of the statement should,

Robert, the second son, M.P. for Colchester and at one time Governor of the East India Company, although by residence a member of the Clapham circle, seems to have been rather different from the rest of the family. He collected a magnificent library, his "villa in Clapham was celebrated for the beauty of its garden and conservatory", and he "lavishly entertained royalty and many others" there with the result that he outran his fortune, tried to recoup it in daring speculations in the funds, failed, and ultimately died in America.[20]

Henry, the youngest son, was born on March 10, 1760. The parents apparently had rather unusual ideas about education, and while they seem to have spared no expense, and even sent their eldest son for three years to the Royal Pedagogue in Halle, Saxony,[21] they took a somewhat unfortunate line in the case of Henry. After eight years at a fairly efficient school run by a Mr. Devis in Wandsworth, where he began to learn Latin at five, he was sent to a Mr. Roberts at Point Pleasant, who

> professed to keep a school different from other schools, and seemed a sort of miracle from the circumstance of his being himself the teacher of every thing. He taught Latin, Greek, French, Rhetoric, drawing, arithmetic, reading, writing, speaking, geography, bowing, walking, fencing. He also gave us a few lessons in Hebrew, and in mathematics.[22]

Henry resided in this academy from his thirteenth to well into his nineteenth year, but because of his superior previous knowledge of Greek and Latin he was tempted to be very idle during the whole of this period. He complains later that he left school with an extremely small stock of knowledge and that he knew little or nothing of English, History, Mathematics, Natural Philosophy, Belles Lettres, and Politics.

---

however, have been obvious from the fact that according to a firmly established tradition a banker (in the strict English sense of the word, as distinguished from a 'merchant-banker') could not become a director of the Bank.

[20] Cf. R. de M. Rudolf in *Clapham and the Clapham Sect*, p. 107; J. C. Colquhoun, *Wilberforce* (London: Longmans, Green, Reader, & Dyer, 1866), p. 270; W. G. Black in *Notes and Queries*, 5th Series, vol. 7, January 6, 1877, p. 6; and *MS. Recollections of Marianne Thornton*, op. cit.

[21] *Book of Yearly Recollections of Samuel Thornton*, p. 1. The University of Halle was then the centre of German Pietism, in a sense a precursor of the Evangelical Revival in England.

[22] *MS. Diary of Henry Thornton*, January 1802, op. cit.

His school years had only been interrupted, in the interval between the two schools, by a family visit to France, where in the company of Cowper's friend, the Rev. Mr. Unwin, they spent some weeks in Paris in 1773.

The two years from the spring of 1778 to the spring of 1780 Henry spent in the firm of his relative, Godfrey Thornton, and then he entered his father's counting house, that is, as he explains,

> a counting house in which he conducts some business in his own name, apart from that of the House of Thornton, Cornwall & Co. There is a proverb that 'Jack of all trades never thrives.' This proverb was verified in my father's case. He was in his private capacity a merchant in general. He made, that is to say, occasional and sometimes large speculations in any article which happened to take his fancy. During the two or three years in which I was his partner he embarked on a great speculation in wheat by which he lost £2,000 or £3,000—in a speculation in Tobacco by which he also lost money; in the sale also of British articles sent to the West Indies. . . .
>
> Mortified to find that little pecuniary advantage was to be expected from my connection with my Father, I gave a very willing ear to a proposition made to me by Mr. Poole of Woodford for entering into a Banking concern with Mr. Down, my present partner. My Father was averse to it, and my Mother also. I did not, however, very greatly respect their judgment and they did not forbid my becoming a Banker. My Father as I suspect chiefly feared that I should be placed under peculiar temptation to keep improper Company by my being a Banker, a point in which he was mistaken. My Mother's prejudices led her to think that to cease being a Merchant in order to become a Banker was to descend in life. She was well read in the *Spectator*, and had learnt to think that Sir Andrew Freeport was one of the first characters in the world.[23]

It was in 1784 that he joined the banking house of Down and Free,[24] which soon became Down, Thornton, and Free, and of which he remained an active partner till his death. Two years earlier, however, he had entered the House of Commons and it was, as he records, partly this fact which recommended him to his partners.

---

[23] *MS. Diary of Henry Thornton,* op. cit. ['Sir Andrew Freeport' was one of the several pseudonyms used by Joseph Addison (1672-1719) in *The Spectator* to denote a fictional London merchant. Freeport was one of the four members of 'The Spectator Club', a mythical group of four 'men about town' supposedly responsible for the publishing of the magazine. -Ed.]

[24] Established in 1773 as Marlor, Lascelles, Pell, and Down.

He had, indeed, made an even earlier attempt to enter Parliament when he was little more than twenty-one. Such an early entry into political life was at that time by no means uncommon. At the elections of 1780 the two friends, William Pitt and William Wilberforce, had both been successful at the age of twenty-one—Wilberforce, a second cousin[25] of Henry Thornton, at Hull, where Wilberforce senior and the father of Mrs. John Thornton were both eminent merchants. When a year later the second seat for Hull became vacant, Henry's ambitious mother urged him to become a candidate. But after a little canvassing he discovered that he was universally expected to give two guineas to every voter, a custom with which he was neither willing nor able to comply, and consequently withdrew. In the autumn of 1782 another vacancy occurred, however, by the death of the member for Southwark, and again his mother urged him on, and prepared the way for him through her connections in Dissenting circles. His father, Henry records,

> appeared to me not at all opposed to my mother's propositions and he gave me a recommendatory letter to Mr. Ellis, the only person in Southwark with whom he was acquainted. My father, however, observed that according to his opinion the only mode in which it was right to enter into Parliament was that of Sir John Barnard, who was riding about Clapham Common while his election was going on, and who instead of soliciting his Electors was solicited by them. I perceived so plainly the impossibility of success in my own case if a principle of this kind was to be prescribed to me, that I considered my father's objections as extravagant, and the evil of the two guineas not subsisting in Southwark I thought little of any other Evils and committed my cause to the hands of a large and self-created Committee which took upon itself to manage my election for me. A very able Lawyer Mr. Serjeant Adair was my opponent. Mrs. Thrale at whose house I dined on this occasion in

[25] William Wilberforce I, the grandfather of the more famous William Wilberforce III here discussed, had married Sarah Thornton, a sister of Robert, the grandfather of Henry Thornton. In the next generation a daughter of Robert Thornton and half-sister of Henry's father, Hannah Thornton, married her cousin William Wilberforce II, an uncle of William Wilberforce III, who spent part of his boyhood in the house of his aunt and there came for the first time under the influence of the Evangelicals. Most of the years of his boyhood were spent in the house of Mr. Joseph Sykes, at West Ella, near Hull, where he grew up with the numerous children of the family, one of whom was to be the future Mrs. Henry Thornton.

company with Dr. Johnson, gave me her support.[26] The dissenters in general were favourable to me. The Thrale party[27] who had supported Lord North in the American war, were most of them also on my side, and the popular sentiment was in favour of a Merchant rather than a Lawyer. Some religious people moreover sided with me for my father's sake, and the known largeness of his charities were a further recommendation. I carried my election by a great majority. . . .[28]

The first vote I ever gave in Parliament [he writes somewhat later in his diary], was in favour of the treaty of peace with America. I immediately became in some measure enlisted with the friends of Mr. Pitt and an opponent of the Coalition party. I divided against Mr. Fox's India Bill (November 1783) and again supported Mr. Pitt on his return to power, except in a few instances.

Thornton's active participation in the debates of these years seems in the main to have been confined to questions of taxation, particularly the discussion of the receipts tax and the shop tax. Even then, as he suggests, his allegiance to Pitt was by no means absolute, and in these years that little but influential group of independent members, the 'party of the Saints', gradually formed, of which Thornton and Wilberforce were for many years to be the leading figures.[29]

In the winter of 1785-6 Wilberforce, after his final conversion to the views of the Evangelicals, had found a retreat in the house of John Thornton, and there the two young men drew close together

---

[26] Cf. the following note by Fanny Burney: December 2, 1782, "Mrs. Thrale had a large party . . . . The rest were: . . . Mr. Thornton, the new member for the borough, a man of Presbyterian extraction upon which he has grafted of late much *ton* and *nonchalance*, and who was pleased to follow me about with a sort of hard and unmeaning curiosity, very disagreeable to me, and to himself very much like nothing. . . ." (*Diary and Letters of Madame D'Arblay* (London: Macmillan, 1904), edited by C. Barret, Preface and Notes by Austin Dobson, vol. 2, p. 130).

[27] Henry Thrale had been M.P. for Southwark from 1768 to 1780.

[28] MS. *Diary of Henry Thornton*, op. cit. The passage quoted in the text continues: "There is no doubt that the law which forbids treating was violated by me on this occasion, a subject into which my Father and Mother did not enquire. Mr. Adair, in the speech which he made on retiring from the Hustings intimated that he might if he pleased set aside my Election by petitioning against me and I believe he took the question of an appeal to the House of Commons into consideration, but that he relinquished his purpose partly on the ground of his party having also treated though in a less degree, and partly on that of my majority proving so considerable that I could not be said to owe my success to this illegal practice. A short time after my Election, but antecedently to my taking my Seat I was invited by a friend to dine at his House in private with Mr. Pitt, and I was much gratified by the idea of being introduced to so great a person."

[29] [See Ernest Marshall Howse, *Saints in Politics*, op. cit. -Ed.]

and round them the 'Clapham Sect' began to form. Looking back many years later,[30] Thornton writes:

> Few men have been blessed with worthier and better friends than it has been my lot to be. Mr. Wilberforce stands at the head of these, for he was the friend of my youth. I owed much to him in every sense soon after I came out in life, for my education had been narrow, and his enlarged mind, his affectionate and understanding manners and his very superior piety were exactly calculated to supply what was wanting to my improvement and my establishment in a right course. It is chiefly through him that I have been introduced to a variety of other most valuable associates, to my friends Babington[31] and Gisborne[32] and their worthy families, to Lord Teignmouth[33] and his family, to Mrs. Hannah More[34] and her sisters; to Mr. Stephen[35] and to not a few respectable members of Parliament. Second only to Mr. Wilberforce in my esteem is now the family of Mr. Grant.[36]

[30] MS. Diary of Henry Thornton, op. cit.

[31] Thomas Babington (1758-1838), landowner in Rothley Temple, Leicestershire, since 1800 M.P. for Leicester, member of Wilberforce's 'Philanthropic Cabinet', prominent abolitionist and writer on education. On Babington and the others mentioned below see the full accounts in John C. Colquhoun, William Wilberforce, His Friends and His Times (London: 1867).

[32] Thomas Gisborne (1758-1846), curate of Barton-under-Needwood, Stafford-shire, lived at Yoxall Lodge which, like his friend Babington's house Rothley Temple, provided frequently a country retreat for Wilberforce and other members of the group; author of Principles of Moral Philosophy (London: T. Bensley, 1789) and An Enquiry into the Duties of Men in the Higher Ranks and Middle Classes (London: B. & J. White, 1794).

[33] Sir John Shore, later created Lord Teignmouth (1751-1834), after early experience in India under Warren Hastings, Viceroy from 1793 to 1798, retired to Clapham in 1802, first President of the Bible Society.

[34] Hannah More (1745-1833), authoress and dramatist, who after a youth in the midst of the London literary circles, as a friend of Garrick, Dr. Johnson, and Horace Walpole, became one of the most influential religious writers and most active advocates of popular education.

[35] James Stephen (1758-1832), Master in Chancery and M.P. for Tralee since 1808, and for East Grinstead since 1812, became interested in the abolitionist cause by experiences as a barrister in the West Indies, later for many years one of the closest allies of Wilberforce.

[36] Charles Grant (1746-1823) lived in Clapham after a long life in India and was one of the most influential directors and at one time Governor of East India Company; father of Lord Glenelg, Secretary for the Colonies, and Sir Robert Grant, Governor of Bombay.

For the early years the names of T. Clarkson[37] and Granville Sharp,[38] while somewhat later Zachary Macaulay,[39] John Venn,[40] William Smith,[41] and John Bowdler[42] would have to be included, to give a fairly complete list of Thornton's closer associates. It was a truly remarkable group of people, whose connections were made even closer by numerous intermarriages between their families,[43] and who to the present day show the strength of their native gifts by the extraordinarily long list of their famous descendants.[44]

Early in 1792 Henry Thornton bought a house at Battersea Rise,[45] on Clapham Common, which had formerly belonged to

[37] Thomas Clarkson (1760-1823), with Granville Sharp and Wilberforce the leading figure in the abolitionist movement.

[38] Granville Sharp (1735-1813), originator of the anti-slavery agitation.

[39] Zachary Macaulay (1768-1838) joined the anti-slavery movement because of experience as an employee on an estate in Jamaica, appointed Governor of Sierra Leone Company by Henry Thornton, and after his return for many years editor of the *Christian Observer*; father of T. B. Macaulay.

[40] John Venn (1759-1813), son of Henry Venn, the author of the *Complete Duty of Man* (London: The Religious Tract Society, 1763), "trusted exposition of the Characteristic theology of the Clapham Sect", Rector of Clapham since 1792. [Grandfather of John Venn (1834-1923), the Cambridge logician and historian. -Ed.]

[41] William Smith (1756-1835), merchant and stockbroker, from 1784 M.P. in succession for Sudbury, Camelford, and Norwich, noted lover of nature and patron of the arts, lived at Clapham.

[42] John Bowdler (1783-1815), lawyer and poet, cousin of Thomas Bowdler of "Family Shakespeare" fame. In John Bowdler's writings Henry Thornton appears under the name of "Sophron".

[43] T. Gisborne married Babington's sister, and Babington Macaulay's, who in turn married, if not a real member of the group, at least a favourite pupil of Hannah More's; James Stephen married as his second wife a sister of Wilberforce who, it will be remembered, was a second cousin of Henry Thornton. James Stephen's son of the same name, the author of the Essay on the Clapham Sect, married a granddaughter of John Venn, whose son Henry was married to Martha Sykes, a niece of Mrs. Henry Thornton.

[44] The most famous of these is of course T. B. Macaulay, who in a school originally provided for negro children but then continued for the Clapham boys had James Stephen the younger, Samuel Wilberforce, the bishop ("Soapy Sam"), and the younger Lord Teignmouth for his contemporaries. In the third generation there is Florence Nightingale, the granddaughter of William Smith, and in addition James Fitzjames and Leslie Stephen, G. O. Trevelyan, A. V. Dicey, and John Venn the logician may be mentioned as figures of great intellectual eminence. Of living authors (1939) the names of Mrs. Virginia Woolf as a descendant of the Stephens and of Mr. E. M. Forster as a direct descendant of Henry Thornton may be added.

[45] A charming description of Battersea Rise (which disappeared only in 1907) is given from her own recollection by Miss Dorothy Pym, another descendant of Henry Thornton, in a book of that title (London: Jonathan Cape, 1934). Photographs of the famous library will be found in *Clapham and the Clapham Sect* (Clapham: Edmund Balwin, 1927), p. 109, and in Telford, *Sect that Moved the World*, op. cit., p. 116. [See also *Henry Thornton of Clapham*, op cit., throughout; *William Wilberforce*, op. cit., pp.

Lubbock, the banker, and for the next five years, till they both married, Wilberforce shared it with him, "contributing so much toward expenses". Two other houses on the estate which Thornton had acquired, Glenelg and Broomfield, were let to two friends, Charles Grant and Edward Eliot, the latter the brother-in-law of Pitt. After Eliot's death in 1797 Broomfield was taken by Wilberforce. Thornton added to his house and it is said that Pitt on one of his visits to his brother-in-law designed the oval library of Battersea Rise, which became the famous meeting-place of the groups. It was here that the campaign for the abolition of slavery was planned and directed and that the numerous other activities of the Evangelical party were discussed.

It is quite impossible to make more than a mere mention in this sketch of the more important movements which the Clapham Sect initiated and in which Henry Thornton took a leading part. Their main achievement is, of course, the abolition of the slave trade,[46] and from the beginning of the association of Thornton and Wilberforce up till the passing of the Act of 1807,[47] the greater part of their energies were devoted to this leading goal. If Wilberforce was the driving spirit, Thornton was the wise and practical counsellor on whom Wilberforce placed absolute reliance. When in 1791 the experiment of settling a number of liberated slaves in St. George's Bay led to the foundation of the Sierra Leone Company, the first of the African Chartered Companies, Henry Thornton became its Chairman; and through all its vicissitudes, till Sierra Leone was taken over as a Crown Colony in 1808, he remained Chairman of the Company, and devoted much of his time to its business and the

116-117; and *Marianne Thornton: A Domestic Biography*, op. cit., chapter 1. -Ed.]

[46] Cf. F. J. Klingberg, *The Anti-Slavery Movement in England*, op. cit., and R. Coupland, *The British Anti-Slavery Movement* (London: Home University Library, 1933). [See now also Roger Anstey, *The Atlantic Slave Trade and British Abolition, 1760-1810* (Atlantic Highlands, N.J.: Humanities Press, 1975) and Christine Bolt and Seymoure Drescher, eds, *Anti-Slavery, Religion, and Reform* (Folkestone, England: Wm. Dawson; Hamden, N.Y.: Archon Books, 1980). -Ed.]

[47] The following anecdote, connected with the final passage of the long fought for bill, which is rather characteristic of Henry Thornton and his relation to Wilberforce, may have a place here. After the division "a good many came over to Palace Yard after the House got up and congratulated [Wilberforce]. John Thornton and Heber, Sharp, Macaulay, Grant and Robert Grant, Robert Bird and William Smith who were in the gallery. 'Well, Henry,' Mr. Wilberforce asked playfully of Mr. Thornton, 'what shall we abolish next?' 'The lottery, I think,' gravely replied his sterner friend" (*Life of Wilberforce*, op. cit., vol. 3, p. 298).

many Parliamentary discussions to which its problems gave rise.[48] And when in 1798 the abolitionists almost despaired of ever succeeding, Henry Thornton revived their hopes by successfully piloting a bill for the exclusion of the slave trade from certain parts of the African coast through the House of Commons, although it eventually failed to pass the Lords.[49]

If this is the best known of the achievements of the group, there are others of not much less importance. Faith in popular education, and sabbatarian zeal, led in 1785 to the foundation of the Sunday School Society of which Henry Thornton was the first President.[50] He provided for twenty-five years the means which enabled Hannah More to run her schools for the poor.[51] And when in 1795 the same old friend[52] embarked upon her *Cheap Repository Tracts*, in addition to writing some of the tracts,[53]

> Mr. T[hornton] and two or three others condescended to spend hours with the hawkers to learn the mysteries of their trade; the result is, we purpose next month to print two different editions of the same tract, one of handsome appearance for the rich, the other on coarser paper, but so excessively cheap by wholesale, as fully to meet the hawkers on their own ground.[54]

With such advice the groups succeeded in selling no less than two million of the *Cheap Repository Tracts* during the first year of

---

[48] On the History of the Sierra Leone Company see F. W. Butt Thompson, *Sierra Leone in History and Tradition* (London: H. F. & G. Witherby, 1926).

[49] That Henry Thornton was the originator of the bill is commonly affirmed in the literature, but not evident from the *Parliamentary Debates*. But according to the *Annual Register* (vol. 40, 1798, p. 237) Henry Thornton moved, on May 4, 1798, "that the House resolve itself into a committee in which he should move to bring in a bill to prohibit the carrying on of the slave trade on the Northern Coast of Africa". See also the *Journals of the House of Commons*, vol. 53, 1797-80, p. 540.

[50] M. G. Jones, *The Charity School Movement* (Cambridge: Cambridge University Press, 1938), p. 152.

[51] Roberts, *Memoirs of H. More* (London: R. B. Seeley and W. Burnside, 1834), vol. 3, p. 451.

[52] "He and H. More are like brother and sister, or mother and son" is the description of the friendship by Lady Hesketh (*Letters of Lady Hesketh to the Rev. John Johnson*, ed. C. B. Johnson (London: Jarrold and Sons, 1901), p. 89).

[53] According to his Diary, in addition to revising for Hannah More some of her own tracts, particularly the *Shepherd of Salisbury Plain* and the *Lancashire Collier Girl*, he seems to have written himself at least three tracts in 1795, one of them containing dialogues and another on the *Religious Advantages of the Inhabitants of Great Britain*.

[54] Hannah More in a letter to Z. Macaulay, dated January 6, 1706 (*Life and Correspondence* (London: R. B. Seely and W. Burnside, 1834), ed. Roberts, vol. 2, p. 460).

their existence. Out of this grew in 1799 the Religious Tract Society;[55] in the same year the Church Missionary Society,[56] and in 1804 the British and Foreign Bible Society[57] were founded by the Clapham group, and in all three organisations Henry Thornton served as Treasurer. And the Charity of the Sect did not remain confined to the English on the one side and the Heathen on the other. When during the Napoleonic wars news came of frightful destitution in Germany, it was again Henry Thornton and Zachary Macaulay who organised public meetings and subscriptions to raise funds for relief.[58]

But we must leave the activities in which Henry Thornton participated mainly as a leading member of a group, and return to the main events of his life and his more personal views and activities in Parliament. He had entered the banking business at the beginning of a period of ten years of great prosperity and rapid expansion of the credit system of England. At the death of his father in 1790, Henry inherited a substantial sum which may well have helped him in building up what appears to have been a comparatively small banking house into one of the largest in the City. Of the three older partners two, of whom he says that

> they both were very kind to me—both however lent no very willing ear to the religious observations which I sometimes endeavoured to press upon them,[59]

died in the first few years of the new century, and, the third being an invalid, left him as the dominant figure in the business. Looking back over his career as a banker he writes in 1809:

> My Banking business has been very profitable to me. I discovered before I entered that the antecedent gains had been extremely small; probably they were not more than £1,500 or £2,000 per year in all of which half had belonged to Mr. Down. The business gradually increased when my name and that of Mr. Free were added to the firm. We owed much to the kindness of our friends

---

[55] See A. de Morgan in *Notes and Queries* (London: Oxford University Press, 1849), 3rd series, vol. 6, pp. 241-246.

[56] E. Stock, *The History of the Church Missionary Society* (London, 1899), vol. 1, p. 69.

[57] W. Canton, *History of the British and Foreign Bible Society* (London, 1899), vol. 1, p. 69.

[58] Lady Knutsford, *Z. Macaulay* (London: Edward Arnold, 1900), p. 310.

[59] *MS. Diary of Henry Thornton*, op. cit., March 21, 1803.

and much also to the circumstance of many country banks rising up at the time, with which we were wise enough to become connected. In the year 1793, a season of great commercial distress, we experienced greater difficulties than most other bankers in consequence of the sudden reductions of very large sums which we had held at interest for some very considerable banks. The evil partly consisted in the inadequacy of our capital. Mr. Down was not at that time very rich and my savings had been far from considerable.

The world naturally expects that a House trusted so largely and conducting such extensive operations, should have funds of its own either in hand or within call, bearing some proportions to its concern and there is something, as I now think, like want of honesty in claiming an almost unbounded credit without laying a proportional foundation for it. The banking business is an extremely desirable one. It is remarkably suited to my infirmity of health, and the Providence of God has dealt most mercifully with me in thus accommodating my profession to my circumstances. My eldest son seems well qualified by nature to take my place in this concern. A little good sense, regular attendance, a spirit of liberality and kindness not degenerating into profusion and servility, together with an exact integrity are the chief points to be regarded.

There is no necessity for becoming an *intimate acquaintance* of all who are disposed to be the good customer of the house. Many of them may be very unfit to be friends. It may be, on the other hand, expedient to cultivate the friendship of a few respectable connections of the House and it will not be difficult to discover which of these are in point of private character the most desirable as guest at our table, or intimate associates in our family . . . .

I have, by the blessings of good Providence, enjoyed a considerable and generally increasing income for the last twenty years. But I have made it my rule not to amass any large fortune. When my father died, I received from him about £40,000, having antecedently derived from him only the very moderate sum of £6,000. My income has grown to £8, 10, or even 11 or 12,000 per an. of which £4 or £5,000 generally suffices for my expenses and about £2 or £3,000 is given in charity. My bounty was much larger before I married and now and then perhaps approached to profusion. The number of my children (now 8) and the infirmity of my health, together with the consideration that some may derive from me a tender constitution, which may be the source of more than ordinary expense, disposes me now to lay by £2 or £3,000 per an. for, in the midst of my compassion for the poor, I desire always to remember that saying of the Apostle "He that provideth not for his own household is worse than an infidel."

It is recorded that till his marriage in 1796 Thornton had made it a rule to give away as charity six-sevenths of his income.[60] His work at the Banking House does not appear to have taken up too much of his time. If we may trust his Diary, to attend there regularly from 11 a.m. to 3 p.m. seems to have been a good intention rarely achieved. And even so, we find occasionally entries as the

[60]This is a statement frequently made in the literature on Henry Thornton. In a letter to *The Guardian* of June 19, 1907, p. 1023, "A Granddaughter of Henry Thornton" gives the following extracts from Henry Thornton's accounts for the four years from 1790:

"Charity £2,260. All other expenses £1,543
"   3,960   "   "   "   1,817
"   7,508   "   "   "   1,616
"   6,680   "   "   "   1,988

and about the following year, 1794, he says in his *MS. Diary*: "I have spent £1,300 this year more than I have got and find I have been indiscreet in my loans of money, especially formerly—

I have spent 2,200 besides 560 repairs, is about	2,800
Clapham House and furniture rent	600
gave in Charity 3,750	- - - - -
lost by old bad debts now wrote off about 1,550	5,300
	8,700

which is about £1,300 more than I have got, but I have been rather imprudent and I ought to trace this to a fault in my character."

In an MS. letter in the British Museum (Egerton Collection, 1966), by Robert Harry Inglis, apparently written shortly after Henry Thornton's death, it is said of him that "he was liberality embodied—his charities were munificent beyond any example as we now know since his death. One of the items of his bounty as it was told me by a common friend who had personal means of knowing it, was £1,400 per annum for the education of pious men for the Church. His charities before his marriage were 10,000 per annum and the most extraordinary part of this is that he gave nothing without enquiry—it was not a large appropriation of a particular sum to the relief of others which satisfied his conscience—he felt that he was not only a Steward to set apart for the general class of indigence a large portion of his means, but that he was equally a Steward in the detailed distribution of it—it was not enough that he did not spend it on himself, but in spending it on others he made it go as far as possible. He therefore gave his time as well as his money—a sacrifice which Mr. Macaulay said he did not think overstated at 5,000 per annum more—as his undivided attention to the business of his Banking house would have enabled him to realise many more profits and to avoid many more losses—if he had left a very large fortune, it might have been said that these charities magnificent as they are were yet mainly his superfluities; but his income was mainly for life and his fortune is comparatively very inconsiderable; but he left his children a name more valuable and an example more precious than any other employment of his time would have enabled him to leave."

following: "I did little yesterday at my Banking House except correcting a Sermon on Self Denial."[61]

Of his business habits two anecdotes have come down to us, one of them referring to an embarrassment similar to that reported above, which occurred during the crisis of 1810. In the autumn of that year

> he was on his road with his family to Scotland. It was a time of severe pressure upon banks and trading interests. Straitened by the obstacles of the war, hampered by the embargoes by which Napoleon had deranged the course of trade, many commercial houses, long reckoned safe, sunk; others could only save themselves by flying to the banks for accommodation. The bank in which Mr. Thornton was a partner felt the pressure, and felt it severely, just after their most able partner had left London for the North. Had Mr. Thornton known what was impending, he would not have absented himself. The news reached him on his route to Scotland, and caused him some embarrassment. To return from a journey undertaken and generally known, would have spread rumours which might have brought on the very crisis that was to be feared. This course, therefore, could not be thought of. He decided to continue his journey, but he opened himself in confidence to one valued friend, and stated his wish that some thousands of pounds might be placed at demand at the disposal of his partners in the bank. No sooner was the hint given than it was met by ample support. Funds poured in from all quarters—Wilberforce, with generous ardour, hastening to lead the way; and the money came in such a flood, that his bank saw itself lifted above the sands on which it was settling, and floated into deep waters with abundant resources.[62]

The other anecdote is told by the younger James Stephen without a date:

> Tidings of the commercial failure of a near kinsman embarked him at once on an enquiry—how far he was obliged to indemnify those who might have given credit to his relative, in reliance, however unauthorised, on his own resources; and again the coffers of the banker were unlocked by the astuteness of the casuist. A mercantile

---

[61] *MS. Diary*, op. cit., January 23, 1795. Shortly after the following entry occurs, February 15, 1795. "Went to Sierra Leone House and attended an hour and a half on Committee of Trade—I think my attendance was useful—It was certainly a self-denial, and yet how pleasant would some people think even my acts of self-denial to be—so favoured am I by Providence."

[62] Colquhoun, *Wilberforce*, op. cit., p. 248.

partnership (many a year has passed since the disclosure could injure or affect any one), which without his knowledge had obtained from his firm large and improvident advances, became so hopelessly embarrassed, that their bankruptcy was pressed upon him as the only chance of averting from his own house the most serious disasters. He overruled the proposal, on the ground that they whose rashness had given to their debtors an unmerited credit, had no right to call on others to divide with them the consequent loss. To the last farthing he therefore dissolved the liabilities of the insolvents, at a cost of which his own share exceeded twenty thousand pounds. Yet he was then declining in health, and the father of nine young children.[63]

As will be seen more fully in the second part of this essay, it was probably the experience of the crisis of 1793 which directed Thornton's mind to credit problems. And in 1797, when the suspension of cash payments by the Bank of England led to separate enquiries by the House of Commons and the House of Lords, we find him prepared to give in his evidence before both committees a most lucid outline of the main ideas, which shows that by this time his thoughts had already crystallised. It immediately attracted wide attention and established his reputation as the foremost authority on these matters.[64] This side of his activities will, however, be taken up in the next section and we must now bring this general account of his life to a close.

Henry Thornton had married in the spring of 1796 Marianne Sykes, like his mother the daughter of a 'Russian merchant' in Hull. It seems that she was a woman of considerable intelligence and education, but like her husband of very delicate health. In spite of this, however, Battersea Rise was soon peopled with nine children who all survived their parents. In the education of his children Henry took a great interest, and it is said that he "endeavoured to interest them at the earliest possible age in politics, and even in

---

[63] J. Stephen, *Essays* (Philadelphia: Carey & Hart, 1843), p. 191. From the last sentence of the passage it appears that the event must have taken place between 1809 and 1815. The first sentence very likely refers to the bankruptcy of his brother Robert.

[64] In the House of Lords Debate on the Bank on May 15, 1797, already, Lord Auckland refers to "Mr. Henry Thornton of whom and of whose evidence it was difficult to speak in terms of adequate respect" (*Parliamentary History*, vol. 23, 1897-8, p. 534).

currency. He wrote a paper advocating this practice, in the *Christian Observer*"[65].

To the busy father the country house in Battersea Rise served, however, only as a retreat from his labours in the City and in Parliament, and during the months when he resided at Clapham he would daily ride on horseback into town. He spent most of his time at a house in King's Arms Yard, Coleman Street, near the seat of his Bank in Bartholomew Lane, and later, when his increasing parliamentary duties made it desirable to live in Westminster, at a house in Old Palace Yard which he had taken over from Wilberforce. His activities and his influence in Parliament, and at the same time his political independence, had been constantly growing since the evidence of 1797 had established his reputation. In that same year he supported Grey's motion for parliamentary reform, and on questions such as abuses in elections and the general abolition of sinecures he frequently found himself in disagreement with the Government. His reformatory zeal led him to support Catholic emancipation at an early stage (1805) and to take a lively interest in questions such as debtors' relief and prison reform. In the great struggle with France all his efforts were directed towards the restoration, and later to the maintenance, of peace. On questions like the attack on Copenhagen he differed not only with the Government but also with members of his closest circle, his brothers, Wilberforce, Babington, and Grant. In the discussion of Pitt's income tax he strongly advocated a graduation of the rate according to the character of the income, and when he failed to carry his point, he silently raised his own payment to the figure to which it would have amounted under his scheme.[66] In the new century, however, his parliamentary activity became more and more connected with the problems of currency and banking. He was a member of the Committee of 1804 on the Irish exchange;[67] he was elected in February 1807 a member of the committee of 21 "to examine and control the several branches of public expenditure", and there took "a considerable lead in the report made by them on

---

[65] Leslie Stephen in the article on Henry Thornton in the *Dictionary of National Biography* (London: Oxford University Press, 1921-2), vol. 19, pp. 781-783, and *MS. Recollections of Marianne Thornton*, op. cit.

[66] There is only a short reference in the report in *Hansard* of his speech on December 22, 1798, to the distinction between fluctuating and fixed incomes, but some additional information can be gathered from J. Stephen's *Essays*, p. 190, L. Stephen's article in the *Dictionary of National Biography*, and an article by Miss J. Wedgwood in the *Contemporary Review*, vol. 68, October 1895.

[67] See *Journals of the House of Commons*, vol. 59, 1803-4, pp. 129-130.

the Bank affairs, by which £240,000 a year has been saved to the state. I had in this case to oppose the views of my family and city connexions."[68] In 1810 at last he took a leading part not only in the work of the Bullion Committee, of which we shall have to speak more fully later, but also in the work of the Committee on the State of Commercial Credit appointed by Perceval's Government a little later in the same year. His active years in Parliament extended just long enough not only to be a member of the Committee of 1813 "to enquire into the Corn Trade of the United Kingdom", but also to speak in the great debate on the Corn Laws in June 1814. This was almost his last speech in Parliament; it was followed by only one a little later in the same month on a bill on London prisons.

During these fourteen years which Henry Thornton lived into the nineteenth century, his work in Parliament and his literary activities must have taken up almost all his time. In the repeated elections of these years, in 1802, 1806, 1807, and 1812, he found it harder and harder to retain his seat with declining majorities. He was not a figure who appealed to the popular imagination, and even though the universal respect in which he was held secured him his seat till his death, his diary shows that he was greatly worried by his declining support. Yet we need hardly be surprised that in times of intense party strife and widespread political corruption to retain his seat was difficult for a man who refused to give undivided allegiance to any party and whose supporters attempted to recommend him to a greedy populace by doggerel verses like these:

> Nor place nor pension e'er got he
> For self or for connexion;
> We shall not tax the Treasury
> By Thornton's re-election.[69]

It has been said by one of the admirers of Henry Thornton that he wrote a good deal, "but nothing likely to descend to posterity".[70] That the *Paper Credit*, the only book[71] which Thornton appears himself to have published, might be an exception probably never

---

[68] *MS. Diary of Henry Thornton*, op. cit., 1809.

[69] *MS. Recollections of Marianne Thornton*, op. cit.; also Colquhoun, *Wilberforce*, op. cit., p. 283.

[70] M. Seeley, *Later Evangelical Fathers* (London: Seeley, Jackson, & Halliday, 1879), p. 36.

[71] See bibliographical notes at the end of this chapter.

occurred to the author of this statement. He clearly had in mind the devotional and more popular writings of Henry Thornton, which, indeed, were voluminous. It has happened to a bibliophile economist[72] that a stout volume of *Collected Works of Henry Thornton, Esq., M.P.*, which he eagerly pulled from the shelves of a second-hand bookshop, proved to contain Family Prayers and Family Commentaries on the Sermon on the Mount and on Portions of the Pentateuch. These strictly religious writings of Henry Thornton were published from his manuscripts after his death by R. H. Inglis. But in addition he wrote a considerable amount for the organ of the Clapham Sect, the *Christian Observer*, which he helped to found and which for many years was edited by Zachary Macaulay. It is said that from 1802, when this journal started, till his death, Thornton contributed no less than eighty-two articles on a wide range of subjects:

> sketches of public affairs, of the state of the parties in the stormy times of 1803, 1806, 1810, and 1813; the difficult questions of the Orders in Council; and the Middlesex election; biographies of Pitt and Fox, written with the thoughtfulness as well as the impartiality of history, critiques on the *Edinburgh Review*, on books, on the temper of religious parties, are interspersed with advice as wise as Addison's, less playful, but more sound.[73]

During these later years of his life Thornton's contacts and influence must have extended far beyond the narrower circle of the Sect. As early as 1800 we find Jeremy Bentham writing to him in connexion with his Panopticon project.[74] And if a difference of religious views had probably prevented closer contacts, he was a well-known and respected figure in the camp of the Philosophical Radicals. Lord Brougham seems to have known him well,[75] and in 1812 we find Ricardo inviting Malthus to dine with him and Thorn-

---

[72] [This appears to refer to Hayek himself. -Ed.]

[73] Colquhoun, *Wilberforce*, op. cit., p. 303.

[74] *Catalogue of the Manuscripts of Jeremy Bentham* in the Library of University College, London, compiled by A. Taylor Milne, University College, London, 1937, pp. 41, 141.

[75] See *Brougham and His Early Friends. Letters to James Loch, 1798-1809*, collected and arranged by R. H. M. Buddle and G. A. Jackson, Privately Printed, 1908, vol. 2, letters of December 14 and 22, 1904.

ton, a dinner party which the busy Thornton asks to have transferred to his house.[76]

It is astounding that all this activity should have come from a man who throughout the greater part of his life seems to have been in exceedingly weak health. But apart from occasional visits to Buxton or Bath, Brighton or the Isle of Wight, enforced by the state of his health, he did not give himself any rest. Even these annual journeys, although often extended to include visits to the sisters More and other friends, were not entirely devoted to recreation. In a letter to Charles Grant written from Buxton in September 1806, Henry Thornton writes:

> Dr. Lovell, whom partly to satisfy the kind anxiety of friends, I consulted about my own health, advised Buxton Waters, and after seeing some beautiful scenes in Monmouthshire and one especially which I never shall forget we moved slowly hither: We bought a grey poney on which my little Girl[77] has cantered many a half stage and I have to thank the poney for having made me much better acquainted with my Daughter than I was before. We have also gone together to see a variety of Manufactures and have been learning to feel for those who dig in mines, who toil in Quarries, perspire in Salt works, wear out their Eyes in looking at Furnaces or pass their whole morning noon and Even in the limited Employment of putting on the head of a Pin, or drawing over and over the same pattern on a piece of China. I fear that the Less pleasant part of Education has been neglected. I trust however that seeing the world in this sense will be very usefull. It also has not a little entertained Mrs. T. and I trust that the View which we have taken of our fellow creatures has inspired some thankfulness for the temporal as well as spiritual Advantages of our own condition.[78]

The anxiety of Henry Thornton's friends was however only too well justified and the lingering complaint, apparently consumption, grew gradually worse. In the autumn of 1814 his constitution finally broke down, and after a prolonged illness he died on January 16, 1815, in his fifty-fifth year.[79]

---

[76] *Letters of David Ricardo to Thomas Robert Malthus, 1810-23*, ed. James Bonar (Oxford: Clarendon Press, 1887), pp. 25-26, December 17, 1812.

[77] This is Henry Thornton's first child, Marianne, then nine years of age.

[78] MS. letter of Henry Thornton to Charles Grant, dated Buxton September 17, 1806, in the possession of Mr. E. M. Forster.

[79] On the day of Thornton's death we find a young T. B. Macaulay writing to Mrs. Hannah More: "Clapham, January 16, 1815. My dear Madam, My mamma was on the point of writing to inform you that a supposed favourable alteration has taken

"A more upright, independent, and truly virtuous man has never adorned the Senate," says the writer of the obituary notice in the *Gentleman's Magazine*.[80] The various attempts to describe his character depict him as a man of almost unearthly goodness. "He has indeed a mind so disciplined and trained," writes one of Thornton's friends to his wife, "so godly, so divested of self, and so active to glorify God and benefit men that a near view of him is a most humbling lesson."[81] James Stephen[82] and J. C. Colquhoun[83] describe the bent of his mind as pre-eminently judicial and "essentially philosophic". But we shall perhaps have a more life-like picture of the man if from the almost unbroken stream of deserved praise we quote the one or two more critical passages. Henry Brougham describes him as "the most eminent in every respect" of Wilberforce's small party,

> a man of strong understanding, great powers of reasoning and of investigation; an accurate and curious observer, but who neither had cultivated oratory at all nor had received a refined education, nor had extended his reading beyond the subjects connected with moral, political and theological learning. The trade of a banker, which he followed, engrossed much of his time; and his exertions both in Parliament and through the press, were chiefly confined to the celebrated controversy upon the currency, in which his well-known work led the way, and to a bill for restricting the Slave Trade to part of the African coast, which he introduced when the abolitionists were wearied out with their repeated failure; and had well-nigh abandoned all hopes of carrying the great measure itself.[84]

place in Mr. Henry Thornton's case. His physicians are still sanguine in their expectations; but his friends, who examine his disorders by the rules of common sense, and not by those of medicine, are very weak in their hopes. The warm bath has been prescribed; and it is the wish and prayer of all who know him that so excellent and valuable a character may be preserved to the world" (*Letters of Hannah More to Zachary Macaulay*, ed. A. Roberts (London: J. Nisbet, 1860), p. 68). Mrs. Henry Thornton followed her husband after a few months and the orphaned children were taken care of by Mr. and Mrs. R. H. Inglis (later Sir Robert Inglis, and M.P. for Oxford), who moved into Battersea Rise and succeeded in preserving it as a centre of humanitarian and intellectual activity. It may be of interest to note that the apothecary Pennington who attended Henry Thornton in his last illness was probably the brother of the economist, James Pennington.

[80] *Gentleman's Magazine*, February 1815, vol. 85, Part 1, p. 182.

[81] H. Morris, *The Life of Charles Grant* (London: John Murray, 1904), p. 177. Letter of Charles Grant to Mrs. Grant of September 1794.

[82] *Essays*, op. cit., p. 189.

[83] *Wilberforce*, op. cit., p. 271.

[84] Henry Brougham, *Historical Sketches of Statesmen who Flourished in the Time of George III* (London: R. Griffin, 1855), vol. 1, article on Wilberforce, p. 346.

And James Stephen at the end of the description of Thornton in his once celebrated essay on the Clapham Sect pictures him as

> Affectionate, but passionless—with a fine and indeed a fastidious taste, but destitute of all creative imagination—gifted rather with fortitude to endure calamity, than with courage to exult in the struggle with danger—a lover of mankind but not an enthusiast in the cause of our common humanity—his serene and perspicacious spirit was never haunted by the visions, nor borne away by the resistless impulses, of which heroic natures, and they alone, are conscious. Well qualified to impart to the highest energies of others a wise direction, and inflexible perseverance, he had to borrow from them the glowing temperament which hopes against hope, and is wise in despite of prudence.[85]

A note may perhaps be added to this on the fate of Henry Thornton's firm. After his death it had become Pole, Thornton, Free, Down & Scott, with Sir Peter Pole as leading partner, and young Henry Sykes Thornton, Henry's eldest son, who was only fifteen at the time of his death, became an active partner early in 1825. The house seems to have greatly prospered—it is said during the years 1818-24 to have yielded 40,000 pounds a year,[86] and it was regarded as "one of the oldest and most extensive Banking Houses in London".[87] It is suggested, however, in some of the contemporary literature that the means of the partners were not fully adequate to the increased volume of business, and that they had invested "in securities not strictly convertible to a larger extent than was prudent".[88] However this may be, when in the late autumn

---

[85] *Essays*, op. cit., p. 193.

[86] J. Francis, *History of the Bank of England* (London: Willoughby, 1845), vol. 2, p. 9.

[87] T. Joplin, *Analysis and History of the Currency Question* (London: J. Ridgway, 1832), p. 206.

[88] See J. H. Palmer's statement in *Report from the Committee of Secrecy on the Bank of England Charter, ordered (by the House of Commons) to be printed June 17, 1833*, Q.607. In a pamphlet by an anonymous writer Henry Thornton is blamed as being responsible for the failure of the firm ten years after his death: "The failure of Pole, Thornton, and Co. is in no degree whatever to be ascribed to their country correspondents, but mainly to the circumstances of that kindhearted, amiable and good man Henry Thornton, having left the concern of Down, Thornton, and Co. in a state of great perplexity, to say no more; and Sir Peter Pole having joined the concern, on the death of Mr. Thornton, in a state that imperatively required the most rigid adherence to pure banking principles, to insure safety and prosperity to the establishment, being weak enough to depart from those principles for the purpose of specula- tion" (*A Letter to the Earl of Liverpool, on the Erroneous Information that His Majesty's Ministers have adopted regarding the Country Banks and the Currency in the Manufacturing*

of 1825 an acute stringency in the money market occurred and a number of the more important country banks failed, suspicion was aroused against the London house which by its extensive connections was bound to be particularly affected by the heavy drain of funds from London. For some time the firm was able to meet the steadily increasing demands; but on the evening of Saturday, December 3rd, the Deputy-Governor[89] of the Bank of England was informed that Pole & Co. were in need of assistance. An emergency meeting of the available directors on Sunday morning decided to put on Monday at the disposal of the firm, against ample security, the sum of 300,000 pounds.[90] And if we may believe a much later report, "it was not thought that the extent of the financial crisis should be known, and before the subordinates of the Bank were in their places, the Governor and the Deputy-Governor themselves counted out and handed over the gold, which was carried away in silence and secrecy".[91] But this only prolonged the struggle for a week and on the following Monday the firm stopped payment[92] with the effect of bringing the panic to its height and causing the closure of several other banking houses on the next day, including one of about equal size, Williams, Burgess & Williams. Although Pole & Co. was ultimately not only found to be fully solvent but even to realise a handsome surplus over its liabilities, it did not re-open. It was in effect merged with Williams & Co., which at the beginning of 1826 re-opened as Williams, Deacon & Co.,[93] and it was in this firm that Henry Thornton the younger spent another fifty-five years

---

Districts, By a Manufacturer in the North of England (London, 1826), p. 11).

[89] The Governor, Cornelius Buller, is reported to have been connected with the House of Pole & Co. by marriage and "other circumstances of relationship".

[90] *Report on the Bank Charter*, op. cit. [see note 88 above] Q.5006.

[91] J. Wedgwood, *Contemporary Review*, vol. 68, October 1895, p. 525.

[92] T. Joplin, in discussing this crisis (*Analysis and History* (London: J. Ridgway, 1832), p. 235), rightly points out that it was similar to that of 1793 in that it was brought about by a contraction of the issues of the Bank of England, and he adds that "Mr. Thornton, being a banker—a partner, it is curious to remark, of the house that failed on this occasion—had his attention particularly called to the subject; and a very considerable portion of his work, on public credit, is devoted to show, that, in a period of panic, the Bank ought rather to lean to the side of enlarging, than contracting its issues."

[93] This is according to a circular dated December 31, 1825, and signed by Robt. Williams and C. M. Williams, a copy of which was kindly supplied to the present author by the Manager of Williams, Deacon's Bank Ltd. Mr. John Deacon who joined the firm at the same time is described as a later partner of Messrs. Baring Brothers & Co., and the Hon. John Thornton Melville, who also became a partner at the same time, was the son-in-law and former partner of Samuel Thornton and apparently related to the Thorntons in other ways also.

of successful banking life till he died in 1881. His relations to another more famous son of a member of the Clapham Sect, his classmate, Lord Macaulay, to whom he acted as banker, will be familiar to many readers of G. O. Trevelyan's *Life of Macaulay*.[94]

II

It is not too much to say that the appearance of the *Paper Credit* in 1802 marks the beginning of a new epoch in the development of monetary theory. Although Thornton's merits have long been overshadowed by the greater fame of Ricardo, it has now come to be recognised[95] that in the field of money the main achievement of the classical period is due to Thornton, and that even the modifications of his theories by his better-known successors were not always improvements. The remarkable fact is that almost as soon as, after a long period of quiescence, circumstances once again made monetary problems the subject of general interest, he was ready to put forward a new body of doctrine which not only provided the framework during the next fifteen years for what may still be regarded as the greatest of all monetary debates, but which also represents the most important single contribution to these discussions.

Since the contributions of Cantillon, Galiani, and Hume in the middle of the eighteenth century little progress had been made in monetary science. Joseph Harris's *Essay upon Money and Coins*, published in 1757-8,[96] which was one of the first systematic treatises on money in the English language, might still be regarded, at the end of the century, as representative of the existing state of knowledge. The suggestive and interesting, but essentially wrongheaded, chapters on money in James Steuart's *Political Economy*[97] had no very wide influence. And the treatment of money in the *Wealth*

---

[94] [Sir George Otto Trevelyan, Bart., *The Life and Letters of Lord Macaulay by his nephew* (Leipsic: Lemmermann, 1876). -Ed.]

[95] The more correct appreciation of Thornton's merits in modern times is mainly due to Professor Jacob Viner's *Canada's Balance of International Indebtedness* (Cambridge, Mass.: Harvard University Press, 1924).

[96] Joseph Harris, *An Essay upon Money and Coins* (London: G. Hawkins, 1757-8).

[97] Sir James Steuart, *An Inquiry into the Principles of Political Economy* (London: A. Millar & T. Cadell, 1767; reprinted Chicago: University of Chicago Press, 1966).

of Nations,[98] which dominated opinion on these matters in the last quarter of the century, contains comparatively little of theoretical interest.[99] But even the descriptive parts of the *Wealth of Nations* were no longer adequate by the end of the century. The twenty years following its appearance had brought gradual but fundamental changes in the structure of the English credit system. The rapid increase in the number of country banks, the abandonment of the issue of notes on the part of the London bankers, the rapid growth of the use of the cheque, and the establishment of the London Clearing House all fall into this period. And it was during the same period that the Bank of England became the Bankers' Bank, the *dernier resort* as Sir Francis Baring described it in 1797,[100] where in an emergency everybody expected to obtain ready money.

Another phenomenon to which Adam Smith had given comparatively little attention was the economic crises which occurred with surprising regularity in 1763, 1772, 1783, and 1793. And in consequence of the changed position of the Bank of England new problems arose on the occasion of these crises. It is said that in the crisis of 1783 the Bank for the first time deliberately and successfully met an outflow of gold by a contraction of credit. Whether or not this was a new discovery, there can be little doubt that ten years later,

---

[98] [Adam Smith, *An Inquiry into The Nature and Causes of the Wealth of Nations* [1776], in *The Glasgow Edition of the Works and Correspondence of Adam Smith*, vol. 2 (Oxford: Clarendon Press, 1976). -Ed.]

[99] On the literature of this period see J. H. Hollander, "The Development of the Theory of Money from Adam Smith to David Ricardo", *Quarterly Journal of Economics*, vol. 25, May 1911. I am here disregarding some of the more interesting French writers of the period, who seem to have had practically no influence on discussion in England (with the exception probably of Turgot). For the same reason I am also neglecting Henry Lloyd's interesting *Essay on the Theory of Money* (London: Printed for J. Almon, 1771), which appears to have remained almost completely unnoticed.

Henry Thornton probably had no very extensive acquaintance with the early literature. A manuscript "list of all the books in the library" of Battersea Rise, drawn up about twenty years after Henry Thornton's death, which presumably contains most of the works on economics which he possessed, and which very appropriately begins with Trimmer's *Economy of Charity* (London: Printed by T. Bensley for T. Longman, 1787), contains from among the early economic works only: the *Wealth of Nations*, Montesquieu's *Spirit of the Laws* (London: Printed for J. Nourse and P. Vaillant, 1750), the *Works* of John Locke (London: Printed for E. Parker, E. Symon, C. Hitch, and J. Pemberton, 1740), A. Anderson, *Origin of Commerce* (London: Printed for A. Millar, 1764), and M. Postlethwayt, *Universal Dictionary of Trade and Commerce* (London: Printed for W. Strahan, 1774). If we add Hume's *Essays* (which would probably not be admitted to so pious a household), these are practically the same books as those quoted in the *Paper Credit*.

[100] Francis Baring, *Observations on the Establishment of the Bank of England* (London: Minerva Press, 1797), second edition, pp. 22 and 47.

in somewhat different circumstances, the Bank applied this method rather harshly.

The years preceding the crisis of 1792-3 had been years of great prosperity, which, in the last twelve months before the crisis, assumed the character of an inflationary boom. The tide had already turned, however, in the last few months of 1792, and the outbreak of the war with France led in February 1793 to a financial panic, caused by the failure first of a well-known house in London, then of a big banker in Newcastle and finally of numerous country banks all over England. The general state of alarm, and the discredit into which the notes of the country banks fell, led to an extensive and prolonged demand for guineas and Bank of England notes. The directors of the Bank, who for the past six months had seen their demand liabilities mount and their cash reserves dwindle, finally lost their heads and suddenly refused to grant further accommodation, leaving "the unfortunate public to shift for itself".[101] The result was an unheard of intensification of the financial panic and the danger of universal failure. After pressure by the Government on the Bank to relax its attitude had failed to produce any result, a rapidly appointed committee of the House of Commons[102] recommended that Exchequer bills to the amount of 5,000,000 pounds should be issued (under the direction of a board of commissioners appointed for the purpose) to provide the mercantile community with the means to raise cash. The mere announcement that this step would be taken went far to stay the panic, and, in fact, only a fraction of the authorised amount of Exchequer bills had to be issued before normal conditions were restored.

This drain on the resources of the Bank of England had occurred at a time when the exchanges were favourable and when in fact gold was being imported in small quantities. It was a classical case of what was later to become known as an 'internal' as distinguished from an 'external' drain. But it took some years more for the Bank of England to learn that the way to meet such an internal drain was to grant credits liberally, and then, in learning this lesson, it forgot that in the case of an external drain exactly the opposite measures were called for.

---

[101] *A Letter to the R. H. William Pitt on the Conduct of the Bank Directors* (London: Printed for J. Stockdale, 1796), p. 11.

[102] See *Report from the Select Committee on the State of Commercial Credit*, April 29, 1793, reprinted in *Irish University Press Series of British Parliamentary Papers*, Monetary Policy, General, vol. 1 (Shannon, Ireland: Irish University Press, 1969), pp. 11-22.

The first two years of the war with France, although free from major financial disturbances, gradually created a situation of considerable difficulty for the Bank. On the one hand expenditure for the English army on the Continent, subsidies to the allies, bad harvests in England, and France's return to a gold currency led to a continual and increasing drain of gold from England. On the other hand insistent and repeated demands from the Government for loans not only made it impossible for the Bank to contract the note circulation, but actually led to a considerable expansion. When finally, towards the end of 1795, the foreign exchanges began to fall rapidly and the export of gold assumed alarming proportions, and repeated protests to the Government had failed to lessen the demands from that quarter, the Bank (which was still prevented by the usury law from charging a rate of interest in excess of 5 per cent) made the sensational announcement, on the last day of that year, that in future

> whenever bills sent in for discount shall in any day amount to a larger sum than it shall be resolved to discount on that day, a pro rata proportion of such bills in each parcel as are not otherwise objectionable, will be returned to the person sending in the same, without regard to the respectability of the party sending in the bills, or the solidity of the bills themselves.[103]

This recourse to a rationing of credit caused renewed stringency in the money market in the spring of 1796 and evoked loud protests from the City. A committee of merchants and bankers even proposed a plan for a new Board of Credit, a kind of rival institution to the Bank of England, which was to relieve the dearth of cash.

It is not easy to reconcile these complaints about the continued scarcity of money during this period with the no less insistent complaints about the high prices, and with the continued unfavourable course of the exchanges. While, however, a really satisfactory account of the exact course of events could only be given after a good deal of research, there can be no doubt that the immediate cause of the final suspension of cash payments by the Bank in 1797 was a renewed internal drain. The latter part of 1796 had brought a new wave of failures of mercantile and banking houses all over the country. The apprehension of a French invasion heightened the

---

[103] See T. Tooke, *History of Prices* (London: Longman, Orme, Brown, Green, & Longmans, 1838), vol. 1, 1838, p. 200.

alarm, and when in February 1797 a single French frigate actually landed 1,200 men in Fishguard in Wales, a run on the Bank of England started, which in the course of a few days reduced its already much impaired reserves by one-half.

It is idle to speculate today as to whether the Bank, if it had continued to pay in cash so long as it could, would have been able to allay the panic before its reserves of coin had been exhausted.[104] The fact is that Pitt, being informed of the state of affairs by a deputation from the Bank on Sunday, February 26, 1797, forbade the directors, by an Order in Council of that date, to continue

> issuing any cash payments until the sense of Parliament can be taken on that subject, and the proper measures thereon, for maintaining the means of circulation, and supporting the public and commercial credit of the kingdom at this important conjuncture.[105]

On the following day the contents of the Order in Council were conveyed to the House of Commons in a special Message from the King, and the House thereupon immediately resolved to appoint a committee "to examine and state the total amount of the outstanding demands on the Bank of England, and likewise of the funds for discharging the same". A Committee of Secrecy of fifteen members was accordingly chosen by ballot on March 1st, and proceeded at once with its task. A special committee was also appointed by the House of Lords on the following day, and on March 7th was supplanted by a Committee of Secrecy of fifteen "to enquire into the causes which produced the Order in Council of 26th of February last".

In the course of March and April both committees took extensive evidence, the Commons committee calling nineteen witnesses and the Lords sixteen. Both committees called largely the same persons, primarily representatives of the Bank of England, merchants, the secretary of the Country Banks Association, and Henry Thornton, who seems to have been the sole representative of the London Bankers. The reason why he was selected is probably that, in addition to his being a member of the House of Commons, his firm

---

[104] As Ricardo later thought it might have done. See *Proposals for a Secure and Economical Currency*, in *Works*, ed. John Ramsay McCulloch (London: John Murray, 1816), p. 406.

[105] The texts of the various documents connected with the Bank Restriction have been conveniently collected together by A. Allardyce, *An Address to the Proprietors of the Bank of England*, third edition with additions (London: W. J. & J. Richardson, 1798).

was particularly widely connected with country banks. The list, which he gave in the course of his evidence, of places in which his bank had country correspondents in 1797 is largely the same as that for 1800, the first year for which we can reconstruct a complete list. In that year, Down, Thornton & Free had altogether twenty-three country correspondents. They were mainly in the Midlands, the North, and Scotland, with a few in the Southwest.[106]

But Thornton had something more to offer than just the knowledge and experience of a banker with wide connections all over the country. It is clear from his evidence that he had already thought deeply about the problems of credit. Indeed, there is some reason for believing, despite a statement in the preface to the *Paper Credit* which gives a contrary impression, that he was perhaps at that time already engaged on a work on the subject. This at least seems to follow from a statement, which we no longer have any means of checking,

> that while, during one of his elections, he had been engaged all day in a hot canvass, toiling through the streets of Southwark, he writes to his wife that he secured a couple of hours in the evening to carry on his work on Paper Credit.[107]

As the elections of 1802 took place some months after the book had appeared, this statement must evidently refer to the elections of 1796, so that Thornton would appear to have worked on the book for six years.[108]

---

[106] I am indebted to Mr. H. A. Shannon for a complete list of the country correspondents of Down, Thornton & Free, and later of Pole & Co., from 1800 to 1825. In 1800, in addition to the places mentioned in the evidence, they had correspondents in Aberdeen, Brecon (Wales), Sheffield, and Stafford. And as regards the towns mentioned in the evidence they now had two correspondents in both Bristol and Edinburgh, but apparently no longer had any in Ashburton and Sleaford (assuming that the bankers in these places mentioned in 1793 were 'correspondents' and not merely 'acquaintances'). The number grew from twenty-three in 1800 to a maximum of forty-nine in 1813, and was still forty-one in 1825 when the firm went out of business. In that year fourteen of their country correspondents seem to have failed or otherwise come to an end, eight to have transferred to Williams, Deacon & Co., and the rest to other London banks.

[107] Colquhoun, *Wilberforce*, op. cit., p. 283.

[108] Certainly the statement cannot refer to an earlier date, for Thornton did not marry until March 1796; nor is there any indication in his diary for 1795 that he was then occupied with questions of this kind.

Whether this is true or not, Thornton's evidence, which is re-printed in full in Appendix I of this volume,[109] gives, in the course of the discussion of the causes of the panic of 1797, a careful analysis of the interrelations between the different parts of the monetary circulation and of the factors determining the demand for the different kinds of media of circulation. Incidentally he also throws a certain amount of light on such problems as the factors which affect "the disposition of persons to detain bank notes", the role of the rate of interest, and in particular the difference between the position of a private banker and the position of the Bank of England. He does not yet, however, deal with the question of the depreciation of the currency and the factors influencing the foreign exchanges, which were to be the main topics of discussion in the years to come, and on which he was to make the major contribution in his book of 1802.

There had been, indeed, even before this time, much concern about the unfavourable state of the exchanges and even suggestions that this might have been due to an over-issue of bank notes.[110] We must not forget that the recent spectacle of the depreciation of the French assignats had made the phenomenon of inflation as familiar to the English public as it is at the present time, and that it certain-ly did not require any very profound knowledge to realise that an increase of paper money would lead to a fall in its value. But at the time of the crisis of 1797, the exchanges had recovered and re-mained fairly favourable for more than two years; and the Bank was even able to replenish its much depleted gold reserves. The restric-tion of cash payments, however, which may have been justified as a temporary expedient, was renewed again and again, and remained in force for altogether twenty-four years.

Up till the end of 1799 it can hardly be said that there existed any appreciable degree of inflation. The demands for accommoda-tion of the Government were kept within fairly narrow limits and, since the general depression of trade also kept private demands for credit low, there was little temptation for the bank to expand its circulation. Towards the beginning of the year 1800, however, the situation altered. Increased war expenditures and the unsatisfactory receipts from the new taxes led to renewed Government borrowing

---

[109] [I.e., *An Enquiry into the Nature and Effects of the Paper Credit of Great Britain.* -Ed.]

[110] Cf. William Anderson, *The iniquity of banking; or banknotes proved to be an injury to the public, and the real cause of the present exorbitant prices of provisions* (London: J. S. Jordan, 1797).

from the Bank on a large scale, and as early as the middle of 1799 the exchanges began to fall and prices to rise. Most attention was attracted by the rise in the price of gold bullion which in the autumn of 1800 reached a premium of 10 per cent. This led to attacks on the Bank in a host of pamphlets. The one which drew most attention was a pamphlet by Walter Boyd, who had already taken a prominent part in the discussion of the measures of 1797, and had become known as one of the sponsors of the proposed rival note-issuing institution.[111] Boyd claimed, with somewhat questionable justification, that it had been reserved to him

> to assign, as the cause of the general rise, which almost all things have experienced within the last two or three years (and which grain, as the article that comes most frequently in contact with money, feels the soonest and the most) the existence of a great Bank, invested with the power of issuing paper, professing to be payable on demand, but which, in fact, the Bank which issues it, is not obliged to pay.[112]

Boyd had the satisfaction that, even before his *Letter to Pitt* appeared in print, his argument was apparently confirmed by a statement which the Bank of England submitted at the request of the House of Commons, and which showed that the note circulation had increased from the date of the restriction to December 6, 1800, from 8.6 to 15.5 million pounds. In the debate in the House which followed, Henry Thornton agreed that

> as to the assertion that the increased issue of Bank paper was the cause of the dearness of provisions, he would not deny that it might have some foundation; but he would contend that its effect was far from being as great as was being alleged; and as to the

---

[111] Walter Boyd, *A Letter to the Right Honourable William Pitt on the Influence of the Stoppage of Specie at the Bank of England on the Prices of Provisions and Other Commodities* (London: Printed for J. Wright by T. Gillet, 1801). See also two earlier pamphlets, *The Cause of the Present Threatened Famine Traced to its Real Source, viz. an Actual Depreciation of our Circulation, Occasioned by the Paper Currency, etc., etc.,* by *Common Sense* (London: R. B. Scott, 1800), and *Thoughts on the Present Prices of Provisions, their Causes and Remedies,* by an Independent Gentleman [John Symmons] (London: T. Reynolds, 1800); and of a slightly later date *Profusion of Paper Money, not Deficiency in Harvests; Taxation, not Speculation, the Principal Causes of the Sufferings of the People, containing . . . and an important inference from Mr. H. Thornton's speech in Parliament on March 26th,* by a Banker (London: Printed for J. S. Jordan by W. Nicholson, printer, 1802). (The reference is actually to Thornton's speech on March 23, 1801, quoted below.)

[112] Loc. cit., p. 60.

depreciation of Bank paper arising from the exchange being against this country, it was at present only 12 per cent and was produced, not by the mismanagement of the Bank, but by the difference between imports and exports, the latter of which had risen above the former from the extraordinary importations of provisions.[113]

There is reason to doubt whether this condensed report of Henry Thornton's speech does justice to his argument. It is clearly unfair to regard Thornton as an apologist of the Bank of England, and the too often repeated accusation of bias is particularly baseless when it is founded on the wrong assumption that he was a director or even Governor of the Bank. It is, nevertheless, evident that he regarded the argument of Boyd and others, who attributed all the difficulties merely to an excessive issue, as unduly simplified and misleading. He was still too much impressed by the acute scarcity of money which had only recently been felt; and events, indeed, proved that before inflation was to set in on a scale such that there could be no doubt about its existence, the pound was to make at least a partial recovery.

It is very likely that, at least in the shape in which it was ulti-mately published, the *Paper Credit* was intended partly as a reply to Boyd. Others, who had attempted to reply, had not been particular-ly successful,[114] and for some twelve months Boyd's argument seemed to hold the field. But when, in February or March 1802, Thornton's work appeared, it immediately took first place and provided the basis from which all further discussion proceeded.

This essay cannot attempt to summarise the argument of the work or even to point out all its merits. It would take a great deal of space merely to mention all the points in respect to which Thornton's treatment constituted an important advance on earlier discussions, and it must suffice to indicate a few passages which deserve special attention. It may be true, as has often been asserted, that his exposition lacks system and in places is even obscure, but

[113] Cf. *The Parliamentary Register; or, History of the Proceedings and Debates of the Houses of Lords and Commons*, printed for J. Debrett; First Session, First Parliament of the United Kingdom and Ireland, vol. 14, vol. 76 of series, 1801, p. 556. The report there is fuller than in *Hansard*. An even fuller report, judging by contempo-rary references, appears to be contained in yet another publication, referred to as *Woodfall's Parliamentary Debates*, which I have not been able to trace. [This appears to have been William Woodfall, *An Impartial Report of the Debates that Occur in the Two Houses of Parliament* (London: T. Chapman, 1794). -Ed.]

[114] See particularly Sir Francis Baring, *Observations on the Publication of Walter Boyd* (London: Printed for J. Sewell, 1801).

too much can be made of this defect. And there will be few readers who will not be impressed by the acumen and the balance of mind displayed throughout the exposition. Thornton's achievement lies much more in his contribution to general theory than in his diagnosis of the situation of the particular moment. And if, as may well be the case, it can be argued that his judgement of the situation of the moment and his forecasts were less correct than those of some of his contemporaries who used cruder reasoning, this does not detract from the lasting value of his work. We have to judge it not as a controversial pamphlet on the questions of the day, but as one of the works in which problems of the moment have led the author to go down to fundamentals and to treat them for their general significance.

It seems that on the whole the arrangement of the book follows the order in which the author's thoughts developed. The first part, after two short introductory chapters, is mainly devoted to pointing out the dangers of an excessive contraction of the issue of paper, and the causes of what became known as an 'internal drain'.[115] It is in this context that Thornton develops his important views about the 'motives for holding' money, the factors which determine the relative demand for the different kinds of media of circulation, and a fairly elaborate theory of the effects of changes in the 'rapidity of circulation'.[116] He discusses the effects of the 'state of confidence' on the willingness to 'provide for contingencies' by holding money or assets which can be more or less easily converted into money, and in certain later passages he takes account of the 'loss sustained by keeping money' and the effects of an increase of money on the rate of interest.[117] And it is in these discussions that he makes his main contributions to the theory of credit properly so-called: that is, to that branch of monetary theory which has only just recently again begun to attract attention under the title of 'liquidity preference'. It is largely in this connexion also that he incidentally provides a great deal of descriptive information on the organisation of the English monetary and banking system. One does not realise how full this description is until one finds it summarised in systematic form in the review article by Francis Horner which has yet to be mentioned. Of special interest in this connexion is the explanation of how "by the transfer of debts in the books of the banker a large

---

[115] Chapter 4.
[116] Pp. 96, 232.
[117] Pp. 83, 91, 96, 232, 234, 235.

part of what are termed cash payments are effected", and the implied recognition of the essential similarity of bank notes and bank deposits.[118]

There are several other little points in these early chapters, such as the remark about the relative rigidity of wages,[119] and the reference to the movement of commodity stocks,[120] which show surprising insight into the problems of industrial fluctuations. But Thornton's best-known achievement does not come until later when he deals with the problems relating to the foreign exchanges. He first takes up this topic in chapter 5, where he treats the effects of an external drain, i.e., an outflow of gold which is primarily caused by an unfavourable change in the balance of trade.[121] This is the situation which he rightly thought to exist in the years immediately before and after the abandonment of the gold standard in 1797. He is fully aware that a relative excess of bank notes "may arise from other causes besides that of a too great emission of paper",[122] and that in such a situation "the bank should not only not increase, but that it should, perhaps, very greatly diminish it, if it would endeavour to prevent gold from going out".[123] His very modern doubts about such a policy of deflation (doubts by reference to which he attempts partly to justify the Bank of England's policy) are "whether the bank, in the attempt to produce this very low price, may not, in a country circumstanced as Great Britain is, so exceedingly distress trade and discourage manufactures as to impair . . . those sources of our returning wealth to which we must chiefly trust for the restoration of our balance"[124] as to frustrate the main purpose.

The problem of the effects of an absolute increase of the circulation, as it was the last to arise in his experience, is also the last to be taken up in his book. What is most impressive here is the methodical development of the argument. He commences by giving a brilliant exposition of the mechanism of the change in relative prices in the two countries concerned, which already contains practically all of the doctrine which, 120 years later, was 'rediscovered' as the purchasing power parity theory.[125] Then after showing

---

[118] P. 101 and footnote on p. 134.
[119] Pp. 119 and 189-190.
[120] Footnote on p. 120.
[121] Footnote on p. 150.
[122] P. 225.
[123] P. 151.
[124] P. 152.
[125] Pp. 198-199.

how a local change of prices in a particular part of any country will soon be corrected by a reduction of sales to, and an increase of purchases from, other parts of the country,[126] he proceeds to apply the same argument to the relations between two different countries.

All of this is, of course, the theory of the mechanism of international gold movements, and of the foreign exchanges, which later became associated with the names of Ricardo and John Stuart Mill. It has now become clear that in so far as Mill (and later Professor Taussig[127]) differed from and improved upon Ricardo they just resumed Thornton's argument. Ricardo's unwillingness to recognise that the excess of the circulation might be an effect as well as a cause of the unfavourable balance of trade, which led him to criticise Thornton at some length,[128] caused this whole theory to remain for a long time in a much more rigid and unsatisfactory form than that which it had originally received at the hands of Thornton.

Great as this achievement is, to many readers Thornton will appear to reach the height of his intellectual power in the penultimate chapter in which he proceeds to meet various objections, and in particular to refute the erroneous argument "that the proper limitation of bank notes may be sufficiently secured by attending merely to the nature of the security for which they are given".[129] It is here that, in summarising earlier points, he sometimes finds the happiest formulations; he also breaks entirely new ground in an attempt to elucidate the effects of a credit expansion in greater detail. He sees that the expansion of credit will in the first instance lead to the employment of "antecedently idle persons", but adds that as these are limited in number, the increased issue "will set to work labourers, of whom a part will be drawn from other, and perhaps, not less useful occupations".[130] This leads him (after some animadversions of Hume's suggestion that it is only in "the intermediate situation between the acquisition of money and the rise of prices that the increasing quantity of gold and silver is favourable to industry") to one of the earliest expositions of what has become

---

[126] Pp. 208-211.

[127] F. W. Taussig, *International Trade* (New York: Macmillan, 1928).

[128] *The High Price of Bullion* (1810), *Works*, ed. John Ramsay McCulloch (London: John Murray, 1810), pp. 268-269. For further criticisms of Thornton's views by Ricardo, see the latter's notes on Thornton's book as reproduced in *Minor Papers on the Currency Questions, 1809-1823*, by David Ricardo, ed. Jacob H. Hollander (Baltimore, Md.: The Johns Hopkins University Press, 1932).

[129] P. 244.

[130] P. 236.

known as the doctrine of 'forced saving'. The "augmentation of stock", which may be brought about by an excessive issue of paper, is due to the fact that the labourer "may be forced by his necessity to consume fewer articles, though he may exercise the same industry" and "this saving" may be supplemented by "a similar defalcation of the revenues of the unproductive members of society".[131] And Thornton is careful to add that the increase in output will never be proportional to the increase in the quantity of money and that therefore a general rise in prices is inevitable.[132]

The discussion of the proper limitation of issues leads on to the second point of primary importance in this chapter, the discussion of the role of the rate of interest. The statutory limitation of the rate of interest which the Bank may charge has the effect, he says, that at times this rate will be much lower than the mercantile rate of profits, and will in consequence lead to an undesirable expansion of credit unless the Bank takes other measures to keep down the volume of credit.[133] This is a remarkable anticipation of the distinction between the market rate and the 'natural' or 'equilibrium' rate of interest which since the work of Knut Wicksell has played such an important role in the discussion of these problems. With this idea, along with the idea of forced saving, Thornton was for the first time in possession of the two main elements which it was left for Wicksell, nearly a hundred years later, successfully to combine into one of the most promising contributions to the theory of credit and industrial fluctuations.[134]

The points we have mentioned, though they are the most important, do not by any means exhaust Thornton's contributions to knowledge. They may, however, serve as an indication of the character of the work which put the discussion of monetary problems on a new plane. Its outstanding merit was soon recognised. On June 28, 1802, we find Jeremy Bentham writing to Dumont:

---

[131] P. 239.

[132] Pp. 239 et seq.

[133] Pp. 253-256.

[134] On the significance of Thornton's views on this point, and the further development of these theories, see the first chapter of my *Prices and Production* (London: Routledge, second edition, 1935 [reprinted New York: Augustus M. Kelley, 1967. -Ed.], and "A Note on the Development of the Doctrine of 'Forced Saving'", *Quarterly Journal of Economics*, November 1932 [also in *Profits, Interest and Investments; and Other Essays on the Theory of Industrial Fluctuations* (London: Routledge & Kegan Paul, 1939; reprinted New York: Augustus M. Kelley, 1969; 1975). -Ed.]

This is a book of real merit—a controversy with him would be really instructive. I have tumbled it over but very imperfectly, that not being the order of the day, and for fear of calling off my attention, and absorbing my capacity of exertion. But one of these days I may not improbably grapple with him. Admitting all his facts, with thanks,—agreeing with him in almost all his conclusions,—but disputing with him what seems (as far as I have yet seen) to be his most material conclusions, viz., that paper money does more harm than good. Here is a book of real instruction, if the French were wise enough to translate it; the style is clear, plain, without ornament or pretension, the reasoning is close.[135]

A fact which was of great importance in leading to the rapid diffusion of Thornton's ideas was that Francis Horner devoted to it, in the first number of the new *Edinburgh Review*, a brilliant article of thirty pages in which, even if he perhaps passed over some of the finer points in Thornton's analysis, he gave an exposition of the main argument of the book in a form which was considerably more systematic and coherent than the original version.[136] Although to some extent critical, he gave the work the deserved praise as "the most valuable unquestionably of all the publications which the momentous event of the Bank Restriction had produced". In particular his reproduction verbatim of one of the most important passages on the effect of price movements on the balance of trade and the foreign exchanges probably exerted as much influence as the book itself.

The developments of the years immediately following the publication of the *Paper Credit* had the result of causing further discussion to centre almost entirely upon the effects of an over-issue on the foreign exchanges and the price of bullion. The immediate cause of the renewed discussion was not so much the situation in England as developments in Ireland. The restriction of cash payments had been extended (merely for the sake of uniformity and despite the fact that the exchanges had been favourable to Dublin) to the Bank of Ireland. This institution seems very rapidly to have taken advantage of the new situation, and in the first six years it quadrupled its note

---

[135] J. Bentham, *Works*, ed. J. Bowring (Edinburgh: Tait, 1838), vol. 10, p. 389.

[136] [*The Edinburgh Review*, vol. 1, no. 1, October 1802, pp. 172-201. Hayek initially intended to reprint Horner's article in his edition of Thornton's work, but, as he writes, "this plan had to be abandoned in favour of the inclusion of Thornton's speeches on the Bullion Report. It is, however, to be hoped that not only this, but also some of the other very interesting articles on economic questions which Francis Horner contributed to the *Edinburgh Review*, will some day be reprinted." -Ed.]

circulation. The result was that by 1803 the rate of exchange on London had fallen by about 20 per cent. The fact that this was due to the mismanagement of the note issue was particularly clear in this case because the exchanges on Belfast, which had its own circulation consisting largely of coin and notes of local banks, had remained at par, and the Dublin exchange showed the same depreciation in Belfast as in London.

Sometime before this, however, and shortly after the appearance of the *Paper Credit*, Henry Thornton had already expressed, in one of the parliamentary debates, his concern about developments in Ireland. In the second reading of the Bank of Ireland Restriction Bill on April 26, 1802,

> Mr. Henry Thornton observed that this bill had been introduced to accompany the restriction on the Bank of England. With respect to the restriction on the Bank of England no danger could result from it; that Bank was a body extremely respectable, who were sufficiently disposed to restrain the circulation of their own paper, and to limit within due bounds the circulation of the country, which they were better enabled to do, as they possessed a monopoly of the issue of paper in the metropolis. With respect to the Bank of Ireland, the case was different; other banks issued paper in the same place where that existed, and a restriction on that bank would therefore be ineffectual. It was important, however, for the House to bear in mind, that too great an emission of paper produced the ground on which the continuance of the restriction on the Bank was founded, as, by raising the price of commodities, it impeded their exportation, and consequently turned exchanges against us. Ireland appeared extremely liable to dangers of this kind; when, however, the discontinuance of the restriction on the Bank of England should be under discussion, the circumstances of the course of exchanges against Ireland ought not to operate as a reason against that discontinuance, and they must provide in that country, as in this, cash for their paper. . . .[137]

As time went on, however, it became increasingly clear that the Bank of England, too, was not keeping its circulation within safe limits. And in April 1804 Thornton (in the marginal annotations of a copy of Lord King's *Thoughts on the Effects of the Bank Restrictions*

---

[137] *Parliamentary Register* (Second Session of First Parliament of United Kingdom and Ireland, vol. 18), vol. 80 of series, p. 95.

which he evidently made for a friend)[138] already expresses his apprehension of the directors of "the Bank perhaps not sufficiently perceiving that a limitation of Paper will improve the exchanges", although he still thinks that, compared with the Bank of Ireland, "the Directors of the Bank of England, if they have erred at all, have erred but a little". But at the same time he admits that

> if the Committee of the House of Commons on Irish Currency now sitting were to state in their Report to the House in distinct language that they are persuaded that a Reduction of Bank Paper must have a tendency to improve the Exchange even this hint coming from such a quarter and applying itself as is necessary to the Bank of England as well as that of Ireland would have all the desired effect.

Of this Committee on the Irish Currency to which Thornton here refers and which had been appointed early in the year Thornton himself was a member. It seems even that he was one of the most influential and active members,[139] and in view of this confessed intention to give a hint to the Bank of England, the Report of this Committee, which has justly been celebrated as anticipating the more famous Bullion Report in almost every important respect, gains still further significance. It is not known, however, what part, if any, Henry Thornton took in the drafting of the Report, and in

---

[138] Lord King, *Thoughts on the Effects of the Bank Restrictions*, the second edition enlarged, including Some Remarks on the Coinage (London: Cadell & Davies, Strand, and J. Debrett, Piccadilly, 1804). See Appendix II [of Hayek's edition of Thornton's book, p. 312], where these manuscript notes are reproduced and a full description of the volume from which they are taken is given. It appears from this that Henry Thornton gave the annotated copy of Lord King's book to a friend, Mr. Scott Moncrieff, whose name also appears in Thornton's diary, who in turn sent it to J. A. Maconochie, evidently the same James Allan Maconochie, advocate and Sheriff of Orkney, who owned the manuscript notes of Adam Smith's Glasgow Lectures (see Edwin Cannan's Introduction to his edition of Adam Smith's *Lectures on Justice, Police, Revenue and Arms* (Oxford: Clarendon Press, 1896), p. xvi). The passages quoted above occur on pp. 29 and 126 of the pamphlet [see pp. 316 and 321 of Hayek's edition of Thornton]. Acknowledgement is due to the Goldsmiths' Librarian of the University of London for permission to reproduce the notes from the copy in his library.

[139] Among the letters of Francis Horner in the possession of Lady Eleanor Langman there is an unpublished letter to his brother Leonard, undated but probably written in April 1804, in which he writes about the Irish Committee: "The inquiries of this Committee will give us a good many curious facts. Thornton attends these constantly; and he understands these matters better than anybody else in London." For this quotation I am indebted to Professor F. W. Fetter, who has had an opportunity to inspect the unpublished letters of Francis Horner.

view of the fact that the Committee counted among its members other competent writers on currency, in particular, Henry Parnell, who in the same year also published a pamphlet on the Irish currency,[140] we cannot even venture a surmise.

Of the development of Thornton's ideas in the next six years we know nothing. Nor is this the place for writing a history of the monetary developments of these years or of the further discussions to which they gave rise. This has been done well by others. Suffice it to say that in 1810 the continued rise of prices and fall of the exchanges caused increasing and widespread apprehension, and that eventually, on a motion of Francis Horner, on February 19th of that year, a Select Committee was "appointed to enquire into the Cause of the High Price of Gold Bullion, and to take into consideration the State of the Circulating Medium and of the Exchanges between Great Britain and Foreign Parts".

Of the deliberations of this famous Bullion Committee, and the exact responsibility of its individual members for the writing of the Report, we also know very little. Francis Horner was elected chairman, and on the twenty-two days (from February 22nd to March 26th) on which the Committee took evidence, he usually took the chair, although his place was occasionally taken by Huskisson and three times by Thornton.

On the drafting of the report there is an oft-quoted passage from one of the published letters of Francis Horner which deserves to be included here:

> The Report is in truth very clumsily and prolixly drawn; stating nothing but very old doctrines on the subject it treats of, and stating them in a more imperfect form than they have frequently appeared before. It is a motley composition by Huskisson, Thornton, and myself; each having written parts which are tacked together without any care to give them an uniform style or a very exact connection. One great merit the Report, however, possesses; that it declares in very plain and pointed terms, both the true doctrine and the existence of a great evil growing out of the neglect of that doctrine. By keeping up the discussion, which I mean to do, and by forcing it on the attention of Parliament, we

[140] H. Parnell, *Observations upon the State of Currency in Ireland and upon the Course of Exchange between Dublin and London* (Dublin: Printed for M. N. Mahon, 1804).

shall in time (I trust) effect the restoration of the old and only safe system.[141]

There is also a somewhat obscure and probably incorrect statement of Colquhoun, who speaks of the "long deliberations in the bullion committee in which Horner and Henry Thornton carried their motions against the Government 11 to 4".[142] As the total membership of the Committee numbered twenty-two, this statement, allowing for a number of absentees, is not absurd on the face of it, although nothing else is known of any motions on which the Committee voted.

The report was not submitted to the House until the evening of the day (June 8th) preceding the prorogation of Parliament. But, it is alleged,

> the substance of the report was immediately circulated in the newspapers and the alarm which it occasioned among the bankers and the merchants, who were accustomed to look to the Bank for discounting their bills, was followed by many failures of mercantile houses in London, as well as of some country banks.[143]

The publication of the report led to an intense discussion of the problems it raised in a host of pamphlets, but as it had been too late to discuss it in the session in which it had been presented, it was some time before it was taken up in the House. In fact, it was not until May 6, 1811, that Francis Horner moved the House into Committee to consider the report. There occurred a four-day debate in which Thornton, Horner, Huskisson, Canning, and a number of the other members of the Bullion Committee took part. A carefully prepared speech which Thornton delivered on the second day, together with another made a week later, was published by him in pamphlet form. This first part of the debate revolved around sixteen resolutions moved by Horner, of which the last and most important proposed

---

[141] Francis Horner to J. A. Murray in a letter dated June 26, 1810, reprinted in *Memoirs and Correspondence of Francis Horner*, ed. L. Horner (London: John Murray, 1843), vol. 2, p. 47.

[142] Colquhoun, *Wilberforce*, op. cit., p. 301.

[143] T. H. B. Oldfield, *Representative History of Great Britain and Ireland* (London: Baldwin, Cradock, & Jay, 1816), vol. 2, p. 345. The crisis mentioned occurred only in September and is the same as that in which, as we have seen, Henry Thornton's firm experienced difficulties, and in which, as may be added here, the firm of his oldest brother Samuel came to grief. See also W. Smart, *Economic Annals of the Nineteenth Century, 1801-1820* (London: Macmillan, 1910), p. 255.

> That in order to revert gradually to this Security, and to enforce meanwhile a due Limitation of the Paper of the Bank of England, as well as of all the other Bank Paper of the Country, it is expedient to amend the Act which suspends the Cash Payments of the Bank, by altering the time, till which the suspension shall continue, from Six Months after the Ratification of a Definitive Treaty of Peace, to that of Two Years from the present Time.

By this time, although he had not altered his theoretical position in any essential respect, Thornton had become thoroughly convinced of the mismanagement of the note issue and the overwhelming danger of an excessive circulation in general, and was no longer afraid to apply the remedy of a severe contraction. His speech, which is really a lecture on the dangers of a paper currency, is particularly interesting for the increased importance which he had now come to attach to the rate of interest. He not only emphasised the power of a high rate of interest to attract gold,[144] but described the whole "subject of the rate of interest" as "a very great and turning point".[145] He supplemented his theory, as given in the *Paper Credit*, of how a rate of interest lower than the mercantile rate of profits led to an indefinite expansion of credit, by a discussion of the effect of an expectation of rising prices on the rate of interest, which in all important points anticipated Professor Irving Fisher's well-known distinction between the real and nominal rate of interest.[146]

In the vote which followed Horner's resolutions were all defeated, the first fifteen (which embodied the theoretical basis of his recommendations) by 151 to 75, the last and decisive one by 180 to 45. And to make quite certain of the victory, Vansittart, for the Government, moved on May 13th seventeen counter-resolutions, which in effect asserted that there was no divergence of value between notes and coin and that the high price of bullion was not due to any over-issue of notes. These resolutions led to a further debate, in the course of which Thornton took the opportunity to reply to a number of objections. The most interesting feature of this second speech is that in it Thornton explicitly retracts "an error to

---

[144] P. 331.

[145] P. 335.

[146] Pp. 335-336. See also p. 339, where Thornton speaks of "a rate of interest lower than that which was the natural one at the moment", and pp. 342-343. [This concept is central to much of Hayek's theoretical work in economics. See this volume, chapter 11, p. 190. -Ed.]

which he himself had once inclined", namely, the idea that an increase of the circulation, by stimulating production, might help to correct the exchanges.[147]

With these two speeches Thornton's known contributions to monetary theory come to an end. If, in the remaining three years of his life, he took any active part in the discussion which continued, nothing has been preserved in print. But although in Parliament his views had been defeated, largely for reasons of high policy, he lived long enough to see them widely accepted. And among those of his contemporaries who took an interest in these matters there existed little doubt that the new body of thought was mainly his creation. Even a comparative outsider, like Dr. Miller in his *Philosophy of History*, did justice to his contribution by describing his book, in 1816, as "forming an epoch in the history of the Science to which it belongs".[148] If some of his fellow economists, and particularly Ricardo, do not appear to have given him full credit and to have mentioned him only to criticise him, we can be sure that this was only due to the fact that among the public for which they wrote they could take a thorough acquaintance with Thornton's work for granted. But the effect was that in the course of time his fame faded before that of men whose contributions covered a much greater part of political economy, and then even the distinct contribution, which was undoubtedly his, began to be credited to his successors. For a long time John Stuart Mill, who in 1848, in his *Principles of Political Economy*, described the *Paper Credit* as even at his time "the clearest exposition that I am acquainted with, in the English language, of the modes in which credit is given and taken in a mercantile community",[149] was the last author to do anything like justice to Henry Thornton. And even Mill does not appear to have been quite aware that in his exposition of the mechanism of international gold movements he followed Thornton more than Ricardo. It was not until just before, and particularly since, the First World War that, with the great interest which a number of American economists (particularly Professors Hollander and Viner) have shown in the history of English monetary policy and monetary doctrines, his importance came again to be fully recognised.[150]

---

[147] This volume, chapter 15, p. 353.
[148] George Miller, *Lectures on the Philosophy of Modern History* (Dublin: Printed by Graisberry and Campbell for John Murray, 1816).
[149] Ashley's edition, footnote on p. 515.
[150] See D in the bibliographical notes at the end of this chapter.

BIBLIOGRAPHICAL NOTES[151]

A. The Works of Henry Thornton. *The Enquiry into the Nature and Effect of the Paper Credit of Great Britain* was published in February or March 1802[152] by J. Hatchard, of Piccadilly, as an octavo volume of 320 pages (I-XII and 13-320), price in boards 7s. An American edition appeared in Philadelphia, 1807, 272 pp., and it was reprinted by J. R. McCulloch in *A Select Collection of Scarce and Valuable Tracts on Paper Currency and Banking* (London: Printed by Lord Overstone, 1857), pp. 137-340. A French translation was undertaken, at Bentham's suggestion (see above), by P. E. L. Dumont, and six extracts of this translation appeared in the *Bibliothèque Britannique ou Receuil*, vol. 21, pp. 408-499, vol. 22, pp. 25-75, 145-216, 301-332, and 413-464, and vol. 23, pp. 3-31. This translation was then published in book form under the title *Recherches sûr la nature et les effets du credit du papier*, etc. (Geneva: De l'impr. de la Bibliothèque Brittanique, 1803), and seems now to be exceedingly rare. A German translation by L. H. Jakob, with notes and appendices, appeared under the title *Der Papier Credit von Grossbrittannien* (Halle: In der Ruffschen Verlagshandlung, 1803).

The Substance of two Speeches of Henry Thornton, Esq., in the Debate in the House of Commons on the Report of the Bullion Committee on May 7 and 14, 1811, were also published by Hatchard, as an octavo pamphlet of vii + 79 pages.

The Catalogue of the Library of the British Museum and the *Dictionary of National Biography* ascribe to Henry Thornton also the authorship of an anonymous pamphlet *On the Probable Effects of the Peace, with Respect to the Commercial Interest of Great Britain* (London: Hatchard, 1802). There seems, however, to be no ground for this ascription and internal evidence makes it rather unlikely that this pamphlet should be by Henry Thornton, since it deals largely with the effects of the peace on particular commodities in which Henry Thornton was not likely to be interested. The author may well, however, have been one of the merchant members of the Thornton family.

Apart from unsigned and mostly unidentified[153] contributions to the *Cheap Repository* tracts and the *Christian Observer*, Henry Thornton appears to have published nothing else. But after his death the following religious writings were edited by the guardian of his children, R. H. Inglis:

Family Prayers, by the late Henry Thornton, Esq., M.P., edited by R. H. I. (London: Hatchard, 1834), xii + 164 pp. This reached its thirty-first edition in 1854, and it has been said that "indeed the use of that book

---

[151] [Supplementary bibliographical notes have now been added throughout the text. -Ed.]

[152] Cf. *Christian Observer*, no. 1, published February 1, 1802, p. 3: "An Essay on Paper Credit by Henry Thornton, Esq., M.P., is expected to appear in a few days."

[153] See, however, above.

was the distinctive sign of true Evangelism" (G. W. E. Russell, *The Household of Faith* (London: Hodder & Stoughton, 1902)).

Family Commentary upon the Sermon of the Mount (London: J. Hatchard, 1835).

Family Commentary on Portions of the Pentateuch, in Lectures, with Prayers adapted to the subject, by Henry Thornton, edited by R. H. I. (London: J. Hatchard, 1837).

The volume entitled *Works of the late Henry Thornton, Esq., M.P.*, is a consecutively paginated reprint of the three works last named (856 pp.) of which only twelve copies were issued.

The *Lectures on the Ten Commandments* contained in the *Commentary on the Pentateuch* were originally written for Hannah More's *Cheap Repository*, and later also reprinted separately with prayers by R. H. Inglis (London: J. Hatchard, 1843).

Finally, a series of seven articles which Thornton had contributed to the *Christian Observer* were republished under the title *Three Female Characters* (London: J. Hatchard, 1846).

All the works of Henry Thornton as well as the *Christian Observer* were published by John Hatchard, the first bookseller of that name, and "a sound evangelical and resident of Clapham".

B. The *Manuscript Diary of Henry Thornton* and other Family Papers. The main source for the present sketch of the life of Henry Thornton are various manuscripts preserved by members of the family which the author has been privileged to use. Among these is a diary kept by Henry Thornton from January 1795 till February 1796 (i.e., the date of his marriage), containing almost daily entries for the first six months, and somewhat more irregular notes made during the later periods, with a few additions made in 1802, 1803, 1810, 1812, and 1814.

In this diary, the original of which is in the possession of Mr. E. M. Forster, Henry Thornton refers to a connected history of his life, which in 1803 he was writing for the benefit of his children. The original of this does not seem to have been preserved, but a copy of it is prefixed to a copy of the diary proper which is in the possession of Mrs. Dorothy Demarest. It was written at intervals between 1802 and 1809 and most of the longer quotations in the text are from this connected history. As, however, all the quotations used were taken from this copy before it was discovered that it contains copies of two different documents, the reference is throughout to the "MS. Diary of Henry Thornton". Earlier authors, particularly the sons of Wilberforce in the *Life* of their father and James Stephen who have used the same documents refer to them as "Private and Conversational Memoranda of Henry Thornton".

The author has also been able to use "MS. Recollections of Marianne Thornton", the daughter of Henry Thornton, written in 1857, and a few family letters, which are all in the possession of Mr. E. M. Forster.

C. Printed Sources on Henry Thornton and the Clapham Sect. The main printed sources on the life of Henry Thornton are James Stephen's essay on the Clapham Sect, first published in the *Edinburgh Review*, vol. 80, 1842, and many times reprinted in his *Essays in Ecclesiastical Biography* (page references in the text are to the Silver Library Edition, 1907, vol. 2) and John C. Colquhoun, *William Wilberforce, His Friends and His Times* (London, 1867). John Telford, *A Sect that Moved the World* (London: C. H. Kelly, 1907), the volume on *Clapham and the Clapham Sect* (Clapham: Clapham Antiquarian Society, 1927), and M. Seeley, *Later Evangelicals Fathers* (London: Seeley, Jackson, & Halliday, 1879) are useful collections of information on the Clapham Sect, mostly from earlier printed sources. The chapter on Henry Thornton in H. R. Fox Bourne, *London Merchants* (London: J. Hogg, 1869, second edition 1876) is unreliable. Some information on Henry Thornton is to be found in two memoirs of other members of his family, namely *The Book of Yearly Recollections of Samuel Thornton, Esq.*, edited for private circulation with a Preface and Introduction by his grandson John Thornton and printed by W. Clowes & Sons, 1891, and in P. M. Thornton, *Some Things we have Remembered: Samuel Thornton, Admiral 1797-1859, and Percy Melville Thornton 1841-1911* (London: Longmans, Green, 1912).

Of the biographies of Henry Thornton's friends those containing most information are *The Life of William Wilberforce*, by his sons R. I. and S. Wilberforce, 5 vols (London: John Murray, 1838); *The Correspondence of William Wilberforce*, edited by the same (London: John Murray, 1840), and *The Private Papers of William Wilberforce*, ed. A. M. Wilberforce (London: T. F. Unwin, 1897); *The Life and Letters of Zachary Macaulay*, by his grand-daughter Viscountess Knutsford (London: E. Arnold, 1901); the *Memoirs of the Life and Correspondence of Hannah More*, by William Roberts, third edition, 1835 (London: R. B. Seeley and W. Burnside, 1835); and the *Life of Hannah More*, by Henry Thompson (London: T. Cadell, 1838).

There are several modern biographies of Wilberforce of which only the one by R. Coupland (1923) need be mentioned. A *Life* of the elder James Stephen has been written by Sir George Stephen (Victoria, 1875) and sketches of his life will be found in the introductory chapters of the biographies of his son of the same name by C. E. Stephen (Gloucester: Printed for private circulation, 1906) and of his grandsons James Fitzjames Stephen, by Leslie Stephen (London: Smith, Elder, 1895), and Leslie Stephen, by F. W. Maitland (London: Duckworth, 1906). Biographies are also available of T. Clarkson, by J. Elmes (London: Blackader, 1854) and E. L. Griggs (London: Allen & Unwin, 1936); of Granville Sharp, by Prince Hoare (London: H. Colburn, 1820) and E. C. P. Lascelles (London: Oxford University Press, 1929); of Charles Grant, by H. Morris (London: John Murray, 1904); of John Shore (Lord Teignmouth) by his son (London: J. Hatchard, 1843); a *Life* of John Venn is prefixed to the collection of his Sermons (London: Printed by Ellerton and Henderson, 1814); and a Memoir of John Bowdler to the edition of his Works (London: G. Davidson, 1857).

D. Works on the Monetary History and Literature of the Bank Restriction Period. 1. *History*: In addition to the well-known works on the history of currency, banking, and industrial fluctuations by T. Tooke, H. D. Macleod, R. Bischop, A. Andréadès, M. Bouniatian, and A. E. Feavearyear the following should be especially mentioned: E. Cannan, Introduction to *The Paper Pound 1797-1821. A Reprint of the Bullion Report*, second edition (London: P. S. King, 1925); R. G. Hawtrey, *Currency and Credit*, third edition (London: Longmans, Green, 1928), chapter 18; W. Smart, *Economic Annals of the Nineteenth Century 1801-1820* (London: Macmillan, 1910); N. J. Silberling, "British Financial Experience, 1790-1830", *The Review of Economic Statistics*, prel. vol. I, 1919; and "Financial and Monetary Experience of Great Britain during the Napoleonic Wars", *Quarterly Journal of Economics*, vol. 38, 1924; A. Cunningham, *British Credit in the last Napoleonic War* (Cambridge: Cambridge University Press, 1910); A. W. Acworth, *Financial Reconstruction in England 1815-22* (London: P. S. King, 1925); G. O'Brien, "The Last Years of the Irish Currency", *Economic History* (A Supplement to the *Economic Journal*), vol. 1, no. 2, 1927; L. Wolowski, *Un chapitre de l'histoire financière de l'Angleterre, La suspension des payments de la Banque et le Bullion Report* (Paris: Bureau de la Revue Britannique, 1865); M. Phillips, *The Token Money of the Bank of England 1797-1816* (London: E. Wilson, 1900); P. Aretz, *Die Entwicklung der Diskontpolitik der Bank von England, 1780-1850* (Berlin: C. Heymann, 1916); E. Kellenberger, "Die Aufhebung der Barzahlung in England 1797 und ihre Folgen", *Jahrbücher für Nationalökonomie und Statistik*, III. F. vol. 51, 1916; J. Wolter, *Das staatliche Geldwesen Englands zu Zeit der Bankrestriktion* (Strasbourg: K. J. Trübner, 1917); A. M. de Jong, "De Engelsche Bank Restriction van 1797", *De Economist*, 72nd year, February-April 1923.

2. *Development of Monetary Theory:* J. H. Hollander, "The Development of the Theory of Money from Adam Smith to David Ricardo", *Quarterly Journal of Economics*, vol. 25, May 1911; J. Viner, *Canada's Balance of International Indebtedness*, 1900-1911 (Cambridge, Mass.: Harvard University Press, 1924); and *Studies in the Theory of International Trade* (London: Harper and Brothers, 1937); J. W. Angell, *The Theory of International Prices* (Cambridge, Mass.: Harvard University Press, 1926); C. Rist, *Histoire des Doctrines relatives au Crédit et la Monnaie* (Paris: Libraire du Receuil Sircy, 1938); A. Loria, *Studi sulla valore della moneta* (Turin: Fratelli Bocca, 1891); G. Krügel, *Der Bullion Bericht* (Rostock: C. Hinstorff, 1930); H. Leroi-Fürst, "Die Entwicklung der Lehre von der Zahlungsbilanz im 19. Jahrhundert bis 1873", *Archiv für Sozialwissenschaften und Sozialpolitik*, vol. 56, 1926; E. Fossati, "Ricardo und die Entstehung des Bullion Reports", *Zeitschrift für Nationalökonomie*, vols 4 and 5, 1933-4.

PART IV

CURRENTS OF THOUGHT
IN THE 19th CENTURY

FREDERIC BASTIAT (1801-1850), JULES DUPUIT (1804-1866), HERMANN HEINRICH GOSSEN (1810-1858)

Frédéric Bastiat[1]

Even those who may question the eminence of Frédéric Bastiat (1801-1850) as an economic theorist will grant that he was a publicist of genius. Joseph Schumpeter calls him "the most brilliant economic journalist who ever lived".[2] For our present purpose, we might well leave it at that. One might even grant Schumpeter's harsh assessment of Bastiat that "he was not a theorist" without seriously diminishing his stature. It is true that when, at the end of his extremely short career as a writer, he attempted to provide a theoretical justification for his general conceptions, he did not satisfy the professionals. It would indeed have been a miracle if a man who, after only five years as a regular writer on public affairs, attempted in a few months, and with a mortal illness rapidly closing in on him, to defend the points on which he differed from established doctrine had fully succeeded in this too. Yet one may ask whether it was not only his early death at the age of forty-nine that prevented him. His polemical writings, which in consequence are the most important ones he has left, certainly prove that he had an insight into what was significant and a gift for going to the heart of the matter that would have provided him with ample material for real contributions to science.

Nothing illustrates this better than the celebrated title of his essay: "What is Seen and What is Not Seen".[3] No one has ever stated more clearly in a single phrase the central difficulty of a rational economic policy and, I would like to add, the decisive argument for

---

[1] This section was originally published as the "Introduction" to a volume containing some of Bastiat's most successful writings for the general public: Frédéric Bastiat, *Selected Essays on Political Economy* (Princeton, N.J.: D. Van Nostrand, 1964), pp. ix-xii.

[2] [Joseph Schumpeter, *History of Economic Analysis* (New York: Oxford University Press, 1954), p. 500. -Ed.]

[3] [In Bastiat, *Selected Essays*, op. cit., pp. 1-50. -Ed.]

economic freedom. It is the idea compressed into these few words that made me use the word 'genius' in the opening sentence. It is indeed a text around which one might expound a whole system of libertarian economic policy.[4] And though it constitutes the title for only one of his essays, it provides the leading idea for many of them. Bastiat illustrates its meaning over and over again in refuting the fallacies of his time. I shall later indicate that, though the views he combats are today usually advanced only in a more sophisticated guise, they have basically not changed very much since Bastiat's time. But first I want to say a few words about the more general significance of his central idea.

This is simply that if we judge measures of economic policy solely by their immediate and concretely foreseeable effects, we shall not only not achieve a viable order but shall be certain progressively to extinguish freedom and thereby prevent more good than our measures will produce. Freedom is important in order that all the different individuals can make full use of the particular circumstances of which only they know. We therefore never know what beneficial actions we prevent if we restrict their freedom to serve their fellows in whatever manner they wish. All acts of interference, however, amount to such restrictions. They are, of course, always undertaken to achieve some definite objective. Against the foreseen direct results of such actions of government we shall in each individual case be able to balance only the mere probability that some unknown but beneficial actions by some individuals will be prevented. In consequence, if such decisions are made from case to case and not governed by an attachment to freedom as a general principle, freedom is bound to lose in almost every case. Bastiat was indeed right in treating freedom of choice as a moral principle that must never be sacrificed to considerations of expedience; because there is perhaps no aspect of freedom that would not be abolished if it were to be respected only where the concrete damage caused by its abolition can be pointed out.

Bastiat directed his arguments against certain ever-recurring fallacies as they were employed in his time. Few people would employ them today quite as naively as it was still possible to do then. But let the reader not deceive himself that these same fallacies no longer play an important role in contemporary economic discus-

---

[4] [The argument of Bastiat's essay is essentially the one adopted by Henry Hazlitt in his *Economics in One Lesson* (new edition, New York: Arlington House, 1979). -Ed.]

sion: they are today merely expressed in a more sophisticated form and are therefore more difficult to detect. The reader who has learnt to recognise these stock fallacies in their simpler manifestations will at least be on his guard when he finds the same conclusions derived from what appears to be a more scientific argument. It is characteristic of much of recent economics that by ever new arguments it has tried to vindicate those very prejudices which are so attractive because the maxims that follow from them are so pleasant or convenient: spending is a good thing, and saving is bad; waste benefits and economy harms the mass of the people; money will do more good in the hands of the government than in those of the people; it is the duty of government to see that everybody gets what he deserves; and so on.

None of these ideas has lost any of its power in our time. The only difference is that Bastiat, in combating them, was on the whole fighting on the side of the professional economists against popular beliefs exploited by interested parties, while similar proposals are today propagated by an influential school of economists in a most impressive and, to the layman, largely unintelligible garb. It is doubtful whether there is one among the fallacies which one might have hoped Bastiat had killed once and for all that has not experienced its resurrection. I shall give only one example. To an account of Bastiat's best-known economic fable, "The Petition of the Candlemakers against the Competition of the Sun", in which it is demanded that windows should be prohibited because of the benefit which the prosperity of the candlemakers would confer on everyone else, a well-known French textbook of the history of economics adds in its latest edition the following footnote: "It should be noted that according to Keynes—on the assumption of underemployment and in accordance with the theory of the multiplier—this argument of the candlemakers is literally and fully valid."[5]

The attentive reader will notice that, while Bastiat grapples with so many economic panaceas which are familiar to us, one of the main dangers of our time does not appear in his pages. Though he has to deal with various queer proposals for using credit which were current in his time, straight inflation through a government deficit seemed in his age not a major danger. An increase of expenditure means for him necessarily and immediately an increase in taxation. The reason is that, as among all people who have gone through a

---

[5] [Daniel Villey, *Petite histoire des grandes doctrines économiques*, third edition (Paris: Génin, 1954), p. 207. -Ed.]

major inflation within living memory, a continuous depreciation of money was not a thing which people would have put up with in his day. So if the reader should be inclined to feel superior to the rather simple fallacies that Bastiat often finds it necessary to refute, he should remember that in some other respects his compatriots of more than a hundred years ago were considerably wiser than our generation.

Jules Dupuit[6]

If one were to judge by the number of republications of works of former economists which have appeared in recent years, one might be tempted to believe that there is an intense revival of interest in classical economics. The Royal Economic Society, the London School of Economics, and one or two enterprising British publishers, as well as Professor Hollander[7] in America and Professor Einaudi[8] in Italy, have recently done much to make important but rare works of this kind available to a wider public. Earlier writers are constantly being rediscovered who still have contributions to make or who at least may claim credit for having anticipated advances which were only later incorporated into the main body of economic doctrine.

In most such cases such early writings have, by the time of their rediscovery, become so inaccessible that it needs the devotion of an enthusiastic editor to make them a part of the living literature of today. But it is not often even then that they are presented to the public in so attractive a form as in Professor Luigi Einaudi's magnificent collection of unpublished or rare writings of economists. And the economic works of the French engineer Jules Dupuit most assuredly deserve to be resuscitated. His articles, published about the middle of the last century in different French technical journals, contain one of the most remarkable early formulations of the

---

[6] [Review of Jules Dupuit, *De l'utilité et de sa mesure*. Écrits Choisis et republiés par Mario de Bernardi (Collezione di scritti inediti o rari di economisti diretta da Luigi Einaudi, vol. 2 (Turin: La Riforma Sociale, 1933). The review was written by Hayek in June 1933 and published in *The Economist Monthly Book Supplement*, June 9, 1934, p. 47. -Ed.]

[7] [Jacob H. Hollander (1871-1940), economist at The Johns Hopkins University, editor of an early edition of Ricardo's letters and Ricardo's *Notes on Malthus* (Baltimore, Md.: The Johns Hopkins University Press, 1928). -Ed.]

[8] [Luigi Einaudi (1874-1961), economist and journalist, Professor of Public Finance at the University of Turin, and later President of the Republic of Italy (1948-55). -Ed.]

marginal utility theory of value and of the modern apparatus of demand and supply curves. W. S. Jevons, who became acquainted with Dupuit's work only some years after he had independently discovered and further developed the same ideas, said in the later editions of his *Theory of Political Economy* that Dupuit "must probably be credited with the earliest perfect comprehension of the theory of utility".[9]

Although we now know that Dupuit was in turn anticipated at least by W. F. Lloyd,[10] and to a certain extent even by earlier writers, there can be no doubt about the originality or the importance of his work. It can also not be said of his work, as of that of most of the other anticipators in this field, that it remained unnoticed. It immediately led to an interesting controversy (also reprinted in Einaudi's edition) and probably influenced contemporary French thought to some extent. Dupuit's influence can, however, quite definitely be traced in the work of L. Walras,[11] who drew his inspiration mainly from his French predecessors, Cournot[12] and Dupuit—and to have influenced Walras means to have influenced all later writers on mathematical economics. In some respects Dupuit had even gone further than the recognised founders of the mathematical school, and at least the fact that he had already formulated the concept of 'consumers' rent', for which credit is generally given to Marshall,[13] deserves mention, even if at present there exists considerable doubt about the value of this particular tool of theoretical analysis. Engineers do not often make good economists. It has even been said that to be trained as an engineer completely incapacitates a person from understanding economic problems. Dupuit,

---

[9] [W. Stanley Jevons, *The Theory of Political Economy*, preface to the second (1879) edition. See the new edition, edited by R. D. Collinson Black (Harmondsworth, England: Pelican Books, 1970), p. 57. Jevons also acknowledged another predecessor; that Gossen's discovery of marginal utility preceded both his and Walras's. See this chapter, page 354. -Ed.]

[10] [William F. Lloyd (1795-1852), Professor of Political Economy at Oxford University. -Ed.]

[11] [Léon Walras (1834-1910), Professor of Economics at the Academy (later University) of Lausanne in Switzerland, co-discoverer of marginal utility analysis in the 1870s with Carl Menger and W. Stanley Jevons, and the founder of modern general equilibrium theory. -Ed.]

[12] [Antoine Augustin Cournot (1801-1877), Professor of Analysis and Mechanics at Lyon University in France, known for his contributions to the theory of duopoly. -Ed.]

[13] [Alfred Marshall (1842-1924), Professor of Political Economy at Cambridge University and founder of the 'Cambridge School' including himself, A. C. Pigou, and John Maynard Keynes. -Ed.]

however, is a splendid—and by no means the only—exception to this rule.

The present edition contains practically all of Dupuit's work on utility and price, written between 1844 and 1854, but none of his numerous later (and much less important) writings on other economic problems. It is not only luxuriously produced and enriched by a contemporary obituary notice of Dupuit from the pen of his colleague, Mahyer, but it also contains a scholarly introduction and ample notes by Mr. Mario de Bernardi, and a complete bibliography of the writings of Dupuit. It is certainly a worthy monument to the memory of a long-neglected economist.

Hermann Heinrich Gossen[14]

Theoretical economics is still a young science. Although a great many of its most important findings were already contained in the teachings of the English classical school of the first half of the last century, it is little more than fifty years[15] since an approach was introduced into our science which made possible its continuing development into a unified, exact discipline. Only with the fundamental ideas developed almost simultaneously at the beginning of the seventies of the last century by the Englishman W. Stanley Jevons,[16] the Austrian Carl Menger,[17] and the Frenchman Léon Walras[18] did it become possible to construct a consistent system of

---

[14] [This essay was first published in 1929 as the introduction ("Einleitung") to the third edition of Hermann Heinrich Gossen, *Entwicklung der Gesetze des menschlichen und der daraus fließenden Regeln für menschliches Handeln* (Berlin: R. L. Prager, 1927), pp. ix-xxiii. Never before published in English, it has been translated and partly annotated by Professor Ralph Raico, whose notes are marked 'Tr.'. -Ed.]

[15] [Written in 1927. -Ed.]

[16] [William Stanley Jevons (1835-1882), Professor of Political Economy at Owens College, Manchester, from 1863 to 1876 and discoverer, with Carl Menger and Léon Walras, of the theory of marginal utility. Among his works are *The Theory of Political Economy* (London and New York: Macmillan, 1871) and *The State in Relation to Labour* (London: Macmillan, 1882). -Tr.]

[17] [Carl Menger (1840-1921), Professor of Political Economy at the University of Vienna, co-discoverer with Jevons and Walras of marginal utility analysis, and the founder of the Austrian School of economics. His major work is *Grundsätze der Volkswirtschaftslehre* [1871], published in English as *Principles of Economics* (Glencoe, Ill.: The Free Press, 1950; reprinted 1981). On Menger, see Hayek's introduction, Carl Menger, *Principles of Economics*, trans. by James Dingwall and Bert F. Hoselitz (New York and London: New York University Press, 1981), pp. 11-36, and the bibliography by Richard Ebeling, p. 10. -Tr.] [See also vol. 4 of *The Collected Works*. -Ed.]

[18] [Léon Walras (1834-1910), Professor of Economics at the Academy (later University) of Lausanne, 1870-92.]

economic theory whose stock of assured results will doubtless form the enduring foundation of all explanations of economic phenomena regardless of changes in approach and methods of research. Both opponents and adherents of the 'subjective' orientation of theoretical economics which those scholars called into being always take the findings of these men as their starting point.[19] This is true even when, as with, for instance, a part of the modern English school, they formally maintain the tradition of the classical school, or even when they believe themselves to oppose the theories of Jevons, Menger, and Walras.

If we date the development of modern economics from 1871, the year of the appearance of the works of Jevons and Menger, this is by no means to say that at the time of the appearance of these works, their key ideas were entirely new. The achievement of these investigators, of Walras, and in part also of the Englishman Alfred Marshall[20] and the American J. B. Clark[21], lies above all in the fact that they made the insight into the nature of economic values which they independently discovered the point of departure for self-contained systems of theoretical economics. Indeed, later research showed that every single one of their basic ideas had repeatedly and clearly been set forth in earlier works, yet did not reach full fruition because they were not carried through consistently. Thus, interesting as the discovery of anticipations of the ideas of the modern schools by older writers may be in general, what they accomplished for economics cannot be compared with the achievement of the founders of the modern schools of thought.

Hermann Heinrich Gossen, whose work is presented to readers here in a new edition by the publishing house of R. L. Prager, forms an exception. The numerous other subsequently discovered precursors of the marginal utility school who anticipated its solution of the problem of value were scarcely aware of what their discovery

[19] [On the differences between Jevons, Menger, and Walras, however, see William Jaffé, "Menger, Jevons, and Walras De-homogenized", *Economic Inquiry*, vol. 14, no. 4, December 1976, pp. 511-524, and Philip Mirowski, *Against Mechanism: Protecting Economics from Science* (Totowa, N.J.: Rowman & Littlefield, 1988), pp. 22-25. -Ed.]

[20] [Alfred Marshall (1842-1924), Professor of Political Economy at Cambridge University from 1885 to 1908, author of *Principles of Economics* (London and New York: Macmillan, 1890). -Tr.]

[21] [John Bates Clark (1847-1938) taught economics at Columbia University from 1895 to 1923. Among his books is *The Distribution of Wealth* (London and New York: Macmillan, 1899), in which he developed a marginal productivity analysis of distribution. -Tr.]

signified for economic theory and failed, in any case, to make it the cornerstone of a system.[22] Instead, in most cases they were content with a brief statement of the causes determining value. Gossen, however, not only accurately perceived the importance of his insights but even, perhaps, stressed them somewhat effusively. He also worked out their application to the most vital problems of theoretical economics and to a series of questions of economic policy to such a degree that even the later founders of the new school, in their own initial works, only partially surpassed him. As far as the substance of his theory went, Gossen could just as well have become the founder of a new school as Jevons and Menger did seventeen years later, and shortly after that Walras, if the form of his presentation and the peculiar fortune of the work had not for a long time kept it from the notice of his fellow specialists.

But before entering into the strange fortunes and ultimate success of his work, we may mention what little is known of the life of the man who—once the general views on the tasks of economics are more firmly established and, consequently, the judgement on the pioneers of this science become more uniform—will probably share with Heinrich von Thünen[23] the honour of being the greatest German economist before the rise of the modern school.[24]

Gossen was born on September 7, 1810, in Düren, in the administrative district of Aachen, the son of the former tax-farmer of the Napoleonic Empire[25] and later administrator of domains, Josef

---

[22] [On the history of marginal utility theory see Emil Kauder, *A History of Marginal Utility Theory* (Princeton, N.J.: Princeton University Press, 1965). Kauder traces the origins of marginal utility to Aristotle. Drawing on the investigations of Aristotle's *Topics* by Oskar Kraus, Kauder demonstrates that Aristotle had at least some knowledge of the law of diminishing utility. Kauder provides English translations of passages from Aristotle, Menger, and Böhm-Bawerk to demonstrate the similarity of their respective arguments. See op. cit., pp. 15-17. -Ed.]

[23] [Heinrich von Thünen (1783-1850), landowner and farmer, author of *Der Isolierte Staat in Beziehung auf Landwirtschaft und Nationalökonomie* [1826-63], translated as *The Isolated State* (Oxford and New York: Pergamon Press, 1966), in which he uses statistics and mathematical techniques to analyse rent, location, wages, and interest. -Tr.]

[24] The biographical data are drawn from the essays of: Léon Walras. "Un économiste inconnu", *Journal des Economistes*, April and May 1885, reprinted in *Etudes d'économie sociale* (Lausanne: Rouge, 1896), pp. 351-374; Oskar Kraus, "Gossen, Hermann Heinrich", in the *Allgemeine Deutsche Biographie*, vol. 55 (Leipzig: Duncker & Humblot, 1910), pp. 483-488; and Gisbert Beyerhaus, "Hermann Heinrich Gossen und seine Zeit", *Zeitschrift für Volkswirtschaft und Sozialpolitik*, N.S., vol. 5, 1926, nos. 7-9. (Beyerhaus, incidentally, overlooked the article by Kraus.)

[25] [Conquered by France in 1794, from 1798 to 1814 Aachen was the capital of the French department of Roer. -Tr.]

Gossen and his wife, Mechtildis, née Scholl. He later spent his early years in Cologne and Muffendorf, under the strong influence of a deeply Catholic environment. Only the emphatic wish of his father, who desired to channel him into the civil service, could induce the youth, attracted as he was to mathematics early on, to take up the study of law. This he appears to have completed only reluctantly and with difficulty. After his school-leaving examination (matura) in 1829, he studied first at Bonn, then in Berlin, and, on passing the examination in 1834, became a law-clerk in Cologne. To judge from the opening words of the preface to his book, by the end of his course of university studies Gossen must already have started working on the problems which would later engross him completely and, after twenty years, bear fruit in the *Entwicklung der Gesetze des menschlichen Verkehrs*.[26] Not long afterwards—according to a likely conjecture by Professor Beyerhaus—he may have become acquainted with English utilitarianism through a translation of Jeremy Bentham's *Principles of Legislation*,[27] which appeared in Cologne in 1833.[28] The influence of this doctrine was indeed decisive for the further evolution of his thought. His acquaintance with the philosophy of Auguste Comte,[29] whose positivism surely had no less of an influence on Gossen's world-view, probably only began, according to Beyerhaus, at a later date.

Distracted as he was by these interests, Gossen required almost seven years for the completion of his practical training. Not until

[26] [Published in English as *The Laws of Human Relations and the Rules of Human Action Derived Therefrom* (Cambridge, Mass., and London: MIT Press, 1983). -Tr.]

[27] [Jeremy Bentham (1748-1832), philosopher, economist, and legal reformer, proposed pleasure, or utility, as the ultimate standard in matters of law or ethics. His *Principles of Legislation* was published in French, as part of Bentham's *Traité de Législation*, edited by Étienne Dumont, in Paris, in 1802. See *Bentham's Theory of Legislation, Being Principes de Législation and Traités de Législation, Civile et Pénale*, trans. and ed. by Charles Milner Atkinson, 2 vols (London: Humphrey Milford and Oxford University Press, 1914). -Tr.]

[28] Loc. cit., p. 536. This assumption of Beyerhaus, who also states that Gossen's dependence on Bentham "extends from the subtlest undertones to literal correspondence", seems to me more likely than the view of Oskar Kraus (*Zur Theorie des Wertes. Eine Bentham-Studie* (Halle: M. Niemeyer, 1901)), to the effect that Gossen was not familiar with Bentham.

[29] [Isidore Auguste Marie François Xavier Comte (1798-1857), positivist philosopher and co-founder of modern sociology along with Henri de Saint-Simon. On Comte's influence on economics see Ben B. Seligman, "The Impact of Positivism on Economic Thought", *History of Political Economy*, vol. 1, no. 2, Fall 1969, pp. 256-278. See also Hayek's remarks on Comte in *The Counter-Revolution of Science* (Glencoe, Ill.: The Free Press; second edition, Indianapolis, Ind.: LibertyPress, 1979), in vol. 2 of *The Collected Works of F. A. Hayek*. -Ed.]

1842 did he take the main examination, after having in the previous year once again pleaded in vain with his father to allow a change of careers, and, in addition, two more years of university study. Gossen only finished the written work and passed the oral examination after another three years, during which he also occupied himself with mathematical astronomy, among other subjects. Thereupon he was appointed government assessor in Magdeburg, later in Erfurt. In this position, for which he had little taste and wherein, moreover, he came into conflict with his superiors, he remained until his father's death in 1847. This event put him in a position to give up his career and dedicate himself completely to his researches. In the same year, in which Gossen also moved to Berlin, there seems to have occurred the great inner crisis to which he alludes at the end of the preface to the book:[30] the renunciation of Catholicism, or, really, of any ecclesiastical faith, and the conversion to that positivist-optimistic, yet deeply religious, view of life that characterises his work. Two years later, in 1849, Gossen once more entered social life for a short time, as director of a hailstorm and livestock insurance company in Cologne, which came into being as a result of the initiative of a Belgian acquaintance of his. The very next year, however, he withdrew from the business, so as not, as Walras reports, to lose too considerable a part of the sums he invested in it, or else, according to Beyerhaus, after the enterprise had ended in a public fiasco. A plan he himself worked out for a 'universal German savings bank', which was to deal with life insurance, remained a mere project. From then until the completion of his book in January, 1853, he lived in Cologne, totally occupied with his work and looked after by his two sisters. In the same year, his health was permanently damaged by a typhus infection, in the wake of which quickly worsening symptoms of pulmonary tuberculosis appeared. Kraus reports that Gossen, as a consequence of this illness, pursued the printing of his work with nervous haste. Thus, according to the contract signed on April 15, 1854, with the commissioned publisher Friedrich Vieweg and Son, Brunswick, the book had to be produced in three months. A Cologne lawyer by the name of Meyer is supposed to have guaranteed the printing costs. The book, however, went totally unnoticed. Gossen died on February 13, 1858, without having lived to see his work, for which he had expected the greatest success, make any mark whatsoever. Bitter

[30] [*The Laws of Human Relations*, op. cit., p. cxlix. -Tr.]

over this failure, just before his death he had copies of the first edition withdrawn from the bookshops.

What was probably to be the first reference to his work in economic literature appeared in the year of his death in a textbook by the Hungarian professor Kautz. In a footnote in the section on demand, Kautz mentions that very recently Friedrich [sic] Gossen, in his book, *Die Entwicklung der Gesetze des menschlichen Verkehrs*, attempted to furnish "a formal theory and philosophy of pleasure (and, what is more, on a mathematical foundation!)".[31] Twelve years pass before we find the next trace of any notice of Gossen's work, in the second edition of F. A. Lange's *Arbeiterfrage*.[32] Since, however, Gossen's ideas were disseminated in the following years through the works of Jevons, Menger, and Walras, not only did these authors consider themselves to be the discoverers of completely new knowledge, but for years there was no one who might have pointed out the agreement between their theories and those of Gossen. It was only some years later that Professor R. Adamson,[33] Jevons's successor at Owens College in Manchester, came across Kautz's reference to Gossen's book, which led him to make inquiries about the work. It took him, however, until 1878 before he was able to discover it in the catalogue of a German bookseller and purchase it. Only later did it come to light that the British Museum had owned a copy of the book since 1865. Adamson immediately informed Jevons, who had only a poor command of the German language, of the discovery and of the book's contents. Jevons, for his part, sent an account of it in September, 1878, to Walras, who had, in the most candid fashion, shortly before conceded to him the priority of his discov-

---

[31] Julius Kautz, *Theorie und Geschichte der Nationalökonomik*. Part I. *Die Nationalökonomik als Wissenschaft* (Vienna: Gerold, 1858), p. 9. In the second part of this work, titled *Die geschichtlichen Entwicklung der Nationalökonomik und ihrer Literatur* (Vienna: Gerold, 1860), there is also a brief citation of Gossen's book among more recent works, on p. 709.

[32] Friedrich Albert Lange, *Die Arbeiterfrage. Ihre Bedeutung für Gegenwart und Zukunft*. Second revised and expanded edition (Winterthur: Bleuler-Hausheer, 1870), p. 125n: "Gossen . . . attempted to establish a rigorously mathematical theory of pleasure and work, starting from the fact that every pleasure of a determinate type is greatest at the moment of its emergence and then begins to diminish. Despite the onesidedness with which the author treats a single topic, the work deserves more attention than has been paid to it so far." Thus Lange appears to have been the first to recognise Gossen's importance. It is remarkable that Menger missed this reference to a kindred effort occurring just before his own book was published.

[33] [Robert Adamson (1852-1902) succeeded Jevons as Professor of Philosophy and Political Economy at Owens College, Manchester, in 1876. He was the author of works on logic and studies of Kant and Fichte. -Tr.]

357

eries. And Jevons now, equally frankly, informed Walras that Gossen had anticipated the ideas of both of them.[34]

The wider public first learned of the discovery of Gossen's book from the preface to the second edition of Jevons's *Theory of Political Economy*, in which a short summary of Gossen's work is given, based on the information conveyed to Jevons by Adamson.[35] Jevons concludes his account of Gossen's achievement with the words: "From this statement it is quite apparent that Gossen has completely anticipated me as regards the general principles and method of the theory of economics. So far as I can gather, his treatment of the fundamental theory is even more general and thorough than what I was able to scheme out."[36] Walras esteemed Gossen's work no less highly. Immediately on receiving word of it, he began to hunt for it among booksellers and libraries, finally acquiring a copy through the Munich librarian Halm. Walras himself relates[37] how (in the first weeks of 1879, the same year that the second edition of Jevons's work appeared), together with his colleague Charles Secrétan,[38] he set about a painstaking reading and complete translation of the work. Investigations regarding Gossen revealed that his nephew, Dr. Hermann Kortum, was a Professor of Mathematics at the University of Bonn. Walras wrote to the latter and in 1881 received a brief biography of the uncle, composed on the basis of his posthumous papers. Walras published excerpts of the biography in the essay cited and intended to append the whole text to the published translation of Gossen's work that had been prepared.[39] To this communication of Kortum to Walras we owe almost all of the little that we know of Gossen's life. In 1880, even before Walras used these facts in the article cited—indeed, before he had even obtained

---

[34] The history of the discovery of Gossen is given by W. Stanley Jevons in the preface to the second edition of his *Theory of Political Economy* (London: Macmillan, 1879) and by Léon Walras in the essay cited earlier.

[35] Loc. cit., pp. xlvii-lii.

[36] *Ibid.*, p. il. In the same year an unsigned account of Gossen's book appeared in the *Journal of the Statistical Society*, vol. 42, September 1879, pp. 727-733, which Vladimir Zawadski (*Les mathématiques appliquées á l'économie politique* (Paris: M. Riviere, 1914)) attributes to G. D. Hooper, and which contains literal translations of large parts of the foreword and the first part of Gossen's work.

[37] Léon Walras, "Un économiste inconnu", op. cit., p. 359.

[38] [Charles Secrétan (1815-1895), Professor of Philosophy at Lausanne, author of *La Philosophie de la Liberté* (Paris: L. Hachette, 1849). -Ed.]

[39] To my knowledge, neither this French translation of Gossen's work nor the full text of Kortum's biography has ever been published. [An Italian translation of Gossen's book by Tullio Bagiotti was published in 1950, *Sviluppo delle leggi del commercio umano* (Padova: Cedam, 1950). -Ed.]

them—he discussed in detail a part of Gossen's theory (his plans for land reform) in an essay on the "Mathematical Theory of the Price of Land and Land Redemption by the State",[40] in which he characterises Gossen's work as "one of the most splendid books in political economy ever written". The actual essay on the "unknown economist", mentioned earlier, which Walras wrote in 1881, he published, with an epilogue, only in 1885, after, as he says, the development of theory in the intervening years had dispelled his fears that he had attached an undue and premature importance to theories in which he was personally interested. In this essay, Walras attempts to give a suitable assessment to Gossen's whole work and to differentiate Gossen's achievement from his own. Like Jevons, he awards Gossen unconditional priority for a major part of his theories, which he believes he needs to supplement only on quite specific points, to be referred to later.[41] In his accolades to Gossen, however, he goes far beyond even Jevons. To Walras, not only do the theoretical arguments of the first part of Gossen's work seem of the greatest importance, but he pays the highest tribute as well to the applications of theoretical doctrines to social questions attempted in the second part. "Thus, to the glory of Copernicus", Walras states, referring to the opening words of Gossen's foreword,[42] "to which he lays claim and which is due him for his conception of the mathematical equilibrium of the economic world, Gossen joins, in my view, something of that of Newton for his solution of the social question. That said, I have nothing more to add in expressing my opinion of his merit."[43]

Gossen was really first introduced into German scientific literature by Friedrich von Wieser.[44] In his *Natural Value*,[45] Wieser develops

---

[40] "Théorie mathématique du prix de terres et de leur rachat par l'état", printed in *Etudes d'économie sociale*, op. cit., pp. 267-350; cf., especially, pp. 170ff. and 338ff.

[41] Loc. cit., p. 361.

[42] [*The Laws of Human Relations*, op. cit., p. cxlvii. -Tr.]

[43] *Ibid.*, p. 369. Cf. also pp. 354f.: "For my part . . . I will say that among the equally numerous examples of scientific injustice, there is none as flagrant as the ingratitude shown to Gossen. This is the case of a man who passed completely unnoticed, and who is, to my mind, one of the most outstanding economists who ever existed."

[44] [On Friedrich von Wieser (1851-1926), one of the founders of the Austrian School of Economics and Hayek's teacher at the University of Vienna, see Hayek's "Friedrich Freiherr von Wieser", *Jahrbücher für Nationalökonomie und Statistik*, 3rd series, vol. 70, no. 2, 1926, pp. 513-530. -Tr.] [To be published in English in vol. 4 of *The Collected Works*. -Ed.]

the law of the diminishing intensity of wants, which forms the basis of the subjective theory of value, in reference to Gossen and under his name. This part of Gossen's theory has since become totally established in the theoretical literature as Gossen's law. In every country, numerous theoreticians have since more or less exhaustively examined and grappled with Gossen. In Italy, in the same year as Wieser, Maffeo Pantaleoni[46] did full justice to Gossen in one of the most brilliant summaries of economic theory that has ever appeared,[47] and soon afterwards Wilhelm Lexis also dealt with him at length in the article on "Marginal Utility" in the *Handwörterbuch der Staatswissenschaften*.[48] From the abundant literature that has sprung up since then, only the most important works can be cited in a footnote.[49]

---

[45] *Der natürliche Werth* (Vienna: A. Hölder, 1889), pp. 6ff. [Friedrich von Wieser, *Natural Value*, ed. William Smart, trans. Christian A. Malloch (New York: G. E. Stechert, 1930), p. 9. -Ed.]

[46] [Maffeo Pantaleoni (1857-1924), professor at various Italian universities, including, from 1901, the University of Rome, attempted to combine marginalist with Ricardian analysis. He interested himself particularly in questions of public finance. -Tr.]

[47] Maffeo Pantaleoni, *Principii di economia pura* (Florence: G. Barbéra, 1889), esp. pp. 38ff., 48ff., 96ff., 100ff., and 132.

[48] "Grenznutzen", in the supplementary volume to the first edition (Jena: G. Fischer, 1895), pp. 422-432.

[49] Besides the works already cited, the following deserve particular mention: F. Y. Edgeworth, "H. H. Gossen", *Palgrave's Dictionary of Political Economy* (London: Macmillan, 1896 and later); G. Sulzer, *Die wirtschaftlichen Grundgesetze in der Gegenwartsphase ihrer Entwicklung* (Zurich: A. Müller, 1895); Winiarski, *Les deux théories d'équilibre économique* (1897); Oskar Kraus, *Zur Theorie des Wertes*, op. cit.; idem., "Die aristotelische in ihrer Beziehung zu den Lehren der modernen Psychologie", *Zeitschrift für die gesamten Staatswissenschaft*, 1905; Rudolf Kaulla, *Die geschichtliche Entwicklung der modernen Werttheorien* (Tübingen: H. Laupp, 1906); Franz Cuhel, *Zur Lehre von den Bedürfnissen* (Innsbruck: Wagner'sche Universität-Buchhandlung, 1907); Lujo Brentano, *Die Entwicklung der Wertlehre* (Munich: Königlich bayerische Akademie der Wissenschaften, 1908); idem., *Versuch einer Theorie der Bedürfnisse* (Munich: Königlich bayerische Akademie der Wissenschaften, 1908), both reprinted in *Konkreten Grundbedingungen Volkswirtschaft* (Leipzig: F. Meiner, 1924); Karl Diehl, "Die Entwicklung Wert- und Preistheorien im 19. Jahrhundert", in *Die Entwicklung der deutschen Volkswirtschaftslehre im 19. Jahrhundert. Festgabe für Gustav Schmoller* (Leipzig: Duncker & Humblot, 1908); idem., *Theoretische Nationalökonomie*, vol. 1, *Einleitung in die Nationalökonomie* (Jena: G. Fischer, 1916); Max Weber, "Die Grenznutzenlehre und das 'psychophysische Grundgesetz'", *Archiv für Sozialwissenschaften und Sozialpolitik*, vol. 29, 1908, reprinted in *Gesammelte Aufsätze zu Wissenschaftslehre* (Tübingen: J. C. B. Mohr, 1922); E. A. Heber, "Die sogenannte Lausanner Schule der politischen Ökonomie", *Zeitschrift für Sozialwissenschaften*, N.S., vol. 1, 1910; R. Liefmann, "Hermann Heinrich Gossen und seine Lehre", *Jahrbücher für Nationalökonomie und Statistik*, 3rd series, vol. 40, 1910; idem., *Grundsätze der Volkswirtschaftslehre*, op. cit.; Franz Oppenheimer, *Theorie der reinen und politischen Ökonomie*, vol. 3 of *System der Soziologie* (Jena: G.

The posthumous renown that Gossen achieved eventually also led R. L. Prager, the successor to his publisher Viehweg, of Berlin, to arrange in 1889 for a new edition of his work, which, as it was put, had been pulped at Gossen's request. As it later transpired, however, this was merely the first edition outfitted with a new title page and wrapper.[50] So few copies of the actual first edition are available in libraries that they scarcely count,[51] and, strangely enough, none of the editions of economic classics up until now has included Gossen's work. Thus the remainder of the original edition, salvaged in this way and put back on the market so little altered in appearance, has constituted until the present edition the sole form in which Gossen's work could be obtained.

Today the vast majority of economists are familiar with Gossen's Law of the Satiation of Wants, and most of them, in addition, with his plans for land reform. But this by no means redresses the wrong that they committed against him during the lifetime of the great man and for decades after his death. Gossen's work contains many more important ideas which later became fundamental to the development of theoretical economics and still merit consideration today. It is as if most readers of his book had confined themselves to the first chapters, those setting out the basic laws of the theory of wants, and only a few later researchers had taken the trouble to study the whole book thoroughly. For this Gossen's form of exposition is surely partly at fault. Not only does it produce a ponderous and long-winded impression through the extended and not always adroit use of mathematical formulae, but, as a consequence of inept organisation, it is also extraordinarily involved. The whole book is written uninterruptedly, without chapter headings or table of contents, and even the few divisions of the text, marked by horizontal lines, separate the different subjects quite inadequately. In the following section of this introduction, therefore, the intention is to

Fischer, 1910 and later); idem., *Wert und Kapitalprofit*, second edition (Jena: G. Fischer, 1922); Roche-Agussol, *Etudes bibliographiques des sources de la psychologie économique chez les Anglo-Américains* (Montpellier and Paris: R.-V. Darsac, 1919), including the more recent relevant English literature; E. Lang, "Der Ertragsverlauf in der Landwirtschaft bei steigendem Aufwand", *Landwirtschaftliche Jahrbücher*, vol. 55, 1920; L. Schönfeld, *Grenznutzen und Wirtschaftsrechnung* (Vienna, 1924); H. Mayer, "Bedürfnis", *Handwörterbuch Staatswissenschaften*, fourth edition (Jena: G. Fischer, 1924); Otto Weinberger, *Die Grenznutzenschule* (Halberstadt: H. Meyer, 1926).

[50] See E. Lang, loc. cit., pp. 395-400, and Beyerhaus, loc. cit., p. 524.

[51] Professor Beyerhaus informs me that the Staatsbibliothek in Berlin owns a copy of the 1854 edition. The British Museum's copy has already been mentioned above.

remedy this deficiency, at least in part, and to give, together with an exposition and appreciation of Gossen's theory and its significance for modern economics, a short survey of the arrangement of the book's contents.

As already mentioned, Gossen's crucial and celebrated discoveries are presented in a few pages at the beginning of the book. Both laws that today bear his name are developed on pages 1 through 24 [1-28],[52] and everything that follows is based on these propositions. After a brief description of his utilitarian world-view, raised to a peculiar pitch of religiosity (pp. 1-4) [1-6],[53] Gossen passes to the investigation of the laws governing the driving force of all human action. This he calls the capacity to enjoy, by which should most probably be understood the capacity to so arrange actions that a person's life pleasure is maximised. At the head of this inquiry he places two statements on the diminution of every pleasure with its continuance or repetition, the first of which, in the formulation given by Wieser in *Natural Value*, is known in the literature as Gossen's Law of the Satiation of Wants, or Gossen's First Law.[54] Wieser there formulated this law as follows: "Within any single period of want every additional act of satisfaction will be estimated less highly than a preceding one obtained from a quantity of goods equal in kind and amount."[55] It was precisely in the recognition of

---

[52] [The numbers in brackets indicate the pages in the new English edition of Gossen, *The Laws of Human Relations and the Rules of Human Action Derived Therefrom*, trans. Rudolph C. Blitz (Cambridge, Mass., and London: MIT Press, 1983), corresponding to the pages in the 1927 German edition. -Tr.]

[53] The following exposition is essentially confined to the substance of the economic ideas in Gossen's book and deals less with the ethical-philosophical conceptions regularly associated with it. The reader wishing further information on the influences discernible here should consult the excellent essay by Beyerhaus, cited above, especially pp. 532f.

[54] Wieser, *Der natürliche Wert*, op. cit., p. 7; Lexis, loc. cit. See also Cuhel, loc. cit, pp. 234ff., who quite correctly remarks that these two propositions should be clearly designated as Gossen's First and Gossen's Second Law of the Decrease of Pleasure [*Genussabnahme*], respectively, as distinguished from Gossen's Law of Value, to be mentioned later. They are further to be distinguished from what Lexis designates as Gossen's *Second* Law, the rule of the proportionate satisfaction of different wants.

[55] In his great work, *Theorie der gesellschaftlichen Wirtschaft*, in the first volume of the *Grundrisse der Sozialökonomie* (Tübingen: J. C. B. Mohr, 1914; second edition, 1924), Wieser offered an improved version of this law. There it reads (p. 148 of the first and p. 24 of the second edition): "In the case of every divisible need the first unit of satisfying goods is desired with the greatest intensity. The use of further units is less intensely desired. Finally, satiety is reached. Beyond this point desire is transformed into aversion." [Friedrich von Wieser, *Social Economics*, trans. A. Ford Hinrichs (London: Allen & Unwin, n.d.), p. 28. -Ed.]

this law, basic to the whole theory of value, that Gossen had numerous predecessors, of whom we shall cite only Aristotle, Bernoulli, and Bentham. But he was the first to perceive its "connexion with the law of economic value and must therefore", to quote Wieser once more, "receive credit for being the scientific discoverer of the law of satiation".[56] Gossen already states the law with the most important qualifications stipulated by later authors. He distinguishes precisely in both propositions between the decrease in pleasure in the case of the continuing satisfaction of a want and in the case of satisfaction at repeated intervals; he stresses that the decrease of pleasure proceeds differently with different pleasures; and he understands that an augmentation of pleasure through practice is also possible (p. 7) [8]. But he also already makes particular use of diagrammatic representation by means of curves, later so popular, in order to illustrate the course of the decrease of pleasure. In this way, he equips himself with the mathematical tool with which he later tries to represent exactly human behaviour determined by the pursuit of the greatest pleasure (pp. 8-10) [9-12]. It should be noticed that Gossen explicitly emphasises (p. 9) [10-11] that nothing can be stated about the shape of these curves from the outset except that they continuously descend, and that he chooses the form of a straight line only for the sake of the greater simplicity in his further exposition. But as so often happens in economics especially, and even with Gossen elsewhere, this unjustified concretisation of assumptions later leads, precisely in his mathematical statements, to results which do not possess at all the universal validity which the author would like to claim for them.

On the basis of this finding, Gossen propounds three theorems (pp. 11, 12, and 21) [13, 14, 25] about the behaviour required to attain the greatest sum of pleasure. Of these, the second, which Lexis has christened Gossen's Second Law (as opposed to the previously mentioned First Law) is by far the most important. Gossen here assumes that the individual is prevented from attaining all pleasures only by the limitedness of the time at his disposal, and for this case he lays down the rule that then the various pleasures will only be effected in part: "in such a manner that the magnitude [intensity] of each single pleasure at the moment when its enjoyment is broken off shall be the same for all pleasures" (p. 12) [14]. With this statement, perhaps the most important in the book, we obtain the bridge that was sought for in vain before Gossen—the

---

[56] *Theorie*, op. cit., pp. 148 and 24 respectively.

bridge between both constituents of value, utility and impediments to its realisation. This bridge is the idea of the margin, which has been assimilated into the literature of economics never again to vanish from it. Gossen carries this idea through in great detail, both algebraically and with numerical examples, always on the assumption that the relation between time elapsed and decrease of utility is of the simplest character, namely linear. Attention should be drawn to the subsequent remarks on the importance of changes in the intensity of a want (pp. 21-23) [25-27] or the emergence of a new want. Gossen then introduces the concept of value, which, entirely in the sense of the modern subjective school, he derives from the utility (the life pleasure) that things of the external world are capable of procuring for us (p. 24) [28-29]. Before entering into the laws of the formation of value, however, he gives (pp. 24-28) [28-32] a classification of goods which is very similar, on the one hand, to Menger's now-famous division into goods of the first and of higher orders, and, on the other, the division into goods which can be utilised alone and complementary goods. In today's terminology, one would have to designate the categories Gossen demarcates as consumption goods, complementary goods (and, indeed, both complementary consumption goods and those production goods whose material enters into the finished consumption goods), and, finally, instrumental production goods, namely so-called fixed capital. Special note should also be taken here of Gossen's observations on the possibility and method of an imputation of value to goods of a higher order (pp. 26-27) [31-32]. The alternative or cumulative utilisability of a good for several wants, which Gossen stresses, has likewise acquired importance in later theory.

In the investigation that follows into the determinants of the value of goods (pp. 28-34) [32-39], Gossen finds that the limitedness of the quantity of the available good restricts the attainable pleasure in a manner similar to the previously examined case of the limitedness of the available time. As a consequence, the goods on hand must be economised in the same way as had been shown for time. The law of decrease of value for every additional unit of quantity of a good, which Gossen propounds here (p. 31) [35], corresponds to the law of marginal utility of the modern subjective school and surely deserved—as Gossen's Third Law—to be highlighted as had the other two. It should be clearly distinguished from the Law of the Satiation of Wants, since the latter is universally applicable to all wants, irrespective of whether they require material objects for their satisfaction. The Third Law, on the other hand, only concerns the importance of given quantities of a good in the realisation of pleasure. Gossen is aware that it is only with this last law that he enters the field of conventional economics. But he wishes to expand this discipline to a general *theory of pleasure* through incorporating all principles of pleasure, including those not conditioned by the limitedness of available goods (p. 34) [38-39].

The next section, according to Gossen's own division (pp. 34-45) [40-53], introduces a new element to be considered in explaining the value of goods: the trouble of the labour of producing them, whose laws are supposed to complete the theory of value. The theory of the importance of the pain of labour for the valuation of goods, and the tenets about the necessary equilibrium between the pain of labour and utility, largely correspond to Jevons's later theory. Particularly notable is the ingenious geometrical representation of the state of equilibrium between utility and pain of labour, which already makes use of the procedure that afterwards became the cornerstone of the mathematical method in economics, the determination of the intersection of two curves representing the two given factors (p. 39) [44]. These observations of the conditions of maximum utility, as well as the following ones on the necessary distribution of labour among the ends in view, rank with the best in Gossen's exposition. Gossen then compares the concept of relative value yielded by the preceding discussion with the prevailing concept of absolute value (pp. 45-48) [54-58], and in the next three sections (pp. 48-55, 55-67, 67-80) [56-64, 65-77, 78-92], applies his theory of economic equilibrium, as we would call it, to a great number of individual cases, in a somewhat wearying recital that ends with the previously selected numerical example.

Up to this point (pp. 1-80) [1-92], the basis of Gossen's investigation has been the state of affairs that Wieser, who follows the same method of decreasing abstraction, has called 'the simple economy', or, rather, a still more simplified condition, namely, the economy of an isolated individual. But after this assumption has served its function in elucidating the laws of economic behaviour and the formation of value, Gossen, like Wieser, relinquishes it and turns to the exchange economy. The next section of his investigation (pp. 80-102) [95-116] begins with a brief presentation of the division of labour, from which Gossen immediately passes to the motives for exchange. In this regard, Gossen, contrary to classical theory, starts from the insight that has become fundamental for the modern school: namely, that the basis of the advantage which exchanging individuals expect from the exchange must be that they assess the exchanged goods differently, one valuing a good higher, the other lower. The theory of exchange that Gossen develops from the basic idea suffers, to be sure, from Gossen's viewing of the utility provided to the participants by the goods to be exchanged as comparable. Respected theoreticians make this mistake even today, but it inevitably undoes any theory of exchange and price. Aggravating this flaw in Gossen's explanation of exchange and price is the fact that it is precisely in this part of his work that the elucidation of what actually exists gets inextricably mingled with the rules he lays down for how things ought to proceed. The decisive statements on the outcome of exchange (p. 85) [100], therefore, in spite of the correct starting point of the inquiry, completely miss the mark. A real explanation of price formation that would constitute a further development of his fundamental ideas is missing entirely, and where there are the beginnings of an explanation of exchange relations curious undertones of the labour theory of value even appear. Following on the theory of exchange is an exposition of the importance of the division of labour and particularly of trade (pp. 88-90) [103-105], which contribute to bringing about the maximum general utility attainable. The last part of this section, reminiscent of Bastiat's doctrine of universal economic harmony, describes how this condition of the greatest happiness for the greatest number is necessarily realised through the free workings of economic forces. Noteworthy here are the observations on the importance of money (p. 93) [108-9] and the repeated remarks on the significance of prices as directors of production.

The subsequent sections on the origin and importance of rents (pp. 102-105, 106-110, 110-112, 112-114) [117-122, 123-127, 128-130, 131-132] and the nature of capitalisation (pp. 114-120) [133-139] are of particular theoretical significance. Then, in a very brief passage, Gossen summarises once again the ultimate determinants of human welfare (pp. 120-121) [143-144], and with this he concludes the genuinely theoretical part of the book, to which however the following three sections, with supplementary remarks, might also be added (pp. 121-128, 128-133, 133-148) [145-151, 152-156, 157-171].

In the first of these, Gossen attempts to show that the intensity of pleasures is measurable, an attempt which Jevons, among Gossen's successors, also tried. The other passages contain practical deliberations on the importance of established findings for the appropriate arrangement of life. While these are quite characteristic of Gossen's outlook, they cannot be gone into here. They lead to the second part of the work, which takes up about half of the volume, containing Gossen's programme for economic and social policy. He starts with a critique of momentous economic errors (pp. 148-191) [172-212], the individual points of which could perhaps be titled as follows: Money as a Measure of a People's Welfare (p. 148) [172]; On the Alleged Duty of the Government to Create Opportunity for Remunerative Work (p. 159) [173]; The True Advantage of Exchange and Trade (p. 158) [181]; On the Apparent Retrogression of the General Welfare (p. 162) [184]; On Counting Capitalised Rents as part of the National Wealth (p. 168) [190]; On Limitations on Interest (p. 172) [194]; Errors of Moralists and the True Religion (p. 186) [207]; and Errors of Educators (p. 189) [210]. There follows a section on the ends of general education (pp. 191-198) [215-221].

The extraordinarily modern ring of many of Gossen's observations on the value of money and currency and monetary policy (pp. 198-228) [222-251] have been unduly neglected. The point of departure of his reflections in this regard, the importance of a monetary value that is subject to no unforeseen changes, his subjective concepts of the value of money (pp. 199-200) [223], as well as his formulation of the quantity theory in terms of the velocity of circulation (p. 201) [225]: e.g., "Accelerating the circulation of money has the same effect as a corresponding increase in quantity"—all of these, many years later, have scarcely been better presented by respected scholars. The brief exposition of the consequences of a paper money inflation (pp. 205-206) [229-230] can also still be considered as exemplary. From among his remarks on monetary policy, special attention should be drawn to his rejection of all paper money (p. 208) [231] and his critique of bimetallism.

His subsequent discussion of "The Necessity of Preserving the Property and Freedom of Action of the Individual from All Restrictions" (pp. 228-238) [252-261], so that the "laws of experiencing pleasure" can fulfil their goal, comprises an extremely liberal programme, culminating in the sentence: "Everything that exists must create the means of its continued existence through itself; otherwise, it does not deserve to exist" (p. 235) [258]. Gossen would have this principle applied also to church, art, and science. This section well displays a trait for which not only Gossen, but, quite unjustly, all the representatives of the marginal utility theory have been reproached (e.g., by K. Diehl),[57] that of trying to derive the necessity

---

[57] [Karl Diehl (1864-1943), German economist who "endorsed the proposition that all economic phenomena were primarily determined by specific forms of social relationships and legal institutions, varying with different epochs and different nations". Karl Pribram, *A History of Economic Reasoning* (Baltimore, Md., and London: The Johns Hopkins University Press, 1983), p. 224. See Diehl's *Sozialwissenschaftliche Erlauterungen zu Ricardo's Grundsetzen* (Leipzig: F. Meiner, 1905-21), and *Die Sozialrechtliche Richtung in der Nationalökonomie* (Jena: Gustav Fischer, 1941). -Ed.]

of a specific programme of economic policy from theoretical findings. In Gossen's case, to be sure, this has its special cause in the peculiar religious outlook that formed the framework for his investigation of the laws of experiencing pleasure. He claimed to see in them the will of the Creator, and knowledge of these laws was supposed to enable us to live in accordance with that will.

Gossen develops further a detailed plan for establishing banks to make public loans (pp. 238-249) [262-273]. This project is intended to realise another presupposition for the most advantageous working of the laws of human relations, in that it is to be made possible for anyone to undertake those enterprises for which he considers himself particularly adapted. Here Gossen's undeniable unworldliness is exhibited with special acuteness. The next section, the last in which a new subject is taken up, is after the first one the best known of the whole book. Here Gossen elaborates (pp. 250-273) [274-295], for the first time in Germany so far as I am aware, a plan for the nationalisation of the landed property in the manner of the present-day land-reform movement.[58] Gossen would have the payment of the land price by the state take place in the form of a long-term amortisation, for which the land's appreciation in value, which Gossen assumes to be roughly constant, is to be utilised. As already mentioned, Walras held this part of Gossen's work in especially high esteem, and in the earlier of his two essays subjected it to a thorough examination and critique. The last two sections of Gossen's work (pp. 273-276, 277) [296-298, 299] contain an exceedingly optimistic survey of the results to be expected for the well-being of mankind if his proposals are carried out, and a call to men to make use of the knowledge that has been discovered in order to achieve the purposes of the Creator.

The aim of the preceding brief overview of Gossen's book has merely been to facilitate the reading of it by bringing out the most important points of the exposition in the sequence in which they appear in the text. A genuine assessment of Gossen's work would have to show in detail to what extent his ideas have proved themselves. It would hence be possible only in conjunction with a description of the present state of economic theory and, for that reason, can scarcely be provided within the framework of an introduction. Some readers will perhaps regret more than this shortcoming the absence of any more extensive introduction to Gossen's not always easily intelligible general outlook and how it was conditioned

---

[58] [This essay was written in 1929. -Ed.]

by the history of ideas, but we have had to dispense with such an account for the same reasons. The few suggestions included in the sketch of Gossen's life will have to make good this deficiency as far as possible. If the preceding remarks have made the essential content of the economic ideas in his work more accessible, they have fulfilled their purpose.

We may add in conclusion a few comments on the relation of Gossen's theory to the various modern schools of economic theory. Its relation to the 'Lausanne' mathematical school, which first gained recognition for it, can scarcely be better expressed than in Walras's own words. In his essay on Gossen he states:

> Gossen and Mr. Jevons discovered the mathematical expression of utility before me and formulated the condition for a maximum of utility in the exchange by an individual of one good for another. This is incontestable. Mr. Jevons seems inclined to concede a certain preeminence to Gossen on the first point and to claim it for himself on the second. He is correct. Gossen only formulated the condition of the absolute maximum; it is Jevons who was the first to formulate the condition of the relative maximum coexisting with the equality of supply and demand. However, both of them stopped there as regards even the case of the exchange of two goods for each other in kind. Neither Gossen nor Mr. Jevons even broached the question of the determination of the market price of each of these two goods by the other under the assumption of an indefinite number of exchangers. That is precisely one of the two questions resolved by me in a paper titled, "Principes d'une théorie mathématique de l'échange" (August, 1873), from which it emerges that the market price is obtained by a rise in the case where effective demand exceeds effective supply and by a fall in the opposite case. Thus there appears, besides the condition of the greatest possible satisfaction of wants, or the maximal satisfaction, the condition of the unity of the exchange relation for all exchangers, or unity of price on the market. The theory of exchange, even in the very restricted case of exchange of two goods for each other in kind, is only complete with these two conditions.[59]

The so-called Austrian school has not been able to associate itself with Gossen's total theoretical system to quite so great an extent as has the modern mathematical school. Its founder, Carl Menger, never expressed himself, to my knowledge, on the relation of his

---

[59] [Léon Walras, *Etudes d'économie sociale*, op. cit., p. 361. -Tr.]

theory to Gossen's.[60] That his successors, particularly Wieser, have done full justice to Gossen and that it is especially owing to the latter that Gossen's name has come to be joined to the first principle of the subjective theory of value was already emphasised at the outset. Because of dissimilarity in methods of presentation, however, the congruence of the two systems is essentially confined to the three fundamental propositions, which were earlier distinguished as Gossen's First, Second, and Third Laws, and to the starting point they provide for the theory of exchange and of the value of money. But even if the agreement between the Austrian school and Gossen's theory does not extend as far as in the case of the mathematical school, nevertheless it too may justly look on him as its most important precursor: the one who set forth its basic ideas not, to be sure, in the most felicitous form, but from beginning to end with the greatest consistency and a solid grasp of their significance.

Just how great the persuasive power of Gossen's ideas is, moreover, is singularly shown by the fact that even pronounced opponents of both the schools in question, who have, as I believe, continued to develop his theory consistently, e.g., Robert Liefmann[61] and Franz Oppenheimer[62], prefer to point up the agreement between their theories and his. Liefmann in particular even wants to lay personal claim to Gossen, as his single genuine precursor. This only proves, of course, that any modern analysis of economic phe-

---

[60] [Menger did in fact make a brief comment on Gossen in a letter to Léon Walras in 1887, sixteen years after the publication of Menger's *Principles*. On the relationship between Gossen and his own work Menger finds "nur in einigen Punkten, nicht aber in den entscheidenden Fragen zwischen uns Übereinstimmung, bez. Ähnlichkeit der Auffassung" (agreement only on some points, but not on those decisive ones between us). See letter of January 27, 1887, in William Jaffé, *Correspondence of Léon Walras and Related Papers* (Amsterdam: North-Holland, 1965), vol. 3, p. 176, letter number 765. Emil Kauder reports that Menger had bought a copy of Gossen's book in 1886 and that he "did not approve of Gossen, rejecting his purely hedonistic approach, his emphasis on labour, and the application of mathematics in the realm of psychology". See Emil Kauder, *A History of Marginal Utility Theory* (Princeton, N.J.: Princeton University Press, 1965), p. 82. These references are provided by Erich Streissler in "The Influence of German Economics on the Work of Menger and Marshall", *History of Political Economy*, forthcoming. -Ed.]

[61] [Robert Liefmann (1874-1941) wrote on trusts and cartels, among other issues. He was noted for emphasising the 'psychological' element in economics, as in his major work, *Grundsätze der Volkswirtschaftslehre*, 2 vols (Stuttgart and Berlin: Deutsche Verlags Anstalt, 1917-19). -Tr.]

[62] [Franz Oppenheimer (1864-1943), a sociologist at the Universities of Berlin and Frankfurt, was the author of *System der Soziologie*, 4 vols (Jena: G. Fischer, 1922-35), and *Der Staat* [1907], published in English as *The State: Its History and Development Viewed Sociologically* (Indianapolis, Ind.: Bobbs-Merrill, 1914). -Tr.]

nomena that aspires to explain them must attach itself to the ideas which Gossen was the first to develop in an adequate form. The fragmentation of theoretical economics into different schools and the varying distribution of emphasis on different theorems that has resulted have prevented a full appreciation of the ideas common to them all—ideas which are to be found joined together for the first time in Gossen. Yet it is hardly saying too much to assert that once the basic framework of economics is placed beyond dispute, as, for instance, has now happened with the theories of mechanics, Gossen will be universally cherished as the first great modern master of this science. In this way, his ideas and his name will have won that degree of imperishability that scientific achievements can attain.

CHRONOLOGICAL LIST OF CONTENTS

CHRONOLOGICAL LIST OF CONTENTS

BIBLIOGRAPHICAL NOTE

In addition to items of ephemeral value, such as short newspaper articles and book notices of a few lines written when Hayek was editing *Economica*, Hayek also wrote many short pieces designed for the general reader which were published as book reviews or as articles in encyclopaedias. The student of Hayek's work may find of some interest the following pieces which are related to the essays in this collection:

"Economics: A Survey", in *Chambers's Encyclopedia*, new edition (New York: Oxford University Press, 1950), vol. 4, pp. 771-775.

"Gossen, Hermann Heinrich", in *The Encyclopedia of the Social Sciences* (New York: Macmillan, 1930-4), vol. 7, p. 3.

"Macleod, Henry Dunning", in *The Encyclopedia of the Social Sciences*, op. cit., vol. 10, p. 30.

"Norman, George Warde", in *The Encyclopedia of the Social Sciences*, op. cit., vol. 11, p. 397.

"Ricardo, David", in *Chambers's Encyclopedia* (London: International Learning Systems Corporation, 1950), vol. 9, pp. 667-668.

EDITOR'S ACKNOWLEDGEMENTS

The Editor expresses his gratitude, first and foremost, to Mr. Peter Klein of the University of California, Berkeley, for his indefatigable efforts in establishing the accuracy of many of the references in this volume. He also wishes to thank his research assistants, Mr. Tim Bryan, Mr. Tim Groseclose, and Mr. Leif Wenar of Stanford University. Thanks are due also to Mr. Jeffrey Friedman of the University of California, Berkeley, and to Ms. Leslie Graves for her careful reading of the manuscript. In addition to her excellent translations, Dr. Grete Heinz provided valuable insight into the milieu of Hayek's early work. Above all, my gratitude goes to Ms. Gene Opton for her exceptional help in preparing this manuscript for publication. They are of course not responsible for any errors that remain.

Material from the Jacob Viner Papers quoted in chapter 6 is published with permission of Princeton University Libraries. The editors would like to acknowledge the generous assistance provided to the Eucken Institute by the Liberty Fund for the preparation of the manuscripts which have appeared in this volume as chapters 9 through 12.

W. W. Bartley, III

INDEX

Rousseau, Jean-Jacques, 104, 116, 250n, 274, 287
Rouxel, W., 259n
Rudolf, R. de M., 299n, 301n
Rufner, Vinzenz, 100
Ruggerio, Guido de, 61 & n
Russell, Bertrand, 62 & n
Ryskamp, Charles, 298n

Sabine, G.H., 115n
Saint John, Henry, *see* Bolingbroke, Lord
Saint-Simon, Henri de, 355n
Sakmann, Paul, 93n, 99
Salin, Pascal, 127n
Salter, Arthur, 29n
Savary, Jacques, 251 & n, 278n, 286
Savigny, 96 & n
Say, Jean-Baptiste, 271n, 289 & n
Schams, Ewald, 261n
Scharfstein, Ben-Ami, 49n
Schatz, Albert, 89n, 99
Schelle, Gustave, 169n, 266n
Schiller, Johann Christoph Friedrich von, 104n
Schiller, Johann von, 44
Schmoller, Gustav, 22n, 294
Schneider, Louis, 96n, 100
Schönfeld, L., 361n
Schrödinger, Erwin, 5
Schumpeter, J.A., 50n, 258 & n, 347 & n
Schwartz, Anna Jacobson, 177n
Schwarz, Pedro, 127n
Scott, Thomas, 299n
Scott, Walter, 272n
Scott, William Robert, 122 & n, 123–124
Scottoni, F., 249 & n
Secrétan, Charles, 358 & n
Seeley, M., 315n, 343
Seligman, Ben B., 355n
Serionne, 269n
Sewall, H.R., 262n, 268
Senior, Nassau William, 223 & n, 224n
Shannon, H.A., 326n

Sharp, Granville, 306 & n, 307n, 343
Shell, Karl, 211n
Sheridan, Richard, 197n
Shore, Sir John, *see* Lord Teignmouth
Silberling, 344
Sinclair, Sir John, 205n
Sismondi, J.C.L. Simonde de, 204n
Sivers, Friedrich von, 253
Skinner, Andrew S., 151n, 178n, 247n
Slotkin, J.S., 97n
Smart, William, 338n, 344, 360n
Smith, Adam, 10, 26, 27 &n, 39, 40n, 76, 88 & n, 89, 90 & n, 91 & n, 96 & n, 99, 101, 106, 108, 117, 118, chapter 8, 151, 164, 178 & n, 180–181, 193–194, 200, 211, 240, 247 & n, 248, 252, 257 & n, 262n, 267, 287–288, 292, 322nn, 336n, 344
Smith, Sydney, 299n
Smith, Vera C. (later Lutz), 127n
Smith, William, 306n, 307n
Sombart, Werner, 68 & n
"Sophron", 306n
Spengler, Joseph J., 155n, 271n
Spring, David, 296n
Sraffa, Piero, 118 & n, 187n, 199n, 200nn, 205n, 206n, 208n, 210nn, 212n, 215n, 219n
St. John-Stevas, Norman, 201n
Stafford, Lord, 272
Stammler, Rudolf, 99
Stamp, J.C., 29n
Stephen, C.E., 343
Stephen, Sir George, 343
Stephen, Sir James, 299n, 305n, 306n, 343
Stephen, James, the younger, 306n, 312, 313 & n, 314n, 318, 319, 342
Stephen, James Fitzjames, 343
Stephen, Leslie, 81n, 255n, 296n, 300n, 306n, 314nn, 343